6695

Contemporary
India—*transitions*

FUNDAÇÃO ORIENTE

The Fundação Oriente is a Portuguese private institution that aims to carry out and support activities of a cultural, artistic, educational, philanthropic and social nature, principally in Portugal and Macao.

Within these general aims, the Fundação Oriente seeks to maintain and strengthen the historical and cultural ties between Portugal and countries of Eastern Asia, namely the People's Republic of China, India, Japan, Korea, Thailand, Malaysia and Sri Lanka.

The Fundação Oriente has its headquarters in Lisbon, Portugal, with Delegations in Macao and Goa (India) and a Delegate in Beijing (China).

Contemporary India—*transitions*

edited by
Peter Ronald deSouza

FUNDAÇÃO
ORIENTE

and

Sage Publications
NEW DELHI/THOUSAND OAKS/LONDON

First published in 2000 by

Sage Publications India Pvt Ltd
M-32 Market, Greater Kailash, Part 1
New Delhi 110 048

Sage Publications Inc   Sage Publications Ltd
2455 Teller Road   6 Bonhill Street
Thousand Oaks, California 91320   London EC2A 4PU

Published by Tejeshwar Singh for Sage Publications India Pvt Ltd, typeset
in 10/12 Book Antiqua by Asian Telelinks, New Delhi, and printed at
Chaman Enterprises, Delhi.

Library of Congress Cataloging-in-Publication Data

Contemporary India — transitions/edited by Peter Ronald deSouza.
    p. cm.
Includes bibliographical references and index.
  1. India — Politics and government — 1947 — Congress. 2. India — Eco-
nomic conditions — 1947 — Congress. 3. India — Social conditions — 1947 —
Congress. 4. India — Civilization — Congresses. I. De Souza, Peter.
DS480.84.C757   954.05'2 — dc21   2000   00–059157

ISBN: 0–7619–9480–7 (US–Hb)   81–7036–968–1 (India–Hb)

Dedication artwork by Shamoli Barreto
Sage Production Team: AshaRani Mathur, Aruna Ramachandran,
                Mathew P.J. and Santosh Rawat

For Edwin —
two friends, two friends

Contents

Goa in Transition

Introduction:
Initiating a Dialogue on India

Peter Ronald deSouza

h alf a century is a long enough historical period in the life of independent India to entice a diverse and multidisciplinary group of scholars to reflect on the details of its biography. Contained within the pages of this biography are stories of constraint and opportunity, advancement and resistance, seduction and illusion, failure and success. These stories constitute a major intellectual challenge, since they require to be not only appropriately framed, a framing that gets mired in the ontological minefield of 'whose India, which India', but also flexibly framed to encourage a dialogue between the various voices of India. Understanding India, therefore, requires us to recognise the existence of many storytellers, for there are many Indias within India.

Fortunately for all of us, such a multidisciplinary group of scholars got an opportunity to initiate such a collective deliberation at a conference organised in Lisbon in June 1998. It was titled *Contemporary India in Transition*. This grand conference emerged from a small wish to begin a new conversation, after nearly four decades of sullen silence, between Goa and Portugal. Modern societies need to talk to each other. We thought we could begin with a conference. The larger canvas of contemporary India was chosen to locate this conversation, as it was only within such a location that the transitions that mark the visual, social and mental landscape of Goa and Portugal would gain some perspective. India was needed to anchor the conversation. Europe was needed to be the site of initiation. That it took place at all was because of the support of a Portuguese foundation, Fundação Oriente, who most readily agreed to sponsor the conference, to transport a group of Indian scholars to Lisbon and to thereby assist, 500 years later, this new voyage of discovery. What began as an idea in the winter of 1997 became a reality in the summer of 1998, when some of India's most eminent intellectuals presented, to a distinguished audience in Portugal, multiple readings of contemporary India in transition.

One may here legitimately ask 'why contemporary India?' 'why transition?' and 'why Lisbon?' Let me answer the last question first. One is tempted to respond rhetorically with 'why not Lisbon?' which seems a perfectly valid response that is both stubborn and challenging, compelling the questioner to look longer and search deeper for an answer. But a more polite response can also be given. The choice of Lisbon had both political and symbolic significance. In the new millennium, India must increase the number of avenues on which it will travel, on which it will announce its arrival from being an ex-colony to being a modern nation responsible for its own destiny. It must stop seeing itself, or being regarded, as an ex-colony. It must be prepared, after half a century, to take it on the chin for its own failures and successes.

Lisbon, symbolically, is an important place to announce this arrival. It is an old capital city, one of the oldest in Europe from where, 500 years earlier, Vasco da Gama set sail to inaugurate the modern encounter of India with Europe. There were many aspects to this encounter, each with its own dynamics, its own personality. While there was suppression and denial, very brutal at times, there was also subversion and challenge, a series of revolts and *satyagrahas*. While there was exploitation, the drain theory, there was also emancipation, the common civil code. While there was coercion there was also cooperation, though perhaps not in equal measure. And then there was the anti-colonial struggle. It has been a complex encounter and we, both in India and Europe, and more particularly in Goa, need to investigate its implications and unravel its many meanings. We need to understand not just the vicissitudes that make up our past, not just the intricacies of the colonial relationship, not just the mysteries of civilisational encounters (Indian political thought from Raja Ram Mohan Roy to Tilak, Gandhi, Nehru and Ambedkar can only be read through this encounter), but also the stirrings of a society negotiating the contours of its own contested future. This understanding, I believe, will best emerge when we adopt a comparative framework, and India and Europe, because of their similar dimension, provide the basis of such a comparison. So Lisbon it had to be.

Then why 'contemporary' India? There are many reasons for this. The first is perhaps our belief that ancient India has been better studied, with Indological studies having a certain presence within the academy in Europe, than contemporary India. Even here one may wonder why the academic signposting of a certain historical period, 'ancient' in India and 'classical' in Europe, is different and whether this difference in naming has less to do with the characteristics of the place and more with the characteristics of the academic mind, a bias of seeing which carries on right through to the western reading of contemporary India. One felt that a set of diverse presentations, of theme, subject and perspective, would go some way towards challenging the stereotypes that persist about India. Such a diverse set of readings would show India to be the intellectual challenge it is and not just another ex-colony somewhere in the orient whose ties with Europe belong only to the past.

This leads to the second reason, which is our belief that a new dialogue agenda must be established where contemporary Europe looks to contemporary India for answers, as does India to Europe. Both entities are experimenting with new forms, a new political union composed of complex accommodations, a new set of institutions regulating multiple demands, and a new set of principles seeking to establish a federal secular state; as they move from a societal space that was multicultural by historical accident into one that is multicultural by political design. As Europe confronts its present it must look at India. And likewise must India. Both have much to share.

The third reason is more straightforwardly academic. Contemporary India has the potential to rejuvenate the social sciences, especially in the west which, I daresay, has lost its engagement with the grand concerns of societal transformation. In the last few decades there has been a subtle shift, a narrowing in the normative

grounding of social theorising, from 'good society' to 'good governance' issues, from value rationality to instrumental rationality. A
consensus seems to have emerged, or rather is being portrayed,
on the big questions of distributive justice, social equality, public
interest, human rights; even on states and markets. This is an
erroneous portrayal. India represents a challenge to this claim of
consensus as there is an intense contest, in both policy and normative terms, around the content of these issues. These remain the
big questions of the social sciences in India. They remain relevant
and central. This collection of articles is therefore an invitation to
the reader to join us in the exploration of the shadows of these
questions, to resist the reductionism that is enveloping the practice
of the social sciences.

  This brings us to the third question, 'why transition?' From the
structure of the book the reader will notice that not only are there
papers on different themes, but the authors also represent different
ideological positions. While this diversity of topic and perspective
may appear to produce a volume that does not hold together, in
terms of a narrow understanding of what it means to hold together—no focussed question running right through all the
papers—this judgement proves on deeper reflection to be mistaken.
There is a coherence in the volume but at a different level. What
binds all the papers together is their engagement with the transition
process under way in India. India is undergoing not a single,
unilinear transition, but a series of transitions. This important
distinction between one and many transitions became apparent
only after the various presentations had been made and the post-
mortems of the conference completed. It prompted us to make
what is a small but significant change in title from *Contemporary
India in Transition*, the title with which we began the exercise, to
the more appropriate one: *Contemporary India – Transitions*. This
reshuffling of words produced not just a more aesthetic title but
also a better signpost since it represents more truly what is contained in the collection. India is undergoing multiple transitions
which can, and should, only be explained from multiple perspectives. And, hence, with this change, another cause of unease
was set at rest.

  Some unease remained nonetheless. Here we have a confession
to make. In the original schema which was presented in Portugal,
there were two significant absences. The Dalit view of transition

was missing and the gender voice was underrepresented. Between the pragmatics of numbers and our eagerness to get the show on the road, a grievous lapse was committed. Perspective was lost. The absence was not noticed in the honest belief that the selection was representative. We were seriously wrong. In retrospect we realise that our lapse itself is significant. We succumbed to the pressure of an instrumental calculus. But wiser after the fact, and since no volume can claim to discuss transitions without these voices, we have sought to remedy the lacuna by inviting chapters on both these themes. The collection, however, I am sure is still incomplete. But for that we will not take the blame. For a dialogue to develop it must be unfinished. And this one has just begun.

In the planning of the conference and the volume, we have accepted that any study of India, however well executed, will soon confront the fundamental problem of the six blind (wo)men and the elephant. Each blind man insists that his description of the elephant is right. Each regards the other as erroneous. And each is both right and wrong. For the elephant is India, a culturally and spatially diverse entity, an ontological conundrum that has been confined by the contingencies of language within a singular label: India. Recognising this, we have sought to skirt the problem by adopting the strategy of a dialogue between groups, viewpoints, subject domains and even societies. We have encouraged this dialogue within each of the five sections of the book as well as between the sections. Dialogue basically recognises the limitations of its own claim while remaining open to correction, extension, modification. This collection of articles is an invitation to a dialogue about India, about issues that are India-specific and also about issues of global concern.

The chapters are grouped into five sections. In the first, *Civilisation in Transition*, the contributions reflect on the changes taking place in the civilisational terrain of India. I realise that the signpost 'civilisational' has politically undesirable overtones, since it is often invoked by the communal right in India, but I have sought to problematise the terrain by the selection of topic and author. There are four contributions here, each speaking from a different direction. From the direction of history is Romila Thapar's opening address at the conference, a magisterial survey of three interpretations of Indian history: colonial, nationalist and post-colonial. Through these readings she shows the links between interests and interpretations, the power that ideas bring to those who produce and control them. She shows how this power has been used to recast knowledge about India and how, with the rise of religious nationalism, the history of India remains a contested space. From the direction of literature and language is U.R. Ananthamurthy's offering, a subtle account of the play between the 'frontyard' and the 'backyard' in India's cultural imagination. Very poetically, he explains how the Indian motto of 'Unity in Diversity' works, in that if one overstresses unity, diversities begin to appear; and likewise with diversity. He discusses the place of the *bhashas* in Indian literature and their contribution to the making of the nation. Chapter 3, by Rustom Bharucha, challenges the elite and establishment representations of Indian culture and advocates an attentiveness to the ignored cultures of groups outside these elite boundaries. He identifies the limitations of the multicultural idea and prefers instead the intracultural, which is politically more acceptable since its primary agencies are more mixed, including non-governmental organisations, citizens' groups and people's movements. Chapter 4 is by Gopal Guru, whose reading of civilisation in transition is one of a cultural space changing, albeit not fast enough, in its constitutive principles from exclusion to inclusion. The silent, suppressed voice of India speaks here. There is no glorification of India's fabled tolerance. It is just a reflective account of the practices and structures of exclusion, political, social, economic and cultural. It is the Dalit voice speaking. Four different voices, all speaking of India in transition.

The second section, *Economy in Transition*, seeks to counterpoise an evaluation of the policy and experience of economic liberalisation with the need to maintain and strengthen the welfare component of the state. India embarked on the path of liberalisation at the beginning of the 1990s. This section contains a view from industry, a comment about agriculture, and an analysis of welfare services. Chapter 5, by S.S. Bhandare, represents the view of corporate India. He presents with great clarity the constraints and impediments Indian industry had to face in the years before liberalisation, constraints which he believes were detrimental to the Indian economy. The new policies of reform will release its productive energy, and when a level playing field emerges (he tells us what this is) the economy will produce the wealth that India needs to take her place in the comity of nations. Chapter 6,

by Bhupat Desai, is a rigorous evaluation of the situation of agriculture and agri-businesses in the context of liberalisation. He
argues that the goal of reduction of absolute poverty can be met
through technical change in agriculture and agri-businesses, which
are people-oriented. He makes the interesting observation that
most food-processing industries and agro-processing industries
in general have had deteriorating growth rates in post-reform
years. Through a marshalling of data ranging from land ownership
patterns, to agricultural output, to consumption patterns, to agro-
based exports, he makes a strong case for greater fine-tuning in
agricultural policy. From hard economics we move to economics
with a human face in Chapter 7 by Ghanshyam Shah. Here the
focus shifts from the instrumentalities of economic productivity
to the instrumentalities of welfare. The chapter very graphically
details the experience of poverty and its cumulative consequences.
It then argues for the continued relevance of the welfare state.
Shah evaluates the various poverty alleviation schemes in existence
in India and argues that in spite of their poor record of delivery,
they still remain the only avenues available to the poor. He presents
the gloomy statistics that the 'proportion of people living below
the poverty line, which had shown a declining trend between 1970
and 1990, has shown an upward trend in 1993–94'. Again, multiple
readings of the transitions in the economy.

The third section, *Polity in Transition*, traverses the terrain from
the adopted constitutional order, through institutions and processes that make up the polity, to the normative agenda for the
future. Chapter 8, by Soli Sorabjee, captures the idealism of the
Constituent Assembly as the various freedoms that were subsequently enumerated in the constitution were debated. He draws
attention to the provisions concerning the freedom of religion, a
freedom which is the subject of contestation today, and states that
the founding fathers very deliberately included the word 'propagate' along with the right to profess and practice. He highlights
some of the innovations of constitutional democracy in India, such
as the redefinition of the principle of *locus standi* and the phenomenon of judicial activism. Chapter 9, by Rajeev Bhargava, engages
with one of the key issues of Indian politics: the place and privileges
of the minorities in India. He makes a case for Muslims having a
general right to their personal laws — because of 'the right to preserve one's culture against potential threat from other cultures' —

but also argues that they do not have a right to all laws they currently happen to have. To do so he evaluates the normative and ontological assumptions of the debate on individual and group rights, and attempts to build a rights-based argument for reform of personal laws while accepting the general case for minority rights. Chapter 10, by Peter Ronald deSouza, is a critique of some of the dominant ways of looking at democracy in India. He suggests that factoring in scale, which is the unique aspect of the Indian project of democracy, would change the way in which democracy is discussed in India. He develops his reading of democracy in India through an analysis of the electoral process and of party politics. Chapter 11, by Nawaz Mody, places on the discourse agenda the question of human rights in India. She traces India's engagement with human rights from its involvement with the UN declaration, through its constitutional provisions, to its dismal record in safeguarding the rights of children and other vulnerable groups. Her contribution is more in the nature of an announcement of a set of concerns, of a fundamental moral commitment that must guide the Indian polity. Behind each of these four chapters is a large and complex debate on the four facets of the Indian polity discussed here.

The fourth section, *Society in Transition*, is the most incomplete. It is a selection of themes within the domain of society that are of significance, that give valuable insights into the changes taking place, and that are being contested and negotiated. Chapter 12, by D.L. Sheth, quite naturally deals with that ubiquitous signature of India: caste. He presents the revolutionary argument that through the processes of (a) de-ritualisation, (b) politicisation and (c) classisation, caste is changing its character in India. These three processes, brought about by the modernisation of India's economy and the democratisation of its political institutions, have resulted in a veritable process of secularisation of caste. Sheth makes his case from extensive survey data collected in 1996. Chapter 13 looks at the changes that have occurred in another important domain of Indian society, the gender domain. Seemanthini Niranjana traces the imprint of these societal changes on women in India. For her the gender question has assumed a rather complex shape within such a context, intersecting with caste, class, regional and religious considerations. These intersections having 'complicated the terms on which women and the conditions of their empowerment can be understood today', Niranjana presents us with a map of these changes. Chapter 14, by Zoya Hasan, takes one aspect of this intersection further as she looks at the debate in India on gender justice and a uniform civil code. Through an analysis of events such as the Shah Bano case, Hasan engages with the debates concerning the trade-offs between group and individual rights. She makes a case for gender justice while still safeguarding the rights of minorities from erosion by the forces of communalism. Chapter 15, by B.G. Verghese, is on a different plane. It examines the status of the media in India and in a globalised world. He argues for the enactment of a Freedom of Information Act and for greater autonomy being given to the government-owned broadcasting corporations. He also briefly raises the issue of foreign control of the media in India. This section takes us from the 'thick' processes under way in society to the more policy-level issues of ideas and the public domain.

The fifth section, *Goa in Transition*, is an indulgence and a concession. Since the venue was in Portugal, where there is a large Goan diaspora who would attend the conference to understand better the transitions taking place in the land of their origin, it was felt appropriate to have a section on Goa. For this diaspora, Goa remained the *Goa Dourada* of yore. They needed to engage with *Goa Indica*. Contemporary Portugal also needed to engage with contemporary Goa for the new conversation to develop a meaningful momentum. This section on Goa has also been included in the book because the audience for the book is not just in Portugal, or Europe, but also in India. Goa is a neglected area of study in India. This small section is intended to combat that neglect. In Chapter 16, Errol D'Souza looks at the state of Goa's finances in the last decade. He argues that the state government is following a myopic policy which is leading Goa into cutting back on development expenditure and into a debt trap. He calculates the cost to the economy of the politics of defection and coalition, and makes the interesting point that it is the politics of concession which has led Goa to its present precarious financial position. Chapter 17, by Maria Ligia Noronha, while using Goa as an illustrative case, seeks to address the problem confronting most developing societies, that of determining the threshold point where there is a trade-off between development and environment. She takes the sectors of mining and tourism to show how weaknesses of government policy undermine the regulatory mechanism. She makes the point that 'institutional capacity has been weak both in terms of ability and willingness to implement these regulations.' The last chapter in this final section by Peter Ronald deSouza is a survey of a decade of politics in Goa, a decade which shows interesting patterns of when, for example, a strong *Bahujan* base becomes a soft *Hindutva* base; and where the politics of pragmatism continues to dominate the politics of ideology. He outlines the social base of politics in the old and new conquests of Goa.

The eighteen chapters in this book cover various domains, address many questions and speak from different viewpoints. At the risk of repetition I must say that what knits them together is their engagement with 'transition' and their commitment to dialogue. Through the different voices emerges a picture of India which, as Mark Twain wrote in his book *More Tramps Abroad* (1897), is 'the country of a hundred nations and a hundred tongues, of a thousand religions and two million gods, cradle of the human race . . . .' And so on. The six blind (wo)men and the elephant . . . .

In conclusion, I should like to return to the motivation that was the basis of the conference and of this book: the initiation of a new dialogue. I must recall with gratitude the complete freedom that Fundação Oriente gave me in designing the theme and selecting participants. Intellectual exchanges between Goa and Portugal in the last four decades have been marked by a stickiness that perhaps can be understood, but whose persistence cannot be justified. A society needs to come to terms with its own history, to create the conditions for critical intellectual explorations of its past. This we have failed to do, a failure that reflects our own lack of confidence. Fundação Oriente broke new ground in taking this risk of organising a conference on India in Portugal. Responsibilities were divided: we at Goa University looked after the scientific aspects; Fundação Oriente, the organisational aspects. There was little reason to cross over. I am indebted to Paulo Varela Gomes, then Delegate of Fundação Oriente in India, for sharing my enthusiasm and doing everything to make the conference possible. He introduced us to contemporary Portugal, and contemporary Portugal to us. I am grateful to his successor Adelino Rodrigues daCosta for giving the intellectual effort a longer life. The emergence of this volume is because he made every effort to work with Sage to bring it out. I owe a special thanks to the Board of Fundação Oriente for their generous sponsorship of the conference. I am particularly indebted to all the contributors who willingly joined me in the pursuit of my wish. I must record my gratitude to Ashwin Tombat who with great meticulousness helped me with the preparation of the manuscript and to Omita Goyal of Sage who closely monitored the evolution of the volume. And finally I owe an unpayable debt to Siddharth, Gayatri and Roshni, my children, who bore with good humour the grumpiness of a *Dada* struggling with an incomplete dream. I hope they will appreciate the virtues of dialogue and the significance of transition. For when they grow up they will realise that my contemporary India is different from theirs.

Civilisation
in
Transition

one

Interpretations of Indian History: Colonial, Nationalist, Post-colonial

Romila Thapar

the modern writing of Indian history dates to about 200 years ago and begins with a disjuncture. When British scholars started asking about histories of India, they were told that there were no historical works as history was a subject which was of no interest to pre-colonial Indian scholarship. This led to the theory that Indian civilisation was unique because it was ahistorical. It had no sense of history. This is a theory which is very widespread and very often accepted, and which some of us are trying to question and, hopefully, to eventually overthrow. As a result of this theory British scholarship took upon itself the task of 'discovering' the Indian past. This, of course, had its own problems and orientations. The disjuncture meant that initially, at least, the European imprint on Indian historical scholarship was extremely strong; slowly and gradually, one can trace the receding of this imprint and the coming of an Indian point of view, as it were. Although, of course, with

This is the opening address given at the conference on *Contemporary India in Transition* held at Lisbon in June 1998.

the consciousness of modernisation, it is very difficult to sharply distinguish between a modern European and a modern Indian understanding of history.

This chapter, therefore, is concerned with a series of questions. How did this disjuncture occur? What is the nature of these imprints? And to what extent is historical interpretation today in India reflective of intellectual concerns which may have a global context but which, nevertheless, grew out of an Indian understanding of both history and of its context?

The Colonial Interpretation

Quite apart from the fact that there was a disjuncture in the late 18th and early 19th centuries, and there was a presumed need on the part of colonial scholars to 'rediscover' Indian history, it is important to note that from the early 19th century onwards, the reconstruction of Indian history was tied to European preconceptions and debates about the Orient. The intellectual history of Europe was therefore extremely pertinent to the interpretation of the history of India, and this is particularly true of the 19th century. Writing about India, thus, was like holding a mirror to European society. India was, to use the fashionable term, the 'Other'; and the 'Other' is always important to understanding the 'self'. This was done through drawing comparisons, and consequently much of the writing, the reconstruction of the Indian past, derived from this concern with how the 'Other', by contrast, had a history which was different from European history.

Apart from these ideological, intellectual concerns, there was also one other very basic concern, which was the colonial belief in knowledge as a source of power. This belief was rampant throughout the 19th century. Knowing the history of an area provided control over it. What Curzon refers to in a famous statement as 'the necessary furniture of empire', a curiosity about the past of the colony, becomes extremely central, and the desire then is to control the colony through re-casting its knowledge about itself and particularly about its past. Colonial historiography, therefore, does have a big agenda and certainly not always a hidden agenda.

The 19th century throws up some very recognisable themes. Initially, there was the activity of what has been called orientalist scholarship. This is a tricky word, because it should not be confused with Edward Said's concept of Orientalism per se. Orientalist scholarship included what Said writes about, but it also included varieties of oriental scholarship; the study of languages, for example, or the study of texts thought to be value-free prior to the theoretical discussion of Orientalism. Orientalist scholarship, as embodied in people like William Jones and in the Asiatic Society in Calcutta, and a number of others, explored the new terrain of the Indian past and tried to link it to the European past. For example, linguistic links were sought between Sanskrit on the one hand and Greek and Latin on the other. This is not something that was developed only by British orientalist scholars; both Italian and, I am told, Portuguese scholars had earlier made these links. It was now developed into a theory, a theory of the interconnection of ancestral languages, and of their monogenesis.

There was also an attempt to draw conceptual and chronological links with Biblical history. The story of Noah's Ark has an almost parallel story in the Indian texts of Manu, of the god Vishnu converting himself into a fish and directing the boat, lodging it on the top of a mountain, and so on. These early scholars saw these connections, linked them immediately to Biblical thinking and tried to produce a chronology that was the equivalent of Biblical chronology.

The focus was essentially on texts that dealt with social laws— for example, the *Dharmashastras*, which focus on the social and ritual obligations of different castes in Indian society — and religious texts. Both were functionally important to understanding the earlier institutions. Their study was thus not just intellectual curiosity, it also had an administrative function. The notion of controlling the society by understanding its earlier institutions became an important item on the intellectual agenda of these scholars.

India was regarded as an exotic area in terms of orientalist scholarship. Not surprisingly, it had a tremendous influence on German romanticism throughout the 19th century. The literary movement of German romanticism was imbued with excitement about the discovery of Sanskrit and what it taught of the Indian past; many thought that it was the Indian present as well. This is in part a reflection of an escape from 19th century European industrialisation and the changes which this industrialisation brought, which were somehow difficult to comprehend. Colonial intervention, therefore, was not concerned with trying to change the society of India or the society of the colony; the intervention was, at this point, without plans for any radical change.

One of the major theories that emerged out of orientalist scholarship which was dominant in the middle of the 19th century and which is now again very prominent particularly with the ideology of *Hindutva* being encouraged politically, is the theory of the Aryan race. This theory was developed in the 19th century, and, in its relationship to Indian history, was intended to explain the origins of Indian society and provide the beginnings of Indian history. It maintains that Indian history begins with the invasion of the Aryans, the superior people who came from Central Asia, subjugated the whole of northern India and established an Aryan civilisation.

The theory evolved in Europe, but it was applied both in Europe and in India. It evolved in Europe through the discussion of what in the 19th century was known as race science, which was concerned with theories of biological race and drew its strength from both natural science and other disciplines. For example, the botanist Linnaeus worked out a whole ordering of genus and species with reference to plants, which was taken as the model for working out genus and species with reference to human groups. Social Darwinism, the theory of the survival of the fittest, was also brought into the discussion. The question of who, in fact, were the fittest, was answered by indicating that the fittest were the European Aryans, because they dominated world civilisation.

Max Müller, the famous German Sanskritist at Oxford, was the first to superimpose this theory of Aryan race on India. The theory basically stated that race and language were identical. People who spoke a particular language inevitably belonged to the same race and, if two languages were similar, then the speakers of those languages belonged to the same race. The argument was that there was a language called Aryan which was spoken by a race called Aryan, and this race traced itself back to the Indo-European people and the Indo-European languages. Equating a language label with a racial label was, of course, a major blunder; and although Max Müller stated that the two had to be kept separate and could not be equated, he nevertheless confused the issue himself. For example, he referred to Raja Ram Mohan Roy, the social reformer of the early 19th century, as a member of the Bengali Indo-Aryan race which spoke Bengali and the Indo-Aryan language.

Further, caste was seen essentially as racial segregation, each caste being visualised as a separate race. It was argued that Indian society was extremely advanced because it had managed to segregate all these racial groups in a social system known as caste. And, of course, the idea of the purity of caste, derived from the Portuguese word *casta* meaning 'pure', gave a certain kind of direction to the way in which studies of caste in the early period were conducted. The upper castes, it was argued, were of Aryan stock, and the lower castes were indigenous and mixed. Thus the theory also influenced ethnology and the discussion of Indian society. Max Müller's statement that the Aryans were of a superior race and had brought civilisation to India was much appreciated by the colonialist historians, who saw in the Aryan conquest of India parallels to the British conquest of India. The comparison was frequently endorsed.

This was not the only trend, however, in the 19th century. There was another group of historians who contested the interpretations of orientalist scholarship. They were known as the utilitarian historians, because they drew much of their inspiration from the writings of the British philosopher, Jeremy Bentham. They took an alternative view to the romanticism of exotic India, emphasising instead the weaknesses of Indian civilisation and society. They argued that there was a tremendous need for rationality and individualism if the society was to progress, the term 'progress' being used very much in its early 19th century meaning. Therefore, there was a need to legislate change. This was a departure from the orientalist scholars, who were quite happy to leave things as they were and simply write about the past of India, about how Indians were all given to loving nature, or, as Max Müller says, meditating peacefully for endless years in their little village communities. The utilitarians maintained that all of this had to be changed, because India was a backward, stagnant society. India was clearly, then, the 'Other' in terms of British society, and it is interesting that much of this writing is as much a critique of British society, in an oblique way, as it is, in fact, a critique of Indian society.

The person best remembered from this group is the historian James Mill, who wrote a massive three-volume history of British India in the early 19th century. This became what has been called the 'hegemonic text' on Indian history. He periodised Indian history into the Hindu civilisation, the Muslim civilisation and the British period. This periodisation became so popular that in the middle of the 19th century, Christian Lassen, an orientalist philosopher in Germany, described the three periods as the Hindu thesis, the Muslim anti-thesis, and the British synthesis.

Mill argued that the pre-British Hindu and Muslim civilisations were not only backward and stagnant, but conformed to the image of 'oriental despotism'. Oriental despotism became the key concept in the 19th century to explain the situation in India prior to the coming of the British. Incidentally, these views also coincided with the views of a number of Christian missionary groups, particularly those working under the aegis of the British administration, who also wanted a major legislation to change the basis of Indian society.

This kind of historical thinking was not something that was abstract or confined only to Britain. It is interesting that both Max Müller and James Mill never actually visited India, although they were frequently invited. This is a very interesting little vignette on the way in which they approached India as a colony. This historical thinking also coincided with a change in colonial policy. We must keep in mind that, by the middle of the 19th century, the British conquest of India had been completed, or more or less so. The emergence of British industrialisation at this time gave rise to the need to reconstruct the economic structure of the colony, so that it would supply resources and provide markets for industries in Britain. Consequently, this historiographic urging for legislative change, for change in the nature and structure of the colony, came in extremely handy for British colonial policy.

Let us also remember that this is the latter half of the 19th century, when aggressive capitalism was changing into imperialism with its much more intensive exploitation of colonies. Therefore, ideologies geared to legitimising change in the colonies became imperative.

Indian society as the 'Other' of Europe was a major theme. This is perhaps best illustrated in the writings of Karl Marx and Max Weber. Marx, in his Asiatic mode of production, argues that Asian societies are distinctively different from European societies, and that they present in some ways the reversal of the explanations that are offered for European history and modes of production. He argues that because there was no private property in land, there were no class contradictions, no dialectic of change, no class conflict. India was, in essence, a stagnant society. Therefore, even though British colonialism did much harm, it was a necessary intervention because it broke the stagnancy of the Indian past. Weber argues that the absence of the puritan ethic in the religions of both India and China was the main reason why capitalism did not emerge at this time in Asia. There was no possibility of accommodating the rationality of economics in Indian religions.

The basic question for both Marx and Weber, and for a number of scholars looking at the Indian past, was why capitalism developed in Europe and not in Asia. The contrast with Europe became a primary concern. Europe was unique because it developed capitalism. There is a noticeable disregard in the writings of Marx and Weber for empirical data which might suggest the contrary. This disregard in itself forms a very interesting subject for study in European considerations of the Indian past. The focus is so concentrated on theory and on contesting theory that empirical data was frequently either marginalised or ignored altogether. The uniqueness of India was said to be caste, there was a considerable emphasis on textual views of caste and, consequently, on the dominance of the idea that Brahminism was responsible for the creation of caste. This emphasis has continued from the early 19th century up to the present. The writings of Louis Dumont, for example, are very much in this tradition.

The Nationalist Interpretation

So much for colonial historiography. Let us turn now to an Indian perspective. Towards the end of the 19th century there emerged the beginnings of what have been called nationalist interpretations of Indian history, interpretations that had become much more forceful by the early 20th century.

The context of nationalist historiography in India was not similar to that in Europe, because it was not initially geared to the emergence of a nation state. This came later. Rather, it grew from an anti-colonial movement for independence. History was used for two purposes. The first was to establish the identity of Indians by asking questions such as who we are, where we began, what we are, what our history is, and how we have arrived at where we are. The second was to establish the superiority of the past to the present. The remote past, referred to by Mill as Hindu civilisation, became the golden age. This was always very convenient, because the more remote the golden age, the more imaginative were its reconstructions, as they could not always be tested factually.

Mill's periodisation of Indian history into Hindu, Muslim and British periods, which many of us are now contesting, was accepted by these historians. A dichotomy was projected of a spiritual India as against a materialist West. This dichotomy is evident in all historiographies of colonial history, and makes for a fascinating comparative study, for example, with the notion of Negritude which developed in African and Caribbean societies.

What the nationalists did not do was provide an alternative theory of explanation for Indian history. While they rejected some ideas like oriental despotism, which they disapproved of, they accepted others like the Aryan theory of race, which they were willing to incorporate. Nevertheless, the fact that they were questioning some of these theories, irrespective of whether they arose out of orientalist scholarship or out of utilitarian writing, meant that a debate had been started. By the early 20th century, it was recognised that history is not unbiased information; it involves interpretation. This was a very major departure from the earlier histories.

Nationalist interpretations gave rise to certain tangential interpretations, emerging partly from its own concerns and partly out of the politics of the 1920s and the 1930s. One of these, regarded as a fringe activity at the time but which has become much more central in the last ten years, was the writing of history based on religious nationalisms and relating primarily to the identities of communities as Hindu or Muslim. This gave rise to communal interpretations of India's past. They were motivated primarily by the politics of the 1920s and the 1930s, and became extremely influential in interpreting the pre-modern period in particular, because it was during this period that the Hindu community and the Muslim community as identifiable communities or, as many people argued, as identifiable nations, were thought to have been established.

Historical explanation from this perspective is based on a single, monocausal explanation, which is always religious. It is either religious confrontation or religious conformity between Hindus and Muslims which is seen as the causal factor in history. This kind of historical writing is opposed to that which examines social and economic history, because the latter shows up the poverty or even the inappropriateness of monocausal explanation. Its prominence in the last ten years is largely the result of the rise of political parties that draw support from religious nationalism, such as the Hindu nationalism of the Bharatiya Janata Party (BJP). Such political ideologies constantly reiterate communal interpretations of Indian history.

These interpretations, I would argue, are in fact distortions of Indian history. They are ideologically limited and intellectually even somewhat illiterate, because history becomes a kind of catechism in which the questions are known, the answers are known, and there is adherence to just those questions and those answers. No attempt is made to explore intellectually beyond this catechism.

The aim is to define the identity of the Indian as specifically Hindu and to choose the one identity. This goes against the grain of Indian civilisation, which has been a civilisation of multiple identities. The potential and actual contestation now is over identities, and the rights of these identities, forgetting that identities in history are never permanent; that they change constantly over time, and that present-day identities cannot in any manner be pushed back onto the past.

The Post-colonial Interpretation

I turn, finally, to post-colonial theories of interpretation. One of the theories that continues or has been revived is the communal interpretation which, of course, has received a lot of political support, but is now becoming a highly contested theory. There have been, however, two other directions in which Indian history has moved, two very interesting and intellectually stimulating directions, unlike communal historical writing.

One of these is was Marxist historical writing, which was a major influence in the 1960s and 1970s. What is interesting about Indian Marxist historical writing is that although it used Marxist analysis, the dialectical method and historical materialism, it moved away from the given patterns that Marx and Engels had worked out for Asian history. For example, the major questioning of the Asiatic mode of production has come from Marxist historians. There has been, therefore, a creative use of Marxist analysis in grappling with the issue of modes of production.

Debates have also centred around questions such as whether Marx's five-stage theory of European history — primitive communism, slavery, feudalism, capitalism, socialism — can also be applied to India, or whether there should be a completely new periodisation, using historical materialism but not necessarily conforming either to the five-stage theory or to the Asiatic mode of production theory.

The focus of these debates, known as the transition debates, has frequently been on periods of change. In the 1970s, the question was whether there had been incipient capitalism in India prior to the colonial expansion in the 19th century. What was the state of the Indian economy? The famous 'drain theory' came into play here, the argument being that with industrialisation in Britain and the latter's need for resources and markets, much of India's wealth was drained away into Britain, fundamentally impoverishing Indian society. In the 1980s, the debate shifted to a different mode of production: feudalism. The debate, in fact, still continues on whether the feudal mode of production existed in India.

The focus of interest therefore has been very much, as is to be expected, on social and economic history, on questioning the existing periodisation. It has encouraged a large number of new trends and departures. It has opened up the study of Indian history, with even people who did not conform to Marxism being influenced by these new perspectives from which history has been viewed. Emphasis has also been laid on recognising the difference between pre-modern societies and modern societies. Are pre-modern societies embedded societies or are they open societies? There has been a focus on pre-capitalist economies and how they differ from modern economies, and on changes in society that go along with the fundamental change from clan to caste. The historical changes within caste have also received attention; this was not the case earlier because of the widespread belief that caste was rigid and frozen and, once it had come into existence, has continued without change. This focus has provided material for comparative histories raising questions for other disciplines: more recently, for example, such questions as religion as a social ideology. Because religion is often reduced to textual study, its dimensions get marginalised.

This approach of seeing religion as social ideology challenges a number of existing theories about the nature of religion.

The other group that has recently played an important part is the group known as the subaltern historians. They are largely historians of modern Indian history who have initiated a new perspective on the study of Indian nationalism, arguing that the studies conducted in the 20th century were dominated by an elitism that focussed on either the colonial state or the indigenous elites, the bourgeois nationalists or the middle class. They stress the need to look at the participation of the subaltern groups as defined by Gramsci. 'History from below' became their slogan.

The subaltern historians use diverse sources, moving away from archives and official papers to a variety of local sources, private and popular. They have also emphasised the importance of the oral tradition as legitimate historical source material. They encourage the investigation of the minutiae of what goes into the making of an event, of the author, of the audience, of the intention. This investigation can be of either a written or an oral text.

This kind of history then challenges the validity of making broad-based historical generalisations. Each study is self-contained. Eventually, there are a large number of well-documented studies with little cross-connection. This, frankly, is the level at which I have problems with this particular group, because I am a sufficiently old-fashioned historian to ask for generalisations. In focussing on the fragment, on the little piece that is being pulled apart, analysed and perhaps put together, there is a tendency to ignore the whole to which the fragment belongs. Is there a nation? Is there a national movement? We do not know, because what these scholars are concerned with is a manifestation of something which is very localised and very minute. It cannot, therefore, provide an alternative theory of nationalism, which may have been the original intention of those who founded the group. There is no framework of explanation which relates itself to a central point and to which each study can refer.

There are multiple readings of texts, and these are encouraged, but priorities regarding these readings are not apparent. This is certainly the influence of post-modernism. I find it difficult to accept, because I do believe that some readings are more significant than others, and do not give equal priority to all readings irrespective of what they are. History then becomes something of a narrative, and there is a return to some 19th century historiography, although of course the context and the framework are different.

What is interesting is that this kind of historical writing has so far had no impact on pre-modern Indian history. This may be because of the nature of sources and the way in which historians handle these sources. It has, however, had a tremendous impact on many aspects of third world history outside India, partly perhaps because it is closely associated with post-modernism in its more recent phase. It therefore has international visibility, and this has encouraged comparative studies which historians are now taking much more seriously.

To conclude, I have tried to suggest that in the modern writing of Indian history, there is a continuing dialogue and debate with colonial interpretations, with nationalist interpretations and with the evolution of theoretical formulations in the post-colonial period. This has resulted in Indian perspectives modifying or altering even the use of theoretical explanations in the histories of other parts of the world. This has not only enriched historical theory, even in areas other than India, but has also sharpened the debate and evaluation of comprehending the Indian past. Hopefully, it has also provided a more perceptive understanding of the past, which I think is essential in order to understand the present.

two

Towards the Concept of a New Nationhood: Languages and Literatures in India

U.R. Ananthamurthy

Some time ago I was in Syria meeting Arab writers from several parts of that country, and most of them asked me this question: 'You have twenty-two languages, but you are one nation, whereas we have one language, one religion, but we are twenty-two nations! How do you explain that?' What follows may provide a tentative explanation of this mystery called the Indian nation. I invoke two names, those of Mahatma Gandhi and Rabindranath Tagore. They provided an idea of the nation which is very different from the European idea of one language, one race, one religion. Hence, although there was an attempt to evolve a European kind of nation, the idea of the nation, which works in all the Indian literatures, was very different. India contains many Indias; that is something one encounters when one looks at literatures in all the twenty-two languages of India. Hence, whatever one can truly say about India, one can also say the exact opposite with equal truthfulness.

According to the 1961 census, there were 1,652 mother tongues, classified under 105 languages. These languages belong to four language families: the Indo-Aryan, Dravidian, Tibetan and Astro-Asiatic. But ninety of these 105 languages are spoken by less than 5 per cent of the population, and by sixty-five small tribes. There are fifteen languages that are written, read and spoken by 95 per cent of the people in India. From this, the country might seem like a Tower of Babel. However, if one knows two or three languages one can get by nearly anywhere in India. One of my pet theories is that in India, the more literate one is, the fewer languages one knows. Those who are literate only in English are tempted to use only English. But in the small town where I come from, one who may not be so literate speaks Tamil, Telugu, Malayalam, some Hindi, and some English. It is these people who have kept India together, not merely those who may know only one language.

People in India have always lived, even in the past, in an ambience of languages. Shankaracharya, the great philosopher who wrote in Sanskrit, must have also spoken Malayalam; he was from Kerala. Ananda Tirtha must have spoken Tulu at home and Kannada in the streets, but he too wrote in Sanskrit. Ramanuja, who must have been profoundly moved by the Tamil saints — they were non-Brahmin saints, and they wrote in Tamil — took a lot from them, but also wrote in Sanskrit.

These philosophers, who propagated the notions of monism, dualism and qualified monism, travelled throughout the country and acquired disciples all over India. They also influenced mystical poets who wrote in the regional languages, and whose utterances became myths and poetry in the languages of the common people which I call the *bhashas*. With such happenings a profound egalitarian impulse entered the hegemonic structure of Indian society. The caste system was questioned not after the Europeans came to India; it had been questioned much earlier. In the 12th century, the great Kannada Vachanakara poet, Basava, got into great trouble for arranging a marriage between a Brahmin girl and a Pariah.

The Buddha, on the other hand, chose not to write in Sanskrit. My friend Ramanujan always called Sanskrit the father tongue, just as English too is now a kind of father tongue. So, the Buddha did not write in the father tongue. The saint-poets of the medieval period in India did not use Sanskrit at all, they used rather the *bhashas*, the languages of India. They were mystics whose experience of God was immediate and not speculative. But they were also deeply concerned with society. Hence, although they were mystics, they were not apart from society. Belonging to different parts of India, these mystics, by opting to use the language of everyday speech to convey their religious experience, actually began to communicate with their gods in the languages of the street and of the kitchen. There was indeed a special language to address God, but by their use of a familiar language, the mystics brought God to the common people. As a direct consequence, their poetry empowered women and the lower castes for the first time. For instance, in Karnataka, menstruating women were considered impure. But the mystics said: 'No, they are as pure as ever,' defying a commonly held belief of the time. Thus, the empowerment of women in India has a history of 800 years.

The spiritual insights and philosophical subtleties which marked Sanskrit, the language of the elite classes, thus became the possession of the Indian *bhashas*. Ever since the medieval period, these *bhashas* have been the conduits of egalitarian passion working through the history of India. It has been a continuous process of inclusion, and not a negation of any language; of Sanskrit in the past, or of the *bhashas*, or of English later on.

The most recent of these great saints, who may be described as one of the great critical insiders of Indian civilisation (I use the term 'critical insider' for many of these people; they are insiders to our tradition, but they are critical of this tradition even if they are within it), was Mahatma Gandhi, who wrote in Gujarati, Hindustani, and also in English.

In our times, English serves the communicative function that Sanskrit did in the past. Hence, the Indian *bhashas*, which had earlier digested the essence of Sanskrit, today cope with the challenges of the West. Thus Kafka, Tolstoy and other European writers have influenced writers in the Indian *bhashas*. In the past it was Sanskrit that our writers had to cope with. A 14th century Kannada writer once remarked that there was nothing left in Sanskrit, as everything had been taken away from it.

I do not use the term 'mother tongue' as it is understood by Europeans. For instance, some of the best Kannada writers speak Tamil or Marathi at home. Although there have been instances of European writers such as Conrad, who wrote in their language of adoption, these cases are very few. In India, however, many writers do not speak the same language in which they may be writing.

I once asked one of the greatest Kannada poets, who used the Kannada language magically, just as Blake used English, whether he had always spoken Kannada. He replied 'No, I spoke Marathi at home, but until I was 12 or 13, I did not know that I was speaking two languages!' He was then a very colourful old man. At that point, his daughter-in-law came into the room where we were talking in Kannada and whispered something in his ear. He turned and spoke to her in Marathi, without realising that he was speaking Marathi. This kind of shift takes place constantly and quite unself-consciously.

A thousand years ago, Pampa, another great Kannada poet (the fact that I cite examples from my language should not be mistaken as chauvinism, it merely gives me a sense of authencity) wrote of Arjuna, his hero. Being a Jain, he could not make Krishna his hero, Krishna being a spiritual figure. He instead made Arjuna the hero of his work, and identified him with his own ruler, the Hindu king Arikesari, who was also his friend. Idealising Arikesari, he created the Hindu king after Arjuna. He also did something very interesting: he mixed his own narrative with that of the *Mahabharata*. He used a new figure of speech, *Samsa Alankara*, which draws very unrealistic equations between a great epic of the past and a contemporary event. Personally I think this a great device, one which Pampa used to voice his worldly concerns. It was a daring initiative, to make one's own river flow into the rivers of the past.

Not only have experiences been transferred from one language into another in a continuous and spontaneous act of translation in the course of daily life, but Indians have also lived simultaneously through many ages. The *Mahabharata* has been used freely for this purpose. Therefore, it is possible to say that apart from the innumerable languages of India, there are, metaphorically speaking, two more languages: the two great epics, the *Ramayana* and the *Mahabharata*. Many Indians, I dare say, have never read these epics. Yet they have encountered them right from childhood, through several modes.

A translator of Indian literature once narrated the following. He was collecting oral stories in the Kannada language. There are a thousand such stories in Kannada, which are sung or narrated from memory by non-literate rural people. In the original episode in the *Ramayana*, Rama advises Sita that she should stay back in the palace and not accompany him to the forest where he has been exiled. He says: 'You do not have to come with me. You are a princess. Your feet are tender and you have been brought up with such care, so do not come to the forest with me. It is for men like me.' But Sita says: 'No, I am your wife, and I should go!' However, in one of the folk stories, when Rama similarly advises Sita, she says: 'In every other *Ramayana* I know of, Rama lets Sita go with him. How can you deny it to me?' Thus India is knit, according to this translator, through an inter-textuality, which occurs not only across the texts which we read, but across oral texts as well. That is why I state that the *Ramayana* and the *Mahabharata* could be two languages which knit India together. This rural Sita is aware that there are other *Ramayanas* without even knowing the names of the authors.

For the modern Indian writer, therefore, there is a confluence of languages: Sanskrit, English, perhaps translations from French and Portuguese, and certainly Russian, because Tolstoy was read even during British rule. English was used not only to read British writers. I do not think Jane Austen ever influenced an Indian writer, but Tolstoy certainly did. English, being a hospitable language offering many translations, was used to read much of the work from Europe.

I wish to emphasise this element of plurality within India. For instance, there was an attempt in Tamil, the oldest of the modern Indian languages, to develop an alternative to Sanskrit poetics and grammar, and also a theory of poetry that was very different. Great writers like Tagore and Gandhi became much more than literary figures for the people who spoke the languages in which they wrote.

An interesting point may be made here. While there are certain metrical compositions which can only be read, there are also compositions, in a certain kind of rhythm, which can be easily memorised. Some of the great poets used rhythmical expressions that enabled a composition to directly enter the memory of the people. There are wonderful memory devices within those metres, and they are present in the common speech of the people.

Literary figures were however generally in the high mode, which is the classical. There are thus two streams entering into India's languages: the classical, and the *desi*, or the indigenous stream. After Kalidasa (this is a daring statement that I make, as I have always done), there had been no great literary figure in India until Kabir came on the scene. What is very interesting here is that at one time a literary figure could emerge only in Sanskrit writing. But later, such a figure appears in the form of Tagore in one of the Indian *bhashas*, Bengali, which is neither as widespread as Hindi nor as ancient as Tamil. One of the Indian *bhashas* like any other, Bengali produced a literary figure equal in stature to Kalidasa, a figure who would be emulated all over India. This must have been due to the spirit of nationalism in those days. Since independence, however, we have again become so Euro-centric that we cannot think of any Indian language producing a literary figure for the whole country. Instead, we borrow our literary figures from Europe.

I would like at this juncture to say something about unity and diversity. Dr Radhakrishnan, the great philosopher, once said at the Sahitya Akademi, the academy of Indian letters, that since all the twenty-four languages are represented there, Indian literature is one, although written in many languages. The use of the phrase 'unity and diversity' in politics and in culture has now become clichéd. In fact, I used to shy away from using that phrase myself, until I suddenly realised it could still be used, if one thinks of it as a process.

If you overstress unity in India, and maintain that there is only one India, then diversities begin to appear. This becomes a political phenomenon too. Thus, after Indira Gandhi, who wanted a strong centre, there have been problems in Hassan (in Karnataka), in Punjab and in Kashmir. It has been argued that as Tamil is older than Hindi, Hindi should not be imposed on Tamil. This could be stretched to mean that Hindi should not be imposed on Bengali, or on Marathi. So, if one overly stresses unity, diversities begin to assert themselves. On the other hand, trying to emphasise diversity, arguing that Indians are all different, and that they have nothing in common, makes me uneasy and I start to feel that there is something common after all between a Bengali and myself and everyone else. We are all Indians. So unity and diversity appear true only in actuality, and in these last fifty years we have seen an on-going drama of unity in diversity.

As far as diversity is concerned, over the last fifty years there have been many attempts at grasping the post-colonial situation. Paradigms have been tried and given up, communities imagined and dissolved, traditions constructed and de-constructed, the principles of unity and of difference alternately appealed to. Further, the western presence has been acknowledged and negated, and radical European concepts and models have alternated with a return to indigenous roots, to the classical and the folk elements of India's heritage. Decolonisation has become a major preoccupation.

Creativity in India has just been released afresh. Literary discourse is marked by the negotiation of the necessary heterogeneity, using a concept of identity that lives through difference and hybridity. Overtime, this hybridity enters the languages. There are a number of words of Portuguese and Arab origin in Kannada, and quite often people speaking that language are not even aware that they are using words from other languages, such is the way with the Indian *bhashas*. The philosophers say that there is a little fire somewhere in the *atma* (soul) which can digest anything, this is known in Sanskrit as the *Jeernagni*, the digestive fire. I consider the Indian *bhashas* the great *Jeernagnis* of India, because they digested Sanskrit at one time, as they digest Europe now. They have been transacting with different languages in this manner all through their history.

A great and new phenomenon in the Indian languages was the *dalits*, the untouchables, beginning to write, first in Marathi, then in Gujarati and now in Kannada, Telugu and Tamil. Thirty centuries of silent suffering, a whole culture of silence, lay behind their articulations of indignation. There is a kind of subaltern protest in their writings. They have succeeded in re-drawing the literary map of their languages by exploring a whole new continent of experience, and also in revitalising language with styles, timbres, words and phrases so far kept out of literary use. The tendency in Indian languages has been that whatever is closest to Sanskrit has been used by the elite groups. When new groups begin to talk, words which have never been used in a literary context enter the literary texts. I shall have something more to say about this phenomenon a little later on.

In addition to this *dalit* literature, India also has a committed feminist literature. Some of the great women writers are Lalitambika

Antarjanam, Mahadevi Varma and Mahashweta Devi. These are not self-consciously feminist writers, but I shall not dwell further on this.

Last of all, let me make a personal statement, since I am myself a creative writer. I feel uneasy when I write just academically, because I may not be handling the issues objectively and rationally. But when I write in a creative idiom, I am more comfortable. So I will end my observations about Indian literature, and how it makes for a new kind of a nation, on a personal note. I use a traditional Indian home, my own childhood home, as a metaphor for Indian literature.

My father and his friends frequented the frontyard of the house, which had a raised urban platform under a country-tiled roof, known in Karnataka as Mangalore-tiled roofs. The upper classes usually have Mangalore-tiled roofs over their homes, while the less well off have round-tiled roofs. In the frontyard of my home, caste was not a problem. My father's non-Brahmin friends in the village came to consult him about auspicious days for weddings and other ceremonies and, more frequently, to settle land-related disputes. They sat around him on coloured mats. The very poor who belonged to the same caste sat on one of the steps leading up to the platform. This was like a porch, a matless, quite cold, but well-swept space.

My father offered everyone palm and betel nut, and even tobacco to chew. This frontyard space, framed impressively by massive, well-carved pillars, was a place of authority, yet cheerful and full of tidings of the temporal world outside and the spiritual world beyond. On auspicious occasions, for example, traditional story-tellers would be invited to recite tales in the frontyard.

As a child I came to know of the affairs of the world, I heard even of Edmund Burke and Gandhi, in this man-dominated front-yard of the house. My father was a self-taught man, literate in English, Sanskrit and Kannada, and therefore an unusual and sought-after scholar in the hilly villages around. He spoke enthusiastically to the villagers of the freedom struggle, then being led by Mahatma Gandhi. And the villagers would gossip, narrating again and again the same stories about the British government and its officers, whom they admired for their efficiency and generosity. On auspicious occasions, some elder or the other who came as a guest to our house would describe the glories of the *Dasara* in

Mysore. Or he would choose an appealing episode from the *Maha-bharata* and sonorously read it out.

There were only men in the frontyard, and if women came at all they were taken inside to a cool dark hall which was the centre of the house, called *nadumane*. If the women were Brahmins they went deeper into the house, to the place for family dining. The spaces of the house had their own meanings, depending on where you were and where you sat. The *nadumane* had coloured bamboo mats spread on a smooth, cold and swept floor. The family dining space, more private, had wooden planks to sit on.

Adjoining this was the most private place of all, the kitchen, which had a niche for the household god, where an oil lamp burnt night and day. Only my mother had free entry into this space; even my father could go there only after he had bathed and removed his everyday shirt. Next to the dining hall was a big bathroom, and near that was a workshed for the servants. Beyond that was the backyard; the most magical space for me. Had I not frequented it and eavesdropped on the gossip there, I would never have become a writer, because I got all my material from the backyard.

Into the backyard came women of the village, either to draw water from the well, or just to talk to my mother, or receive a gift of leftover special food which my mother would give them unsolicited. These used to be gracious moments of kindness and friendship and courtesy among the women. A woman might refuse politely, but my mother would keep talking and say 'not for you, but for your child!' After the exchange of such civilised courtesies, much more would take place in the backyard as the women relaxed and the conversation became more intimate.

My mother was ritually more orthodox than my father, who drank coffee and who knows what else in the town. Yet, in the backyard, caste barriers among women were forgotten and they would confide the secrets of their sexual lives. I heard a lot as a child about the sexual life of women, and about affairs in the village. So I knew that no matter what was presented in the front, the spiritual India, there was something else at the back, even in the village. This is how writers are made, in the backyard, not in the frontyard of civilisation. The frontyard produces only professors!

Women would talk of the everyday sorrows of the complicated relationships between men and women, and speak of bodily aches and pains that would never get cured and could never be shared with their menfolk. The world of the frontyard and the world of the backyard were such different worlds! The backyard world was not only the secret world of women. Here mother cooked delicious smelling dishes from herbs and leaves that grew beneath the untended bushes. Only my mother knew them by their names, and every small thing that grew had a name which never entered the learned dictionaries of my language.

My grandfather would also venture into the backyard to collect roots and leaves of plants as medicine for the sick in the village. It was taboo to reveal these names, which were mostly in Sanskrit, or even to identify the plants. Such medicines were effective only if secrecy was observed. Today, I wish secrecy had been observed, because, under globalisation, most of those medicines are going to be American medicines and will cost large amounts of money to obtain.

Grandfather used to assure me as a child that he would pass on to me the secret knowledge when I grew up. But I grew up to be a different kind of person because of the influence of my father's frontyard, where the use of Sanskrit led to Anglicisation and worked on me to make me modern. So the education that began in the frontyard of my traditional home finished in England and America, the great frontyards of modern civilisation.

The Indian literatures in the *bhashas* have a frontyard and a backyard as well. I use the word *bhashas* since I do not like the word 'vernacular'. It is a very condescending word and should never be used. Nor am I happy with the word 'regional language'. One does not call Portuguese a regional language, so I do not want to call any of my languages a regional language. All the languages of the world are also regional languages. Even the word 'dialect' I do not like, for it is of dubious usefulness. For if a dialect has an army and a national poet, then it becomes a language.

Which is the frontyard of India's *bhashas*? I will take the example of Kannada, my own language. The frontyard had Sanskrit literature of pan-Indian fame. But it had a secret backyard, fragrant, fertile and neglected. Here one could find the innumerable indigenous folk and oral traditions in Kannada, the *desi* traditions. The classics in Sanskrit constitute the *marga*, the great road. *Desi* and *marga* are actually the words used by Pampa a thousand years ago. His genius lay in the telling combinations he made of the two, and what he did had implications for the treatment of his themes; it was not just an aesthetic exercise.

The universal truths celebrated in Sanskrit literature were not only given a local habitation and a name but, cohabiting in Kannada with the folk imagination, they became pulsatingly alive. The two worlds of the frontyard and the backyard have been meeting ever since in Kannada literary works. The backyard is inexhaustible. From it, as literacy spreads, more and more people emerge into the frontyard of all civilisations, like the *dalits* and women today, bringing memories and desires to integrate with the mainstream of the frontyard literature, the world literature. The backyard, which is still the world of women, of secret therapeutic herbs, and roots and tendrils for the creation of new dishes, keeps literature in the *bhashas* continuously supplied with fresh themes and stylistic patterns.

Sanskrit as a language had no backyard of its own. It had to admit the *bhashas* of the backyard to ensure the survival and continuity of its spiritual substance. In the *bhashas* of India, the frontyard contains the classical literature, Sanskrit literature. However, what dominates the goings-on in the frontyard of our lives is not just the Sanskrit classics. There is also the powerful presence of English, the language of modernity. But neither Sanskrit nor English has any power if isolated from the *bhashas*, in fact they are impotent if they fail to interact with the world of the backyard.

Literatures in the *bhashas* have also constituted themselves as literary traditions, in search of their own particular royal highways. Tamil and Kannada have searched actively, and discovered their royal highways. A royal highway is meant for those who can compete with the classical Sanskrit tradition. What happens then to the backyard? The linguistics of cultures such as those small, powerless castes and their areas are undermined in the process. Yet while these sub-groups can be undermined, they cannot be destroyed. When the royal highway becomes pompous and loud and artificially rhetorical, and therefore solely a voice of public emotion, it loses the flexibility and truthfulness of common speech. It is at such moments of cultural crisis that the traditions in the backyard make a comeback and revitalise our languages. This was what Blake and Hopkins did to the English language in their own country, what in India has been done with much greater consequence for our culture by poets such as Tukaram, Basava, Mirabai and Kabir. When such people speak the language, they bring new life into the languages.

Women have without doubt been empowered by the great saint-poets of India. So it is misleading to speak about literature in the Indian *bhashas* without recognising its intimate relationship with larger political and cultural questions. The tradition of lively dia-lectical contention between the royal highway and the indigenous in India will be marginalised if globalisation encroaches upon everything; if everything loses out to the corporate world. That is the danger in India today. Even Yadavs, who are supposedly born into the lowly but noble caste of Krishna in India, have begun to rule in the manner of barbarians. Even the so-called sons of the soil, such as the Shiv Sena in Mumbai, seem only too eager to sign a memorandum of understanding with polluting and exploitative industries which threaten to deplete the fertile backyard. There is still a fertile backyard. But if this continues, there will be no place for either a leisurely frontyard, or for a dark and fertile backyard, in the industrial and corporate no man's land which we increasingly inhabit in India today.

three

Cultural Transitions in India Today: From the 'Himalayas' to 'Dharavi'

Rustom Bharucha

I shall begin on a somewhat deceptive note with a Himalayan perspective of Indian culture — a perspective that is often used to uphold an intrinsic multiculturalism of India that is rarely theorised, problematised or even named. Sanctified by the *mantra* of 'unity in diversity', this intrinsic multiculturalism is assumed by the agencies of the state as the 'natural' inheritance of every Indian citizen, the organic outcome of '5,000 years of uninterrupted civilisation', as our former culture secretary recently put it (Singh 1998).[1] This inheritance can be quantified with any number of cultural diversities embodied in a rich panorama of traditional performances, folk theatres, oral narratives and epic spectacles, which are alive in different states of vibrancy in relation to the process of modernisation, which is far from complete in India. While we have every reason to be proud of these pre-modern legacies of culture, we should not lapse — as we so often do — into a kind of self-congratulatory complacency by which we allow these diversities to be hegemonised by the state, frustrating in the process any real activisation of the respect for differences, without which no pluralist society worth its name can be said to exist.

If we could come down from these make-believe 'Himalayas' and take stock of *where* we are and *who* we are as citizens of this nation called India; if we could acknowledge that 'culture' is not an atavistic inheritance of primordial blood ties, bonds and loyalties, but a spectrum of dialogic relationships; if we could recognise more concretely that 'culture' is not just what exists in me and what exists in you, but what could exist *between* me and you — if we could grasp the legitimacy of these principles, we would be compelled to acknowledge our profound ignorance of the cultural diversities surrounding us. Not only are we ignorant of the diversities in a neighbouring state (as in the north-east of India, which is almost entirely isolated from the rest of the country), we could be ignorant of the diversities within the boundaries of our own state in some tribal, *dalit* or indigenous community.

While this ignorance gets masked in metropolitan areas through a tacit indifference to other cultures, it is legitimised by the absence of any real infrastructure for the exchange of cultures across regional and linguistic borders. Tellingly, there is no national infrastructure for the translation or learning of other regional languages in what is supposed to be the most multilingual nation in the world. Likewise, there are no structures for the actual collaboration of different cultural practices across regional states, apart from spectacles like the Festivals of India and the Republic Day Parade, in which our diversities are summarily 'unified'.

In the absence of an interactive, cognitive respect for cultural differences, therefore, our diversities cannot be assumed to constitute a plurality, which is better read as a secular wish-fulfilment, an *idee fixe* which exists in our heads, without being adequately mobilised or confronted in everyday life. Our diversities, I would further contend, are marked, sealed, bordered, hierarchised and regionalised. Consciously or unconsciously, with or without a defined ideology, most of us would define our cultural identities as Indians by affiliating ourselves to specific regional geographies, cultures and languages, which are assumed to be coterminous. These regional identifications (Bengali, Marathi, Tamil etc.), which are predominant in Indian cultural discourse today, have been hegemonised since independence by elite constituencies. Not only do these constituencies assume a knowledge of what constitutes the culture of a particular region, they also control the representation of indigenous, *dalit* and tribal cultures that lie within the geographical boundaries of their states. These marginalised cultures contribute to the valorisation of regional categories, even as their communities are demeaned by upper-caste patriarchies in everyday life. We need to acknowledge, therefore, that there are internal cultural differences within regional constructions of culture that are rarely confronted; indeed, they are more often than not silenced.

Another way of marking cultural identity would be through the specific caste affiliations of *jati*. Here one has to puncture the pervasive and increasingly oppressive myth of tolerance that is assumed to exist through the intrinsic plurality of the Hindu pantheon constituting multiple faiths and beliefs, which has accommodated diverse foreign cultures over centuries. While expansive structures for the accommodation of cultural difference (and syncretism) do exist in several Hindu popular traditions and cultural practices, one can never afford to forget the divisiveness of caste which prohibits and inhibits human, cultural and social relationships for millions of low-caste people, particularly in the rural areas, at the most rudimentary levels of inter-dining and inter-marriage. At the level of cultural practice as well, there are strong taboos that continue to prevent low-caste groups from participating in performances and community celebrations as dancers, singers, actors and even spectators. These exclusions are part of larger ritual sanctions ensuring the hierarchy of castes.

If we have to valorise the multicultural tolerance of Hinduism, therefore, let us not forget the racist intolerance that is built into the hegemony of caste, by which upper-caste ideologies like *Hindutva* have no difficulty in propagating 'one nation, one language, one culture'. Furthermore, instead of regarding *Hindutva* as a perversion of modernity, as some anti-secularist communitarian thinkers would like us to believe, it would be necessary to acknowledge that the foundations of its ethos are embedded in the very discriminations and injustices sanctified by the caste system and other patriarchal agencies.

The irony here is that the very differentiations of social injustice and disparity enable us to speak about Indian cultural diversities with such virtuosic variety. Indeed, as Kumkum Sangari (1995) has argued so forcefully, these differentiations can be said to *produce* diversities in their own right. And yet, the irony is that if one had to counter these disparities and injustices through a process of democratisation, one could be accused of neutralising these diversities and of undermining the cultural identities of underprivileged communities. It is not surprising, therefore, that the attempt to link social disparities to cultural diversities is often circumvented.

In addition, there is an attempt to authenticate the essentially 'Indian' condition of cultural coexistence, and in the process to disparage the emergent multicultural movements in western societies, which for all their democratic pretensions have merely succeeded in dividing entire communities—against each other, within themselves. At one level, this divisiveness is undeniably true if one considers that multiculturalism might never have entered the western vocabulary had it not been for the realities of immigration and the influx of labour from the ex-colonial countries from the late 1950s onwards. Only after these immigrants sought their rights as citizens in these ostensibly democratic societies did the monocultural, monolingual, monoreligious premises of western democracies become explicit. For instance, there is a law against blasphemy in Britain, but it applies exclusively to Christianity and not to any other religion. So how multicultural is this system of law? In the name of respecting pluralities and cultural differences, it could be argued that multiculturalism in western societies has broken the class solidarity of diverse working-class immigrant communities; it has tokenised minorities on a selective basis; and in its most destructive manifestations, it has functioned, as Slavoj Zizek (1997) has put it, as 'an inverted, self-referential form of racism—a racism with a distance'.[2]

We might accept the duplicities of multiculturalism in the West, but these should not legitimise the absence of a democratic multicultural policy in India on the grounds that any such policy can only succeed in further dividing communities. This is a cynical argument to my mind that overlooks the very real necessity of developing a more vibrant plurality in India that could counter the 'one nation, one language, one culture' agenda of *Hindutva* through the mobilisation of diversities and respect for differences, which need to be interrelated.

Instead of pursuing this undeniably difficult task, which needs to be contextualised within the fractured, disparate and incomplete process of secularisation in Indian society, there is an increasingly conservative retreat into the imagined virtues of cultural self-sufficiency, not just by orthodox, communal and fundamentalist forces, but by a growing number of communitarian thinkers and activists, who tend to privilege the narrative of community. This narrative could be a lot more violent and unjust, specifically in relation to minoritarian and gender rights, than is often acknowledged. I should add here that there is an extraordinarily thin line between fetishising self-sufficiency within the narrative of community and upholding a range of chauvinisms, insularities and patriarchal oppressions which can very implicitly feed the communal scenario by which entire communities are 'othered'.

I also believe that it is not particularly viable to uphold cultural self-sufficiency in an age of globalisation, particularly within the context of the ubiquity—or invasion—of the satellite networks in India. Whether we like it or not, we have now been exposed to 'the world' with a vengeance—or, let us say, the world as interpreted by Rupert Murdoch and his allies. The reality is that we do not exist in this world, except in the context of disasters, plagues, riots, the occasional miracle and, more recently, the nuclear blasts. Undeniably, there is a discrepancy at work here insofar as we seem to have internalised at unconscious levels our own *absence* in this world, which could be producing complexes and resentments that have the potential to be communalised. This internalisation of our absence in the global order, however, has yet to be studied adequately at psychological and political levels.

More explicitly, there is another discrepancy at work that functions at an economic level. Surely it is not 'culture' that concerns Murdoch and Co. but the extension of an apparatus for the propagation of global capitalism and the 'goodies' that go with it. This propagation is legitimised through the pluralist slogan of the market affirming 'the right to choose', which amounts to no choice at all for millions of people who lack the basic economic capacities to purchase the commodities of their desires. This does not stop them, however, from fantasising these desires and entering into all kinds of voyeuristic relationships with them. So there can be any number of beverages and colas that can be consumed on TV, even if there is no water in millions of homes. But as a media analyst from the First World once put it to me: 'I wouldn't worry too much about that if I were you. You've got to give people time to read these images and work out their own equations with them.'

Working out the images, of course, is not going to help people get water, but that's not the analyst's problem.

So what is the problem? The contamination of our minds, moral degradation? No, I think our *bharatiya sanskriti* is contaminated in its own right at many indigenous levels. The real problem has to do with the blatant injustice relating to disparities in the dissemination of cultures at global, national and local levels. While we are being bombarded by the cultures of 'the developed world', our knowledge of the cultures in our neighbouring states or within the boundaries of our own states remains exactly where it was; it could even have regressed. It is this imbalance in the transmission of cultures that is resulting in a breakdown of our social ecology.

To address this breakdown, it is at once expedient and necessary to develop the possibilities of intracultural linkages. At an ideational level, the 'intra' and the 'multi' share the same political space insofar as both are concerned with the possible mobilisation, translation and exchange of regional and local cultures across borders within the larger framework of the nation-state. The difference could be that while the primary agency of multiculturalism remains the state, which has the power and indeed the onus to order differences — and minoritarian ones in particular — within the prescribed norms of citizenship, the agencies of intraculturalism are more diverse, diffused, autonomous. Besides, while functioning within the framework of the nation-state, they also have the oppositional capacity to work against its globalising and fascist tendencies. Among these agencies I would include NGOs, voluntary associations, social action groups, and citizenship and civil society initiatives, all of which have been influenced by the primary source of democratisation in India today — the people's movements — out of which are emerging new cultures of struggle. The potential to link these cultures of struggle could be the most potent form of interculturality in India today.

When I use the term 'cultures of struggle', I am not referring to the instrumentalist agency of culture in any struggle, through street plays, posters, placards, graffiti, protest songs, though obviously these are extremely vital for any movement. I am referring to something more fundamental and harder to put in words, which gets to the very crux of the transition between the narratives of community and citizenship. This transition, which lies at the very heart of the postcolonial predicament in India today, manifests itself through the emergence of new identities and subject-formations that are in the process of dislodging (though not necessarily displacing) those primary ingredients of 'community' as determined by caste and religion. Now, through the convergence of new affiliations and commitments around specific struggles like the environment, social justice and the right to information, we are seeing the formations of new cultures which are admittedly processual, always in danger of breaking down, reverting to older, more monolithic notions of 'community', and which are not free of their own sectarianisms. Nonetheless, these cultures exist and continue to grow in unprecedented ways, countering the imagined stabilities of an intrinsically multicultural, 'eternal' India.

Tellingly, these cultures of struggle are most consolidated in the much-maligned metropolises of India where, through the intensities of migrancy and the sheer violence and arbitrariness of the forces of capitalism, we encounter the emergence of new localities, which are almost held together by the density of their differences. Now it is no longer a question of upholding the liberal myth of the intrinsic accommodativeness of Indian peoples, which enables them to 'get along with each other' *despite* their differences. Today we need to emphasise the sheer struggle for survival which compels wide cross-sections of the Indian population to live and *fight* together *through* their differences. Fighting together could be as vital for intraculturality today as living together.

One of the most vital sites of intracultural struggle and survival could be Dharavi, Asia's largest slum situated in Mumbai, sometimes described as a mini-India, which has attracted people from almost every community in the subcontinent, practising a variety of religions and faiths, engaged across classes in the pursuit of different industries, businesses and handicrafts. It has been particularly stirring to see how Dharavi has rallied during and after the Mumbai riots in December 1992 – January 1993, following the demolition of the Babri Masjid. There is much evidence of its social togetherness in the concrete efforts made by neighbours across communities to help rebuild each other's homes, which had been demolished during the riots, along with damaged shrines and mosques. Inter- and intra-communal dialogue to pre-empt violence has also been initiated through civic societies like the *mohalla* (neighbourhood) committees.[3]

Out of these committees have emerged the most inventive subaltern cultural initiatives, like the enormously popular image depicting four young boy-priests with the slogan *Hum Sab Ek Hain* (We Are All One). This is a very different image, in its 'technicolour secularism', its grit, immediacy, mode of production and dissemination in working-class communities, from the images of 'national integration' on television and the metropolitan anti-communal imagery of activist groups like SAHMAT.[4] Grassroots secular images like *Hum Sab Ek Hain* have succeeded in infiltrating communalised spaces, apart from countering the 'saffronisation' of religious festivals like the Ganapati Pooja, which is celebrated with great fervour in the state of Maharashtra. The elephant-headed god, the patron saint of the arts, the official scribe of the *Mahabharata*, is also iconised by the extremist Hindu communal party, the Shiv Sena, which was largely responsible for masterminding the riots in Mumbai.

हम सब एक है ।
धारावी मोहल्ला एकता समिती, मुंबई

In this collision of details—Ganapati, the Shiv Sena, the riots— it becomes evident that the cultural transitions in contemporary India are at once extreme and volatile, as gods get appropriated by political parties and are transformed into communal icons. For every sacred symbol in India today, there is a potential political sign. Secular activists have no other option but to re-appropriate both the symbols and the signs — sacred and secular — that have been taken over by the propaganda and rhetoric of *Hindutva*. Likewise, there is an obligation to uphold the heterogeneity of public space and culture, which cannot be controlled or censored by any one party or organisation, under any one philosophical, ideological or pseudo-religious framework. This means that we have to protest against the increasing invasion of cultural spaces like art galleries, which have been attacked because the allegedly blasphemous painter in question (M.F. Husain) happens to be a Muslim. Nor have the recitals of popular *ghazals* been spared, because the singer (Ghulam Ali) happens to be from Pakistan. And, of course, we are now getting used to the banning of cricket matches with Pakistan in Mumbai, because the Führer in question believes that they are anti-national and unpatriotic.

The reality is that these systematic encroachments on the rights of public culture are blatantly anti-democratic. This leaves us with no other option but to fight the communalisation of our culture in all its manifestations. But how do we fight? With what weapons? Which resources? In these concrete questions, the agendas of intra-culturalism and secularism converge, opening new concerns not only of cultural practice but of political responsibility and self-renewal. It seems to me that as cultural workers we run the real risk today of allowing our most autonomous concepts of culture to be consumed in politics — and not just any politics, but a particularly insidious form of sectarian violence. How do we resist this violence without 'internalising the aggressor'? How do we counter the Other without being 'othered' in the process, or, worse still, by allowing ourselves to be absorbed in the Other? How do we continue to remind ourselves that there are many other ways of practising, conceiving and imagining culture that are not determined by the dominant dichotomies of our times?

Perhaps the critical task for cultural workers today lies in activising the imagination through a re-invention of the secular imaginary, which can help us not only to counter the violence of our times but also to strengthen our own increasingly precarious inner balances. In countering the disruption of the social and political ecologies of our world, let us not forget the ecology of the self, without which no social or political transformation is ultimately sustainable or renewable.

Notes

1. See my review of Singh (1998) in Bharucha (1998a) for a critical elaboration on the multicultural inanities upheld in the official cultural discourse of the Indian state.
2. For a detailed exposition on the racist dimensions of multiculturalism in relation to Eurocentricity and the 'problem of universality', see Bharucha (2000: 34–39).
3. An analysis of the *mohalla* committees within the larger process of secularisation in post-Ayodhya India can be read in Bharucha (1998b).
4. For a critique of SAHMAT's metropolitan secular aesthetic in relation to its exhibition *Hum Sab Ayodhya* on India's pluralist cultural traditions, see the section on SAHMAT in Bharucha (1998c: 52–74).

References

Bharucha, Rustom. 1998a. 'Culture and Power', *Sangeet Natak*, No. 127–28.
——. 1998b. 'The Shifting Sites of Secularism: Cultural Politics and Activism in India Today', *Economic and Political Weekly*, Vol. 33, No. 4, pp. 167–80.
——. 1998c. *In the Name of the Secular: Contemporary Cultural Activism in India*. New Delhi: Oxford University Press.
——. 2000. *The Politics of Cultural Pratice: Thinking Through Theatre in an Age of Globalization*. London: The Athlone Press and The University of Wesleyan Press; New Delhi: Oxford University Press (forthcoming).
Sangari, Kumkum. 1995. 'Politics of Diversity: Religious Communities and Multiple Patriarchies', *Economic and Political Weekly*, Vol. 30, No. 51, pp. 3287–310.
Singh, B.P. 1998. *India's Culture: The State, the Arts and Beyond*. New Delhi: Oxford University Press.
Zizek, Slavoj. 1997. 'Multiculturalism, or, the Cultural Logic of Multinational Capitalism', *New Left Review*, No. 227, September–October.

four

Dalits: Reflections on the Search for Inclusion

Gopal Guru

f or the dalits, who constitute 15 per cent of India's population,
the struggle for moral equality, for equal recognition as men
and women, has been long and painful. This is because the structures of hierarchy and segmentation, and the accompanying
cultural and behavioural codes, still persist in India today, more
than fifty years after independence. Although some dalits are
included at some level in the opportunity structures, thanks to the
interventionist policies of the welfare state, their exclusion by and
large in many vital fields remains profound. This exclusion is
'profound' in the sense that dalits still feel psychologically, socially,
politically, emotionally, economically and, of course, culturally
excluded from the mainstream of Indian life.

One can look at this exclusion in terms of the loss of control
over 'time' and 'space'. This is a negative exclusion which constitutes the life-world of the dalit and can be contrasted with the
privileged, and hence positive, exclusion of the twice-born. As far
as the dalits are concerned, the privileged exclusion of the twice-
born is a logical necessity for the latter's consolidation. For the

twice-born, to be excluded from the social situation of *shudras* and the *ati-shudras* is itself a self-affirmation. The need for the twice-born to maintain this privileged exclusion is further reinforced by their fear of losing their prized place in society if they become polluted. Thus, the condition of privileged exclusion is a matter of anxiety for the twice-born. They seek therefore to perpetuate a structure of self-affirmation through privileged exclusion, a structure which has been maintained by the brahmin and the kshatriya by denying dalits control over their own 'time' and 'space'. Let me illustrate my point.

Historical Background

If we look at it from a critical distance, 'time' and 'space' have never historically belonged to the dalits. During feudal times, for example, the exclusionary paradigm was characterised by the absence of the language of rights. Dalits only dealt with the language of obligation. This led to the misrecognition of their human worth. The language of obligation entailed only negative rights, 'what could *not* be done, enjoyed, claimed', which amounted to their humiliation within the Hindu social order. Dalits' rights, during the feudal period, were negative in that they were entitled only to certain demeaning rights, like the 'right' over the hide and the flesh of dead cattle, the 'right' over the leftover food and cast-off clothes of the feudal lord. In addition to these 'rights' the dalits also had certain judicial rights; they were entitled to adjudicate in matters of litigation with respect to land, a right which had only spiritual value, in the sense that they were required to act as arbitrators in land disputes between the two upper caste feudal lords without, however, having any access to land themselves. Thus, dalits were spiritually included in the economic system while being materially excluded from holding any worthwhile assets in land.

The starkness of this social order of exclusion is best illustrated by the practice of 'Hindu internment', which confined the dalits within fixed boundaries. They were not allowed to leave these areas — internment camps called *mahar/mangwada* in Maharashtra, *halgweri* in Karnataka, *cheri* in Tamil Nadu — without the permission of the upper castes, who policed the boundaries of the camp with physical force and also with the ideology of purity–pollution.

Thus, the dalits were ghettoised in space, a physical and cultural confinement within a territorial area that was stigmatised by the upper castes. They had no freedom to walk on the main streets of the villages or small towns, and even if they had to walk through these streets in the service of their feudal lords, they were supposed to clean those streets with brooms which were tied to their waists in order to erase their polluting footprints. Dalits were thus prisoners of space. In other words, freedom of space was denied to them.

The feudal social order also denied dalits any sense of time. During the feudal period, they possessed a very vague sense of time. Under the *jajmani* system dalits were supposed to perform the *vetbegari* — forced and unpaid labour — without any sense of time. They were in the service of the feudal lords who employed them round the clock, except during times when the appearance of the dalit was considered dangerously polluting. For example, during the Peshwa rule in Pune in 18th century Maharashtra, the brahmin-led feudal state imposed a time limit on dalits, under which they could enter public streets that went through the high caste locality only around noon. This particular time limit was imposed because during this hour the dalit's shadow would be shortest, and hence would have the least chance of polluting the upper caste. This meant that the beautiful mornings and cool evenings were denied to dalits; the scorching afternoon remained their lot. In this sense as well, therefore, dalits had no control over time. On the contrary, their time was policed by the upper castes.

The exclusion of the dalits was, of course, cumulative as they were also excluded from the more dignified occupations and from education. This exclusion was achieved by the upper caste by making available to dalits only those occupations which were considered defiling, such as tanning of leather, scavenging and leatherwork. The dalits were also excluded from the field of politics and from the cultural and social life of the feudal world. In this regard, one can argue that this exclusion was a result of brahminical cunning. On the one hand the exclusion of the dalit was achieved by ghettoising him/her through defiling occupations, and on the other the knowledge system of the dalit was appropriated and resignified, as, for example, happened in the case of music and singing. Thus, for dalits, Indian history has represented their complete exclusion from a knowledge system that actually belonged to them. They were not only obliged to render their services to the feudal lords, without any access to the power structure, but also had to face profound exclusion from other important spheres of the life-world. In other words, dalits had no sense of power. What they had was only a sense of patronage, of being eternally grateful, an attitude of supplication and subservience that crushed them morally.

With the arrival of colonial power, however, the dalits began experiencing a kind of inclusion, both in terms of 'time' and 'space'. For example, they were able to enjoy some kind of freedom to move in the streets of cities and towns without fear of brahminical policing. They also got the opportunity to enter the institutional structure of education and other colonial institutions such as the army. They were also allowed inclusion in the British bureaucracy. Certain principles of standardisation of life made it possible for them to seek *some* inclusion, however small, in the political, economic and social life of the colonial world. But the process of empowerment was too slow for the dalit to enjoy the full range of rights available to others. The independence of the country and its adoption of a constitution ensured, at least theoretically, the equal distribution of rights to everyone without any distinction of caste, race, class, religion and gender. This made possible a more inclusive common life than was possible in feudal society.

After independence, the democratic aspirations of dalits could be met partially in the sense that they could participate as equal citizens in the political process of the country. They also benefited from the process of democratisation of bureaucratic structures through reservations and, more importantly, through the adoption of universal adult franchise. Through these opportunities, legal, administrative and institutional, dalits were able to establish some amount of control over time and acquire some kind of secular space in a 'civil society' that was forced to become, if not more tolerant, then at least more benign. They could now seek to change their occupations. They could attempt to get into more secular occupations in the tertiary sectors. They could send their representatives to decision-making bodies at all levels, local, regional and national. But the experience of fifty years of democracy in India has remained a mixed blessing for the dalits. The fruits of democracy still elude them in many respects, particularly when seen in terms of time and space. One cannot confidently say that independence has enabled them to achieve complete control over their time, or that it has enabled them to destroy the strictures of Hindu internment and to acquire a hold over secular spaces; these practices of control and exclusion still persist across India, as can be seen in the abuse suffered by dalit political leaders. The extent of their democratic empowerment and the nature of the freedom they have enjoyed during the last fifty years remain to be properly assessed. In the following section, I shall examine some of these issues in greater detail. I shall attempt a social auditing of Indian democracy.

Social Auditing of India

Let me begin with the argument that Indian democracy has, by and large, failed to enable dalits to achieve control over their time and space. One can argue that in certain parts and sectors of the Indian economy, dalit workers and agricultural labourers have been able to gain some control over their time from the rich farmers; for example, in the form of fixed working hours in the agricultural sector. They are, however, unable to retain control over this time, which they have achieved through struggle and not through the benevolence of their employers. Do they have the freedom to change their employers on the grounds that the latter do not observe the terms mutually agreed upon? The answer, unfortunately, has to be given only in the negative. The dalit, in fact, has to pay for her freedom twice. She has to sell her labour as a commodity only in order to buy the commodity that is necessary for her physical survival. Thus, she pays twice; first by labouring for longer hours with sometimes more than one employer, and second by working more than one shift. Does the dalit therefore enjoy the freedom to control her time? In fact, because of the inflation in the prices of essential commodities, the unequal relationship that exists between the dalit's purchasing power and the prices of commodities that she needs makes it more difficult for her to maintain control over her time. This aspect of purchasing power, and the corresponding price mechanism, ultimately decides the time factor for the different consumer classes. (I hate using the word 'consumers' for those poor who normally have nothing to consume.)

The Indian markets or the weekly bazaars usually have specific time slots depending on the purchasing capacity of the consumers.

For example, the prime hour will be reserved for rich people, who go to the market during the time when the fruit, fish and vegetables are fresh. The vendors, understanding both the tastes and the purchasing capacity of the rich, inflate the prices almost arbitrarily. This privileging of market time, which undermines the chances of bargaining and operates in a way which suits the dictates of both the rich market-goers and the shrewd vendors, by implication keeps the dalits or the poor out of this prime market time. The lack of purchasing power makes the impoverished dalits effect tactical and strategic entries into the market. They enter only during the time (mostly towards closing-time for the bazaar) when commodities are cheaper and less valuable in terms of nutrition. In a sense, the poor depend on the vulnerability of vendors who, owing to the perishable nature of their commodities, are finally compelled to sell them at throwaway prices. Saturday and Sunday markets in some areas should thus be regarded as culturally and socially inferior because spurious and second-hand commodities are sold. It is the poor dalit who participates in these markets. Thus, the unequal relationship in the marketplace not only denies a good quality of life to the dalits, it also seriously questions the mainstream notion of time and freedom, and hence of democracy. This situation, where control over time is conditioned by control over purchasing capacity, comprehensively rejects the fragmentary view of time. Actually, the situation of dalits or, for that matter, of the poor in general, exposes the bourgeois notion of time as misleading, in the sense that the dalit might gain control of time in one sphere of life but loses it in another. It is important to understand time in terms of its totality, which shows the domination of the rich over time.

It is not only from regulated time that the dalits find themselves excluded, but also from territorial space. These spaces are both economic and geographical. In the first case, the dalits are excluded from the better jobs, and ghettoised in occupations that are considered polluting, such as scavenging, tanning and leatherwork. Even in the public sector, dalits are excluded from the decent sections and segregated in areas where others do not like to go. For example, in the soap factory, they are concentrated in sections where the worker is supposed to touch the tallow that is used in soap manufacturing. This exclusion from the more respectable jobs is a historical reality as far as dalits are concerned. It was common practice in the Bombay textile mills for dalits to be excluded from the weaving sections. This exclusion was sought by upper caste workers on the grounds that dalits, if allowed in this section, would pollute the entire fabric. The workers in this section were supposed to link broken thread with the bobbin by sucking the thread through it. However, the real reason for this exclusion was material, in the sense that jobs in the weaving department were relatively better paid, and the Maratha workers, though they did not have the required skill, occupied these jobs. Thus, untouchability was used as a weapon to exclude the dalit. It is interesting to note in this regard that untouchability came in quite handy to the British who used dalits to collect revenue in Madras presidency. Pariah dalits were sent for this purpose on the assumption that they were very good at collecting revenue dues and taxes, since the wealthy upper castes would pay up on the spot just to keep the dalit revenue collectors out of their houses.

The notion of purity–pollution has also been responsible for keeping dalits out of the hotel industry. They can be associated with the industry, but only as servants who at best are allowed to clean the dishes. However, they are excluded from the kitchens as well as from high-profile positions in the hotel industry because of the ideology of pollution. (In such a situation, it would be interesting to know what happens to the reservation quota in catering colleges across the country.) There do not seem to be any enterprising hotel owners from within the dalit community. This exclusion is replicated in other parts of the industrial sector, especially in the private sector, which is not concerned with reservations and will not respect the complex methodology required to assess the merit of the dalit. The dalit, therefore, is confined to the vulnerable public sector, which is shrinking. However, they will continue to find employment and be ghettoised in the sanitary sections of these sectors in which, even today, their percentage exceeds their proportion in the population. In addition to this exclusion, in every city dalits face a territorial exclusion as they tend, out of a sense of insecurity, or rather out of social security, to remain within localities comprising dalit households. In mixed localities, they feel psychologically isolated and alienated. In such cases they prefer to stay in government colonies, which again affirms the structures of exclusion. One must grapple here with a paradox. Although the state promises the dalits respite from the socially hostile upper

caste civil society through preferential policies, in certain cases
the government is helpless in assisting dalits in their fight against
residential exclusion.

The state's inability to handle those upper castes who attach
negative meaning to dalit residents is evident in the field of education. Education and its institutions are considered progressive
agents of civil society, especially by those who champion the idea
of emancipatory resources of civil society. One must therefore ask:
how effectively have these educational institutions helped the
dalits overcome their exclusion? How effectively have dalits found
inclusion on their own terms? The answer unfortunately is in the
negative. Educational institutions, as open centres of power, are
supposed to confer a sense of democracy and active citizenship
on all persons within them, including dalits. In practice they have
replicated the structures of exclusion. In some medical colleges,
for example, dalits have been ghettoised in one portion of the
hostel, and pushed to the filthiest corner of the dining hall. In
Kanpur, several years ago, dalits were ghettoised in a DAV college.
Such experiences of exclusion have also been faced by dalit
teachers, who in one case were ghettoised in one building in a
premier university of the country. This building is ironically called
'Mandal Manzil', where dalit, tribal and OBC teachers were to be
housed. They refused to occupy the building. In villages, dalits
are still banished to 'areas of darkness' like the *wadas* and *cheris*
mentioned earlier. In urban centres they are ghettoised within
'modern institutions' riddled with social stigma. These institutions
are created at the initiative of the state. Thus are born backward
class hostels, school social welfare departments, SC/ST commis-
sioners and different Ambedkar foundations, all of which, paradoxically, perpetuate the sense of exclusion. Any offers made to
dalits to occupy such institutions only reinforce the sense of exclusion that they feel so deeply. This only goes to show how policy-
making by the state is still trapped within an elitist mindset, and
even when it seeks to redress disadvantage through preferential
policies such as dalit hostels, it does so within a framework of
charity and not one of creating a culture of equal worth and equal
citizenship.

This language of patronage deepens the feeling of exclusion,
particularly when the state apparatus, in patronising tone, cites
all that it has done for the dalits. The state's claim that 'we have

made provisions for the dalits' implies that the dalits are a liability for the state. Its duty then emerges from a feeling of liability, rather than from a desire for redressal of wrong. Just as the existence of *wadas* and *cheris* defines the main upper caste village in rural areas, the emergence of city slums, which are by and large the lot of the dalit, perpetuates a profound sense of exclusion in the cities. In fact, urban slums have become necessary zones of accommodation for pauper criminals and unemployed dalits. This zoning is done in the interest of preventing social unrest from assuming dangerous proportions. It is in terms of this self-enlightened interest that slum improvement schemes are undertaken by the state. Ragpicking has been given a modern name by some NGOs, who call it 'self-employment'. Thus, democracy in India has created an indistinct mass: a population without resources and social attachment, a class which has found itself abandoned or which has been made temporarily mobile as migrant labour.

Democratic practices are supposed to involve a process of transformation that takes place through the opening up of opportunities to participate, the inclusion of excluded voices, democratising access to the media, politicising the depoliticised, empowering the powerless, and reducing political dependency by transforming a passive citizenship into an active one. However, in Indian democracy, by and large, it is the dominant political force that has always defined and decided the political agenda of the dalits. The dalit has come to be the compulsion of competitive politics that is ultimately dominated by non-dalit political parties. For dalits seeking political mobility, empowerment through sponsorship by a political party is really exclusionary and humiliating. For they will always feel morally crushed under the burden of the patron's obligation. This sponsored mobility is doubly humiliating when the dalit is sponsored by a *Hindutva* party, as he or she then succumbs to the party that has historically sought to humiliate dalits. In such a scenario, dalits have made only a 'guest appearance', either in the election manifestos of different parties, or in the proceedings of the legislature. In other words, in Indian democracy, the dalit issue has received only token representation, and hence dalits are excluded from participatory political life. So much so that they are denied the political opportunities that would have given them a definite feeling of inclusion, like the dalit sarpanch who was denied the opportunity to hoist the flag on independence day. The bureaucracy at the panchayati raj level makes decisions ignoring the dalit sarpanch. In some extreme cases, the panchayati raj bureaucracy has gone to the extent of removing the entire dalit population from census records. This is done with the intention of denying dalits the government help that is their due.

Dalit empowerment, in the formal sense of the term, was premised on the argument that 'power belongs to no one and that those who exercise power do not possess it; that they do not, indeed, embody it'. Democracy is thus regarded as inaugurating a sharp break with the past. What is radical, and indeed unprecedented, in modern democracy is its shift of sovereign power to an abstract site or an empty place: a shift manifested at the level of politics in the perpetual rule-governed contest for power. In other words, the exercise of power in democracy is subject to procedures of periodical redistribution, which implies an institutionalisation of conflict in a space, since sovereign power cannot be occupied or embodied by any individual or group in society. Thus, power is a zero-sum game that takes place in an empty space. Within this understanding, parliaments and assemblies become empty places that keep attracting people such as Mayawati and Kanshi Ram. In this particular sense, democracy does not decide beforehand the conditions of exclusion and inclusion of any social group seeking power. It assumes that everyone has the chance to fill the empty space. It is for this reason that Mayawati and Kanshi Ram are attracted by this theoretical indeterminacy. But is there really an empty place at the practical level? When answered in caste and class terms, it is clear that the *empty* space has always been occupied by the upper castes and upper classes of this country.

It is interesting that the real site of power is always occupied by the dominant. Hence, when the dalit reaches parliament, she has hardly any chance of being allotted an influential portfolio. It is always the case that relatively less important portfolios, like social welfare, are assigned to the dalit. The social welfare department is often exclusively manned by dalits. The late Babu Jagjivan Ram could not become the prime minister of this country. In parliament, dalits feel excluded from the proceedings because of the power hierarchy that exists here as well. The very structure becomes so intimidating that the dalits feel marginalised. They have to seek representation through the more powerful members of the party to which they belong. Thus, parliament also serves as a site for harbouring the hierarchy of power relations. In our democracy, dalits feel excluded from the political process as they hardly take part in the active political life of the country. Within parliament, dalits watch helplessly proceedings that concern even dalit issues. Due to this withdrawal, tactical or forcible, dalit issues are excluded or kept in cold storage. For example, the SC/ST commissioner's report is passed ritualistically, without any discussion, or the time allotted to it is too short. In this regard, it is interesting that the SC/ST Order (Amendment) Bill was introduced only in 1976, during the Emergency. The Maharashtra government could not immediately implement the democratically taken decision to rename the Marathawada university after Dr B.R. Ambedkar; it took more than fifteen years to implement that decision. In such a situation, the dalits do not feel that they matter in the political process. They take their political direction either from their bosses in the community or from their upper caste political bosses. Invariably somebody else does the political thinking for the common dalit. They are thus culturally constructed into objecthood. This means that they are turned into a vote bank, are defined by people from outside, are painted as inferior objects in the political museum. To add insult to injury, they are finally stigmatised as passive citizens. In addition, dalits face direct exclusion from local power structures. They are often forcibly prevented from taking part in the electoral process of the country, or forced to vote for a particular party. They are prevented through intimidation from joining or occupying public office, or are represented by proxies in political office.

Sometimes the state, particularly when it has a racist or fascist design, uses directly humiliating methods to seek the exclusion of certain sections of society. For example, a state with the *Hindutva* agenda uses the language of secondary citizenship to keep Muslims on permanent probation with regard to their loyalty to the nation. In similar fashion, such a state seeks to exclude dalits, either by treating them as second class citizens or by attaching negative meaning to the cultural symbols that are so dear to dalits and that seek to accord a universal meaning to dalit identity. For example, the BJP–Shiv Sena coalition government in Maharashtra attempted to segregate the dalit by prescribing blue uniforms for dalit pupils, whereas it recommended white shirts and khaki shorts for non-dalit pupils. Although the order was finally withdrawn owing to pressure from dalits, its intention of attaching a negative, stig-matising meaning to the colour blue was confirmed. Blue is a natural colour, but it is negatively signified by the saffron govern-ment only to exclude what it considers the wretched, despicable lot that follows Ambedkar.

Indian democracy has not so far created the social conditions for dalits to realise their cultural aspirations. They feel completely excluded from cultural life as they are invisible in both the print and electronic media. This obviously happens due to the upper caste — particularly *Hindutva* — domination of public cultural re-sources like radio and television. It is the upper castes who appear and reappear on a regular basis in the print media, on television and on other media channels. Every small detail of the lives of cultural czars is covered on television, while even major events relating to the dalits are ignored by the media. Events that portray them in an adverse light, however, are promptly reported. Ac-tually, some dalits are trapped by the lure of media glamour, for example, the incident involving Kanshi Ram and media persons a few years ago in Delhi. The cultural landscape of the society is the preserve of the dominant in that society, and the dalits, who do not have independent cultural resources like radio or TV, as the blacks do in the USA, are excluded even from the so-called high-level debates that take place on dalit issues. While they do find some representation in the cultural life of the country, one does not know how authentic this representation is.

The Search for Active Citizenship

On the basis of the preceding discussion, one can draw the rather uneasy conclusion that the present form of democracy has not been able to expand the social basis of dalit political aspirations. In such a situation, can civil society expand the social basis of the demo-cratic imagination of the dalits? Or should one invest faith and confidence in the state for such expansion? If the 'state' is preferred to 'civil society', how does one come to terms with the experience of the last fifty years which shows that if the state is pressed into service, it ends up producing only passive citizenship among the dalits? Should one go beyond the state for the expansion of the democratic realm? As far as the dalits are concerned, the answer cannot be given in a straightforward manner. This is because they are not in a position to believe in the intention and the capacity of civil society to give a definite lead to the issue of active citizenship among the dalits in particular and others in general.

Dalits will have to seek active citizenship both within and beyond the state. Active citizenship has to be sought beyond the state because the power structures still underpin and renew unequal, and hence exploitative, social relationships. This by definition, therefore, limits the role of the state which acts as a filter that includes only a few, and that too only periodically, within its gamut of power, while it regularly excludes the vast majority of dalits and the poor. Thus, the process of inclusion is slow and limiting, while exclusion is speedy and widespread. In any case this process of inclusion, due to its ideology of patronage, tends to create only passive citizenship. Logically, therefore, this supplants the need for active citizenship that necessarily prompts both the cognitive and emotional responses of the collective subjects to the immediate world. Its reconstruction, through the negative hermeneutics of suspicion, resists any temporary accommodation with provisional achievement, such as those of dalit elites, in the process of human emancipation. In other words, active citizenship is aimed not at provisional inclusion but at fundamental alternation on the basis of reciprocal recognition rather than modernist triumphalism that seeks more to limit than expand the social base of the democratic imagination. This notion of citizenship does not deny the citizen a radical role as an agent actively intervening in the historical process.

Active citizenship has to be motivated by the notion of empowerment not as provisional accommodation, but more as a critical concept that enables the dalits, or for that matter any agency in question, such as women and tribals, to interrogate the power structures that trample the victim. Dalit citizens become active in resisting the power relations that are close to them, and subsequently try slowly, and also dialectically, to remove the cataract of illusion from the lenses of the dalit vision and to see clearly the complex interconnections between the local centres of power and those located at a great distance. In other words, the precondition for the emergence of active citizenship is not the profound satisfaction of a temporary triumphalism, but the creative disenchantment that shows emancipatory concern and also criticises the established social vision. Active citizenship should have two normative aims. The first is removing the dilemma that suggests the necessity of being bound only by the weak and attenuated bonds of inclusion and yet of presupposing a strong state, capable of protecting the person of the dalit in an increasingly casteist and violent society and of assisting him amidst an increasingly uncertain economy that tends to subvert their sense of time and secular space. The second, which results from the first, is achieving a sense of active citizenship that works towards the ultimate removal of the burden of those conditions that force the dalit to define all 'time' and 'space' in terms of necessity and not of choice. Thus, positive citizenship involves the promise of a positive utopia as against the negative nostalgia that has never belonged to the dalit.

Economy
in
Transition

five

Economic Progress in the Context of Industrialisation and Globalisation

S.S. Bhandare

Since independence, India has made considerable progress in terms of diversification of its economy, industrialisation, technological development and the growth of real gross domestic product (GDP) and per capita income. This has been accompanied by a noticeable improvement in social indicators, including the spread of literacy, reduction in infant mortality, expansion of health facilities, creation of modern temples of scientific, technical and management education, and even a dent, albeit not so significant, in the massive problems of poverty and unemployment. The recent nuclear tests have, no doubt, been the cause of international concern and criticism, but they have conclusively proved the great scientific and technological capability of India. What has been achieved may not be glorious, but it can certainly make anyone proud, particularly because all these gains have been secured within the framework of democracy, in a country of striking contrasts and enormous ethnic, linguistic and cultural diversity. We also cannot overlook the adverse interruptions caused by frequent external tensions and shocks, such as outbreaks of conflicts with neighbours, oil shocks and financial turmoil. Internally too, the growth process has never been consistently smooth and steady; indeed, the economy has experienced intermittent ups and downs in agriculture and industry, as well as frequent forex crises and bouts of inflation.

A span of fifty years may not be very long in the life of an independent nation. And it is surely just an insignificant dot in the history of civilisations. But witness the metamorphosis in the global scene during this period. The crude military parity between the Soviet Union and the United States has suddenly disappeared, leaving virtually a single military superpower, the United States, whose economy is also in good shape. In the post–World War II period, we have seen the accentuation of the Cold War till the 1980s and its sharp retreat thereafter. We have seen the emergence of military blocs such as NATO, CENTO and SEATO, which are being rapidly overwhelmed by trade blocs or economic unions like NAFTA, EU, ASEAN, APEC and SAPTA. We have witnessed the building of the Berlin Wall, its destruction and the consequent unification of East Germany and West Germany. We have seen the initial success of communism under the leadership of the USSR, and its subsequent total retrenchment, thanks to the collapse of the USSR and Eastern Europe. In this period, over forty countries embraced democracy, as the world simultaneously experienced the triumph of the free enterprise system. *The Economist* (1994) proclaimed: 'Now more than three billion people in Asia, Latin America and Eastern Europe have joined the rich world's one billion or so, in the market-economy club.'

This period has also been characterised by the relative decline of the US and Europe in terms of their respective contributions to world economy and trade. Simultaneously, there has been a strong emergence of Asia, due not only to Japan's spectacular achievements till the 1990s, but also to the achievement of the high performing Asian economies (euphemistically called the Asian Tigers) and of China during the last two decades or more. Of course, the Asian currency crisis in the latter half of 1997 imposed an inevitable brake. But can there be any denial of the likely resurgence of the Asian Tigers after the painful process of their economic restructuring is complete, say in the next two or three years? Thus, not only has the global political balance undergone transformation through a series of political events, but the global economic balance has also undergone profound changes.

Equally importantly, there is an increasing degree of economic interdependence. World trade has expanded at a much faster pace than the world economy. The role of capital flows is becoming more dominant than that of trade. Also, significant shifts are taking place in trade and capital flows. Transnational companies (TNCs) and their foreign affiliates are increasingly influencing the size and nature of cross-border transactions. Consequently, markets for goods, services and factors of production are becoming global. Kenichi Ohmae (1995) very perceptively highlights how nation states, once efficient engines of wealth creation, are losing their ability to generate real economic activity. He contends that four great forces — capital, corporations, consumers and communications — have combined to usurp the economic power once held by the nation states.

The process of transition of a large part of the world from communism to capitalism, from commanding heights to market-driven economic systems, from authoritarianism (or dictatorship) to democracy, has obviously been arduous. Simultaneously, the rules of the international economic system, which were written after World War II and based on the Bretton Woods agreement, have undergone a dramatic transformation. The General Agreement on Tariffs and Trade (GATT) is behind us, and the World Trade Organisation (WTO) regime has already been in operation for several years. Rules, procedures and institutions designed for the global economy in the post–World War II scenario have long ceased to be meaningful and relevant. As the world moves towards a more liberal democracy, an ever greater role for the free market system, privatisation and rapid globalisation, what progress has India made in the fifty-odd years of its independence?

Historical Perspective: A Unique Model of a 'Mixed' Economy

Around 1951, when independent India launched on its process of economic planning, there were stimulating debates on alternative approaches to development strategies. These included the famous

Bombay Plan prepared by prominent industrialists. But the most conspicuous were

> three streams of thought permeating the Independence movement. One of the streams was that the state will have a most decisive, perhaps a full say in all economic matters, much in the same mould as the planning experience of the erstwhile Soviet Union during the '20s and '30s. The second approach was to provide support to small and village industries without disturbing the institutional set up in order to achieve village *swaraj*, on the lines of a typical Gandhian prescription. Finally, there were many who favoured the idea that private enterprises should flourish, since modern industries were established and sustained during the days of the British Raj by Indian industrialists of rare vision and patriotism. If one could have combinations of these approaches, clearly there were more than three choices for independent India to make (Vasudevan 1997).

The architecture of India's development strategy was surely influenced by various such ideological thought processes of those times. However, the ultimate framework of planning was based essentially on the famous blueprint prepared by Mahalanobis, which influenced India's path to development for the next thirty-five years.

> It focused on the need to achieve self-sufficiency in the production of capital goods as the first priority with a view to enhancing the output of consumer goods at a later stage. In the original paper, Mahalanobis presented a two and a four sector model with technical coefficients and a growth path. Questions of resource availability, inflation and employment were neglected (Vasudevan 1997).

Eventually, the process of learning in the early phase of economic planning led to the evolution of India's own unique model of a 'mixed' economy. This model survived the vicissitudes of both internal socio-economic events and external shocks. India had completed the implementation of seven five year plans (including the plan holiday period of 1966–69), when the new economic reforms ushered in in July 1991 brought about a virtual paradigm shift.

It is imperative to understand the reasons why India came to embrace its unique concept of mixed economy. First, the experience of the colonial regime, which made economic consolidation and resurgence the topmost priority. It was perceived that such tasks could not be accomplished by the initiatives and efforts of the private sector alone. Second, the immensity of the social responsibilities of the state to deal with problems of poverty, unemployment, population, illiteracy, regional imbalances and so on. Third, the inadequacy of existing physical infrastructure (power, roads, railways, ports, telecommunications) for building a modern economy. Obviously, infrastructure development, requiring massive capital investment and long gestation periods, could not have been undertaken by the private sector. Fourth, a sense of uncertainty about (indeed the lack of credibility of) the efficacy of the free enterprise system in delivering the goods. Last, the international economic and political situation which created 'cruel dilemmas' about aligning with any dominant ideologically oriented system, be it capitalist or communist. The non-aligned middle path approach with a strong bias towards the public sector thus became the driving force of India's unique concept of the mixed economy.

Dominance of the Public Sector

With the concept of mixed economy at the centre of the development process, the public sector came to assume 'commanding heights'. It became a powerful mechanism for promoting economic growth as well as improving the socio-economic condition of the people. Over time, the scope and dimensions of the public sector expanded so rapidly as to encompass not only government departments, but also government companies in both the central and the state sectors, irrigation and power projects, railways, post and telegraph, ordnance factories and other departmental undertakings. The public sector further expanded its dominant position through nationalisation in the spheres of banking and insurance, and by setting up new institutions (the Industrial Development Bank of India [IDBI], the National Bank for Agriculture and Rural Development [NABARD] etc.) offering various financial services.

More importantly, because the industrial sector was to play a key role in the achievement of socio-economic changes, the role of the public sector was guided principally by the Industrial Policy Resolution of 1956. This empowered the public sector to play a strategic and exclusive role in the development of seventeen industries for well over three decades, from 1956 to 1991. The industries covered were aircraft manufacturing, shipbuilding, heavy machinery, heavy electricals, core mining, generation and distribution of electricity, basic metals, air transport etc. The public sector progressively assumed a prominent role in many other important industries and services as well, leaving private enterprise the opportunity to make only a supplemental contribution. Admittedly, the remaining industries, like aluminium, chemicals, fertilisers, machine tools, road transport and sea transport, were left to the initiative of the private sector. With regard to foreign capital, the industrial policy insisted upon the Indianisation of ownership and effective control of industries, while recognising the necessity of securing the participation of foreign capital and enterprise for fostering industrial development.

In substance, in striking similarity with many other countries emerging from the yoke of colonisation, policy makers in independent India stressed the need for rapid industrialisation of the economy with an emphasis on basic and heavy industries, the development of which came within the domain of the public sector. With such a dominating role, the public sector's share in investments and output in the Indian economy grew fairly rapidly during the first four decades of planning. Consequently, there was a corresponding shrinkage in the contribution of the private sector.

Thus, the public sector's share in the GDP rose sharply from 8 per cent in 1960–61 to 19.7 per cent in 1980–81 and further to 24.6 per cent in 1990–91. Not only in overall GDP, but also in the gross value of output from industry, the public sector's share witnessed a rapid increase from 8.5 per cent in 1960–61 to 27.5 per cent in 1990–91. In spite of this spectacular growth, there simultaneously occurred a sharp reduction in its contribution to gross domestic savings, from 20.6 per cent in 1960–61 to as little as 4 per cent in 1990–91. The savings performance of the public sector left much to be desired. Indeed, it continues to adversely affect the overall savings ratio of the economy. Hence, the savings–investment gap in the public sector, which was already very large in the 1960s, rose progressively in subsequent decades. Thus, the gap between gross capital formation and savings in the public sector was 23.6 per cent in 1960–61; it increased to 25.2 per cent in 1980–81, and further to 35.2 per cent in 1990–91 (Bhandare 1996; GOI 1997–98).

To meet the resource needs of economic development as well as its own ever-growing obligations of administration, defence, subsidies and welfare activities, the government made enormous inroads into the savings of the economy. Apart from taxation, its massive capital-raising activities were made possible through internal and external borrowings. This is reflected in the rapid growth of governmental indebtedness over the years. To illustrate, the total outstanding liabilities of the central government expanded more than sixty-four-fold from Rs 119.64 billion in March 1966 to Rs 3,142.58 billion in March 1991, and further to Rs 7,732.41 billion by March 1998. As a ratio of GDP, government liabilities increased from 45.7 per cent in 1965–66 to 58.7 per cent in 1990–91, but declined to 55 per cent in 1997–98 (Bhandare 1996; GOI 1997–98).

All this severely impinged on the private sector's contribution to the economy. Given the ever-expanding financial needs of the government, it was felt imperative to curb and control the private sector's demand for resources. This was sought to be achieved through stringent policy instruments like industrial and import licensing, monopolies legislation, high incidence of taxation, credit controls, foreign exchange rationing, capital issues regulations, selective imposition of the convertibility clause in the disbursement of financial assistance and so on. In short, a stringent 'financial repression' accompanied the strong physical controls on the activities of the private sector.

Indian Growth Experience up to the 1980s

Against this backdrop of economic planning and the industrial policy framework, it is essential to bring out the salient features of India's growth performance spanning the first four decades (1950–51 to 1990–91) after independence, prior to the launching of the new economic policy in July 1991. Undoubtedly, this continues to be an area of intense research and fascinating debate. The basic question being evaluated repeatedly is: what is the long-term trend growth rate of the Indian economy? Also, are there any distinctive phases in the pattern of growth? Several experts have sought to conceptualise the growth trajectory of the Indian economy in terms of transitional dynamics from one crisis to another.

However, for the purpose of our simplistic analysis, we have made our own 'periodisation' scheme consisting of three distinctive parts: first, from the base year of the First Five Year Plan, i.e., 1950–51 till 1980–81 — this period roughly fits the description of the 'Hindu rate of growth' syndrome, so aptly termed by Raj Krishna; second, from 1980–81 to 1990–91 — the decade of high growth rate broadly reflecting the process of gradual liberalisation, and also the beginning of a simmering crisis culminating in the initiation of major economic reforms in July 1991; third, the on-going period of reforms which promises a take-off to a sustainable high growth rate in the Indian economy. Such a periodisation of the growth experience is convenient for the purpose of identifying major turning points or significant trends. This approach seeks to avoid the analytical sterility of viewing the entire period as one of stereotypical, uniform continuity. At this stage, we confine ourselves to the description of the significant features of the growth experience in the first two phases (see Appendix 5.1).

- First, the long-term trend in the real GDP growth rate of the economy over a period of forty-seven years (1950–51 to 1997–98) works out to 4.3 per cent per annum. Within this, the first prolonged phase recorded the Hindu growth rate of 3.6 per cent, while the second phase (1980–81 to 1990–91) showed noticeable improvement at 5.7 per cent per annum.
- Second, if one takes into account the annual growth in population of 2.1 per cent during the first phase, the rise in real per capita income of 1.2 per cent per annum was meagre. The Indian planners had envisioned a doubling of per capita income in fifteen years, but this could not be realised due to low overall economic growth in the context of a population explosion. In fact, it has taken India almost forty-two years to achieve this feat, while the Asian Tigers achieved miracle growth rates in a much shorter time-frame. Incidentally, to quote *The Economist* (1994):

> After the industrial revolution took hold in about 1780, Britain needed 58 years to double its real income per head; from 1839, America took 47 years to do the same; starting in 1885, Japan took 34 years; South Korea managed it in 11 years from 1966; and, still more recently, China has done it in less than 10 years.

Thus, India's achievement pales into insignificance, although it is quite satisfactory when seen against the backdrop of the country's performance in the hundred years prior to its independence.

- Third, the second phase (1980–81 to 1990–91) witnessed an acceleration in the growth of real per capita income to over 3.1 per cent per annum, made possible entirely by striking improvements in overall economic growth, with virtually no change in the growth rate of population.

- Fourth, the sectoral composition of the Indian economy experienced remarkable transformation throughout this period. As a result of the emphasis on industrialisation, the industrial sector registered about a five-and-a-half-fold expansion or an increase of 5.8 per cent per annum in the first phase and an accelerated 7.8 per cent per annum in the second phase. The progress of industry in the second phase reflects the positive impact of the early process of economic liberalisation. Consequently, the share of industry in the overall economy rose progressively from 14 per cent in 1950–51 to 26 per cent in 1980–81, and further to 29 per cent in 1990–91.

- Fifth, the agricultural sector, despite considerable progress in terms of increase in productivity, crop diversification, technological changes and the Green Revolution, recorded a relatively modest growth performance primarily due to intermittent droughts and setbacks to capital spending. In the first phase, agricultural production increased by only 2.2 times or by 2.7 per cent per annum, while in the second phase the progress was noticeably better at 3.8 per cent per annum. However, it needs to be emphasised that the performance of the agricultural sector, in particular of foodgrains production, has been ahead of population growth, thereby enabling the country not only to be self-sufficient, but also to effectively tackle the question of supply management and food security in a consistent manner for the last two decades and more. Indeed, in the 1980s, for the first time in India's history, the agricultural growth rate was significantly higher than the population growth rate. But the divergence in the rates of growth of industry and agriculture led to a sharp contraction in the share of agriculture in the overall economy from 55 per cent in 1950–51 to 38 per cent in 1980–81 and 31 per cent in 1990–91.

- Sixth, this period also saw the strong emergence of the services sector, whose share in real GDP expanded consistently from about 30 per cent in 1950–51 to 40 per cent in 1990–91. Although public administration and defence services were important parts of the tertiary sector, banking, insurance, transport, communication and trade activities also made remarkable progress.
- Last, the external sector was very subdued in the first phase, due to export pessimism on the one hand, and a strong bias towards import-substitution on the other. However, since the beginning of the second phase, the external sector has gathered momentum. The overall ratio of external trade (exports *plus* imports) to GDP, having declined from 13 per cent in 1950–51 to as low as 7.3 per cent in 1970–71, improved gradually thereafter to 14.1 per cent in 1990–91.

To summarise the economic developments in India over this period of four decades (1950–1990), we shall quote the very precise observations of Jagdish Bhagwati (1998):

We had started out in the 1950s with:

- high growth rates
- openness to trade and investment
- a promotional state
- social expenditure awareness
- confidence that poverty would be seriously dented by growth
- macro stability
- optimism; and hence
- the admiration of the world.

But we ended the 1980s with:

- low growth rates[1]
- closure to trade and investment
- a licence-obsessed, restrictive state
- inability to sustain social expenditures
- loss of confidence in the efficacy of growth in reducing poverty
- macro instability, indeed crisis
- pessimism; and therefore
- marginalisation of India in world affairs.

Economic Crisis of 1990–91 and Reforms

The sustainability of the strategy of high growth of the economy in general, and industry in particular, achieved in the 1980s, was challenged in the very beginning of the 1990s. The crisis had been simmering since the mid-1980s, with the government relying heavily on domestic and foreign borrowings. The aftermath of the conflict in the Middle East (the Iraqi invasion of Kuwait), and the resultant steep rise in oil prices, dealt a major blow to macro-economic management. All these events culminated in a crisis of high fiscal deficit, escalating inflation and setback to balance of payments, leading to a rapid depletion of foreign exchange reserves. Thus, the ratio of the central government's fiscal deficit to GDP reached an all-time high of 8.3 per cent in 1990–91; the rate of inflation touched a peak of 17 per cent in August 1991; and forex reserves dropped to a meagre one billion dollars by March 1991, sufficient to meet only about two weeks of imports. India was at the edge of a precipice; it could have even become a defaulter in meeting its international financial commitments.

There were various other major distortions and deficiencies in the economic system, some of which still continue. The industrial policy regime pursued relentlessly from 1965 to 1990 (with the notable exception of limited liberalisation in the 1980s) fostered fragmentation of capacities, stagnation in total factor productivity, a high-cost and inefficient industrial structure, costly import-substitution and export pessimism. This situation had various implications:

- First, given the relatively slow industrial growth, with only a few bright patches in between, India's status as an industrial power in the league of nations saw a decline. Thus, in the mid-1960s, India was ranked eighth largest in the world in terms of GDP, tenth largest in terms of value of industrial output and the nineteenth largest exporter. But its position dropped continuously thereafter, and even with the recent improvement in growth performance it was ranked (in 1996) fourteenth largest in terms of GDP, fifteenth in industry and thirty-first in exports. Many other countries in Latin America and Southeast Asia have overtaken India in the last two or three decades.

- Second, it also led to declining productivity across a number of industries and a higher incremental capital to output ratio. Isher Ahluwalia (1998) points out that over a prolonged period from 1960 to 1980, the total factor productivity growth (TFPG) in the organised manufacturing sector witnessed a secular decline of 0.5 per cent per annum. During the same period, several other countries, notably Japan and South Korea, secured an average annual TEPG of between 3.1 per cent and 5.7 per cent. It was only during the period 1981–89 that TFPG in the organised manufacturing sector in India scored gains of 2.7 per cent per annum.
- Third, since employment prospects are inextricably linked with productivity considerations, Indian industry came to acquire an anti-employment bias. In fact, there was resistance to productivity improvement among workers. Moreover, stringent labour legislation (like the lack of an exit policy) affected the flexibility of management in industrial restructuring.
- Fourth, structural deformities and policy rigidities contributed to the proliferation of industrial sickness. This has become pervasive across ownership (public and private), across industries, across states and across scales (small, medium and large). Of course, industrial sickness is not a phenomenon unique to India, but what is damaging is the lack of an expeditious and effective restructuring process, and the consequent lock-up of enormously scarce financial resources in persistently loss-making enterprises. The economy has, thus, been deprived of opportunities to effect economically viable industrial restructuring.
- Fifth, public sector enterprises (PSEs), considered to be the driving force of industrialisation and economic expansion, in fact became a major drag on the economy. Out of 239 PSEs, as many as 101 were loss-making units in 1995–96 with aggregate losses of Rs 48.26 billion. The profitability profile of PSEs was far from encouraging; the ratio of their net profits to capital employed hovered in the low range of 2–4 per cent for a very long time before improving gradually to 5.7 per cent in 1995–96. The initial exuberance about PSEs entering new areas of industrial and technological developments withered away as a number of problems began to manifest themselves in many enterprises. Thus, a number of PSEs suffered due to low productivity, poor

project management skills, overmanning, lack of technological upgradation, inadequate attention to R&D, etc.

- Last, for the economy as a whole, the incremental capital–output ratio (ICOR) increased sharply, from 3.92:1 during the period 1951–52 to 1964–65, to 5.66:1 during the period 1965–66 to 1975–76, before declining gradually to 4.48:1 in 1976–77 to 1991–92 and further to 4:1 during 1992–93 to 1995–96. The average ratio for the entire period 1950–51 to 1995–96 worked out to a high of 4.88:1. Incidentally, during this entire period, India more or less consistently improved her domestic savings ratio from 10.4 per cent of GDP in 1950–51 to 26 per cent in 1995–96. In substance, as Jagdish Bhagwati (1998) aptly observes: 'The weak growth performance reflects, not a disappointing savings performance, but rather a disappointing productivity performance.'

In short, structural rigidities rooted in the inward orientation of the policy regime rapidly eroded the competitiveness of the economy in general and industry in particular, as India persisted with rigid industrial and import-substitution policies when most other developing economies had embarked on an aggressive export-led growth path. Therefore, it became crucial to regain lost ground and to catch up with many other faster-growing developing countries. For this purpose, it was imperative to carve out a strategy for a sustainable growth momentum with true self-reliance. This formed the basis of the new economic policy aimed at achieving fiscal stabilisation with structural adjustment.

Dimensions of the Paradigm Shift

Thus began the new transition—a paradigm shift in India. I shall refrain from defining the specific details of the new policy framework. Suffice it to say that, quite apart from the immediate task of macro-economic stabilisation, sweeping changes have been made since July 1991 in industrial, trade, tariff, investment, financial and tax policies. The three buzzwords continue to be Liberalisation, Competition and Globalisation. These are not meaningless terms, but symbolise a metamorphosis in the economic environment. The clear objectives are: to deregulate the economy, to reduce the role of the public sector, to unleash private initiative and enterprise, to accelerate economic growth, to meet the challenges of global competitiveness and, of course, to ensure social equity and justice.

Paradigm Shift

Industrial Liberalisation

- Abolition of industrial licensing except in nine industries.
- Exclusive public sector reservation limited to four industries against seventeen previously.
- Drastic dilution of legislations such as the Monopolies and Restrictive Trade Practices (MRTP) Act and the Foreign Exchange Regulation Act (FERA).
- Automatic approval for foreign direct investment (FDI) up to 51 per cent of equity in fifty-one, and up to 74 per cent in nine specified industries.
- Foreign Investment Promotion Board specially constituted to promote FDI in areas of strategic importance and requiring large investments.
- Substantial opening up of infrastructure to domestic private sector and foreign direct investment.

The reform process has indeed already been in operation for ten successive years with commendable progress, especially in the area of industrial policy. As a result, in a crude manner of estimation, (*a*) over four-fifths of industrial activity is free from any licensing restrictions; (*b*) over two-thirds of the industrial sector is open to foreign investments through the automatic approval route; and (*c*) the exclusive role of the public sector is limited to perhaps less than one-sixth of the industry as against half previously. Not only the virtual abolition of an industrial licensing regime, but also the massive dilution of monopolistic legislation has been a striking feature of the new policy. Thus, monopolistic companies do not require the prior approval of the central government to expand by establishing new undertakings, mergers, amalgamations and takeovers. In short, the objective of industrial reforms is to eliminate entry barriers and alter the incentive structure so that markets and prices guide private and public investments and corporate policies. The long pending basic conditions for industrial restructuring have, thus, been ushered in.

Alongside industrial liberalisation, the reform of the external sector (the trade regime) has occupied pride of place in India's structural adjustment programme. The basic thrust is on shifting from inefficient, non-competitive import-substitution to a capable and competitive export-oriented growth strategy.

Paradigm Shift

Opening up of the External Sector

- Rupee devaluation of 20 per cent in early July 1991, and a gradual changeover to market-determined exchange rate.
- Full current account convertibility of the rupee in August 1994.
- Sharp rationalisation and remarkable reduction in customs tariff.
- Long-term Export–Import (EXIM) policy: phasing out of (a) quantitative restrictions; (b) discretionary controls; and (c) canalised items of trade, etc.

At the same time, to support the growth momentum of industry and the external sector, there has inevitably been a need for an investment and growth promoting tax policy.

Paradigm Shift

Investment and Growth Promoting Tax Policy

Rationalisation and simplification of the tax system:
- Personal income tax: top rate reduced from 56 per cent in 1990–91 to 30 per cent.
- Corporate tax: (a) domestic companies from 51.75 per cent to 35 per cent; and (b) foreign companies from 74.75 per cent to 48 per cent.

Excise duty:
- Fewer product classifications/fewer rates: range 8 per cent to 18 per cent; in a few cases going up to 30 per cent.
- Across-the-board extension of Modified Value-Added Tax (MODVAT).
- Gradual shift towards VAT.

Customs Duty:
- Rationalisation into fewer rates.
- Maximum rate reduced from 300 per cent to 40 per cent. Most rates now range from 10 per cent to 25 per cent.
- Trade weighted rate 27 per cent.

The financial system plays a critical role in channelling resources to the real sector of the economy, comprising agriculture, industry, infrastructure and external trade. Progressive liberalisation has taken place in this sector during the last decade. The overwhelming objective has not only been to enhance the operational efficiency of the financial system, especially of the banking sector, but to expand the availability of resources to business and industry at competitive costs. Undoubtedly, fiscal consolidation is an integral part of this process. Accordingly, over the last few years, some fiscal correction has taken place, but the problem is far from resolved.

Paradigm Shift

Financial Sector Liberalisation

- Progressive deregulation of deposit and lending rates of banks.
- Sharp reductions in the Statutory Liquidity Ratio (SLR) and the Cash Reserve Ratio (CRR) allowing banks greater freedom in the deployment of lendable resources.
- Promoting integration of the money and foreign exchange markets.
- Strengthening the banking system through (a) capital adequacy; (b) prudential norms of accounting; and (c) greater autonomy and freedom to banks.
- Allowing the setting up of private sector banks and foreign banks.
- Major capital market reforms including: (a) free pricing of equity; (b) allowing foreign institutional investors (FIIs) entry to portfolio investment; (c) allowing the corporate sector to access Global Depository Receipts (GDRs)/External Commercial Borrowings (ECBs), etc.

The discussion so far is by no means exhaustive, pointing out only the most significant illustrative features of the new economic policy. How the Indian economy has shaped up during this period of transition certainly makes for very fascinating reading.

Post-reforms Achievements

At the time of writing, another coalition government, comprising eighteen parties, is in power in India; its predecessor, which lasted about two years, was a fourteen-party coalition government. The constituents of the new government span virtually the entire spectrum of political, economic and social opinion. Even such divergent combinations have shown their commitment to reforms, and therefore it can be said with complete confidence that economic liberalism is now built into the Indian ethos. Let us now proceed to review the key economic performance indicators during this on-going third phase, beginning with the crisis year of 1991.

- First, the overall economy, in terms of real GDP, recorded an impressive recovery after the first two years of reforms. In fact, during the three-year period 1994–97, real GDP growth averaged a high 7.5 per cent per annum. Shankar Acharya (1995) observes: 'The rapidity and strength of India's recovery stands out in any international comparison with other developing countries that embarked on post-crisis reform programmes, and provides an eloquent tribute to the quality of India's reform strategy.'

  There was, however, a setback in 1997–98, when the growth rate decelerated to 5 per cent. This is attributed to (a) negative growth of the agricultural sector; (b) sharp deceleration in the industrial sector; and (c) overall sluggish performance of the external sector.

- Second, though this slowdown was quite worrisome, it was not all that depressing either in the context of global trends or of India's own long-term trend growth rate.[2] However, all sections of Indian society—those in business and industry, economic planners, policy makers, politicians of all hues and the middle classes—have expressed their serious concern. Indeed, it is now taken as axiomatic that India must achieve an annual sustainable 7 to 8 per cent real GDP growth. This is in itself a remarkable transition in the mindset of the Indian society from the erstwhile Hindu growth rate syndrome.

- Third, the industrial sector, which was virtually stagnant in the crisis year of 1991–92, recovered strongly to achieve over 12 per cent growth in 1995–96. This spectacular performance was brought about both by stimulation of consumption and by an investment boom. However, industrial growth thereafter slowed down to 7.1 per cent in 1996–97 and further to 4.2 per cent in 1997–98. There were clear indications of a sectoral slowdown, but not of a general recession. The deceleration has been attributed mainly to the impact of (*a*) overhanging over-capacity, causing intense domestic competition; (*b*) competition from imports; (*c*) sharp contraction in the capital expenditure of the government in real terms under the compulsions of managing the fiscal deficit; (*d*) high real interest rates; (*e*) sluggish exports, and so on. But the most striking feature of the industrial scenario has been the accentuating pains of industrial restructuring. Having pointed out that Indian industry is witnessing a period of savage competition, F.A. Mehta (1994) observes:

> How much competition now impacts Indian industry can best be illustrated by the fact that prices of several products/commodities in India, but particularly of steel, petrochemicals, paper, aluminium and so on, have begun to be governed not only by the internal forces of demand and supply, but more by global prices. This can be easily demonstrated by comparing the changes in prices of major commodities with those of their prices in the international market.

He further suggests that 'in a fiercely competitive environment, the name of the game is restructuring. One company after another would be compelled by forces of competition to restructure their organisations managerially and financially . . . . Restructuring will assume various forms like mergers, acquisitions, divestitures, and so on.'

- Fourth, in response to the process of liberalisation, there was a spectacular investment boom during the period 1993–96. To some extent, investment activity, particularly in the industry and infrastructure sectors, received a setback in the next couple of years. But the overwhelming fact is that, in terms of the Industrial Entrepreneurial Memoranda filed by Indian industries, the total investments proposed from the inception of reforms till January 1998 were of the order of Rs 6,004.53 billion. Likewise, the data on all the investment proposals (including the infrastructure sector), compiled separately by the CMIE, showed that in April 1998, the value of investments was Rs 12,397.45 billion, of which almost 43 per cent was under implementation. India has been able to mobilise significant foreign capital by way of FDIs ($7.9 billion) as well as portfolio investments through FIIs ($9.1 billion) and GDRs ($7.8 billion). In all, therefore, since the launch of the reforms, India has received cumulative foreign investment of over $25 billion.

- Fifth, yet another remarkable feature of this third phase has been the resource-raising efforts of the capital market during the post-reforms period. In 1980–81, it was difficult for the corporate sector to raise a capital of more than Rs 3.5 billion. This figure had already increased to Rs 109.20 billion in 1990–91, but most spectacularly to Rs 486.3 billion in 1994–95. However, there has been a major setback since then, and capital raised in 1997–98 was only Rs 313 billion. It is evident, however, that Indian capital markets have come of age, and quite apart from their potential to generate a quantum of capital, there have been significant qualitative improvements in their functioning, including regulatory systems, emergence of promotional and regulatory institutions and greater consciousness among investors of the alternative investment opportunities.
- Sixth, there has been a perceptible improvement in the management of inflation; the average inflation rate which was at the peak level of 13.7 per cent in 1991–92 declined to 4.8 per cent in 1997–98. In short, India's growth performance is also associated with better control over inflation.
- Seventh, the most striking achievement in the post-reforms period relates to the sustained recovery and viability of the external sector. Export growth, which averaged over 20 per cent during the three-year period 1992–93 to 1995–96, no doubt slowed down to 5.3 per cent in 1996–97 and 2.6 per cent in 1997–98. Likewise, the growth of imports also slowed down from an average of about 18.5 per cent to 6.7 per cent and 5.8 per cent respectively during the same periods. But what is of even greater significance is the reduction in current account deficit from the crisis level of 3.2 per cent of GDP in 1990–91 to an average level of about 1.5 per cent during 1995–98.
- Eighth, India has been managing its external debt prudently. In fact, in absolute terms, external debt declined from the peak of $99 billion in March 1995 to $93 billion in September 1997. The ratio of external debt to GDP, in fact, declined even more sharply from 36 per cent to 24 per cent over 1994–98. Similarly, the ratio of debt-service payments to current receipts was reduced from 35.3 per cent in 1990–91 to 18.3 per cent in 1997–98. The proportion of short-term debt has been quite low at

around 7 per cent of the total debt. This is in contrast to the high proportion of short-term debt in most of the Southeast Asian countries which recently experienced a major currency crisis.

- Ninth, forex reserves (excluding gold and Special Drawing Rights [SDRs]) were built up more or less consistently after the period of crisis, from $2.2 billion in March 1991 to a healthy $26 billion by March 1998. These reserves are sufficient to meet any contingency of excessive speculation or volatility of the type that afflicted Southeast Asian countries during the latter half of 1997. The present level of forex reserves can finance India's import requirements for about seven months.
- Tenth, exchange rate management witnessed a smooth transition after the deliberate devaluation in response to the crisis in July 1991. India now has full current account convertibility and a market-determined exchange rate system. Of course, currency fluctuations are an integral part of the new scenario, but what stands out is the effective management of a stable and steady exchange rate behaviour even in the midst of the Asian currency turmoil. India has also prepared a road map to capital account convertibility, but this will certainly require strengthening the fiscal–financial nexus, and a greater degree of confidence in the financial sector. The recent events in the Asian currency markets have underlined the imperative of a cautious and gradualistic approach in this area.

Many more such indicators of the beneficial impact of reforms in India so far may be listed. However, suffice it to say that no other country that has gone through the process of major structural change has, in its initial period of transformation, made so many gains with so little pain. Equally significant are the qualitative improvements in the industrial sector owing to the scaling down of import barriers, the growing presence of multinational corporations (MNCs) and foreign direct investments. These changes may not immediately impact on growth performance, but they are too precious to be ignored. Indian industry is becoming increasingly conscious of its price–cost structure, norms of productivity, scales of operations, areas of core competitiveness, priorities of investments, strategic alliances, mergers and amalgamations and so on. In such an environment, the consistency of high industrial growth and corporate profitability performance cannot be taken for granted. Consequently, there is going to be an intensification of pressures to improve productivity and efficiency in the use of resources.

In short, India's macro fundamentals are, by and large, sound and strong. At the same time, the process of economic liberalisation continues unabated, irrespective of the change in the colour and composition of the new coalition government. There can be a re-calibration of reforms, or a slight moderation in their pace, but there are unlikely to be any compromises on the major thrust and direction of reforms.

Structural Changes and Corporate Restructuring

Let us now turn to the structural changes in Indian industry. Un-doubtedly, industrial and trade policies within the framework of Indian planning encouraged diversification of the industrial sector. This is evident from the changing composition of the Indian indus-trial sector. At the time of independence, India inherited an indus-trial structure dominated by light consumer goods industries such as textiles and sugar. Although the first steel plant had been set up, and there had been some limited development of engineering in railway workshops and assembly plants, these industries had only a small role to play. As pointed out earlier, the successive five year plans adopted after independence followed policies of self-reliance in the form of import-substitution-oriented industrial-isation through protective tariffs and restrictive import controls. These policies were combined with public investment policies aimed at setting up new industries. The result was substantial di-versification.

However, structural changes within the industrial sector have also meant that traditional industries such as textiles and sugar (part of food products) are now making much smaller contributions than in the early 1960s, while the machinery and equipment indus-try as well as chemicals and chemical products have emerged as important segments of manufacturing. To illustrate, textiles, the largest traditional industry with a contribution of 29 per cent in the total value added in 1960–61, has lost its relative importance. According to the revised index of industrial production, its weightage worked out to only 5.5 per cent of the total value added in 1993–94. By contrast, the increased importance of basic metal and capital goods industries reflects the heavy industry bias of Indian industrialisation. The rising importance of chemicals and chemical products reflects on the one hand the growth in the fertiliser and pharmaceutical industries, and on the other the growth of petrochemicals after the discovery of offshore oil in India in the 1980s. There has also been a strong emergence of new sunrise industries like automobiles and electronics (including computers and telecom equipment) during the 1990s. In all, India's industrial structure is clearly much more diversified than that of most developing countries.

With the onset of economic liberalisation in the 1990s, further structural changes are being generated within the industrial sector. Recent data on value added for the manufacturing sector and its components, however, are not available to ascertain the extent of such changes. Some indications can be had from the direction of the Industrial Entrepreneurs' Memorandum (IEMs) as well as of sector-wise FDI approvals. It is evident from the distribution of the IEMs and FDIs together that in the post-liberalisation period, core and infrastructure sectors (including power, telecom, metallurgical industries, oil refineries, cement, fertilisers etc.) are attracting the most investments. This is followed by capital goods and machinery, chemicals, consumer goods (including textiles, food processing etc.) as well as transportation.

Concomitant with the structural changes in industry, pressures on corporate restructuring have already started intensifying at the micro level. As a matter of fact, Indian corporations are at a historical crossroads. The old order has changed, giving way to a new paradigm. Corporations have to undertake modernisation and build up economies of scale to achieve cost competitiveness as the fight for market share becomes tougher. Benchmarking for quality, price and delivery schedules on the basis of international norms has become an imperative, but this alone does not ensure prospects of penetration into the global market. The whole series of accreditations of the International Organisation for Standardisation are vital, but they do not guarantee instant success. Re-engineering and downsizing are becoming the need of the hour, but the support of the employees and trade unions cannot be taken for granted. At this stage, there is also evidence of another important feature in operation: the irrational exuberance that characterised the response of the Indian corporate sector to economic liberalisation during 1993–97, is giving way to a sobering evaluation of the long-term economic prospects. Of course, one of the most important factors responsible for this change is a painful realisation of the risks of overestimating market size. Indian companies are facing situations of sharp conflict. While modern concepts like core competency and competitive focus are increasingly becoming relevant, for the erstwhile diversified corporations (the products of 'the licence permit raj'), it is a painful and massive exercise to divest of unrelated business areas. These and many other such dilemmas at present confront the process of corporate restructuring.

However, this does not undermine the aspirations of both the Indian corporations and policy makers of placing India Inc. on the global canvas. Way back in 1994, the then finance minister Manmohan Singh had observed in his budget speech: 'Looking ahead, I have a vision of our industrial firms acquiring a global reach and their names becoming household words in far-off distant lands.' Some time ago, in a similar vein, he said: '. . . India would have its own MNCs in due course of time to effectively challenge the foreign companies.' Needless to say, the underlying sentiment is shared by Indian industry in general and by the private corporate sector in particular. But there is a long journey ahead for everyone concerned in the pursuit of the objective of a resurgent India.

Drive towards Globalisation

Let us then evaluate the implications of globalisation. We live in an era in which world trade is expanding at a faster pace than world output; capital flows are overwhelming world trade; daily transactions in foreign exchange exceed manifold the average daily world output as well as world trade. The WTO regime is endeavouring to continuously expand the scope of multilateralism, not only in the trade of goods and services, but also in the area of investment. The spectacular progress of information technology has transformed world financial markets into virtually a single entity, with a phenomenal increase in cross-border capital flows as well as in the operation of MNCs. In such a rapidly globalising environment, India obviously cannot keep itself aloof and alienated. It is evident from the World Bank's 1996 report on Globalising

Economic Prospects that 'many of the countries that are insufficiently integrated with the world economy are among the poorest.'

In fact, recognising the crucial link between globalisation and economic growth, India is revitalising its efforts to get the best out of the inevitable process of globalisation, even if at the cost of some compromise or sacrifice. The country has already traversed a long distance from its erstwhile 'export fatalism' syndrome that clearly reflected the earlier belief that export stagnation was inescapable for a country like India. This attitude led to import-substitution forming an integral part of foreign trade, industrial and investment policies. Consequently, India lost the opportunity of exploiting foreign trade as an engine of economic growth. As a result, the country's share in world exports declined sharply from about 2 per cent in 1950–51 to 0.4 per cent in 1980–81, and it hovered at around this level throughout the 1980s. After the inception of reforms, this share gradually scaled up to 0.7 per cent in 1997–98. At the same time, the ratio of exports to India's GDP, which had declined from 6.5 per cent in 1950–51 to 4.9 per cent in 1980–81, recovered steadily to 6.2 per cent in 1990–91, and to 10 per cent in 1997–98. Likewise, the ratio of imports to GDP improved from 8.1 per cent in 1990–91 to over 11 per cent in 1997–98. Nevertheless, foreign trade intensity (exports *plus* imports as a ratio of GDP) continues to be very low in comparison with most export-led economies.

During the last four-and-a-half decades, the growth of world trade has been significantly higher than that of world output. World exports rose from $61 billion in 1950, to $315 billion in 1970, to $3,447 billion in 1990, and further to $5,295 billion in 1997. The share of world exports in world output grew from 6 per cent to 16 per cent over this period. The high performing Asian economies have consistently secured tremendous gains through dynamic and vibrant export-led growth strategies. Some of the Latin American countries like Argentina, Brazil and Mexico have also done well in their export performances. In his study, Deepak Nayyar (1996) points out that eleven countries, comprising these three Latin American countries and Korea, Hong Kong, Taiwan, Singapore, China, Indonesia, Malaysia and Thailand, accounted for about 30 per cent of the total exports from developing countries during 1970–80. Their share rose to 59 per cent in 1990 and further to 66 per cent in 1992. He also observes:

The same countries, excluding Korea, were also the main recipients of foreign direct investment in the developing world accounting for 66 per cent of the average annual inflows during the period 1981–1991. There is no firm data on the distribution of portfolio investment, but it is almost certain that the same countries, described as 'emerging markets' were the destination for an overwhelming proportion of portfolio investment flows to the developing world.'

It is evident, therefore, that till the early 1990s India could not take advantage of the opportunities arising out of global markets for goods, nor secure foreign investments and technology or financial flows of any significant measure when the going was good for at least about a dozen other developing economies. But globalisation cannot be an unmixed blessing, especially for a country like India, where erroneous policies have brought about certain serious distortions and deformities. To secure gains from globalisation, there has to be in place a swift response mechanism that will serve to transform India from a high-cost, low-productivity and low-global-intensity economy into a low-cost, high-productivity and high-global-intensity economy. There has to be an efficient system for restructuring Indian industry and Indian firms, which grew under a protective umbrella that shielded them from both local and global competition, now that they have to encounter falling tariff and non-tariff barriers as well as the substantive entry of foreign direct investment and MNCs. F.A. Mehta expressed the fears of Indian industry in October 1994 as follows:

> Does it make any sense, is it realistic, is it fair that Indian industrial enterprises, which for 40 years have been deliberately kept small and 'pigmitised' by a number of governmental policies should be exposed, within a matter of four years, to competition from the global giants?

There were also fears that Indian industry would be swamped by the MNCs' growing presence. The fact is also that while global trade is being driven by the emerging philosophy of multilateralism under the WTO, there has come into existence a fragmentation of trading nations among competing trading blocs.

As a result, in the early stages, there were some genuine apprehensions and several imponderables regarding the globalisation process, yet India has made encouraging progress through its gradualistic approach. Witness the significant increase in the external trade intensity of the economy, the growing reliance on foreign capital inflows, the promising new opportunities for FDI, the globalisation of the Indian capital markets and the increasing number of Indian joint ventures being set up abroad. More importantly, Indian industry and especially corporate management has recognised the need for incorporating global factors into its mindset while making decisions relating to investment, acquisition of technology, marketing or finance. There is now a growing compulsion on Indian industry to attain international competitiveness. It is encouraging to see how India Inc. is striving to achieve economies of scale, benchmarking of cost, quality and prices, product differentiation and strategic focus. Indeed, the process of industrial restructuring is already under way in a variety of dimensions including constant upgradation and modernisation of technology and building up of core competency.

In spite of these favourable responses, there is often a legitimate clamour for a 'level playing field' which, in its extreme formulation, is a cry for *Swadeshi*. The underlying principle, as defined by the *National Agenda for Governance* prepared by the present coalition government, is that 'India shall be built by the Indians.' At the heart of this demand is the concern of Indian industry and Indian firms that they do not enjoy a similar business environment to that which FDIs and MNCs have in their respective countries. The case for a level playing field has been advocated on several major considerations.

- First, while there has been progressive reduction in the customs tariff, no corresponding rationalisation has taken place in the area of excise and other indirect taxes. Indeed, despite efforts to streamline the excise duty structure, domestic indirect taxes are still characterised by anomalies and problems of cascading.
- Second, despite liberalisation of the financial sector, India's real interest rates are sizeably higher than those prevailing in other competing countries.
- Third, infrastructural inefficiencies and constraints are adversely impacting the performance of Indian industry. As a matter of fact, the system of cross-subsidisation in the pricing of major inputs like power, fuel and transportation is at the cost of Indian industry.
- Fourth, bureaucratic systems and procedures have yet to be streamlined and, as a consequence, substantive transaction costs have to be borne by industry.

- Fifth, the inflexibility of labour legislation (for example, the lack of an exit policy) hinders the critical process of industrial restructuring.
- Last, but not least, the whole range of legislative and administrative frameworks for dealing with the problem of industrial sickness has been found wanting, thereby affecting the move towards competitive industrial restructuring.

It is not surprising, therefore, that the *National Agenda for Governance* states: 'We will carefully analyse the effects of globalisation, calibrate the process of it by devising a timetable to suit our national conditions and requirements so as to not undermine but strengthen the national economy, the indigenous industrial base and the financial and services sectors.' In short, while India has embarked on the path of globalisation, it still has many hurdles to clear.

Predicaments

In substance, managing the transition of the contemporary Indian economy, despite the fact that some remarkable success has already been achieved, is not going to be easy. Several major problem areas have to be dealt with, and hard core reforms require immediate attention and implementation. At present, the economy is also besieged by a severe overall economic slowdown, sectoral industrial recession, sluggish exports, a high fiscal deficit and other problems. There is a sense of despondency with regard to the immediate investment outlook. The economic sanctions imposed in the aftermath of the nuclear tests compounded this predicament.

In this context, recognising the essence and imperatives of the policy initiatives, the *Economic Survey 1997–98* suggests:

> On the policy side, therefore, measures should embrace a broad array and include: steps to boost export growth, to revive the primary capital market, to encourage higher private and public investments to relieve infrastructure bottlenecks and boost demand for core industrial sectors, and fiscal and monetary policies aimed at moderating real rates of interest and ensuring adequate availability of productive capital to industry. The climate for industrial investment and growth can also be greatly enhanced through bold economic policy initiatives. Economic reforms play a vital role not only

by directly stimulating higher productivity and efficiency, but also by keeping confidence high and boosting investment intentions of entre-preneurs. Reforms of inappropriate policies, unproductive govern-ment programmes and inefficient public organisations and projects can generate hope and confidence in a more productive future.

Just as it is imperative to progress with further reforms at the level of the central government, so also there is an urgency to initiate measures at the level of the various states. Indeed, with decentralisation of economic power gaining momentum in recent years, the states bear growing responsibilities. In particular, in the vital area of infrastructure development, massive private sector investments must be made in the near future. For this purpose, it is necessary to create an enabling, investor-friendly environment. Significant reforms that need to be undertaken include: (*a*) changes in the framework of policy covering pricing, institutional and regulatory reforms to translate private sector interests in investing in infrastructure into commercially viable ventures; and (*b*) improvements in the state's capacity to manage commercially enforceable contracts. In areas where the public sector still remains important, such as roads and urban services, an environment conducive to efficient public investment becomes necessary. Therefore, there is a continuing need to restructure public expenditure both of the centre and the states, that will necessitate aggressive privatisation, reduction in non-merit subsidies, downsizing of bureaucracy and elimination of other wasteful spending. Indeed, in the long run, this approach alone will make room for high priority programmes, not only in public infrastructure, but also in the social sector covering public health, education and poverty alleviation programmes. In the absence of progress in these areas, management of the success of reforms will be greatly impaired.

More importantly, the *Economic Survey 1997–98* also contends that

while there has been substantial progress with delicensing industry and foreign trade, the 'controls mindset' remains influential and the 'inspector raj' continues to flourish. Fresh initiatives are necessary to reduce the role of these factors in industry, agriculture, trade, infrastructure, finance and social services, in order to unleash the productive energies and capacities of economic agents in all these areas.

All these are formidable tasks which need to be dealt with by policy makers and economic administrators, as India moves into the 21st century.

Concluding Observations

The on-going process of reforms, the changing pattern of income distribution and the shift towards market-driven systems of resource allocations have already set in motion certain vital cumulative trends in the Indian economy. Borrowing the concept from John Naisbitt, we would like to conceptualise them as emerging Indian megatrends, which bring out the essence of the underlying transition. We believe that these megatrends are becoming the driving force of the Indian economy in general, and of Indian industry in particular. They will transmit their impulses and shocks to various industries. As a consequence, at the micro level, there are likely to be continuous disturbances and discontinuities accompanying the painful process of restructuring. At the same time, these megatrends may have the strength and potential to drive the Indian economy towards a high growth trajectory of at least 7 per cent real GDP growth accompanied by a double-digit figure for industrial growth. This, surely, is the most central of the medium-term objectives of India's policy makers, advocating the cause of economic development with social justice.

It is not necessary to identify the specific elements of each aspect of these megatrends. Suffice it to say that there is a convergence of several push and pull forces in the emerging socio-economic scenario of the country. Thus, economic policy is subject to a series of compulsions, such as the urgency of fiscal consolidation, evolving workable political governance and responding to pressures from international institutions like the World Bank, the International Monetary Fund and the WTO. Further, the political process also suggests that electorates have rejected the erstwhile ideological stridency and have preferred centrist solutions to socio-economic problems. Likewise, the emergence of the middle class, the spread of entrepreneurship and the communication revolution have made it imperative to move from domination by the centre to decentralisation. With the reduced role of the central government, states are becoming the powerful focus of economic activities.

The process of accelerated growth is giving rise to an articulate middle class. We are also witnessing the growth of consumerism and modernism. Indeed, consumerism is creating compulsive pressures of competitive market positioning, quality consciousness, creation of brand equity (loyalty) and continuous efforts towards value addition. At the same time, the emergence of an equity cult will necessitate an efficient financial system and transparency in corporate management. Corporate structure will also have to reflect the impact of entrepreneurial explosion. We shall not only see the growth and diversification of the existing mature companies, but also the rapid emergence of young, high-tech, innovative companies.

The process of urbanisation is bringing about the emergence of metro growth clusters. Push and pull factors operate in the creation of these new centres of industrialisation as well as of growth and prosperity. It is evident that purchasing power in urban areas is significantly higher than in rural areas. Business and industry are closely evaluating the emerging prospects on the basis of these trends.

One of the megatrends is the intensification of global competition. India is adjusting itself swiftly from its previous mould of import-substitution to export-promotion. With the opening up of the Indian markets, the pressure on Indian industry is building up through growing imports and easy access to foreign technology and capital. Indian industry has to recognise the imperatives arising out of growing foreign trade intensity, and evaluate the implications of the changes in the world economy due to the dominance of MNCs, the convergence of the multilateral trade system under the WTO regime and regional trade blocs, as well as the upsurge of emerging markets.

The message in all of these events is clear: the frontiers of the public sector will decline; the private sector will become the engine of economic growth; the pressure on industry from the growing middle class with its ethos of consumerism and the equity cult will increase; and global integration will bring with it both threats and opportunities. In the ultimate analysis, both the Indian economy and Indian society will have to respond to the compulsions of the three great ideas of modern civilisation—democracy, the free market system and globalisation—as India enters the new millennium.

Notes

1. The 1980s saw higher rates of growth than the 'Hindu growth rate' of 3 to 3.5 per cent achieved during the preceding two decades but, as has been often pointed out, this was based on excessive internal spending and both internal and external borrowing, and hence was clearly unsustainable. In fact, it led directly to the huge external crisis that forced the reforms of July 1991 and thereafter.
2. Since then, there has been a welcome recovery in the growth performance of the Indian economy. Real GDP increased by 6.8 per cent and 6.4 per cent in 1998–99 and 1999–2000 respectively. In particular, after a prolonged period of recessionary trends, the industrial sector achieved a handsome 8 per cent growth in 1999–2000.

References and Select Bibliography

Acharya, Shankar. 1995. 'The Economic Consequences of Economic Reforms', Sir Purushottamdas Thakurdas Memorial Lecture, The Indian Institute of Bankers, Mumbai.

Ahluwalia, Isher Judge, and I.M.D. Little. 1998. *India's Economic Reforms and Development: Essays for Manmohan Singh.* New Delhi: Oxford University Press.

Bhagwati, Jagdish. 1998. 'The Design of Indian Development', in Isher Judge Ahluwalia and I.M.D. Little, eds, *India's Economic Reforms and Development: Essays for Manmohan Singh.* New Delhi: Oxford University Press.

Bhandare, S.S. 1996. 'Privatisation: The Indian Experience', *Journal of Management*, Vol. 6, No. 1, June 1996.

Government of India (GOI). *Budget Papers 1997–98.*

Mehta, F.A. 1994. 'The Local and Global Challenges before the Indian Industry', Mohan Kumaramangalam Memorial Lecture, Administrative Staff College of India, Hyderabad.

———. 1996. Are There 'Basic Fundamentals' behind the Present 'Industrial Recession'?

Nayyar, Deepak, 1996. 'The Past in Our Present—Globalisation', *Indian Economic Journal.*

Ohmae, Kenichi. 1995. *The End of the Nation State: Rise of Regional Economies.* Harper Collins, USA.

The Economist. 1994. 'A Game of International Leapfrog', London.

Vasudevan, A. 1997. RBI Occasional Papers, Vol. 18, Nos 2–3, June–September 1997. Reserve Bank of India, New Delhi.

Appendix

INDIAN ECONOMY: KEY PERFORMANCE INDICATORS (1950–51 TO 1997–98)

Key Indicators	Unit	1950–51	1980–81	1990–91	1997–98	per cent CAGR[1]		
						Phase I 1950–51 to 1980–81	Phase II 1980–81 to 1990–91	Phase III 1990–91 to 1997–98
Population	Mn	359.0	679.0	839.0	966.0	2.1	2.1	2.0
Real GDP (at factor cost)	Rs crore[2]	42,871.0	122,427.0	212,253.0	311,828.0	3.6	5.7	5.6
GDP (at current prices)	Rs crore	8,979.0	122,427.0	477,814.0	1,264,580.0	9.1	14.6	14.9
Real per capita income	Rs	1,127.0	1,630.0	2,222.0	2,847.0	1.2	3.1	3.6
Per capita income at current prices	Rs	239.0	1,630.0	4,983.0	11,132.0	6.6	11.8	12.2
Index of agricultural production	1981–82=100	46.2	102.1	148.4	171.0	2.7	3.8	2.0
Foodgrains production	Mn tonnes	50.8	129.6	176.4	195.0	3.2	3.1	1.4
Savings ratio	per cent GDP	10.4	21.2	24.3	26.0	–	–	–
Investment ratio	per cent GDP	10.2	22.7	27.7	27.5	–	–	–
Central government expenditure	Rs crore	504.0	22,500.0	104,973.0	243,195.0	13.5	16.7	12.7
Government indebtedness (total liabilities)	Rs crore	2,865.0	59,449.0	314,258.0	773,241.0	10.6	18.1	13.7
Money supply (M3)	Rs crore	2,280.0	55,774.0	265,828.0	820,299.0	11.2	16.9	17.5
Aggregate deposits	Rs crore	881.0	39,233.0	199,643.0	601,348.0	13.5	17.7	17.1
Bank credit	Rs crore	547.0	27,265.0	125,575.0	321,813.0	13.9	16.5	14.4
Inflation: WPI[3]	1981–82=100	16.9	89.9	182.7	329.8	5.7	7.3	8.8
CPI[4]	1982=100	17.0	81.0	193.0	365.0	5.3	9.1	9.5
Index of industrial production	1980–81=100	18.3	100.0	212.6	316.90	5.8	7.8	5.9

(Table contd.)

(Table contd.)

IIP: Use based	(weights percent)						
Basic goods	(39.4)	–	100.00	213.10	335.20	–	7.90	6.70
Capital goods	(16.4)	–	100.00	291.70	385.30	–	11.30	4.10
Intermediate goods	(20.5)	–	100.00	176.90	278.50	–	5.90	6.70
Consumer goods	(23.65)	–	100.00	189.00	273.40	–	6.60	5.40
Durables	(2.55)	–	100.00	359.70	637.60	–	13.70	8.50
Non-durables	(21.1)	–	100.00	168.30	229.40	–	5.30	4.50
Selected Industries							
Coal	Mn tonnes	32.30	113.90	211.70	296.00	4.30	6.40	4.90
Cement	Mn tonnes	2.70	18.60	48.80	83.10	6.60	10.10	7.90
Finished steel	Mn tonnes	1.00	6.80	13.50	23.10	6.60	7.10	8.00
Electricity	Bn kWh	6.60	119.30	289.40	421.30	10.10	9.30	5.50
Fertilisers	Lakh tonnes	0.18	30.10	90.50	130.60	18.60	11.60	5.40
Passenger cars	('000s)	7.90	31.30	181.80	399.80	4.70	19.20	11.90
Commercial vehicles	('000s)	8.60	71.70	145.50	229.40	7.30	7.30	6.70
Exports	$ bn	1.30	8.50	18.10	34.00	6.50	7.90	9.40
Imports	$ bn	1.30	15.90	24.10	40.80	8.70	4.20	7.80
Trade balance	$ bn	–	-7.40	-6.00	-6.80	–	-2.10	1.80
Forex reserves (end March)	$ bn	1.90	5.90	2.20	25.90	3.80	-9.40	42.20
Foreign exchange rate	($=Rs)	4.80	7.90	17.94	37.16	-1.65	-7.87	-9.88

[1] CAGR: Compound Annual Growth Rate
[2] Rs 1 crore = Rs 10 million
[3] WPI: Wholesale Price Index
[4] CPI: Consumer Price Index

six

Agricultural and Agri-business Issues under Economic Liberalisation

Bhupat M. Desai

the new economic policies that have reduced protection to industry and trade have a direct bearing on agricultural incentives.
Barter terms of trade (that is, prices received to prices paid) for
farmers are expected to improve leading to technical change and
growth in agriculture (Ahluwalia 1996; M. Singh 1995). This outcome, along with devaluation, delicensing and dereservation, is
expected to accelerate growth, investment and exports of agri-
business industries (see, for example, Ahluwalia 1996; Bhagwati
1998; Joshi and Little 1998; M. Singh 1995; Srinivasan 1998). The
question is: has this occurred?

Agricultural performance in the post-reform period has deteriorated despite improvement in already favourable relative prices.
This is because these prices have an *a priori* ambiguous impact on
agricultural growth due to substitution, income and wealth effects
which work in opposite directions (Desai and D'Souza 1999; Desai
and Namboodiri 2000). It is also because agricultural performance
is predominantly governed by non-price factors like technology

and infrastructure-led government investment, rather than by relative prices (Desai 1997a and b; Rao 1997). Agri-business performance, being intimately linked to agriculture, lacks broad-based improvement. In fact, mainstream agro-processing industries and major farm input industries have shown a lower growth in the post-reform period.

Nonetheless, these policy changes are a step in the right direction, as they provide a more enabling environment for a better response. But the paradigm of economic liberalisation contains certain elements that are potentially harmful. These include, for example, relaxation/removal of the ceiling on land ownership in agriculture, and deregulation of interest rates. The former is a questionable policy since it may adversely affect smaller farmers, who are preponderant in Indian agriculture. This, in turn, leads to inefficiencies, as scale economies in agriculture are insignificant and these smaller farmers are efficient (Rao 1994, 1997). The deregulation of interest rates is unwarranted because of the absence of subsidy/tax, and the prevalence of scale economies in (rural) banking (Bhattacharjee et al. 1999; Desai and Namboodiri 1996). While land ceilings have not been changed much, interest rates have been deregulated, leading to a higher and more unstable interest rate structure (Desai 2000; Nachane et al. 1997).

The following section briefly sketches the importance of agriculture and agri-business. The strengths and weaknesses of agriculture and its recent performance are then discussed with a view to analysing what past and recent policies have accomplished. This is followed by a discussion of 'strategy' options available for agricultural growth. Policy 'instruments' required to implement the 'strategy' of technical change in agriculture are discussed next. The discussion then moves to changes in demand in agri-business. This is followed by an analysis of how these changes, and the supply of raw materials from agriculture, have impinged on the performance and opportunities of agri-business industries. Both agri-input and agro-processing industries are then considered, followed by a concluding section.

Importance of Agriculture and Agri-business

In the early 1990s, the value added in agriculture was Rs 1,880 billion, while that in major agri-input and agro-processing industries in the 'organised' sector was Rs 30.43 billion and Rs 211.20 billion respectively.

Agriculture contributes about one-third of the national income and employs close to two-thirds of the country's workforce. The share of value added by two agri-business industries (the major farm input and agro-processing industries) in national income is over 4 per cent, and their share in the workforce is over 6 per cent. In value added in manufacturing, however, the share of these two industries is close to 45 per cent, and their share in employment in this sector is over 50 per cent. Agricultural exports account for about 25 per cent of total exports, while imports constitute about 7 per cent of all imports.

While the share of crop-agricultural output in agricultural production is 72 per cent, livestock products and fisheries contribute 25 per cent and 3 per cent respectively. Food processing industries account for about two-thirds of agro-processing output. Most agricultural commodities other than foodgrains are processed. But food processing industries in the 'organised' sector procure only about 25 per cent of primary food commodities. Many food commodities are at present underutilised by processing industries. For example, about two-thirds of paddy production is still milled by hullers, which gives an extremely low recovery of rice. In the case of oilseeds other than groundnut and soyabean, processing is accomplished by mechanical expellers or *ghanis* which yield a recovery rate that is lower by 4 to 14 per cent. In the case of animal products and fisheries, modernised processing is still negligible. Further, only 1 per cent of the production of fruits and vegetables is currently processed, while 15 to 20 per cent of the production is wasted at the farm and in handling.

Thus, agriculture and agri-business industries are sizeable not only in national accounting terms but also in terms of their ramifications for the entire economy. Agro-processing industries (AMPS) provide a forward linkage (FWL) to agriculture (APS), while farm input industries (AIS) provide a backward linkage (BWL) to this sector, as is shown diagrammatically in Figure 6.1.

FIGURE 6.1

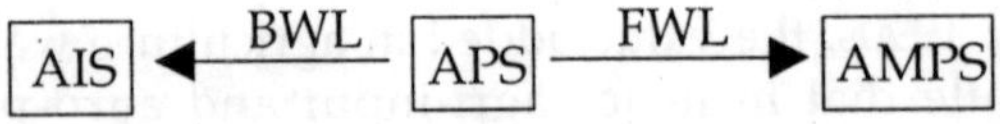

Strengths and Weaknesses of Agriculture

Strengths

Agriculture is the single largest private sector in India in which decision-makers are rational, efficient and responsive to change. Most of the 109 million farm households in the country are owner-operated. Even in eastern India, where tenant farmers are more numerous, there has of late been an accelerated growth in crop yields, and in agricultural production in general (Saha and Swamination 1994). Long-term agricultural growth in the post-independence period was close to 3 per cent per annum, higher than the 2 per cent growth in population. Indeed, agricultural growth in the 1970s and 1980s became broad-based in terms of crops/enterprises, farms and regions (Ray 1998; Sawant 1997; Sawant and Achutan 1995). The annual compound growth rate of crop-agricultural output from the mid-1980s to the mid-1990s was 3.58 per cent. Growth in milk production was 4.5 per cent per annum during this period, while that of annual meat production was 7.6 per cent, and that of egg production 5.68 per cent (Ranjhan 1997). The fisheries sub-sector also recorded better growth during this period: 6.71 per cent for inland fisheries and 6.18 per cent for marine fisheries (Dehadrai 1997).

Second, agriculture in India is diversified due to the presence of varied agro-climatic conditions, ranging from tropical but highly humid and sub-humid to tropical semi-arid and arid. Farmers diversify also to minimise risks, which are greater in agriculture compared with industry on account of weather dependency. Moreover, diversification is found both in crop farming and in the allied sub-sectors of livestock and fisheries, where the farming of even subsistence crops like paddy and wheat for the market rather than for own consumption is now more common (NABARD 1995). Indeed, this diversification is more often a 'complementary' process that is consistent with agriculture's resource endowments.

Third, this 'complementary' nature of the production process is common knowledge among the farming community. Thus, the output response is larger than the sum of effects of each input used singly (Ishikawa 1967; Mellor 1966). This then facilitates the higher growth not only of agricultural output but also of employment. The annual compound growth rate of both agri-cultural output growth and farm employment elasticity were much higher in the post–Green Revolution period than in the period prior to mid-1960s. Agricultural output grew at 3.41 per cent after the Green Revolution, and employment elasticity during this period was 1.37 per cent. Before the mid-1960s, the annual compound growth rate of agricultural output in independent India was 2.05 per cent, and employment elasticity was 0.52 per cent (Desai 1997a; Desai and Namboodiri 1998a).

As in Japan, Taiwan and South Korea, the average size of farms in India is small. Smaller farmers have higher land productivity and efficiency in general (see, for example, Chattopadhyay and Sengupta 1997). Moreover, land ownership inequality is neither very high, nor is it increasing much (see Table 6.A.1). Average farm size in 1992 was a little over 1 hectare. Over 80 per cent of farmers have less than 2 hectares of land, and over 35 per cent of land overall. Another 15 per cent have 2 to 10 hectares with close to 50 per cent of total agricultural land. Thus, the small and medium-size peasantry dominates land ownership distribution (see Table 6.A.2).

Agriculture in post-independence India has thus demonstrated long-term growth rates and resilience unheard of by international and historical standards. Harnessing the potential of its strengths requires overcoming six weaknesses that we discuss next.

Weaknesses

As stated earlier, the misplaced reliance of macro reforms on im-proving relative prices for technical change[1] and growth in agri-culture is a contemporary weakness of Indian agriculture. Tables 6.A.3 and 6.A.4 clearly show that despite improvement in the already favourable relative prices, growth in most of the non-price factors, like area under high-yielding varieties (HYV), fertiliser use, gross irrigated area, electricity use and plan expenditure on agriculture, and therefore in agricultural production and product-ivity, in the post-reform period was much lower than in the five years preceding reforms.[2] This is despite more favourable weather in the post-reform period. Moreover, the rural poverty ratio has also increased (see Table 6.A.3). Aggregate agricultural supply response to relative prices has a negative *net* impact of substitution, income and wealth. Moreover, this response has long been known to be price-inelastic because of three factors that are unique to agriculture. These are: (*a*) fixed land supply; (*b*) resource specificity, which means that the crop pattern is governed by agro-climatic factors in addition to demand conditions; and (*c*) initial lower input intensity. Even the enterprise/crop-mix has not shifted much from low-yield/value to high-yield/value enterprises in the post-reform period, as it is also 'relatively more' governed by non-price factors than by relative prices (see Tables 6.A.5 and 6.A.6).[3] But the overall supply elasticity for non-price factors is over three times larger than for relative prices (Krishna 1982). Further, the growth of non-price factors is largely determined by public goods that constitute the basic production infrastructure and R&D for agriculture.

Agriculture's weather dependency is a self-explanatory weakness. But this is not unique to India. What is interesting, if not unique, however, is that Indian agriculture has become weather-resilient over time (Mahendradev 1987; Ray 1998). This has resulted largely from two major sources. One of these is the farmers' improved knowledge of how to deal with the vagaries of the weather. Incidentally, India's 142 million hectares of net cultivated land is approximately equally divided between low, medium and high rainfall zones in the country (see Table 6.A.7). The second factor is the increase in irrigated farming. Such farming now accounts for over one-third of total cultivated land. This proportion ranges from 60 to 90 per cent in the northern states of Punjab, Haryana and Uttar Pradesh; from 15 to 40 per cent in the southern states of Karnataka, Andhra Pradesh, Kerala and Tamil Nadu as well as Goa; from 8 to 43 per cent in eastern states such as Assam, Mizoram, Orissa, West Bengal and Bihar, and also in Himachal Pradesh and Jammu & Kashmir; and from 15 to 29 per cent in the western states of Maharashtra, Madhya Pradesh, Gujarat and Rajasthan (Table 6.A.8). Despite these inter-state differences in irrigated farming, locational differences in agricultural productivity and production in various states have decreased over time (Desai and Namboodiri 1997b; Ray 1998). Both government investment and farmers' investment facilitated by crop loans and rural credit for irrigation and electricity have contributed to improving weather resilience.

Another weakness of agriculture in India is that it does not have developed markets for modern farm inputs, credit and perishables like horticulture, fisheries and, to an extent, milk. But this is being overcome by government policies for rural credit, for opening the farm input distribution business to the private sector, and encouraging the private sector as well as commodity-based co-operatives in agro-processing.

A further weakness of Indian agriculture is that it is geographically dispersed and isolated. Roads, transportation and communication infrastructure development are still not as broad-based as they should be (see Table 6.A.9).

Although at independence India abolished the absentee landlord (*zamindari*) system in agriculture, the land tenure structure remains inimical to technical change and capital formation especially in eastern and central India as also in some pockets in the rest of the country. Furthermore, concealed tenancy is quite common although it is legally prohibited. As a result, farmers' incentives are endangered. Fragmentation of land is on the rise due to the sub-division of families and due to the population pressure in general.

The last but not the least important weakness of agriculture in India, as anywhere in the world, is that, unlike the industrial and service sectors, it is subject to Ricardo's Law of Diminishing Returns. Overcoming this weakness requires shifting the production function upward and to the right through technological innovations. Such a technical change has occurred in India, as will be shown later. But in more recent times, both land productivity and total factor productivity growth have receded (Desai 1994; Desai and Namboodiri 1997b) (see Tables 6.A.10 and 6.A.11). This suggests the need to introduce another broad-based Green Revolution. What its precise nature could be is the subject of the next section.

Agricultural Growth 'Strategy' Options

Three options for enhancing growth are extensive farming, intensive agriculture and technical change. In the 1950s, extensive farming through bringing hitherto uncultivated land under the plough was the dominant 'strategy', while in the early 1960s the emphasis was on intensive agriculture through increased cropping intensity and the use of some market-purchased inputs. Around the mid-1960s, technical change was epitomised in miracle seeds that were highly responsive to (irrigation) water and fertilisers.

Combined with market-purchased inputs and extension services, this eventually ushered in the Green Revolution. This technical change has been land- and labour-augmenting, with complementary capital requirements (tractors, irrigation pumpsets etc.), besides being divisible and scale neutral. Although the initial response of smaller farmers to this technology was not encouraging, it was just a question of time before they caught up with it.

While technical change shifts the production/cost function upward/downward, under both extensive farming and intensive agriculture, the movement is along a given function which leads eventually into the trap of diminishing returns (Desai 1997b).

As shown in Table 6.A.11, the relative share of total factor productivity (meaning technical change) in agricultural output growth was only a little over one-fourth in the pre-1965 era. But this has since improved to close to 43 per cent.[4] In the initial stages of the Green Revolution, total factor productivity was not only higher but even increasing until around the mid-1970s (Table 6.A.11). Since then, however, it has receded. This suggests that the sharp distinction required between intensive agriculture and technical change was probably blurred. There is a need to restore this distinction by emphasising a proactive role of the new knowledge as an input along with the other inputs in which the new technology is embodied.

To illustrate, while greater use of fertilisers/pesticides may be important, their doses, combination, and method and timing of application also require fine-tuning.[5] The same applies to irrigated farming, and also to the horsepower, size and after-sales services of tractors, pumpsets, etc. (Desai and Namboodiri 1997b). While such fine-tuning is important, it is equally important to explore new developments in technology based on bio-technology, genetic engineering and other such emerging frontiers in scientific knowledge.

Yet another question is whether a future Green Revolution should be only seed-centred, or both seed- and resource-centred. The latter is the superior option, as it would satisfy a high degree of technical complementarity that is unique to agriculture. There are also two other reasons. First, in most semi-arid and arid areas, the binding constraint is a natural resource that requires technology which centres around the watershed, soil conservation, checkdams etc., to harness as well as develop a healthier soil-moisture regime.[6]

Second, it has a better potential to infuse a process of sustainability in agriculture necessary to protect the interests of future generations.

Extensive farming is no longer feasible as most land frontiers have been exhausted, while intensive agriculture is both economically and environmentally unsustainable. But the strategy of technical change that is land- and labour-augmenting as well as both seed- and resource-centred is agro-economically the most preferred alternative. Moreover, such technical change alleviates poverty, for it increases production at reduced unit costs and/or prices in real terms, which benefits the poor most, besides being consistent with agriculture's resource endowments, farm size and employment needs (Desai and Namboodiri 1998b).

Policy 'Instruments' for Technical Change in Agriculture

Earlier studies suggest that non-product-price policies are 'relatively more' potent 'instruments' for technical change in agriculture (see, for example, Dantwala 1967, 1986; Desai and Namboodiri 1997b, 1998a; Krishna 1982; Thamarajkshy 1994).[7] Such policies may be categorised into three types. First, R&D, extension services and farm input (industries), all of which have a direct bearing on technical change in agriculture. Second, economic policies of government investment, input subsidies and agricultural taxes. And third, institutional policies of rural credit, agro-processing (industries) and land reforms. While we propose to discuss farm input industries and agro-processing industries in the sections on agri-business, the other types of policy are briefly sketched below.

The present level of government expenditure on agricultural R&D and its transfer is only 0.43 per cent of agricultural GDP, and needs to be raised to the internationally recommended norm of 2 per cent (Desai and Namboodiri 1998a; Pal et al. 1997). This is justified as the internal rate of return on this investment is as high as 20 to 21 per cent for the sector as a whole, in addition to a much higher rate for some individual commodities such as wheat and paddy (see, for example, Desai and Namboodiri 1998a; Kumar and Mruthyanjaya 1992; Kumar and Rosegrant 1994; Rosegrant and Evenson 1994). Further, this investment should be for developing and transferring new technologies which are both seed- and resource-centred. Lastly, the organisation of this investment should be location-specific, decentralised and accountable. It should also significantly improve the ratio of extension workers to farmers, which is now 1:800/1000.

In terms of the economic policy of government investment in and for agriculture, what is needed is to aggressively increase its present share of about 22–24 per cent (Desai 1997b). The policy must prioritise: agricultural research and extension; the public sector seeds industry; irrigation and watersheds, rural electricity, soil and water conservation and soil testing laboratories; the allied sub-sectors of dairy, fisheries and forestry; rural roads and communications; regulated markets; support institutions such as those for rural credit; land reforms; and poverty alleviation. The present level of farm input subsidies (such as subsidies on fertilisers, irrigation and electricity) is well within 10 per cent of agricultural production permitted under GATT. But these subsidies need to be rationalised through appropriate pricing to contain their future burden as well as their possible adverse implications for farmer-level efficiency. Taxes on agriculture such as land revenue and betterment levy need upward revision, as they have not been changed for a long time. Levy on agri-business companies is also legitimate, as they too have benefited from public R&D in agriculture. Voluntary mobilisation of resources from farmers to match the contribution of government investment for production infrastructure should also constitute an economic policy.

As far as institutional policies for rural credit are concerned, four changes are needed. One, all credit institutions should have partial rather than full deregulation for loans above Rs 0.2 million. Such a policy is quite common for critical sectors like agriculture, exports and infrastructure. This may be because these sectors have more complex externalities and market imperfections, and hence require a more stable regime of cost of credit. Two, the central bank should devise additional tiers/slabs of loan amounts under the present slabs of up to Rs 25,000, and from Rs 25,001 to Rs 0.2 million. This is because most loans (except those for tractors, sprinklers, and borewells) come under the first slab which has an interest rate of about 12 to 13 per cent. This makes for an interest rate structure that is conducive neither to the viability of credit institutions nor to the borrowers' ability to pay (Desai 2000). Three, increases in lending interest rates must be restrained, as neither is there any subsidy, nor do the unit (i.e., average) total costs of credit institutions show an increasing trend. And four, these institutions must have more de-bureaucratised, decentralised and de-politicised management.

Three policies are needed in the case of land reforms. One, the existing ceiling on land ownership must be vigorously implemented.[8] Second, tenancy must be legitimised, as this would improve the incentives and security of tenants. Third, land fragments must be consolidated into a compact block, as it would make farming more viable.[9]

The non-product-price policies proposed have the potential to alleviate the six weaknesses that seem to constrain more rapid technical change in agriculture. What has been outlined above makes a clear distinction between policy 'strategy' and the 'instruments' to achieve it, a distinction which has been lost in the wake of liberalisation.

Changes in Demand for Agri-business Products

Technologically dynamic agriculture provides a market for agribusiness in both farm inputs and agro-processed products (Mellor 1976). Whether this has occurred, and what the demand for these products has been during the pre- and post-reform periods, are concerns which we address now.

Demand for Farm Inputs

Six intermediate inputs in agriculture are irrigation, electricity, diesel oil, fertilisers, current repairs and pesticides. The share (percentage) of all such inputs increased from barely 3.70 per cent in the early 1950s to 34 per cent in the early 1990s (see Table 6.A.12). Due to non-availability of data, however, these figures exclude seed and livestock feed some of which is purchased from the market. But even their share must have increased due to the emergence of new seeds and animal breeds. Yet another set of inputs purchased from the market includes pumpsets, tractors, threshers and other such farm assets (see Table 6.A.13).

Annual compound growth rates of some of these capital inputs and the six intermediate inputs ranged from 6 to 13 per cent during the 1980s (see Tables 6.A.12 and 6.A.13). These were higher than the growth rates for all intermediate inputs taken together. In the 1980s, growth rates in excess of 8 per cent were registered by fertilisers, irrigation, electricity, electric motors, diesel oil, tractors and current repairs and maintenance. These high growth rates as well as the high shares of inputs emerged only after the Green Revolution in the mid- to late-1960s.

The share of the six market-purchased inputs as well as their growth rates were somewhat higher in the post-reform period than in the pre-reform period (see Table 6.A.12). But this rise is associated mainly with electricity, irrigation and pesticides, rather than with all the six modern inputs. The growth of fertilisers and, to an extent, that of other (conventional) intermediate inputs has been poorest (see rows 1 and 8 in Table 6.A.12). Given the technical complementarity in agriculture, this suggests a relatively poor performance of agriculture in the early 1990s, as noted earlier.

Three sets of factors may have been responsible for the decline in the importance of fertilisers and other intermediate inputs. First, the ad hoc changes in policy for farm input subsidies. Second, the decontrol of prices of phosphorous and potash fertilisers, but not of nitrogenous fertilisers (see, for example, Desai 1997b; Narayan and Gupta 1997). Third, the misconceived policy of relying on (barter) terms of trade for growth in investment as well as agriculture. These forces have also led to an adverse ratio of NPK fertilisers, with consequent undesirable implications for soil health. As will be shown later, these policies have also not much encouraged growth in the fertiliser industry or in the farm inputs industry in general (ibid.).

Thus, the new economic policies have arrested commercialisation and technological transformation of agriculture. Moreover, the farm inputs market (especially fertilisers) has become nonconducive to the growth of these industries, notwithstanding the positive initiatives of dereservation and delicensing of such industries as seeds and pesticides.

Demand for Agro-processed Products

As economy-wide data on demand for these products from the rural sector are not available, we first analyse the sample survey data (Table 6.A.14). Consumer demand for agro-processed products has become more diversified in rural India. While in both rural and urban areas, the share (percentage) of consumer rupees spent on cereals has declined over time, the extent of this decline is greater in the rural sector. The products whose shares have increased are pulses (legumes), milk and milk products, meat, eggs and fish, vegetables and fruits, edible oils, and other foods such as sugar (see Table 6.A.14). Indeed, even the share (percentage) of other foods in urban India in 1989–90 declined. But urban consumers' demand for such processed foods as breakfast cereals, packaged foods and beverages, and pre-cooked foods has increased. Nonetheless, these changes in the post-reform years have not accelerated growth in demand for all foods, as the consumers who provide this demand are a small constituent of the overall market (see columns 4 and 7 for rows 5–8, 11, 12 and 16 in Table 6.A.15). Indeed, for all agricultural commodities taken together as well as for all foods, the annual compound growth rates in the post-reform period are marginally lower (see columns 4 and 7 in rows 12 and 20 in Table 6.A.15). The food products for which post-reform growth rates are significantly higher include oils and oilseeds, meat, eggs and fish, other foods and hotels and restaurants. This, together with the increased growth rate for clothing, suggests that the improved demand base is much narrower for agriculture and for food in particular.

Both all-India and rural and urban demand patterns thus reveal diversification in demand for food and agricultural products from cereals to other more income-elastic commodities. But the post-reform growth rates as well as the shifts in these patterns are neither high nor broad-based. Consequently, as will be shown later, most food-processing and agro-processing industries in general have shown deteriorating growth rates in post-reform years.

Performance and Opportunities of Agri-input Industries

Modernised agriculture cannot exist without such farm input industries as seeds, fertilisers, pesticides, implements and machinery, electricity and feed for livestock. India is no exception to this rule, though most of these inputs have emerged significantly only after around the mid-1960s. Even now, they do not form part of mainstream manufacturing, mainly because of the prioritisation of heavy and capital goods industries by the industrialisation policy since the mid-1950s. While private sector industries have emerged in farm implements and machinery, both private and public sectors exist for seeds and pesticides, and private, public and co-operative sectors co-exist in the fertilisers industry. Data on these industries are available only for fertilisers, pesticides, implements and machinery, and electricity.

Table 6.A.16 gives the annual compound growth rates of energy generated, and of invested capital, output and value added for fertilisers and pesticides as well as for agricultural machinery and parts, for the pre- and post-reform years. It reveals that all these growth rates, except that of value added from fertilisers and pesticides, were lower in the post-reform period. The pesticides industry in particular was an exception, perhaps because multinational corporations (MNCs) entered it. Another farm input industry which has attracted MNCs is seeds (especially of fruits and vegetables).[10] Both these farm input industries require much less capital than fertilisers and farm machinery (see Table 6.A.17 for some sample-based data).[11] Moreover, their financial performance in the early 1990s was better to some extent (Table 6.A.17). Although a sample of fertiliser manufacturing firms has shown a reasonably good financial performance (Table 6.A.17), the performance of the fertiliser industry as a whole in the post-reform period has deteriorated (see Tables 6.A.16 and 6.A.18). This may be because some units have outdated technology and depleted plant and machinery. It may also be that the better-performing firms have benefited from the increase in fertiliser subsidy after the initial reduction in the wake of reforms, and from the overall positive policy environment that these reforms have introduced.[12]

It may be premature to project that farm input industries may not grow rapidly in the future. But their sustained high growth will require higher priority for agriculture and agriculture-led industrialisation[13] policies, rather than for the heavy and capital goods policy orientation pursued so far. This is because both these sectors are intimately linked, as has been stated earlier.

Performance and Opportunities of Agro-processing Industries

Agro-processing industries change the time, form and place utilities of agricultural commodities. This is largely because production of these commodities arises once or twice in a year, though their use is more continuous. Agro-processing in the household or 'unorganised' sector is still common for some foodgrains, though the 'organised' sector is now growing. Private, public, joint and co-operative firms co-exist in this sector. Co-operatives are more common in perishables like sugarcane and milk, though they are region-specific, as in Maharashtra and Gujarat.

The post-reform performance of all agro-processing industries taken together in the 'organised' sector has deteriorated in terms of invested capital, output as well as net value added in real terms. All the food processing industries taken together have also registered a similar post-reform performance, though their net value added growth rate has been better (see Table 6.A.19).[14] Such net value added performance is largely associated with the processing of fruits and vegetables, fish, sugar, coffee and, to an extent, grains and pulses (Table 6.A.19), many of which have high value added processing. For most of these better-performing processed food products, consumers' budget share (percentage) has also increased, as noted earlier.

The processing performance of fruits and vegetables in the post-reform period has improved in terms of invested capital, output, net value added and nominal rupee values of exports (see Tables 6.A.19 and 6.A.20). Two innovative features have emerged in the processing of certain fruits and vegetables. One of these is contract farming, under which a processing firm supplies farm inputs, extension services etc., and procures farm produce from the farmers.[15] The other feature is tertiary processing, such as pre-cooling and refrigeration, rather than secondary processing in the form of canned fruits and juices. Both innovations seem to be mutually beneficial to farmers and processors, and also to the economy at large. However, they have emerged only on the periphery of major towns that are well connected to market centres.

Processing of grains and pulses and of coffee have shown improved growth performances of both output and value added, but not of invested capital. The dairy products processing industry has posted a better performance in terms of invested capital and output, but not in terms of value added. The fisheries processing industry has performed relatively well in terms of invested capital and value added, but not of output in real terms. Production of sugar and brown sugar (*khandsari*), like that of fruits and vegetables processing, has seen a better growth of invested capital and output as also of value added (Table 6.A.19). Despite better commodity-specific performance, neither the food processing industries as a group nor the agro-processing industries in general have recorded better growth in the post-reform period. This may be because these commodities do not account for a large share in these industries, or in the enterprise mix of the agricultural sector.

Post-reform growth rates of export quantities have been better for coffee, spices, rice, fish and preparations, and cashew kernels (see Table 6.A.20). Higher growth rates in rupee values in nominal terms have been recorded by meat and preparations, jute manufactures and fruits and vegetables. But cotton yarn and apparels, which has the largest share (percentage) in agro-based exports, has a lower growth rate in the post-reform period (Table 6.A.20). Lastly, the share (percentage) of agro-exports in total exports has also declined in the post-reform period, though the nominal rupee value of these exports has recorded a higher growth rate.

Thus, the better-performing food and agro-processing industries, being still not in the mainstream enterprise mix of agriculture, have not compensated for the lower growth performance of the other agro-processing industries as a sector. However, as stated earlier, opportunities for growth do exist in these industries. Proactive policies to harness such opportunities are needed, as these industries tend to be labour-intensive, as well as located closer to their raw material sources and hence eminently suitable for rural-led industrialisation. While the new economic environment provides a better framework to develop them, this may not by itself be enough if agriculture-led economic growth is not promoted as a priority through broad-based and rapid technical change in both the agri-business and farm sectors.

Concluding Observations

Resolving agriculture and agri-business issues is not an end in itself. It is a means to an end. This is because agricultural and agri-business growth is a vehicle to achieving the larger goals of employment-led economic growth, poverty alleviation and self-reliance.[16]

The new economic policies merely aim at economic growth and poverty alleviation, besides achieving sound macro aggregates. But they do not raise the issue of the composition of growth. Indeed, since independence, no political party or Planning Commission or government has even raised this issue. Yet all of them have voiced their great compassion for rural folk and sworn by poverty alleviation. While this may be a pre-condition to what policies may be formulated and implemented, it is certainly not sufficient for evolving policies that have a better scientific temper.

Perhaps for the first time in 1998 India had a political coalition and government that stated that economic growth was affected by both industrialisation and agriculture. Also perhaps for the first time, it was stated in the National Agenda that the government would increase plan allocation to agricultural development to 60 per cent. These pronouncements are indeed very welcome. Before they become rhetoric rather than practice, the government needs to urgently apply scientific temper to the allocation and mobilisation of resources for various sectors. This would require:

- prioritising objectives;
- prioritising composition of economic growth;
- prioritising policy 'strategy' and 'instruments'; and
- involving the people at large in this process.

This chapter, in considering the agriculture and agri-business sectors, proposes a shift in the paradigm of economic growth and poverty alleviation as follows. On the objective of poverty alleviation, it 'prioritises' absolute poverty[17] reduction as a primary goal, since resources are limited. On the composition of economic growth, it 'prioritises' agriculture and agri-business-led growth rather than 'heavy and capital goods'-oriented industrialisation. This is because growth of the former kind is people-oriented. On policy 'strategy' it 'prioritises' technical change in both the agriculture and agri-business sectors, as this is both economically most efficient and environmentally more sustainable. And on policy 'instruments' it 'prioritises' non-product-price policies, since prevailing supply–demand conditions would have potentially healthy incentive effects. These non-product-price policies should consist of government expenditure (including selective subsidies) on basic production infrastructure and R&D for both agriculture and agri-business, rural credit for both these sectors, tenancy reforms and land consolidation in agriculture, as well as implementation of existing ceilings on ownership of land. Organisation of institutions for all this must be more decentralised, de-bureaucratised and accountable. These paradigm shifts are also justified by the slackening of economic growth,[18] adverse changes in its composition, and increasing poverty in the post-reform period.

Notes

1. Desai and Namboodiri (1998a) show that *a priori* total factor productivity (i.e., technical change) and relative prices have no unidirectional positive association. This is because when these prices improve, farmers' incomes increase with a consequent rise in consumption, and hence saving and investment for technical change decrease. Thus, this negative impact could offset the positive incentive effect of relative prices on saving and hence on technical change. The authors also provide empirical evidence from twenty-five years of the post–Green Revolution period to prove this.
2. Similar empirical evidence also holds for a state-level analysis conducted for Gujarat (Desai and Namboodiri 1997a).
3. These tables reveal some shift in favour of high value enterprises and yet the growth rates have deteriorated. Moreover, such a shift was initiated much before the reforms.
4. In the USA, total factor productivity accounts for over two-thirds of the growth in agricultural output.
5. Extension services on such scientific agronomic practices should also cover other inputs such as organic manure, (irrigation) water regime, and the implements required to apply various inputs.
6. Ralegan Sidhhi is a village in Maharashtra state where such a watershed-based technology was combined with seed-centred

technology, which dramatically improved agricultural productivity and production, returns and self-reliance, besides reducing poverty (NABARD 1995).

7. Product price support policy must follow rather than precede technical change, as prevailing demand–supply conditions being price-inelastic would provide the incentives. But when technical change occurs, prices crash, which may then arrest future growth in agriculture.

8. At present, this ceiling for irrigated land varies from 3.60 hectares in Jammu & Kashmir to 12.14 hectares in Maharashtra, while for unirrigated land it ranges from 4.86 hectares in Kerala to 70.82 hectares in Rajasthan. Area declared surplus under these ceilings accounts for 18.45 per cent of land owned by farmers with more than 10 hectares. Most large-sized farms are in regions where agroclimatic resources are relatively inferior. Radical ceiling is not suggested also because available surplus land is unlikely to be sufficient to meet the demand of those who are land-hungry (Datta and Desai 1998).

9. States like Punjab, Haryana, Uttar Pradesh and Maharashtra, where this has been done, have greatly benefited from such a policy.

10. In 1992, for mainstream crops, seeds production constituted less than 1 per cent for linseed to over 59 per cent for sunflower seeds requirement. Inadequate availability of seeds and extension services and low density of distribution channels are the other serious problems (Singh and Asokan 1997).

11. Another farm input industry with lower capital intensity is small hand- and bullock-drawn farm implements that are eminently suitable to agriculture that is small in size. Scientifically better designs for these have been developed but they are yet to be transferred for mass scale production. Public policy to encourage such production needs to be more proactive.

12. Small and medium-size firms in major farm input industries (especially pesticides and farm implements and machinery) seem to have had relatively better financial performances, in terms of growth in turnover, gross profit margin and return on investment (see, for example, Desai and Parmar 1998).

13. Such industrialisation is termed as the 'Textiles First' Strategy. It gives highest priority to industries which produce (a) non-durable consumer goods like textiles, sugar, edible oil, tea, coffee, grains, dairy products, cigarettes, footwear, paper and pharmaceuticals; (b) intermediate goods like chemicals and dyes; (c) light engineering products like pumps, sewing machines and bicycles; (d) simple

equipment and machinery like looms, lathes and boilers, required in consumer goods industries (Oza 1997). What may be required is relatively higher priority for this strategy, and some of the industries that produce infrastructural inputs, compared with other capital goods industries.

14. But annual growth in employment (mandays) in both food processing and agro-processing industries was lower in the post-reform period, being 3.09 per cent versus 5.34 per cent for the former, and 1.93 per cent versus 4.34 per cent for the latter. Only in dairy, fruits and vegetables and hydrogenated and vegetable oils industries was this employment growth significantly better in post-reform years.

15. This is true of the processing of sugarcane, milk and some oilseeds undertaken on a co-operative basis (see, for example, Desai et al. 1991).

16. There is no trade-off between agricultural growth and alleviating poverty. Indeed, the two goals are complementary. Punjab, the heartland of the Green Revolution, not only has the lowest poverty ratio, but also a decline in the absolute number of people below the poverty line (see, for example, Mellor and Desai 1986; Rao 1997; Shergill and Singh 1995).

17. Two concepts of poverty are absolute poverty and relative poverty. The former refers to the percentage of people below the poverty line corresponding to some minimum calorie intake. The latter refers to inequality in distribution of income and wealth, which is governed by both economic and non-economic factors such as education and health that have an economic result only in the medium to long run. When the absolute poverty objective is prioritised, it does not suggest that the education and health sectors will not receive attention. Rather, these sectors will receive 'selective' emphasis, such as primary rather than higher education, free education of the girl-child linked to her family's economic status, and so on. Similar rationalisation in government expenditure on agriculture is also needed by discontinuing crop insurance, and making capital subsidies for farm assets like sprinklers target-group-specific. Crop insurance is commercially unviable, and does not bring significant productivity and production gains (Desai 1989).

18. National income growth rate at 1980–81 prices from 1986–87 to 1990–91 was 7.06 per cent, while in the five years after reforms were initiated it was 6.23 per cent. The corresponding growth rates for real per capita national income were, respectively, 4.81 per cent and 4.24 per cent.

References

Ahluwalia, Montek S. 1996. 'New Economic Policy and Agriculture: Some reflections', *Indian Journal of Agricultural Economics*, Vol. 53, No. 3, July–September 1996.

Bhagwati, Jagdish. 1998. 'The Design of Indian Development', in Isher Judge Ahluwalia and I.M.D. Little, eds, *India's Economic Reforms and Development: Essays for Manmohan Singh*. New Delhi: Oxford University Press.

Bhattacharjee, Sourindra, Bhupat M. Desai and Gopal Naik. 1999. 'Viability of Rural Banking by the Nationalised Commercial Banks in India', *The Indian Economic Journal*, Vol. 47, No. 1, pp. 24–41.

Chattopadhyay, Manabendu and Atanu Sengupta. 1997. 'Farm Size and Productivity: A New Look at the Old Debate', *Economic and Political Weekly*, Vol. 32, No. 52, 27 December 1997.

Dantwala, M.L. 1967. 'Incentives and Disincentives in Indian Agriculture', *Indian Journal of Agricultural Economics*, Vol. 17, No. 2, April–June 1967.

———. 1986. 'Technology, Growth and Equity in Agriculture', in John W. Mellor and Gunvant M. Desai, eds, *Agricultural Change and Rural Poverty*. New Delhi: Oxford University Press.

Datta, Samar K., and Bhupat M. Desai. 1998. 'Status and Impact of Land Reforms and New Technology on Agricultural Development', in Ghanshyam Shah, ed., *Land Reforms*. Surat: Centre for Social Studies, South Gujarat University.

Dehadrai, P.V. 1997. 'Growth in Fisheries and Aquaculture: Resources and Strategies', in Bhupat M. Desai, ed., *Agricultural Development Paradigm for the Ninth Plan under New Economic Environment*. New Delhi: Oxford and IBH.

Desai, B.M. 1989. 'Is Crop Insurance an Answer to India's Agricultural Development?' *Nirnay*, Vol. 4, No. 3, September 1989.

———. 1994. 'Contributions of Institutional Credit, Self-finance and Technological Change to Agricultural Growth in India', *Indian Journal of Agricultural Economics*, Vol. 49, No. 3, July–September 1994.

———. 1997a. 'Budget: A Retrograde for Agriculture', *Vikalpa*, Vol. 22, No. 2, April–June 1997.

———. 1997b. 'Agricultural Paradigm: A Synthesis', in Bhupat M. Desai, ed., *Agricultural Development Paradigm for the Ninth Plan under New Economic Environment*. New Delhi: Oxford and IBH.

———. 2000. Challenges before the RFIs under the Financial Sector Reforms and Management Strategy to Implement Them. Paper presented at the Seminar on Rural, BIRD, Lucknow, 29–30 April 2000. Mumbai: NABARD (forthcoming).

Desai, Bhupat, and Errol D'Souza. 1999. 'Economic Reforms, Terms of Trade, Aggregate Supply and Private Investment in Agriculture', *Economic and Political Weekly*, Vol. 34, No. 20, 15–21 May 1999.

Desai, Bhupat M., and N.V. Namboodiri. 1996. 'Whither Rural Financial Institutions?' *Economic and Political Weekly*, Vol. 31, No. 31, 3 August 1996.

———. 1997a. 'Developing Agriculture in Gujarat: A Strategic Perspective for the Ninth Plan', *Economic and Political Weekly*, Vol. 32, No. 13, 29 March 1997.

———. 1997b. 'Strategy and Sources of Growth in Crop-Agriculture', in Bhupat M. Desai, ed., *Agricultural Development Paradigm for the Ninth Plan under New Economic Environment*. New Delhi: Oxford and IBH.

———. 1998a. 'Determinants of Total Factor Productivity in Indian Agriculture', *Economic and Political Weekly*, Vol. 32, No. 52, 27 December 1998.

———. 1998b. 'Policy Strategy and Instruments for Alleviating Rural Poverty', *Economic and Political Weekly*, Vol. 33, No. 41, 10 October 1998.

———. 2000. 'Farmers' Response, Prices and Government Expenditure Analysis under WTO Framework for Developing Agriculture', in S.K. Datta and S.K. Deodhar, eds, *Impact of WTO Agreements on Indian Agriculture*. New Delhi: Oxford & IBH (forthcoming).

Desai, Bhupat, and D.S. Parmar. 1998. Profile and Performance of Some Farm Input Subsidies. Working Paper, Ahmedabad Centre for Management in Agriculture, Indian Institute of Management, Ahmedabad.

Desai, B.M., V.K. Gupta and N.V. Namboodiri. 1991. *Food-Processing Industries: Development and Financial Performance*. New Delhi: Oxford and IBH.

Ishikawa Shigeru. 1967. *Economic Development in Asian Perspective*. Tokyo: Kinokuniya Bookstore.

Joshi, Vijay, and I.M.D. Little. 1998. *India's Economic Reforms: 1991–2001*. New Delhi: Oxford University Press.

Krishna, Raj. 1982. 'Some Aspects of Agricultural Growth, Price Policy and Equity in Developing Countries', *Food Research Institute Studies*, Vol. 18, No. 3.

Kumar, Praduman, and Mruthyanjaya. 1992. 'Measurement and Analysis of Total Factor Productivity Growth in Wheat', *Indian Journal of Agricultural Growth*, Vol. 47, No. 3, July–September 1992.

Kumar, Praduman, and Mark W. Rosegrant. 1994. 'Productivity and Sources of Growth for Rice in India', *Economic and Political Weekly*, Vol. 19, No. 53, 31 December 1994.

Mahendradev, S. 1987. 'Growth and Instability in Foodgrains Production: An Inter-state Analysis', *Economic and Political Weekly*, Vol. 22, No. 39, 26 September 1987.

Mellor, John W. 1966. *The Economics of Agricultural Development.* Ithaca, NY: Cornell University Press.

——. 1976. *The New Economics of Growth.* Ithaca, NY: Cornell University Press.

Mellor, John W., and Gunvant M. Desai, eds. 1986. *Agricultural Change and Rural Poverty.* New Delhi: Oxford University Press.

Nachane, D.M., A.V. Karnik, and N.R. Hatekar. 1997. 'The Interest Rate Imbroglio', *Economic and Political Weekly*, Vol. 32, Nos 20–21, 17 May 1997.

Narayan, Pratap, and Uttam Gupta. 1997. 'Emerging Perspectives in the Fertiliser Sector', in Bhupat M. Desai, ed., *Agricultural Development Paradigm for the Ninth Plan under New Economic Environment.* New Delhi: Oxford and IBH.

National Bank for Agriculture and Rural Development (NABARD). 1995. *Watershed Development in Ralegan Siddhi: A Special Study.* Special Studies Series No. 1, Pune, NABARD.

Oza, Ajay N. 1997. 'Role of Agriculture in Industrialisation', in Bhupat M. Desai, ed., *Agricultural Development Paradigm under New Economic Environment.* New Delhi: Oxford and IBH.

Pal, Suresh, Alka Singh, and Dayanath Jha. 1997. 'Levels of Agricultural Research Investment: Lessons for the Future', in Bhupat M. Desai, ed., *Agricultural Development Paradigm under New Economic Environment.* New Delhi: Oxford and IBH.

Ranjhan, S.K. 1997. 'Livestock Industry Perspective: Issues and Policies', in Bhupat M. Desai, ed., *Agricultural Development Paradigm under New Economic Environment.* New Delhi: Oxford and IBH.

Rao, C.H. Hanumantha. 1994. *Agricultural Growth, Rural Poverty and Environmental Degradation in India.* Mumbai: Oxford University Press.

——. 1997. 'Inaugural Address', in Bhupat M. Desai, ed., *Agricultural Development Paradigm under New Economic Environment.* New Delhi: Oxford and IBH.

Ray, S.K. 1998. Sources of Change in Crop Output. New Delhi: Institute of Economic Growth (unpublished).

Rosegrant, Mark W., and Robert Evenson. 1994. Total Factor Productivity and Sources of Long-Term Growth in Indian Agriculture. Paper presented for IFPRI/IARI Workshop on Agricultural Growth in India, New Delhi, 1–6 May 1994.

Saha, Anamitra, and Madhura Swaminathan. 1994. 'Agricultural Growth in West Bengal in the 1980s', *Economic and Political Weekly*, Vol. 29, No. 3, 26 March 1994.

Satyasai, K.J.S., and K.U. Viswanathan. 1997. Commercialisation and Diversification of Indian Agriculture. Occasional Paper 5, Mumbai, NABARD, October 1997.

Sawant, S.D. 1997. 'Performance of Indian Agriculture with Special Reference to Regional Variations', *Indian Journal of Agricultural Economics*, Vol. 52, No. 3, July–September 1997.

Sawant, S.D., and C.V. Achutan. 1995. 'Agricultural Growth across Crops and Regions: Emerging Trends and Patterns', *Economic and Political Weekly*, Vol. 30, No. 12, 25 March 1995.

Shergill, H.S., and Gurmail Singh. 1995. 'Poverty in Rural Punjab: Trend over Green Revolution Decades', *Economic and Political Weekly*, Vol. 30, No. 25, 25 June 1995.

Singh, Gurdev, and S.R. Asokan. 1997. 'Seed Industry: Problems and Prospects', in Bhupat M. Desai, ed., *Agricultural Development Paradigm under New Economic Environment*. New Delhi: Oxford and IBH.

Singh, Manmohan. 1995. 'Inaugural Address', *Indian Journal of Agricultural Economics*, Vol. 50, No. 1, January–March 1995.

Srinivasan, T.N. 1998. 'India's Export Performance: A Comparative Analysis', in Isher Judge Ahluwalia and I.M.D. Little, eds, *India's Economic Reforms and Development: Essays for Manmohan Singh*, New Delhi: Oxford University Press.

Thamarajkshy, R. 1994. *Intersectoral Relationships in a Developing Economy: The Indian Experience*. New Delhi: Academic Foundation.

Appendix

TABLE 6.A.1
LAND OWNERSHIP INEQUALITY: 1956–57 TO 1992

Years	Gini Ratio	Percentage Area Owned by Households at the Top	
		1 per cent	5 per cent
1956–57	0.7511	18.41	42.71
1961–62	0.7114	16.51	38.56
1971–72	0.7062	15.20	37.66
1982	0.7076	14.35	37.55
1992	0.7132	13.83	37.50

Source: Adapted from Table 3 in H.R. Sharma, 'Land Reforms: Status and Opportunities', in Bhupat M. Desai (ed.), *Agricultural Development Paradigm for the Ninth Plan under New Economic Environment*, New Delhi: Oxford and IBH, 1997.

TABLE 6.A.2
OWNED AND OPERATIONAL¹ LAND DISTRIBUTION IN 1992

Farm Size Categories (ha)	Ownership			Operational		
	No. of Households (mn)	Land (mn ha)	Average Farm Size (ha)	No. of Households (mn)	Land (mn ha)	Average Farm Size (ha)
Landless	–	–	–	5.921 (5.42)²	0.825 (0.68)	0.14
Up to 1.00 (marginal)	65.273 (66.42)	19.867 (16.94)	0.30	70.567 (64.60)	23.831 (19.56)	0.34
1.01 to 2.00 (small)	15.563 (15.84)	21.822 (18.59)	1.40	15.622 (14.30)	22.561 (18.52)	1.44
2.01 to 4.00 (semi-medium)	10.985 (11.18)	28.837 (24.57)	2.62	10.807 (9.89)	28.420 (23.33)	2.63
4.01 to 10.00 (medium)	5.393 (5.49)	30.600 (26.07)	5.67	5.297 (4.85)	30.306 (24.88)	5.72
Above 10 (large)	1.058 (1.09)	16.228 (13.83)	15.34	1.023 (0.94)	15.883 (13.03)	15.52
All	98.272 (100)	117.354 (100)	1.19	109.237 (100)	121.826 (100)	1.12
Gini ratio		0.5969			0.5905	

Source: Adapted from Tables 5 and 7 in H.R. Sharma, 'Land Reforms: Status and Opportunities', in Bhupat M. Desai (ed.), *Agricultural Development Paradigm for the Ninth Plan under New Economic Environment*, New Delhi: Oxford & IBH, 1997.

¹ Operational land is owned *plus* leased-in *minus* leased-out land.
² Percentages in parentheses.

TABLE 6.A.3
AGRICULTURAL PERFORMANCE IN PRE- AND POST-REFORM PERIODS

Details	Pre-reform: 1986–87 to 1990–91	Post-reform: 1991–92 to 1995–96
1. Average of index of wholesale prices of agriculture to index of wholesale prices of manufacturing (terms of trade for agriculture with base 1981–82)	110.40	113.80[1]
2. Annual compound growth rate (%) in these relative prices for agriculture	−1.57	−0.43[1]
3. Annual compound growth rates (%) in:		
3.1 HYV area	4.23	3.89
3.2 Fertiliser Use	10.78	2.86
3.3 Gross irrigated area	3.94	2.40[1]
3.4 Electricity use in agriculture	13.99	12.29
4. Annual compound growth rates (%) in:		
4.1 Real plan expenditure on agriculture and rural development at 1980–81 prices	1.72	3.10
4.2 Real plan expenditure on agriculture alone at 1980–81 prices	1.04	0.81
5. Annual compound growth rates (%) in:		
5.1 Real total institutional rural credit issued during the year	−2.12	5.80
5.2 Real total institutional rural credit outstanding	2.16	1.56
6. Annual compound growth rate (%) in:		
6.1 Foodgrains production index	6.36	2.57
6.2 Non-foodgrains production index	8.60	4.44
6.3 Agricultural production index	7.69	3.34
6.4 Gross real value added (GDP) from agriculture at 1980–81 prices	6.29	3.70
6.5 Net real value added (NDP) from agriculture at 1980–81 prices	4.36	2.74
6.6 NDP from agriculture at current prices	12.58	9.67
7. Rural poverty ratio (%)	36.60	39.88[2]
8. Urban poverty ratio (%)	35.22	32.17[2]

Source: Adapted from Bhupat M. Desai, 'Budget: A Retrograde for Agriculture', *Vikalpa*, Vol. 22, No. 2, April–June 1997.

[1] These are for four years as data for 1995–96 are not available.
[2] These are for three years each as data for other years are not available.

TABLE 6.A.4
AVERAGE ANNUAL COMPOUND GROWTH RATES (%) IN YIELD PER HECTARE OF
MAJOR CROPS IN PRE- AND POST-REFORM PERIODS

Crops	Pre-reform: 1986–87 to 1990–91	Post-reform: 1991–92 to 1995–96
High value crops		
Paddy/rice	5.24	2.09
Wheat	4.15	1.78
Oilseeds	6.72	4.01
Cotton	10.27	2.64
Sugarcane	2.50	1.80
Low value crops		
Jowar (sorghum)	8.58	2.55
Bajra (millet)	15.82	2.50
Pulses (legumes)	3.35	1.34

Source: Fertiliser Statistics, New Delhi: The Fertiliser Association of India, 1996–97.

TABLE 6.A.5
AGRICULTURAL OUTPUT AT 1980–81 PRICES: COMPOSITION AND ANNUAL
COMPOUND GROWTH RATES IN PRE- AND POST-REFORM PERIODS

Details	Pre-reform: 1987–88 to 1990–91		Post-reform: 1991–92 to 1994–95	
	% Share to Total	Annual Compound Growth Rate	% Share to Total	Annual Compound Growth Rate
High Value				
Paddy/rice	16.52	8.64	16.38	3.76
Wheat	9.79	4.90	10.06	5.94
Oilseeds	9.53	10.78	10.22	4.32
Sugarcane	7.13	7.56	7.18	3.43
Cotton	2.91	17.84	3.11	5.59
Drugs and narcotics	1.73	6.48	1.66	−0.18
Condiments and spices	2.02	2.73	2.04	6.24
Fruits and vegetables	8.66	4.53	9.03	6.47
Milk and milk products	14.49	5.13	15.21	4.42
Eggs	0.88	6.67	0.95	5.43
Marine fish	0.88	14.24	1.01	11.13
Total	**74.54**		**76.85**	

(Table 6.A.5 Contd)

(Table 6.A.5 Contd)

Low Value				
Coarse cereals	5.73	9.28	4.93	2.78
Pulses (legumes)	5.07	7.57	4.52	5.55
Inland fish	1.32	7.42	1.54	8.57
Total	12.12		11.09	
All	100.00	6.56	100.00	4.36

Source: National Accounts Statistics, Central Statistical Organisation, Ministry of Planning and Programme Implementation, Government of India, New Delhi (various issues).

TABLE 6.A.6
SHIFT IN CROP PATTERN IN PRE- AND POST-REFORM PERIODS

Crops	Pre-reform: % to Total Cropped Area for Triennium Ending				Post-reform: % to Total Cropped Area for Triennium Ending
	1956–57	1969–70	1978–79	1988–89	1992–93
High value					
Paddy/rice	23.13	24.17	24.92	25.69	26.01
Wheat	9.09	9.74	13.58	14.89	14.72
Oilseeds	9.07	10.09	9.66	10.01	11.58
Sugarcane	1.35	1.53	1.90	2.05	2.28
Cotton	5.78	5.21	4.78	4.37	4.64
Drugs and narcotics	0.71	0.65	0.69	0.76	0.83
Condiments and spices	0.29	0.29	0.29	0.23	0.26
Potato	0.20	0.33	0.44	0.56	0.62
Banana	0.11	0.14	0.16	0.19	0.23
Plantations	0.31	0.28	0.27	0.32	0.42
	50.04	52.43	56.69	59.07	61.59
Low value					
Maize (corn)	2.74	3.64	3.64	3.68	3.64
Jowar (sorghum)	12.49	12.28	10.08	9.88	8.16
Bajra (millet)	8.30	8.25	6.95	6.77	6.37
Pulses (legumes)	16.74	14.69	14.69	14.35	14.71
	40.28	38.86	35.36	34.68	32.88

(Table 6.A.6 Contd)

(Table 6.A.6 Contd)

Source: Adapted from Bhupat M. Desai and N.V. Namboodiri, 'Strategy and Sources of Growth in Crop-Agriculture', in Bhupat M. Desai (ed.), *Agricultural Development Paradigm for the Ninth Plan under New Economic Environment*, New Delhi: Oxford & IBH, 1997.

TABLE 6.A.7
DISTRIBUTION OF NET SOWN AREA ACCORDING TO AVERAGE ANNUAL RAINFALL

Average Annual Rainfall (mm)	Net Sown Area (mn ha)
Below 750	48.4 (33.92)[1]
750 to 1,150	50.8 (35.60)
Above 1,150	43.5 (30.48)
Total	142.7 (100.00)

Source: Fertiliser Statistics, New Delhi: The Fertiliser Association of India, 1980–81.

[1] Figures in parentheses are percentages.

TABLE 6.A.8
PERCENTAGE OF GROSS IRRIGATED AREA IN GROSS SOWN AREA IN VARIOUS STATES IN 1992-93

States	Percentage	States	Percentage
North		Manipur	40
Haryana	78	Meghalaya	19
Himachal Pradesh	17	Mizoram	8
Jammu & Kashmir	41	Nagaland	27
Punjab	95	Orissa	26
Uttar Pradesh	64	Sikkim	13
South		Tripura	11
Andhra Pradesh	40	West Bengal	29
Karnataka	24	**West**	
Kerala	16	Goa	22
Tamil Nadu	49	Gujarat	29
East		Madhya Pradesh	22
Arunachal Pradesh	14	Maharashtra	15
Assam	15	Rajasthan	29
Bihar	43	**All India**	35

(Table 6.A.8 Contd)

(Table 6.A.8 Contd)

Source: *Indian Agriculture in Brief,* 25th edition, Directorate of Economics and Statistics, Ministry of Agriculture, Government of India, New Delhi, 1994.

TABLE 6.A.9
ACCESS TO VILLAGES BY ALL-WEATHER ROADS IN VARIOUS STATES IN 1987-88

States	*Percentage of Villages Connected with All-Weather Roads*
Andhra Pradesh	43.0
Assam	64.6
Bihar	34.9
Gujarat	73.6
Haryana	99.1
Himachal Pradesh	43.1
Jammu & Kashmir	59.9
Karnataka	32.9
Kerala	100.0
Madhya Pradesh	23.4
Maharashtra	52.9
Orissa	15.1
Punjab	98.8
Rajasthan	21.2
Tamil Nadu	63.2
Uttar Pradesh	42.8
West Bengal	41.4
All India (including other states)	**40.7**[1]

Source: *Statistical Outline of India,* Mumbai: Tata Services Ltd, 1994-95.

[1] For 1991-92 it is provisionally estimated at 46.2 per cent.

TABLE 6.A.10
ANNUAL COMPOUND GROWTH RATES (%) IN LAND PRODUCTIVITY AND ITS
VARIOUS COMPONENTS

Periods	Total Effect	Pure Yield Effect	Crop Pattern Effect	Location Effect	Interactions	
					Crop Pattern and Yield	Location and Yield
1954–57 to 1967–69	2.318	1.921	0.331	0.087	−0.090	−0.024
1967–69 to 1976–79	3.250	2.221	0.736	0.071	0.271	0.173
1967–69 to 1986–89	2.751	1.896	0.554	0.041	0.474	0.172
1967–69 to 1990–93	2.845	2.103	0.597	−0.012	0.482	0.136

Source: Bhupat M. Desai and N.V. Namboodiri, 'Strategy and Sources of Growth in Crop-Agriculture', in Bhupat M. Desai (ed.), *Agricultural Development Paradigm for the Ninth Plan under New Economic Environment*, New Delhi: Oxford & IBH, 1997.

[1] Land productivity is defined as gross value of output at constant prices per hectare of gross cropped area. This productivity is decomposed into (a) pure increases in yields of individual crops in different states; (b) changes in crop pattern; (c) shifts in location of area under individual crops; (d) interaction of yield and crop pattern; and (e) interaction of yield and location. The methodology is index-based and is explained in the source.

TABLE 6.A.11
ANNUAL COMPOUND GROWTH RATES OF TORNQUISH-THEIL INDEX (TTI) OF AGRICULTURAL PRODUCTION, TOTAL FACTOR PRODUCTIVITY (I.E., TECHNICAL CHANGE),[1] LAND, LABOUR, INTERMEDIATE INPUTS AND CAPITAL IN PRE- AND POST-GREEN REVOLUTION (GR) ERAS

| Details | Pre-GR | Post-GR | | | | | Both Eras: |
	1950–51 to 1965–66	Entire Post-GR 1966–67 to 1989–90	I 1966–67 to 1973–74	II 1974–75 to 1979–80	III 1980–81 to 1984–85	IV 1985–86 to 1989–90	1950–51 to 1989–90
Agricultural output growth (% point)[2]	2.05	3.41	1.98	4.25	3.68	4.49	2.97
Total factor productivity (TFP) growth[1]							
(a) Absolute contribution (% pt)	0.56	1.45	0.84	1.71	1.38	1.33	1.12
(b) Relative contribution[3] (%)	27.32	42.62	42.12	40.24	37.60	29.63	37.72
Land, i.e., gross sown area growth							
(a) Absolute contribution (% pt)	0.37	0.36	0.40	0.40	0.42	0.16	0.36
(b) Relative contribution[3] (%)	18.05	10.56	20.28	9.34	11.31	3.61	12.12
Labour growth							
(a) Absolute contribution (% pt)	0.70	0.93	0.26	1.36	0.75	2.01	0.82
(b) Relative contribution[3] (%)	34.15	27.37	13.28	32.06	20.31	44.78	27.61
Intermediate inputs growth[4]							
(a) Absolute contribution (% pt)	0.21	0.40	0.25	0.22	0.86	0.84	0.42
(b) Relative contribution[3] (%)	10.23	11.83	12.69	12.14	23.36	18.75	14.14

(Table 6.A.11 Contd)

(Table 6.A.11 Contd)

Private capital growth[5]							
(a) Absolute contribution (% pt)	0.10	0.16	0.13	0.13	0.20	0.10	0.14
(b) Relative contribution[3] (%)	4.88	4.69	6.63	3.10	5.61	2.29	4.71
Public capital growth[5]							
(a) Absolute contribution (% pt)	0.11	0.10	0.09	0.13	0.06	0.04	0.11
(b) Relative contribution[3] (%)	5.37	2.93	5.01	3.18	1.81	0.94	3.70

Source: Adapted from Tables 2 and 3 in Bhupat M. Desai, 'Contributions of Institutional Credit, Self-finance and Technological Change to Agricultural Growth in India', *Indian Journal of Agricultural Economics*, Vol. 49, No. 3, July–September 1994.

[1] TTI for technological change (TFP) is an index of growth in all output *minus* that in all inputs, i.e., land, labour, intermediate inputs, private capital and public capital. In logarithmic form it is given by:

$$\ln (TFP_t/TFP_{t-1}) = \tfrac{1}{2}\ (R_{jt}+R_{jt-1})\ \ln (Q_{jt}/Q_{jt-1})\ minus\ \tfrac{1}{2}\ (C_{it}+C_{it-1})\ \ln (X_{it}/X_{it-1})$$

where R_j and C_i are, respectively, revenue and cost shares of various commodity outputs and inputs, and Q_j and X_i are these commodities and inputs at 1980–81 prices.

[2] Agricultural output includes all crops, livestock products and fisheries.

[3] Relative contribution is the per cent share of absolute contribution in agricultural output growth.

[4] Intermediate inputs include seeds, organic manure, fertilisers, pesticides, diesel, electricity and irrigation charges.

[5] Capital includes farm equipment and tools, public and private irrigation, livestock, land improvements, farm houses and inventories.

TABLE 6.A.12
INTERMEDIATE INPUTS OF AGRICULTURE: PROFILE AND ANNUAL COMPOUND GROWTH RATES (ACGR, %)
DURING PRE- AND POST-REFORM PERIODS
(RUPEES MILLION AT 1980–81 PRICES)

Inputs		Pre-reform				Post-reform
	1951–52 to 1954–55	1961–62 to 1964–65	1971–72 to 1974–75	1981–82 to 1984–85	1987–88 to 1990–91	1991–92 to 1994–95
1. Fertilisers						
(a) Average amount	580	2,825	11,532	33,875	56,610	86,237
(b) % to total	0.92	3.69	11.67	17.91	17.07	16.18
(c) ACGR	18.44	18.68	2.85	9.30	12.23	2.39
2. Irrigation charges						
(a) Average amount	312	440	1,110	1,577	2,695	3,942
(b) % to total	0.49	0.57	1.12	0.83	0.81	0.74
(c) ACGR	2.24	12.55	1.08	6.33	7.27	10.92
3. Electricity						
(a) Average amount	32	175	1,127	3,652	6,907	11,795
(b) % to total	0.05	0.23	1.14	1.93	2.08	2.21
(c) ACGR	10.35	5.89	15.39	9.18	1.37	29.89
4. Diesel oil						
(a) Average amount	65	177	23.67	7,580	13,575	29,245
(b) % to total	0.10	0.23	2.39	4.01	4.09	5.48
(c) ACGR	16.93	11.90	9.08	9.87	20.51	15.73

(Table 6.A.12 Contd)

(Table 6.A.12 Contd)

5. Current repairs and maintenance						
(a) Average amount	1,327	1,902	3,905	10,717	24,485	43,625
(b) % to total	2.10	2.49	3.95	5.66	7.38	8.18
(c) ACGR	0.53	4.46	13.53	15.23	17.86	13.70
6. Pesticides						
(a) Average amount	22	330	2,285	3,740	5,325	8,177
(b) % to total	0.03	0.43	2.31	1.98	1.61	1.53
(c) ACGR	12.93	10.43	41.80	13.50	−0.31	23.57
7. Six major market-purchased inputs						
(a) Average amount	2,338	5,849	22,146	61,141	109,575	183,021
(b) % to total	3.70	7.64	22.58	32.32	33.04	34.32
(c) ACGR	5.65	12.14	13.25	10.55	13.02	15.36
8. All intermediate inputs[1]						
(a) Average amount	63,212	76,465	98,855	189,182	331,567	533,087
(b) ACGR	3.57	1.70	2.77	8.68	11.46	11.11

Source: National Accounts Statistics of India: 1950–51 to 1995–96, Mumbai: Economic and Political Weekly Research Foundation, October 1997.

[1] This includes seeds, organic manure, feed for livestock and market charges in addition to the six market-purchased inputs.

TABLE 6.A.13
AGRICULTURAL MECHANISATION

Year	Percentage of Electric Motors	Diesel Engine Pumpsets per 1,000 ha of Net Sown Area	Electric Engine Pumpsets per 1,000 ha of Net Sown Area	Tractors per 1,000 ha of Net Sown Area
1962	46.5	1.72	1.49	0.23
1972	55.0	11.04	13.48	1.22
1982	60.3	21.16	32.17	4.21
1988	62.9	30.47	51.80	7.98
ACGR in the 1980s (%)	9.1	6.27	8.26	11.12

Source: Basic Statistics relating to India, Mumbai: Centre for Monitoring Indian Economy (various issues).

TABLE 6.A.14
RURAL AND URBAN DEMAND PATTERNS FOR CONSUMER PRODUCTS IN 1961–62, 1970–71 AND 1989–90 (SAMPLE AVERAGE RUPEES PER CAPITA FOR 30 DAYS)

Items	Rural			Urban		
	1961–62	1970–71	1989–90	1961–62	1970–71	1989–90
Percentage to total						
Cereals and substitutes	40.18	40.04	24.08	23.20	22.93	14.28
Pulses (legumes)	4.16	4.42	4.60	2.88	3.33	3.57
Milk and milk products	6.75	8.58	9.68	9.45	9.48	9.91
Meat, eggs and fish	na	2.83	3.62	na	3.60	3.83
Vegetables and fruits	na	3.57	4.80	na	4.56	4.90
Edible oils	na	4.81	7.11	na	6.34	7.22
Other foods	na	9.26	10.39	na	14.17	11.81
All foods	68.89	73.58	64.28	60.02	64.41	55.52
Non-foods	31.11	26.42	35.72	39.98	35.59	44.48
All commodities	100	100	100	100	100	100
	(21.63)	(35.31)	(189.46)	(31.20)	(52.85)	(298.00)

Source: National Sample Surveys on Consumer Expenditure, Central Statistical Organisation, Ministry of Planning and Programme Implementation, Government of India, New Delhi (various issues).

TABLE 6.A.15
PRIVATE FINAL CONSUMPTION EXPENDITURE: PATTERN AND ANNUAL
COMPOUND GROWTH RATES (ACGR) IN PRE- AND POST-REFORM PERIODS
(RS MILLION AT 1980–81 PRICES)

Items	Pre-reform: 1986–87 to 1990–91			Post-reform: 1991–92 to 1995–96		
	Annual Average	% to Total	ACGR	Annual Average	% to Total	ACGR
1. Cereals and bread	248,180	17.38	2.21	278,064	16.06	1.77
2. Pulses (legumes)	32,096	2.25	3.71	31,662	1.83	0.21
3. Sugar and gur (Molasses)	78,480	5.50	4.02	88,120	5.09	3.65
4. Oils and oilseeds	68,024	4.76	4.59	78,320	4.52	6.00
5. Fruits and vegetables	70,106	4.91	8.12	87,650	5.06	4.61
6. Potato and other tubers	17,668	1.24	3.26	20,542	1.19	3.14
7. Milk and milk products	111,418	7.80	3.16	138,876	8.02	3.24
8. Meat, eggs and fish	42,518	2.98	5.49	58,200	3.36	6.91
9. Coffee, tea and cocoa	11,950	0.84	2.63	13,426	0.78	2.48
10. Spices	16,806	1.18	2.14	21,402	1.24	0.07
11. Other foods	5,044	0.35	6.35	6,564	0.38	7.23
12. All Foods	702,292	49.18	3.69	820,736	47.39	3.24
13. Beverages	17,796	1.25	–4.72	16,378	0.95	–0.15
14. Pan and other intoxicants	8,252	0.58	5.41	9,924	0.57	6.12
15. Tobacco and its products	23,218	1.63	3.68	28,812	1.66	7.29
16. Hotels and restaurants	14,168	0.99	8.32	20,700	1.20	12.48
17. Foods, beverages and tobacco (12+13+14+15+16)	765,726	53.62	3.57	896,550	51.77	3.54
18. Clothing	165,354	11.58	4.41	190,634	11.01	5.45
19. Footwear	10,416	0.73	11.09	11,124	0.64	3.37
20. All agriculture (17+18+19)	943,096	66.04	3.96	1,098,310	63.42	3.87
Total	**1,428,102**	**100.00**	**4.67**	**1,731,816**	**100.00**	**4.76**

Sources: National Accounts Statistics, Central Statistical Organisation,
Ministry of Planning and Programme Implementation, Government of India, New Delhi (various issues).

TABLE 6.A.16
ANNUAL COMPOUND GROWTH RATES (ACGR) OF SOME FARM INPUT
INDUSTRIES IN PRE- AND POST-REFORM PERIODS

Details	Pre-reform 1987–88 to 1990–91	Post-reform 1991–92 to 1994–95
1. Energy generated for		
(a) Agriculture	12.76	12.10
(b) All sectors	9.50	7.06
2. Fertilisers and pesticides[1] at 1980–81 prices		
(a) Invested capital	10.86	2.72
(b) Output	18.48	−2.10
(c) Net value added	11.03	20.46
3. Agricultural machinery and parts[1] at 1980–81 prices		
(a) Invested capital	9.17	5.61
(b) Output	16.19	−0.12
(c) Net value added	25.23	2.57

Sources: *Economic Survey: 1996–97*, Ministry of Finance, Government of
India, New Delhi; and *Annual Survey of Industries*, Central
Statistical Organisation, Ministry of Planning and Programme
Implementation, Government of India, New Delhi (various
issues).

[1] Separate data for these two industries are not available. Moreover, the
pre- and post-reform years for these industries are, respectively, 1988–
89 to 1990–91 and 1991–92 to 1993–94, as data for more recent years
are not available. The wholesale price index with 1981–82 as base for
chemical and chemical products and for machinery and machine tools
has been used to derive growth rates at constant prices for fertilisers
and pesticides and for agricultural machinery and parts respectively.

TABLE 6.A.17
FINANCIAL PERFORMANCE OF SOME FARM INPUT INDUSTRIES IN THE EARLY 1990s

Details	Seeds [5][1]	Pesticides [14]	Fertilisers [21]	Agricultural Implements and Machinery [10]
1. Average total sources of funds (Rs Mn)	215.0	843.9	6,696.0	6,103.2
2. Average paid-up capital (Rs Mn)	25.1	82.9	1,078.6	215.9
3. Average sales (Rs Mn)	257.5	1,214.3	4,894.0	4,119.2

(Table 6.A.17 Contd)

(Table 6.A.17 Contd)

4. Annual compound growth rates (%) between 1991 and 1995 for				
(a) Sales[2]	15.37[3]	9.67	9.28	4.83
(b) Exports[2]	–	8.24	38.52	0.60
(c) Gross profit[2]	11.34[3]	22.82	15.02	18.37
5. Average of financial ratios				
(a) Inventory turnover	2.60	5.30	6.61	5.61
(b) Gross profit margin (%)	21.52	13.73	19.74	9.84
(c) Net profit to sales (%)	3.96	10.35	13.02	6.83
(d) Return on capital employed (%)	20.05	21.17	16.94	20.54
(e) Return on net worth (%)	14.88	20.11	19.00	27.80

Source: Adapted from Bhupat M. Desai and D.S. Parmar, 'Profile and Performance of Some Farm Input Industries', Working Paper, Ahmedabad: Indian Institute of Management, 1998.

[1] Figures in brackets denote the number of companies or corporations.
[2] Deflated by the wholesale price index of foodgrains, chemicals and machinery with 1981–82 as base.
[3] These are based on data for two units, as data for others are not available.

TABLE 6.A.18
FINANCIAL PERFORMANCE OF FERTILISER INDUSTRY IN PRE- AND POST-REFORM PERIODS

Details	Pre-reform 1989–90 to 1991–92	Post-reform	
		1992–93 to 1994–95	1995–96 to 1996–97
1. Raw material productivity, i.e., gross value added per rupee of raw material cost	0.65	0.62	0.70
2. Gross sales to gross fixed assets (%)	4.52	1.00	1.07
3. Profit after tax to gross sales (%)	4.50	2.64	4.36
4. Return on investment (ROI, %)	9.02	10.50	14.78
5. Return on equity (ROE, %)	5.42	5.29	14.52
6. Net working capital cycle length (days)	167	176	157

Source: Adapted from Ajay Kumar Virmani, 'Structure, Conduct and Performance of Fertiliser Industry', Ahmedabad: Indian Institute of Management, 1998 (unpublished).

TABLE 6.A.19
ANNUAL COMPOUND GROWTH RATES IN INVESTED CAPITAL, OUTPUT AND NET
VALUE ADDED IN FOOD AND AGRO-PROCESSING INDUSTRIES IN PRE- AND
POST-REFORM PERIODS

Industry Type	Pre-reform 1988–89 to 1990–91			Post-reform 1991–92 to 1993–94		
	Invested Capital	Output	Net Value Added	Invested Capital	Output	Net Value Added
Percentage per year at 1980–81 prices						
1. Agro-processing industries	22.68	21.90	21.61	19.68	12.80	19.34
2. All food processing industries	14.49	10.30	4.93	7.87	4.07	12.93
3. Grains and pulses	9.83	2.44	0.89	5.79	8.31	1.20
4. Manufactured and dairy products	−2.41	3.03	6.74	16.77	17.28	1.85
5. Canning and preservation of fruits and vegetables	−5.34	−10.21	10.97	35.73	20.75	65.02
6. Slaughtering, preparation and preservation of meat	26.34	25.96	19.64	65.42	15.93	0.95
7. Canning, preservation and processing of fish	8.67	13.52	−5.10	25.68	9.96	8.29
8. Manufacture of bakery products	15.94	11.37	8.97	0.23	4.17	6.34
9. Manufacture and refining of sugar	17.61	5.17	−15.25	7.17	3.17	27.72
10. Production of sugar, *boora* and *khandsari*	3.46	−4.97	−18.66	5.96	14.44	33.80
11. Manufacture of cocoa, chocolate etc.	23.30	26.99	51.30	−2.21	2.81	3.98
12. Manufacture of hydrogenated oil and *vanaspati*	8.43	0.37	0.81	2.59	−6.96	−1.57

(Table 6.A.19 Contd)

(Table 6.A.19 Contd)

13. Manufacture of other edible oils and fats	40.49	43.82	68.75	7.32	−1.08	20.38
14. Tea processing	7.49	18.08	30.51	9.66	−67.27	−0.33
15. Coffee curing, roasting and grinding	25.37	−18.98	−30.38	12.89	36.40	55.38
16. Other food processing	6.59	6.81	6.94	3.19	41.92	5.35
17. Manufacture of cotton textiles	4.51	8.30	17.04	14.71	1.20	4.92
18. Manufacture of jute and other fibres	6.83	20.28	11.47	−0.09	4.92	1.86
19. All manufacturing	11.27	11.33	12.08	10.23	9.24	16.30

Source: *Annual Survey of Industries*, Central Statistical Organisation, Ministry of Planning and Programme Implementation, Government of India, New Delhi (various issues); *Economic Survey: 1996–97*, Ministry of Finance, Government of India, New Delhi.

Note: Nominal values are deflated by index of wholesale prices of food products and of textiles for food and non-food processing industries with 1981–82 as base.

TABLE 6.A.20
GROWTH AND PATTERN OF AGRO-BASED EXPORTS IN PRE- AND POST-REFORM PERIODS

Commodities	Pre-reform 1986–87 to 1990–91		Post-reform 1991–92 to 1995–96	
	Annual Compound Growth Rate in Export Quantity(%)	Percentage Share in Rupee Value of All Exports	Annual Compound Growth Rate in Export Quantity(%)	Percentage Share in Rupee Value of All Exports
1. Coffee	5.77 (−0.48)	1.34	10.98 (49.93)	1.07
2. Tea	0.94 (18.03)	3.48	−6.99 (−0.71)	1.51

(Table 6.A.20 Contd)

(*Table 6.A.20 Contd*)

3. Oil cakes	27.47 (40.24)	1.87	4.74 (22.41)	2.51
4. Tobacco	−0.71 (10.11)	0.81	−4.20 (−2.75)	0.56
5. Cashew kernels	6.86 (8.05)	1.60	75.86 (18.75)	1.39
6. Spices	3.25 (−5.33)	1.29	9.39 (20.25)	0.77
7. Sugar and molasses	84.26 (111.19)	0.09	−11.78 (6.17)	0.35
8. Raw cotton	8.51 (34.80)	1.21	−26.18 (−10.12)	0.42
9. Rice	16.20 (21.36)	1.62	55.10 (46.36)	2.47
10. Fish and preparation	−13.56 (15.12)	3.08	33.56 (27.26)	3.55
11. Meat and preparation	na (15.96)	0.47	na (27.24)	0.50
12. Fruits and vegetables	na (11.39)	0.80	na (24.00)	0.73
13. Other pro- cessed food	na (25.22)	0.78	na (19.94)	0.58
14. Cotton yarn and apparel	na (30.49)	6.03	na (29.37)	7.75
15. Jute manufacturers	na (6.24)	1.21	na (12.89)	0.63
16. All of the above	na (18.95)	25.76	na (25.23)	24.79

Source: *Economic Survey 1986–87 to 1995–96,* Ministry of Finance, Government of India (various issues).

Note: na = not available. Figures in parentheses are annual compound growth rates of rupee values in current prices of agro-exports.

seven

Poverty Alleviation Programmes in India

Ghanshyam Shah

O n the eve of independence fifty years ago, Pandit Jawaharlal Nehru, the first prime minister of India, said in his famous *Tryst with Destiny* speech:

> The future beckons to us. Whither do we go and what shall be our endeavour? To bring freedom and opportunity to the common man, to the peasants and workers of India, to fight and end poverty and ignorance and disease, to build up a prosperous, democratic and progressive nation, and to create social, economic and political institutions which will ensure justice and fullness of life to every man and woman.

These objectives have been embodied in the Constitution of India. The Directive Principles of the constitution direct that 'the State shall strive to promote . . . a social order in which justice, social, economic and political, shall inform all the institutions of the national life' and, in particular, shall ensure 'that the citizens, men

and women equally, have the right to an adequate means of livelihood'. It is time, after five decades of independence, for retrospec-
tion. To what extent has India attained these objectives? What are
its achievements and failures? This essay presents a bird's-eye view
of the country's efforts in the alleviation of poverty.

India has undoubtedly made significant progress in several
social and economic spheres during the last five decades. The
country has nearly the largest pool of scientific humanpower in
the world. The Eighth Five Year Plan of the Government of India
asserted that 'we now have a robust and resilient agricultural economy with self-sufficiency in food production. Moreover, we have
built a diversified industrial and service structure and have a large
pool of skilled manpower and ample entrepreneurial capabilities.'
Per capita income rose from a mere Rs 238.83 in 1950 to Rs 9,321.41
in 1996. Gross domestic product increased from Rs 93.66 billion in
1950–51 to Rs 10,985.76 billion in 1995–96, at current prices. India
possesses a sophisticated industrial structure. Food production in
the country increased from 50 million tonnes in 1950 to 152.37
million tonnes in 1983–84, and further to about 188 million tonnes
in 1994–95. Though the population multiplied, per capita availability of foodgrains also increased over a period of time, from 394.9
grams per day in 1951 to 474.2 grams per day in 1994 (GoI 1998;
UNIDO 1997). One has every reason to be proud of these achievements, but the country's record in reducing poverty is not that encouraging. The performance on this front does not correspond with
its achievements in other spheres. India, at independence, was one
of the poorest countries in the world. Its rank has not improved
much in the five decades since. The size of the overall population
living below the poverty line (313 million) has not substantially
changed, though the proportion of people living below the poverty
line has declined in the last three decades. Poverty continues to
remain a major challenge.[1]

This chapter is divided into three parts. The section that follows
describes the nature of poverty in India. Various programmes and
legislations aimed at improving the condition of the poor are then
critically analysed. The last section discusses the major challenges
facing the country in dealing with the problem of poverty in a
liberalised, market-oriented economy.

Who Are the Poor?

The Government of India has identified the poor as those who do not get the minimum required calories per day to keep body and soul together. The minimum food requirement is 2,400 calories per capita per day in rural areas and 2,100 calories per capita per day in urban areas.[2] In order to get the minimum food to meet the required calories, the estimated income requirement is Rs 229 and Rs 264 per capita per month at 1993–94 prices in rural and urban areas respectively. That is, a family of five requires an income of at least Rs 1,150 (rural) or Rs 1,300 (urban) per month.[3] Those who have less income than this are considered as living below the poverty line. All the poor do not, however, share the same conditions. They may be divided into four strata. Nearly 2 per cent of poor households, having no earning member, live in destitution. Fourteen per cent are paupers, 38 per cent are very poor, and 46 per cent are poor (Khanna 1988). Again, all those households considered to be above the poverty line are not rich. There is a sizeable stratum of households, whose annual income is between Rs 13,000 and Rs 20,000, struggling very hard to stay above the poverty line. In adverse situations, they are likely to fall below the poverty line.

In general, agricultural labourers, forest labourers, small and marginal farmers, a section of village artisans, non-farm manual labourers and workers in the unorganised sector in urban areas are poor. They belong to various social, linguistic and religious groups. A large number of them are also socially and culturally oppressed by the propertied classes. In terms of caste and community, they belong mostly to the Other Backward Castes (OBCs), Scheduled Castes (SCs), Scheduled Tribes (STs) and religious minority communities, mainly the Muslims. The OBCs and SCs occupy low social positions in the caste hierarchy and have been deprived of certain opportunities to improve their socio-economic condition (Shah 1987). The SCs, also known as ati-sudras or dalits, suffer from the stigma of untouchability. Traditionally, their touch and even their shadows were considered polluting to caste Hindus. The STs have remained outside the mainstream of economic development, and their culture has been looked down upon by the dominant classes.

On an average, agricultural labourers get between Rs 15 ($0.40) and Rs 40 ($1) per day, varying from season to season and area to area. In Kerala, Goa and Punjab, their wages are high, but in Orissa and Madhya Pradesh, they often work for Rs 15 or less per day. According to the observations made by the National Commission on Rural Labour (NCRL), workers in some parts of Bihar and Uttar Pradesh received only Rs 3 ($0.08) as wages per day in 1989–90. The rural lábourer does not get work around the year. On an average, a male worker finds work for 230 days in a year.[4] Sometimes the poor are compelled to sell blood, kidneys or other parts of their bodies to get some money.

Some of them, out of desperation, borrow money from landlords or moneylenders in the slack season to meet their day-to-day needs of food or medical treatment, and/or to meet their social obligations. In return, they agree to being bonded for many years at low wages.

> Chataru, son of Radhe (in Madhya Pradesh), is 30 and had taken Rs 250 and a *mond* (20 kg) of grain from Raghusar Yadav to buy medicines for his ailing father, who died for want of proper medical care. Chataru has been working with Yadav for the last 11 years and does not know if the loan has been cleared or not as yet. He is not aware of the interest rate but says that his master will take care of that. His wife Bhano also works in Yadav's house and gets morning breakfast at their place. They have been allotted 10 *bighas* (5.7 acres) of land and are given one *seer* (500 g) of *dal* or barley as daily wages. When asked if they could work elsewhere, Chataru replied that he has to take permission from his master (LBSNAA 1996).

There are 2.6 million bonded labourers in India, each working for several years for the same master at either very low wages or none at all (GoI 1991).

Wherever possible, small and marginal farmers as well as landless labourers migrate to distant places in search of employment. They return home during the monsoon to cultivate whatever little land they have. After the monsoon, they migrate again. There are nearly two million inter-state migrant workers occupied in agricultural and non-agricultural sectors such as brick kilns, construction works — roads, railways, buildings, dams, canals — and mines, fishing, etc. (Shah et al. 1991). Many of them are employed through contractors and sub-contractors. These workers are rarely paid the stipulated wages or given other benefits prescribed by the government. A committee appointed by the High Court in Gujarat observed in the case of migrant workers working in sugarcane farms:

> The general attitude of the management towards the workers in almost all the factories (sugarcane) are not of normal nature. These workers are not practically recognised as human beings . . . the workers were given treatment as if herds of animals are being organised in certain groups to be carried away from one place to another. The security staff used to move with sticks in their hands and always used insulting and sort of abusive language whenever they had to deal with the harvest workers (Shah et al. 1991)

Regarding the living conditions of migrant labourers working in stone quarries near Delhi, the Supreme Court Commission observed:

> Whether away from the site or on it, the *jhuggis* (huts) are an insult to human dignity. All of them are so low the human being is almost reduced to a four-legged creature. . . . In some of the *jhuggis* entered by the commissioners for having the first hand accounts from the freshly injured as also to talk to the womenfolk, the injured could barely sit up on a cot without touching the roof. The women do their chores bent almost half or in a sitting posture. Almost as a mark of their economic bondage, no miner can stand up erect in these *jhuggis* to say: 'I am a human being' (Shah et al. 1991).

Jan Breman, an eminent anthropologist, gives a vivid description of how migrant sugarcane labourers in south Gujarat are circulated from field to field, from sugarcane factory to factory and also from one place to another, resulting in their pauperisation. He notes in his field diary:

> . . . close to Bardoli station several beggars were sitting together under a tree. They were turned away from Unai and came here the day before yesterday. The company consists of a man with a completely petrified leg, his old mother who is senile, and a young blind man who has lost his previous guide, and tacked on to this pair several months ago. They are preparing a meal from refuse collected in the street and food leavings they have begged. The man lived earlier in a village near Songadh, but lost his land there (it remains unclear why and to whom). For many years afterwards he worked here in the neighbourhood, in stone crushing, until an accident

brought that to an end. He cannot return to his village. There is no one there to take care of him. He can manage well enough by begging, at least so long as he is able to move around (Breman 1985: 258–59).

Poverty is multidimensional. Merely low incomes and calories do not explain the nature of poverty. On an average, the poor have a larger family size than do the middle classes. It is not that they do not understand the importance of family planning. But their rationale for family size is different from that of the urban educated. For the poor, a child is a helping hand, rather than just another mouth to feed. A child is also social security for old age. Moreover, as the survival rate of their children is low, poor people have a tendency to one or two more children as a safety net. The poor do not send their children to school regularly. A child in a poor family is compelled to earn at an early age to supplement the family income. In India, there are more than 20 million child labourers. Though many of these children do get enrolled in school, more than 50 per cent either do not attend, or drop out before completing their primary education.

FIGURE 7.1
THE VICIOUS CIRCLE OF POVERTY

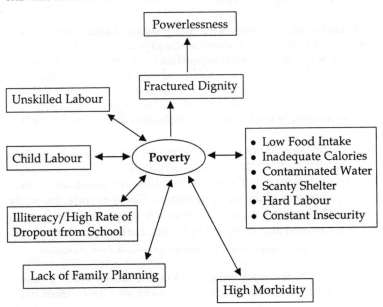

As a rule, the poor are looked upon with contempt and pity. They are hated, and frequently harassed and humiliated. They are often made to feel as if their poverty is the result of their deeds — present and past. In the process of deprivation and destitution, their dignity as human beings is often violated by those who hold power and property — the police, businessmen, etc. Out of desperation, some resort to begging. One comes across beggars in all towns and cities in India. According to Saathi, a non-governmental organisation (NGO), 20,000 to 30,000 girls beg in the city of Mumbai. Sangita is one of them. She

> begs at Chhatrapati Shivaji Terminus (CST), Mumbai's main railway terminus. The slender, short-haired girl in a large, long frock, lives on the station with her bald and ill mother. Her father, who had elephantiasis and begged to support the family, died six months ago. Then Sangita, 8, and her mother lost their tenement in distant Kalyan and came to CST to try and survive (Joshi 1998).

As the buying capacity of the poor is weak, their consumption of pulses, the prices of which have gone up, has declined sharply in the last two decades. Hence, their intake of protein and calories is low. C. Gopalan remarks:

> We are therefore, witness to the cruel paradox of satisfactory buffer stocks of foodgrains on the one hand, and pockets of undernutrition on the other. India's nutrition problem is thus not so much one of lack of foodgrains at the overall national level, but of lack of adequate access to food . . . (at least) 30 per cent of poor households whose family incomes are so low, that even if 70 per cent of their family incomes is spent on food, nutritional needs are not met (Gopalan 1983).

Most of the poor do not get potable water, not to speak of sanitary facilities, throughout the year. Consequently, they are vulnerable to various diseases. Public health facilities are inadequate to meet the requirements of the vast population. Consequently, mortality and morbidity rates among the poor are very high. The story of Rakku, narrated and analysed by Sheila Zurbrigg, presents a picture of how poor agricultural labourers suffer and struggle:

> Rakku, her husband Karrupaiya and three children live in a small mud and thatch home. She cooks and looks after the children and

also works in the paddy field with her husband during the harvest season from morning to evening . . . . Ever since the boy was born, Rakku had dreamed of her son going to the village school to learn to read and write. But four years before, her husband was forced to sell their small piece of land and such dreams had vanished in the need for his son's earnings for the family . . . Ponnu, a daughter aged four looking after the younger brother of one year when the parents work in the farm.

The baby had diarrhoea . . . . Throughout the night the diarrhoea continued . . . next day the village midwife gave some medicine which remained ineffective. Rakku borrowed money for bus fare to reach the hospital in a nearby town. After all hassles, when she reached the hospital at nine in the morning, the hospital gate was closed. She got in the hospital by paying bribe of Rs 1 to the gate keeper.

. . . after examining the baby, the doctor asked if there had been blood or large worms in the child's diarrhoea and how long the child had diarrhoea. When Rakku replied to his last question he looked up impatiently, saying: 'Three days you waited to get treatment for the child? Look at the dehydration!' . . . Rakku did not reply. For the only answer was her poverty, and how could she explain that to him? How could she explain what it meant to her family to be missing the field work even for a single day? How could she explain that money borrowed for the journey would be paid back from their small store of grain which was already far too meagre for the family? . . . the nurse placed a needle into a vein in his leg and connected it to the 'glucose water' above . . . . By evening some strength had returned to the child's body. The diarrhoea had stopped and late night the nurse removed the needle from the baby's leg.

. . . early the next morning the child was discharged, despite some diarrhoea having started again during the night . . . the journey back to her village was as full of despair as the journey into the city had been frightening the day before. The child's diarrhoea had started again — the watery diarrhoea so common to undernourished children when their bodies and stomachs are too weak to absorb the food they are given. It was the chronic diarrhoea of malnutrition . . . . Next day early morning, there was no life left at all in the child . . . (Zurbrigg 1991).

The poor are not only economically badly off, but they are also vulnerable to diseases, and unable to send their children to school. Their children begin to work at an early age. They do not feel the need to control the size of their families. Their living conditions are deplorable.

Measures for Poverty Alleviation

Capital accumulation is a major function of the modern state. India is no exception. 'In the initial stage', the First Five Year Plan noted, 'the accent of endeavour must be on increased production—because without this no advance is possible at all.' The country has followed the path of capitalist economic development with 'equity and justice'. The five year plan documents have set out objectives, strategies and programmes for the country's development. The First Five Year Plan (1951–56) declared that 'the central objective of planning in India is to raise the standard of living of the people and to open to them opportunities for a richer and more varied life.' With this as the broad objective, the removal of poverty has remained one of the main concerns of the Government of India since independence. The state has followed various strategies to attack poverty on various fronts. The measures for alleviation of poverty may be broadly classified into three categories (see Figure 7.2):

- Structural transformation
- Remedial/protective legislation
- Target group programmes

FIGURE 7.2
POVERTY ALLEVIATION MEASURES

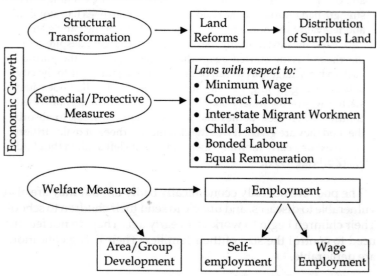

Structural Transformation

During the colonial period, peasant (including tribal) uprisings against the feudal lords, the alien administration and state oppression were widespread in the subcontinent, particularly from the mid-19th century onwards. The Congress Party channelised a section of peasant unrest, in particular that of the middle peasants, into the freedom struggle. The party advocated land reforms in the 1930s to change agrarian production relationships. After independence, several legislations were enacted to change the feudal mode of production by eliminating intermediaries between the state and the cultivators. These legislations aimed at changing agrarian relationships and enhancing agricultural production. The land reforms did to some extent provide land to some tenants — nearly three million tenants and share-croppers acquired ownership of land by the mid-1970s. The contribution of the reforms in facilitating the green revolution — thus boosting agricultural production — in different parts of the country is significant. But all aspects of reforms have not been carried out.[5] Remnants of feudalism and absentee landlordism continue in several federal states. More importantly, the legislation imposing a ceiling on the ownership of land has been sabotaged by the bureaucracy and by political leaders who belonged to the landed class. The Sixth Five Year Plan (1980–85) admitted:

> The progress of taking over and distribution of ceiling surplus land has been tardy. Out of about 15.74 lakh [1,574,000] hectares declared surplus in different states, as in March 1980, only about 9.56 lakh [956,000] hectares have been taken possession of by the states and about 6.79 lakh [679,000] hectares distributed (GoI 1981: 114–15).

By the end of December 1995, 2.09 million hectares of land had been distributed among 5.05 million beneficiaries (Haque 1997). All beneficiaries did not get the necessary infrastructural facilities to make agriculture viable, such as ploughs, bullocks and irrigation. However, the poor who received land with inputs were able to improve their economic condition.

Remedial/Protective Legislation

The first important legislation to provide legal protection against exploitation to the poor was the Minimum Wages Act, 1948. Later, a number of legislations to protect the rights of the poor against exploitation were enacted. These include the Bonded Labour System (Abolition) Act, 1976; the Equal Remuneration Act, 1976; the Contract Labour (Regulation and Abolition) Act, 1970; the Inter-state Migrant Workmen (Regulation of Employment and Conditions of Service) Act, 1979; and the Child Labour (Regulation and Abolition) Act, 1986. A special administrative machinery has been created to supervise the implementation of some of these Acts. But most federal states have not even established the machinery for implementation of the Inter-state Migrant Workmen Act. More often than not, these Acts have proved to be impotent in providing protection to the victims. The NCRL notes that the rural labour administration to supervise the implementation of the Minimum Wages Act has not been effective:

> At the state level, the Secretariat, which deals with the determination of the wage, is not well equipped and the officers have short tenures. The subordinate officers have very little interest in the subject of minimum wages . . . . In agriculture, where the bulk of employment on minimum wages is located, ignorance prevails. Briefly the ground situation can generally be described as lack of understanding, absence of skills and motivation, inadequate and poor supervision and unimaginative deployment of men (GoI 1991).

The government also advocated the need for organisations of the poor to enable them to assert their rights. This was one of the objectives of adult education programmes in the mid-1970s. Besides encouraging NGOs, the state also provided financial support in 1981 to rural organisers for organising the rural poor. But the scheme did not work (Hirway and Abraham 1990; see also Nadkarani et al. 1991).

Target Group Programmes

Initially, policy makers assumed that increased production would create more employment opportunities, and that the benefits of development would trickle down to all strata of society. This would improve the standard of living of all. It was within this philosophy that community development programmes were formulated. The fallacy of the assumption was realised within a decade, as the benefits of development were cornered by the dominant strata of society and deprived groups were left high and dry. The rural and urban poor began to revolt, often taking a violent and extra-constitutional course against local dominant groups and the state. The 1960s were a decade of large-scale unrest in rural areas and assertion of rights by tribals, *dalits* and OBCs, leading to political turmoil. The state had to contend with the rising aspirations of the masses and also win over the deprived groups. Hence, for the first time, a special reference to weaker sections appeared in the Fourth Five Year Plan (1969–74): a reference to SCs and STs. In the context of rising political turmoil—agrarian unrest, a split in the ruling Congress Party, anti-price-rise students' movements etc.—the Fifth Five Year Plan made special reference to the issue of removal of poverty. The Plan stated: 'Removal of poverty and attainment of economic self-reliance are two strategic goals that the country has set for itself. Our plans derive their basic in-spirations from these objectives.' It further noted:

> The existence of poverty is incompatible with the vision of an ad-vanced, prosperous, democratic, egalitarian and just society implied in the concept of a socialist pattern of development. In fact, it holds a potential threat to the unity, integrity and independence of the country. Elimination of poverty must, therefore, have the highest priority (GoI 1975).

The Government of India has formulated more than fifty pro-grammes targeting the poor to alleviate poverty. In course of time, some have changed their nomenclature, and some have merged with each other. These programmes are of two types:

- Area/group development programmes
- Welfare programmes

AREA/GROUP DEVELOPMENT PROGRAMMES

Development schemes focusing on poor cultivators, such as the Small Farmers' Development Agency (SFDA), and the Marginal Farmer and Agricultural Labour Agency (MFALA), were for-mulated under the Fourth Five Year Plan. The purpose of these schemes was to provide infrastructural inputs in the form of subsidy and credit to boost agricultural production. Moreover, development programmes such as the Drought-Prone Area Programme, the Desert Development Programme and the Hill Area Development Programme were formulated to meet the special needs of backward regions. Along with increasing the productivity and income of the local people, the programmes aimed at countering the endemic poverty caused by hostile agro-climatic conditions and degeneration of the eco-system. The main activities developed in these areas were: irrigation, soil and moisture conservation, afforestation, grassland development, construction of water harvesting structures, animal husbandry, roads, health services etc.

The Integrated Tribal Development Programme (ITDP), focusing on income generation and afforestation, came into existence to cater to the special needs of tribal people. A special administrative structure has been created in each state under a project administrator to formulate and implement the ITDP. Though these programmes are not well co-ordinated, they have to some extent created the necessary infrastructure in backward regions, and catered to the culture-specific needs of tribals and other groups.

WELFARE PROGRAMMES

Welfare programmes function broadly under the Integrated Rural Development Programme (IRDP), first introduced in 1976. The main objective of the IRDP is to transfer productive assets and thus broaden the resource base of families living below the poverty line. The following guidelines were provided for the preparation of plans to attain this objective:

- The Action Plan must provide gainful employment and increase the purchasing power of the rural poor, in particular, the landless labour, marginal farmers, artisans and women;
- employment generation programmes must spring from scientific resource utilisation strategies so that the short- and long-term goods of development are mutually supportive;
- the programmes should be simple in operation and economically viable, so that they are quickly capable of achieving self-reliance and self-replication; further, external inputs of humanpower and material should be introduced in a manner such that they are self-eliminating and not self-perpetuating; and

- the major thrust of the programme should be the effective utilisation of the most priceless of all resources, namely the human resource through new skills, education and economic emancipation (Swaminathan 1982: 32).

The IRDP has launched three types of programmes: (*a*) the Minimum Needs Programme; (*b*) self-employment programmes; and (*c*) wage employment programmes. The **Minimum Needs Programme** (MNP) aims at improving quality of life and providing infrastructural support including social services to other programmes of poverty alleviation. The major components of the Minimum Needs Programme include elementary education, rural health, rural water supply, housing assistance to rural landless labourers, environmental improvement of urban slums and nutrition. As these schemes are not specifically targeted at the poor, even the limited achievements of the MNP have not directly benefited the poor, except in the case of housing assistance.

The main objective of the **self-employment programmes** is to generate income through productive asset and skill endowment. The programmes include Training of Rural Youth for Self-employment (TRYSEM), providing loan and subsidy for development of land including irrigation, seeds and fertiliser, and/or for undertaking non-farm enterprises, providing raw material and market etc. During the Sixth Plan period, Rs 16.61 billion was spent on these programmes, as against the target of Rs 17.67 billion, implying a 94 per cent achievement. During 1985–90, 39 per cent of the beneficiaries belonged to SC/ST. Their proportion rose to 47 per cent in 1992–93. Around 51 per cent of the families assisted under the programme were provided assets is the primary sector, about 40 per cent in the tertiary sector, and 9 per cent in the secondary sector. During 1992–93, subsidy disbursed per family under various primary sector heads was Rs 2,324, and under tertiary and secondary sector heads Rs 2,211 and Rs 1,993 respectively. Credit per family during this period was around Rs 5,000. A recent survey shows that 10.24 per cent of the families received more than Rs 11,000 and 29 per cent received Rs 6,000 or more from the assets (GoI 1996).

The **wage employment schemes** include the National Rural Employment Programme (NREP), the Rural Landless Employment Generation Programme (RLEGP) and the Jawahar Rozgar Yojana.

Under these schemes, the poor are provided employment during the slack season. They are employed in repairing and construction of roads, village tanks and school buildings, afforestation, etc. These programmes also aim at creating assets for rural people. Some states have also launched employment programmes for the rural poor. The Employment Guarantee Scheme (EGS) in Maharashtra is one very important and relatively successful programme. The EGS provides, on an average, 105 days of employment per person to beneficiaries and contributes about 36 per cent of their family income (Acharya 1989). Though this is not sufficient, it is certainly critical for the poor. Indira Hirway et al. (1990) observe

> ... that the rate of unemployment (usual status unemployment rate) in Maharashtra has declined from 5.160 in 1973 to 3.44 in 1978 and 3.99 in 1983 for males, and from 5.93 in 1974 to 4.09 in 1978 and to 2.69 in 1983 for female labourers. And this has happened when the all-India rate (of unemployment) for males has increased and for females has declined only marginally.

A number of studies on IRDP, NREP, EGS etc. point out that these programmes do assist the poor in surviving during the slack agriculture period, and also help some to rise above the poverty level. However, these studies also highlight the weaknesses of the delivery system, the weakness or absence of co-ordination among various agencies, and factors such as corruption. Some of the major weaknesses of these programmes are outlined below.

First, the programmes are formulated, perhaps inevitably in the present economic structure, at the higher levels by the bureaucracy, politicians and social workers (including NGO activists). The formulation of these programmes often ignores the marketability of the production. Despite all talk about 'people's participation', the beneficiaries are rarely consulted or allowed to express their felt needs. Poor people might ask for land to grow foodgrains, but instead receive milch animals without the facilities for fodder. They are given sewing machines to stitch clothes, but there are not enough clients who can afford to buy their products or pay for their services (Sainath 1996). Any cost–benefit analysis of these programmes will show that they can hardly withstand market forces. They are not profitable. More often than not, they cannot compete with the sophisticated production of large factories (Shah and Chaturvedi 1983). Consequently, most of these economic activities survive only so long as they are subsidised.

Second, though the IRDP has created employment outside agriculture, it has not succeeded in diversifying the rural economy as beneficiaries have not been able to set up sound productive units under the programme. V.M. Rao in his study on Karnataka (1989) argues: 'The types of activities selected by the beneficiaries in the non-agricultural sector are mainly in the area of petty trade, service or low productivity and low investment-based manufacturing activity. Such activities are incapable of diversifying the economy.' Moreover, the IRDP is not linked with the economic growth process.

Third, these programmes are individual-oriented, and therefore limited in their coverage. Those who are covered are unable to face market forces with their limited capital and assets. They are not assured of raw material, and are unable to compete with the products of the organised sector. Their bargaining power as producers and sellers is negligible. They become gradually more frustrated and helpless.

The IRDP is neither a great success nor a total failure. It has some positive achievements to its credit in terms of helping the poor. The various anti-poverty programmes, though they have enabled the poor to remain alive — to get two square meals a day — have not been powerful enough to eradicate poverty. Many of those whose incomes have risen above the poverty line constantly fear that they may, under any slightly adverse situation — drought, inflation, riots — slip back below the poverty line. Notwithstanding these limitations, the importance of poverty alleviation programmes (PAPs) for mitigating the wretched condition of the poor in a country with widespread under-employment cannot be ignored.

The Challenges Ahead

During the Sixth and Seventh Plan periods combined, about 4.38 million families crossed the poverty line (Figure 7.3). In other words, the IRDP helped about 9.34 per cent of poor households to cross the poverty line in a span of ten years. It may also be added that in 1983, the proportion of rural households who reported that they could have two square meals per day was 81 per cent. The proportion of such families increased to 93 per cent in 1993. That is, only 7 per cent reported that they did not have enough to eat (Mahendradev and Ranade 1997). This is a small but welcome achievement, brought about by PAPs and economic growth.

FIGURE 7.3
HEADCOUNT RATIO OF POVERTY IN INDIA, 1951–92

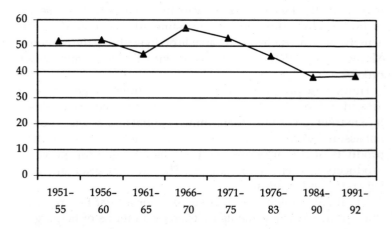

Source: Martin Ravallion and Gaurav Datt, 'India's Checkered History in Fight Against Poverty', *Economic and Political Weekly*, Vol. 31, Nos 35–37, 1996.

The question that concerns us is: what is happening and what will happen to the poor under the new market-oriented economic policy that the country has been following since 1991? The immediate impact has not been positive. The proportion of people living below the poverty line had shown a declining trend from 1970 to 1990, but there has been an upward trend in 1993–94. One may argue that it is too early to link the rise in poverty with economic reforms, which began only in 1991 (Sen 1996; Tendulkar and Jain 1995). But even the champions of economic reform agree that disparity of wages, income and wealth is a 'necessary part of the transition'. They also grant that increased inequality can raise poverty 'in the short run' (World Bank 1996). How 'short' is the short run, and for how long will the 'transition' continue?

Meanwhile, farm and non-farm sector employment has not visibly improved. On the other hand, more and more land is being acquired for industries and other projects (GoI 1994). Tribals and poor peasants are being deprived of their sources of livelihood and forced to migrate (Fernandes and Mohammad 1996). Moreover, large agriculturists not only follow capital-intensive farming but also pressurise the state to do away with land ceiling laws, building up a strong advocacy of large-sized farms (Ahluwalia 1997). Industrial growth is increasingly capital-intensive, using large and sophisticated technology, which has adversely affected employment opportunities. Amidst the euphoria over growth and globalisation, poverty alleviation has been displaced from the priority agenda. Safety nets, though talked about, are yet to be worked out effectively. In this situation, can the political system contend with the widespread dissatisfaction and rising aspirations of the masses?

Notes

1. For a discussion of various policies, see Shah (1994).
2. There are differences of opinion regarding estimates of people living below the poverty line. See Bagchi and Roychoudhury (1989), Minhas et al. (1991) and Tendulkar and Jain (1991).
3. Families living in rural areas whose annual family incomes were less than Rs 11,000 at 1991–92 prices were classified by the Planning Commission in 1993 as families living 'below the poverty line'. See GoI (1996).
4. The number of days of wage employment fluctuates from time to time. See GoI (1991).
5. Landlords in many regions, though not everywhere, became rich peasants and/or continued to remain absentee landowners. Their political power has not reduced substantially.

References

Acharya, Sarthi. 1989. *Intervention into Labour Market: Case Study of the Maharashtra Employment Guarantee Scheme*. New Delhi: IRTEP.
Ahluwalia, Montek. 1997. 'New Economic Policy and Agriculture', in Raj Kapila and Uma Kapila, eds, *Indian Economy Update*. Delhi: Academic Foundation.

Bagchi, Amaresh, and Uma Roychoudhury. 1989. 'Poverty Measures as an Index of Backwardness and Their Relevance for Tax Devolution', *Economic and Political Weekly*, Vol. 24, No. 15, 15 April 1989.

Breman, Jan. 1985. *Of Peasants, Migrants and Paupers: Rural Labour Circulation and Capitalist Production in West India*. Delhi: Oxford University Press.

Fernandes, Walter, and Asif Mohammad. 1996. *Development Induced Displacement in Orissa 1951–1995*. Delhi: Indian Social Institute.

Gopalan, C. 1983. 'Development and Deprivation: Indian Experience', *Economic and Political Weekly*, Vol. 18, No. 51, 17 December 1983.

Government of India (GoI). 1975. *The Fifth Five Year Plan*. Planning Commission, Government of India, New Delhi.

——. 1981. *The Sixth Five Year Plan*. Planning Commission, Government of India, New Delhi.

——. 1991. Report of the National Commission on Rural Labour, Vol. 1. Ministry of Labour, Government of India, New Delhi.

——. 1994. National Policy for Rehabilitation of Persons Displaced as a Consequence of Acquisition of Land. Draft Paper, Ministry of Rural Development, Government of India, New Delhi.

——. 1996. Concurrent Evaluation of Integrated Rural Development Programme (September 1992 to August 1993): A Report. Ministry of Rural Areas and Employment, Government of India, New Delhi.

——. 1998. *India 1998: A Reference Annual*. Ministry of Information and Broadcasting, Government of India, New Delhi.

Haque, T. 1997. Relevance of Land Reform in the Wake of Economic Liberalisation. Paper presented at the Workshop on Land Reforms, Land Reform Unit, LBS National Academy of Administration, Mussoorie, 18–19 January 1997.

Hirway, Indira, and Joseph Abraham. 1990. *Organising Rural Workers – The Gujarat Government Experience*. Delhi: Oxford and IBH.

Hirway, Indira, et al. 1990. 'Anti-poverty Programmes', in Report of the National Commission on Rural Labour, Vol. 2. Ministry of Labour, Government of India, New Delhi.

Joshi, Sharmila. 1998. 'The Beggar Child: For a Few Coins a Day . . .', *The Times of India*, Mumbai, 24 April 1998.

Khanna, Indrajit. 1988. Revised Strategy and Restructuration of IRDP in the Seventh Plan. Workshop Paper, Ministry of Rural Development, Government of India, New Delhi.

LBS National Academy of Administration (LBSNAA). 1996. 'Bonded Labour System: A Case Study', in *Case Study IAS Professional Course*, LBSNAA, Mussoorie.

Mahendradev, S., and Ajit Ranade. 1997. 'Poverty and Public Policy', in Kirit Parikh, ed., *Indian Development Report, 1997*. Delhi: Oxford University Press.

Minhas, B.S., L.R. Jain and S.D. Tendulkar. 1991. 'Declining Incidence of Poverty in the 1980s: Evidence Versus Artefacts', *Economic and Political Weekly*, Vol. 26, Nos 27–28, 6 July 1991.

Nadkarani, M.V., et al. 1991. 'Organisation of Rural Labour and Role of Government, Unions and Voluntary Agencies', in Report of the National Commission on Rural Labour, Vol. 2. Ministry of Labour, Government of India, New Delhi.

Rao, V.M. 1989. 'Decentralised Planning: Priority Economic Issues', *Economic and Political Weekly*, Vol. 24, No. 25, 24 June 1989.

Sainath, P. 1996. *Everybody Loves a Good Drought*. New Delhi: Penguin Books.

Sen, Abhijit. 1996. 'Economic Reforms, Employment and Poverty: Trends and Options', *Economic and Political Weekly*, Vol. 31, Nos 35–37, September 1996.

Shah, Ghanshyam. 1987. Caste and Poverty. Paper presented at the Workship on Poverty in India, Queen Elizabeth House, Oxford, 2–5 October 1987.

——, et al. 1991. 'Migrant Labour in India', in Report of the National Commission on Rural Labour, Vol. 2. Ministry of Labour, Government of India, New Delhi.

——. 1994. 'The Prime Minister and the "Weaker Sections of Society"', in James Manor, ed., *Nehru to the Nineties: The Changing Office of Prime Minister in India*. London: Hurst.

Shah, Ghanshyam, and H.R. Chaturvedi. 1983. *Gandhian Approach to Rural Development*. Delhi: Ajanta.

Swaminathan, M.S. 1982. Report of the Expert Group on Programmes for Alleviation of Poverty. Planning Commission, Government of India, New Delhi.

Tendulkar, S.D., and L.R. Jain. 1991. 'Change in Number of Rural and Urban Poor between 1970–71 and 1983', *Economic and Political Weekly*, Vol. 26, Nos 11–12, 2 March 1991.

——. 1995. 'Economic Reforms and Poverty', *Economic and Political Weekly*, Vol. 30, No. 23, 10 June 1995.

United Nations Industrial Development Organisation (UNIDO). 1997. *Industrial Development: Global Report, 1997*. New Delhi: Oxford University Press.

World Bank. 1996. *World Development Report 1996: From Plan to Market*. Delhi: Oxford University Press.

Zurbrigg, Sheila. 1991. *Rekku's Story: Structures of Ill-Helath and the Source of Change*. Bangalore: Centre for Social Action.

Polity
in
Transition

eight

The Constitutional Order in India: A Framework for Transition

Soli J. Sorabjee

I t was on a cold, wintry day, on 9 December 1946 in New Delhi, that the first meeting of the Constituent Assembly was held for framing free India's constitution. The members were faced with a truly daunting task, if one considers the various religious and linguistic minorities in the country whose interests had to be protected, the innumerable castes and sub-castes as well as the different regions and states whose rights had to be safeguarded in and by a constitution with a federal structure. The task of negotiating a constitution was made more difficult because during the negotiations Gandhiji was assassinated, and India was confronted by a great exodus of people from across the border, by a partition that engendered widespread violence and bloodshed and by a turmoil that produced a great human tragedy. But through all this, the work went on and the task was accomplished. It took exactly two years, eleven months and seventeen days. On 25 November 1949, the Constitution of India was finally framed.

The Indian constitution is the longest in the world. I do not say that this is an asset; I merely mention a fact. The constitution, as

most people are aware, is the basic law of the land, which sets up
the system of government. India's is a parliamentary system based
on the Westminster model. It provides for distribution of powers
between the union and the states, and then between different institutions set up by the constitution. There are the legislative, the
executive and the judicial wings of the state. But the Indian constitution is not an exclusively legal instrument. It is also a social document which reflects the ideals and values of the people who gave
themselves this constitution. These are reflected in the preamble
to the constitution, which promises to secure: 'Justice, social, economic and political; liberty of thought, expression, belief, faith and
worship; equality of status and of opportunity; and to promote
among them all fraternity, assuring the dignity of the individual.'

There are 395 articles in the Indian constitution. I shall at this
point touch upon certain salient features that are called, in the
language of Indian constitutional jurisprudence, the essential or
basic features of the Indian constitution. The first of these is the
acceptance of the principle of Rule of Law. This means that any
executive action or decision prejudicial to the interests of any individual must have the backing of law, the sanction of some legislative
authority. For example, the denial of a passport to an individual
cannot be at the whim of the passport officer; there must be a law
that provides the grounds for refusal to issue that passport. A
demonstration in the streets cannot be prohibited by the police
commissioner, or the minister, or simply by writing a letter, unless
such action is supported by law.

The Rule of Law actually existed in India even before the constitution was framed. It was an established principle of British jurisprudence, which has been adopted and elaborated upon. Its basic
purpose is to check and minimise executive arbitrariness. The Rule
of Law is a sworn enemy of caprice. One may recall the famous
story which, possibly, like all stories about Voltaire, is apocryphal.
Voltaire was jailed in the Bastille for a poem he did not write,
whose sentiment he did not share, and whose author he did not
know. Yet he was imprisoned, because some official believed that
Voltaire should be in prison. There was no Rule of Law. Voltaire
is supposed to have said, when he came to England, that he now
breathed the fresh air of liberty because he knew that in England
there was such a thing as the Rule of Law. This is the first basic
principle which runs through the Indian constitution. Any action,

any decision, must have the authority of law; law made by parliament or by the state legislatures. The definition of law includes subordinate legislation.

The second basic feature of the constitution is its democratic charter. The constitution provides for periodic elections in which people aged 18 years and above can vote without any discrimination on the basis of race, religion, sex or other qualification. No educational or property qualifications are required. There has been some criticism, which I regard as rather elitist, which says that people must be educated in order to vote, or that people who vote must have some sort of property rights to make Indian democracy really functional. However, past experience, especially in 1977 and onwards, has shown that the so-called illiterate Indian voter is as shrewd if not more so than the 'cocktail party', intellectual set, and recent events have confirmed this. There is clearly little need to interfere with the principle of universal adult suffrage, in spite of all its shortcomings.

The Indian constitution further guarantees certain 'basic human rights'. Known as fundamental rights, these are elaborated in Chapter III of the constitution. Foremost is the right of equality and the guarantee of non-discrimination. Certain sections of Indian society, such as the Scheduled Tribes and the Scheduled Castes (earlier known as untouchables) as well as the Backward Classes, have suffered economic and social discrimination for centuries. In order for these sections to enjoy true equality, and not merely legal or formal equality, the constitution makes provision for what is known as protective or compensatory discrimination. These measures are meant to give such persons certain advantages in respect of government employment or seats in educational institutions, in order to help them overcome the effects and consequences of past discrimination practised against them and their antecedents. Of course, the basic idea is that such protection should only be afforded till the stage is reached when they can compete on equal terms with the rest of the population. Care must be taken that compensatory discrimination does not become a permanent feature, because it was never intended to be one. But a furious controversy rages as far as these provisions are concerned. Many people think, in my opinion without justification, that in some cases they have amounted to reverse discrimination.

Equally significant among the fundamental rights is the guarantee of freedom of speech and expression, which has been judicially construed to include freedom of the press. Although the latter has not been specifically mentioned as a fundamental right, the Supreme Court held in a very leading case brought to it by Romesh Thapar that freedom of press is implicit in the guarantee of freedom of expression. Apart from guaranteeing life and liberty, the constitution also provides for freedom of conscience, freedom of religion, and the fundamental right of linguistic and religious minorities to establish and administer educational institutions of their choice. I shall dwell in particular upon these latter fundamental freedoms.

It is interesting to know the historical background of these two fundamental rights. The rights of freedom of religion and freedom of conscience are guaranteed to every individual, and not only to citizens. Even a non-citizen has the right to profess, practice and even propagate religion. The Constituent Assembly debates included much discussion of the fact that the right to propagate religion includes also the right to convert, in a lawful manner and not by force or deceit. The founding fathers of the constitution were aware that Indian society contains certain faiths, such as Christianity and Islam, that are proselytising in nature, that is, proselytisation is one of their basic tenets. Therefore, the word 'propagate' was deliberately included in this article (Article 25). The national constitutions of many other countries provide for the right to practice, profess, and even manifest religious beliefs in public. But the right to propagate is a signal contribution of India's Constituent Assembly.

Another article (Article 30) guarantees the right of religious and linguistic minorities to establish educational institutions of their choice in order to transmit their culture — their way of living — through such institutions. Before the constitution came into being, there existed separate electorates for Christians and Muslims. An appeal was made to these communities to give up their separate electorates in the cause of national integration. They acquiesced, because they were satisfied with the guarantee of these two fundamental rights, which were of utmost importance to them.

The next basic feature of the Constitution of India is secularism. Essentially, secularism in India is guaranteed by two basic constitutional provisions: equality and the freedom of religion, and a provision that prevents the state from levying any taxes on the promotion of any particular religion. Secularism in the Indian context is neither anti-god, nor anti-religion. It has two facets. On the one hand, an individual is free to profess and practise his or her religion subject, of course, to public order, morality and health, without interference by the state. This is not, therefore, an unlimited freedom; no freedom under the Indian constitution is unlimited and absolute. On the other hand, the state must not, directly or indirectly, take any measures to promote any particular religion; it must observe a strict neutrality. The state cannot thus subsidise the translation of the Bible or the Quran or the Gita into different languages, because this would constitute indirectly promoting a religion, and thereby not adhering to the norm of strict neutrality. This is the philosophy of secularism that underlies the constitution. In practice, however, these provisions are sometimes overlooked and in certain instances have even been challenged in courts of law.

These fundamental rights would remain rights only on paper were they not judicially enforceable by an independent judiciary with the power of judicial review. The Indian constitution contains a specific provision that any law or executive action that violates any of the fundamental rights can be struck down by a court. The judiciary has been performing this task since 1950, when the constitution came into operation.

Courts in India have safeguarded minority rights, specially the rights of educational institutions, under Articles 29 and 30. Any attempt by a state to interfere with the autonomy of religious educational institutions has been struck down. The courts have been vigilant so far, and will no doubt stay vigilant in striking down legislative and executive measures that tend to erode the autonomy of religious educational institutions.

A burning issue in India today is that of judicial activism or judicial hyper-activism, on which I shall now dwell. The traditional rule of *locus standi* asserts that if an individual's rights are affected, the court cannot be approached by another individual on the former's behalf. However, it was realised in India that, in a country afflicted by mass illiteracy, where large sections of the population are disadvantaged, exploited and oppressed, it would be ridiculous to insist that each member of such a class should approach the court individually. Therefore, courts in India have liberalised, or if I may say so revolutionised, the traditional concept of *locus standi*.

Today, the legal position is that any person or organisation acting
bona fide in the public interest may approach a court for vindication
of the rights of other members of society who, because of economic
or social disabilities, are unable to gain access to the courts.

Several beneficial consequences have resulted from this position.
Take the instance of the prisoners in jails in Bihar who had been in
prison for longer than the maximum periods of conviction they
would have received upon sentence. The Supreme Court, on being
approached by a human rights activist lawyer, intervened. It made
inquires, gave directions and, as a result, hundreds of prisoners
who had overstayed the maximum period of sentence for their
crimes were released. The case of young children working in factories in hazardous occupations is similar. Out of economic necessity,
their parents were forced to have them placed in such employment.
This suited the factory owner, who could exploit the children. The
factory inspector was complicit. Some bold and sensitive non-
governmental organisations (NGOs) approached the court and
pointed out that the laws protecting these children were being
flouted, resulting in the violation of human rights. Again, the court
intervened, in this case to rescue the children from their plight.

The upshot is judicial dynamism — judicial sensitivity to fundamental rights. In the early 1950s and 1960s, the emphasis was more
on property rights and land rights. But today, the judiciary takes
human suffering seriously. The orders and directions issued by
the courts have resulted, at least for a few Indians, in translating
fundamental rights from dry, 'parchment' promises into a living
reality.

I recount here an instance of environmental jurisdiction. Life is
a fundamental right guaranteed by the constitution. The courts
have interpreted 'life' not merely to mean physical existence but
to include quality of life, the right to live with dignity. This means
the right of every citizen to pollution-free air and pollution-free
water. Environmental jurisprudence has been built up in India
today through this creative judicial interpretation. A number of
factories which did not install the necessary anti-pollution measures have been closed down. Plants that were devastating the
atmosphere have been controlled, owing to the judiciary's interpretation of the constitution.

This is not a satisfactory solution, because it is really the duty
of the executive to see that the laws passed by parliament are

enforced. But if the executive is remiss in its implementation of the laws, the judiciary cannot prevaricate. It must act. And courts in India have actually been very active in this field. Thus the controversies about judicial activism.

Another chapter of the constitution contains the Directive Principles. Directive Principles are in the nature of social and economic rights. The constitution says that although they are not enforceable through a court of law, it shall be the duty of the government to enforce and implement them. The Directive Principles include, for example, the right to education, the right to a living wage for workers, the right to medical relief and adequate nutrition. However, here again the courts have — through judicial interpretation — incorporated some of these Directive Principles into the chapter on fundamental rights, by giving a broad meaning to the expression 'life'. The right to live with dignity means the right to medical health; it means a living wage for workers. This is another way by which the courts have been making some of these social and economic rights available to the Indian people.

I turn now to the framework for transition. The most important task in this framework is to strengthen democracy. The basic postulate of any democracy, its *sine qua non*, is accountability and transparency. This accountability and transparency are ensured, or at least facilitated, by two institutions in particular, among others. One is a free press, and the other an independent judiciary. The press enforces accountability on government and public functionaries by exposing corruption, deception and maladministration. It does this by providing relevant information about the workings of the government and of public officials. The press enables citizens to make informed and intelligent decisions. In a true democracy, it is the business of the press to censure the government. It is not the business of the government to censor the press.

At the same time, the press has a duty to disseminate a plurality of views from divergent and antagonistic sources, especially the views of the vulnerable, the views of those who are otherwise inarticulate, who do not have big businesses or vested interests in their support. The Freedom of Information Bill was drafted in June 1998 and should be presented in one of the coming sessions of the parliament. The Freedom of Information Bill, when it becomes an Act, will go a long way towards ensuring transparency, because its basic philosophy is that disclosure is the rule, while withholding information is the exception. There have to be exceptions on account of national security and other concerns. Having been on the committee myself, I remember how, once we started on the exceptions, the list became longer and longer until the original objective of freedom of information was lost sight of. So we had to go through the list again to try and narrow it down, limiting exceptions to the minimum possible. Two values must be reconciled: the right of the people to freedom of information, and the rights of the government and other organisations and interests. One of the most difficult tasks was to reconcile freedom of information with the right to privacy. Thank God, we do not have anything like the hounding of Princess Diana in our country. The culture of our country would really be repulsed by what happened in England.

An independent judiciary also enforces accountability by enforcing the basic tenet of the Rule of Law, which is: 'However high you may be, the law is above you.' Take the instance of the spate of cases against ministers and prime ministers that proceeded at a very tardy pace. The investigating authority, which was under the control of the prime minister's office, was not keen to pursue these investigations to their logical conclusion. Again, a public-spirited person went to the Supreme Court to claim that although these were serious charges, these matters had been pending for months and years with little being done to resolve them. The court sprang into action and directed the investigating authorities to carry out their duties under the criminal procedure code, irrespective of the high status of those involved. The authorities were asked to expedite their investigations, and to report to the court about the course of these investigations. It is no surprise, therefore, that the judiciary is unpopular with politicians and ministers. In fact, if this were not so, the independence of the judiciary would be cast in doubt!

We are going to have a Bill called the Lok Pal Bill in our parliament, which is something like an Ombudsman Bill. The Lok Pal will look into allegations of maladministration, and corruption against ministers, including the prime minister. One of the greatest evils in Indian society is corruption. Although this is a global phenomenon, it has assumed menacing proportions in developing countries. This Bill is a parliamentary effort to supplement the judicial effort.

The electoral process is a crucial matter for a democracy. It must be rid of the elements of money and muscle-power, which are not conducive to free and fair elections. It may, however, be said with confidence that, considering the scale and vastness of the exercise of holding general elections in India, elections on the whole have been free and fair. Of course, there have been disturbances and incidents. But by and large its elections should be a matter of pride for India, particularly because the transition from one government to another takes place smoothly. That does not mean, however, that electoral reforms are not necessary. In speaking of India, its problems and transition, it should never be forgotten that the founding fathers deliberately, consciously, chose the democratic path for solving India's many problems. Democracy may have its shortcomings and deficiencies, but they chose not to follow the path of dictatorship.

One of India's greatest problems is the size of its population. This cannot be remedied by enforcing compulsory sterilisation, because such a method goes against the lesson taught by Gandhiji, the father of the nation: that the end does not justify the means. Laudable ends may not be achieved by employing illegitimate means. And therefore, it takes time to solve the various problems besetting India. Democracy is not like instant coffee: one cannot solve all problems in a single day if one takes care to be true to democratic principles and to respect human rights. That does not mean, nor should it be understood to mean, that efforts to strengthen democracy should be lessened. On the contrary, the one thing that is necessary in secular, democratic India is social justice. Without social justice, to my mind, many of the fundamental rights would not have the meaning and the value they possess. The vast disparities of wealth and income must be minimised, with social justice as a cornerstone. To achieve this end, however, constitutional and democratic means and methods must be adopted. Only then can one make democracy, and the human rights guaranteed in the constitution, real and meaningful to the multitudes of humanity in India. This is a daunting task, perhaps more daunting than that which confronted the founding fathers of India's constitution on that cold and wintry day of 9 December 1946. But I am an optimist, and I have no doubt that with the requisite will and spirit, and the goodwill of friends, India shall achieve that goal. India shall overcome.

nine

Do Muslims Have a Right to Their Personal Laws?

Rajeev Bhargava

t he Indian constitution recognises two distinct kinds of rights. First, rights that can belong only to individuals. For example, the right not to be subject to bodily harm, or be detained arbitrarily, or prosecuted for expressing dissent against the state. Second, rights that can only belong to groups. The right to preserve one's culture against potential threat from other cultures, particularly a dominant culture, can be possessed only by a collectivity. The framers of the Indian constitution introduced both these rights not in the innocent belief that they sat harmoniously with one another. They did so because of their conviction that the identities of persons are constituted in part by their membership in groups and in part independently of them. They gave rights to individuals to counter the potential oppression of the state as well as of

This chapter relies on the arguments of my book *Individualism in Social Science* (1992) and two articles, 'The Democratic Vision of a New Republic: India, 1950' (1999a) and 'Should We Abandon the Majority–Minority Framework?' (1999b). This is a slightly revised and shorter version of Bhargava (1999b).

communities. But they also grasped that an individualist ethic alone cannot fight hierarchical and competitive communalism. To do so, we require an egalitarian communitarianism to which group rights are central.

In what follows I try to lend further support to this very significant dimension of the Indian constitution. Although my views concerning group rights have a more general application, my specific objective in this chapter is to defend two related claims. I argue that Muslims have a general right to their personal laws, but I also defend the view that they do not have a right to all laws they currently happen to have. As such, I distinguish my position from both the endorsement of a uniform civil code as well as from a blind ratification of the status quo on Muslim personal laws. In short, I defend the view that Muslim personal laws need to be reformed.

Cultural Rights of Groups

What do Muslims as a group have a right to? In the present context, group rights are the rights of a group to the survival, maintenance and creative renewal of its cultural resources. Therefore, Muslims as a distinct cultural and religious group have a right to the survival and renewal of their own cultural resources. There are two distinct aspects of this right. The first has to do with the content of their culture, the second with the manner in which this content is generated and nourished. If Muslims have a right, then it is the right to be the guardians of the content of their culture, as well as the right to make decisions on how best this content is to be preserved. In India, this cultural right can be decomposed, I believe, into four parts. First, the right to their language, or rather languages. The mother tongue of Muslims varies from region to region in India (Kashmiri, Malayali, Tamil Muslims) and this right, the right to the protection of their mother tongue, they must share with people of other faiths. There is then the language of their religious instruction, Arabic. And finally, the language of their literati, Urdu, a unique hybrid of *Farsi* and local dialects of Hindi, spoken in North India even by non-Muslims. Thus, Muslims also have a distinct right to the protection of Urdu and of their language of religious instruction. Second, the right to their cultural heritage, to ensuring that it is passed on from one generation to another. Though separate educational institutions are not necessary for this purpose, necessities of institutional design dictate that they have their own educational institutions. Third, the right to the protection of their places of worship. This should be taken care of in India by the fundamental right they have as individual citizens. But in view of the destruction of the Babri Masjid, this may be deemed a separate right. Finally, a right to their own personal laws, such as laws pertaining to family, marriage, divorce, maintenance, inheritance, child custody and adoption.

Of these, the right to their personal laws has become more significant in India. For a number of reasons which I cannot go into in this essay, Muslim identity in India is identified with their personal laws, and the right to the maintenance of cultural resources has come to mean the right to the maintenance of existing personal laws. The question: 'Should we abandon the majority–minority framework?' then amounts to the question: 'Should there or should there not be separate personal laws for Muslims?' It is, therefore, to this that I now turn.

I begin with a brief outline of the content of these laws. For my limited purpose I need refer to only four aspects. The first has to do with inheritance. Muslim personal law requires that women get a share of the parents' property, albeit roughly half of the amount granted to male descendants. The other three aspects relate to marriage, divorce and maintenance. Of these, polygamy is much talked about and I shall say nothing more on it. The position on *talaq* is familiar too: if convinced that the marriage has broken down, the man can quietly pronounce divorce which becomes effective only after the period of *iddat* (roughly three months). If the man has not retracted during this period, the marriage is dissolved, though this need not be permanent; provided the woman agrees, the man can revive the marriage. This renewal, however, can occur only twice in the lifetime of the couple. With the third pronouncement of *talaq*, the marriage is irrevocably dissolved. If divorced, the woman must be paid her *mehar* (her share in matrimonial property). She also gets alimony, but only till she is re-eligible for marriage, which, once again, is in roughly three months.[1]

Do Muslims have a right to *these* laws? Opinion on this has for long been sharply divided. Modernists in India, Muslims as well as Hindus, Sikhs and Christians, have firmly demanded the abolition of separate personal laws for religious minorities, and the institution of a uniform civil code on liberal grounds of justice for women *qua* individuals (I refer to this position as A). Pitted against them are conservatives (B), who obdurately seek the strict maintenance, indeed a further extension, of existing separate personal laws for each religious group (they cannot stomach diversity in customs that more freely indulge in inter-cultural borrowing). I believe that neither of the two positions is satisfactory. There are many reasons why this is so, and I undertake to identify them below. For the moment, I wish to emphasise that despite the opposition between A and B, the two viewpoints share a number of assumptions. First, an ontological assumption that to treat groups as irreducible is to view them as organisms of which individuals are functional parts, and that therefore they necessarily subsume individuals within them. Second, the normative assumption that if groups have a value, it must always be greater than the value of individuals who make up the group; that group interests always override individual interests, including, when necessary, the material interests of individuals. Advocates of position A associate these assumptions with a defence of group rights and counter it. One objection is that groups cannot have rights, simply because they have no irreducible existence. Since minority rights is a species of group rights, there cannot, it follows, be irreducible minority rights, or a separate right to personal laws either. A second objection is grounded in normative considerations. Whatever the truth or falsity of ontological individualism, groups have no moral worth (value) independent of the individuals who compose them. Since only entities with moral worth have rights, groups and therefore minorities have no rights. Proponents of B, working with the same framework, affirm the two assumptions. So, despite sharing the same framework at some level, A and B conflict because A denies these assumptions and B affirms them. I believe by challenging the very framework embodying these assumptions, we can reject both A and B. It can then be shown that a proper understanding of some of the basic features of groups, ignored by both the positions, enables us to arrive at an alternative position C, that reconciles A and B and seeks reform, not abolition, of these laws. I support one version of position C below. But first I try to demonstrate why A and B are mistaken; in particular, to show how some crucial issues elude both positions, and how they misunderstand the precise character of threats to the survival of individuals and groups.

The Ontological Assumption

Are groups reducible to the individuals who compose them? Some advocates of position A, believing it to be necessarily committed to ontological individualism, argue that they are so reducible. Now, ontological individualism is the view that only human individuals exist, and that groups are a mere aggregation of individuals. Here the term 'individuals' refers to distinct biological organisms with mental states, the contents of which are individuated internally; without reference to external, more particularly social, relations. Groups are thought to be an aggregate of individuals who possess distinctively human attributes prior to their relations with other individuals. I believe this view is false. First, the content of relevant mental states is individuated at least partly by reference to social contexts, meaning in relation to the mental states of other individuals, or to wider practices involving several individuals. So at least some attributes of individuals already presuppose the presence of social relations and, in particular, of groups to which those individuals belong. Second, to see groups as aggregates is to get the specific ontology of groups completely wrong. Groups are neither aggregates nor sets of individuals, but distinct wholes with individuals as their parts. Let me elaborate on this just a bit.

The difference between wholes, sets and aggregates is as follows. Unlike aggregates, wholes are extremely sensitive to the relationships between their parts. A cluster of stars is a cluster precisely because of its arrangement. If the arrangement breaks down, an aggregate still exists but the cluster has disappeared. Likewise, groups of human individuals are individuated by their relations. When these relations are destroyed, we are still left with an aggregate of individuals, but the group has ceased to exist. It follows that groups are not mere aggregates.[2] Nor are wholes identical with sets. The difference is this. Wholes tolerate identity-preserving changes, sets do not. If one item of the set is taken away, an altogether different set emerges. This is not true of wholes. Take away any particular star from a constellation, and the latter remains the same as long as another star replaces it in the same arrangement.

Groups of human individuals have the same property. For example, the identity of a university is not changed when the current set of students, teachers and fellow-workers leaves and is replaced by a different set. It is the institutional arrangement that individuates the university.

I am not claiming that all attributes of human individuals depend on groups, nor that they depend exclusively on specific groups. There is a perfectly coherent sense in which humans *qua* biological organisms exist without membership in any group. Some properties of human individuals, their bodily movements and non-attitudinal mental states exist and make no reference to groups. Human beings have sentient life without groups; many of their bodily needs, their felt pain and pleasures, inhere in them without groups. Indeed, I accept that in some ways these properties of individuals are more basic. Social or group properties supervene on these material biological properties. This does not threaten the non-individualist, however. For he does not claim that the source of all properties of individuals resides in groups. It is the individualist who claims that all social properties are reducible to individual ones and that groups are mere aggregates of individuals. The non-individualist can deny this without a commitment to a stronger collectivist thesis.

The Normative Assumption

I believe the foregoing has a bearing on normative issues. The falsity or implausibility of ontological individualism also contributes to the invalidation of value-individualism. However, I shall not try to show this here. Instead, I shall accept the view that a commitment to value-individualism is independent of one's affirmation or denial of ontological individualism. But is value-individualism plausible?

Value-individualism is the view that (*a*) only lives of individuals have ultimate value; and (*b*) collective entities derive their value from their contribution to the lives of individual human beings (Hartney 1991: 297). I believe these claims to be implausible. But let me first remove the unhelpful vagueness that plagues them. The claim (*a*) is ambiguous between lives of individuals understood (*i*) aggregatively or (*ii*) holistically, and between lives understood (*iii*) purely materially or (*iv*) also socially. The claim (*b*) clarifies how precisely, for value-individualism, (a) is to be grasped. In (a), individuals are to be understood aggregatively, but by lives of individuals is meant both the material and social lives of individuals. I take it that value-individualism is the claim that only lives of individuals aggregatively understood have ultimate value, and that collective entities derive their value from the contribution they make to each of these lives. In arguing against this claim, I shall contrast it with two perfectly sensible claims that I endorse. First, the material lives of individuals understood aggregatively have basic value, and (some) collective entities also derive value from their contribution to such lives. Second, some aspects of the lives of individuals have an ineliminable collective dimension and value. With respect to these dimensions of human lives, any talk of collective entities deriving their value from the contribution they make to individual lives is either incoherent or a matter of further convention and belief, and has no basis in hard facts about individuals. In short, if individuals are conceived holistically and their social lives are the focus of our concern, then (a) is true but (b) is incoherent or false.

It is clear, however, that, once we remove the term 'only' from its substantive claim, it is possible to recognise a partial truth in value-individualism. Indeed, some very powerful moral claims emerge from this recognition: many of our absolute prohibitions such as 'do not kill' or 'do not cause pain or suffering to others', as well as positive moral claims derived from the basic needs of others, have this individualist basis. I suspect their impersonality is also grounded in these properties. In other words, I agree with the view that pain and pleasure, primitive comforts and discomforts and the satisfaction of basic needs possess not only agent-relative but also agent-neutral value (for example, the pleasures of food, drink, sleep, sex, warmth and ease; the pains of injury, sickness, hunger, thirst, excessive cold or heat and exhaustion) (see Nagel 1986: 156–66). This is what gives credence to the claim that 'just as we have more reason to help someone get enough to eat than to help him build a monument to his God — even if he is willing to forgo the food for the monument — so he may have more reason to help feed others than to build the monument, even if he cannot be faulted for starving himself (ibid.: 172).[3] I accept that the reasons grounding these claims are also group-neutral. When a person abstracts from all his social properties he will still have a residue of properties in which value inheres directly, a value that derives neither from God nor from interaction with other individuals. This value can be a reason grounding the further value of collective entities. If the value of collective entities is partly derived from these basic individualist values, then it follows that such collective values never constitute a sufficient reason for overriding basic individualist values. What appears not to follow from this claim is that collective entities have no other (non-derivable) values. Value-individualism is false because it claims to be exhaustive: not all our interests *qua* human beings are adequately captured as facts about individuals, and the value of these interests is not grounded in aspects of individual lives when construed purely individualistically.

One more point. In one sense it is true that groups are just individuals acting. This claim is not as trivial as it first appears. It is not trivial if the plural term 'individuals' is taken not aggregatively but as 'several individuals with (fairly) thick relations to each other'. It is even less trivial if many of the properties of individuals emerge from such relations. For then an individual with such properties, even when he is not perceptibly acting with others in a group, presupposes social relations, meaning some group. I believe most of our distinctively human desires (interests), and most of our human capacities, including the capacity to assess the worth of these desires, are properties of this kind. Since interests of individuals and, I guess, part of the complex capacity to endow them with value (therefore, distinctively human values) are generated within groups, and partly only when people are acting as groups, it follows that groups have some value which is not reducible to, or simply derivable from, the value that individuals have independent of groups. These include not only values that individuals realise only with others (participatory or irreducibly social values, like Waldron's example of conviviality, or irreducibly collective games such as cricket and football; or our interest in belonging, in self-government or life in a cultured society); but also those that individuals appear to achieve on their own. (These include building a monument to one's God, leading rational, autonomous rather than heteronomous lives, speaking English rather than German, refusing to eat beef, creating or appreciating music, painting etc.) Such social properties (values), I have claimed, supervene on, but are for that reason irreducible to, the material or biological properties of individuals, and therefore of group-independent individuals.

However, critics may not be satisfied with this. They might argue that, after all, even these values are values *for* individuals. Once again, this claim needs disambiguating. I agree that all these values exist for social individuals, that is, for individuals *qua* members of groups, but disagree that they exist for individuals outside of these groups or for members conceived independently of their groups. Looked at thus it is better to say either that with respect to these collective dimensions of their lives, values are derived from collective entities or that the value of collective entities just is a value for collective entities, namely groups or individuals acting as members of groups. I cannot help repeating that value-individualism appears trivially true when its claims are ambiguous between individuals understood holistically and individuals understood aggregatively. But it is decisively false when individuals are construed aggregatively. It is not true that the ultimate reason for the need to protect all collectivities is their contribution to the welfare of each individual conceived independently of all groups.

I know that by now individualists must be itching to register protest. Does this not raise the familiar spectre of collectivism? I think not. First, my defence of collective values must not be conflated with what I call the subsumption thesis. According to the subsumption thesis, the description of the well-being of an individual is exhausted by the description of his well-being as a member of any group to which he belongs. The overall well-being of the individual is just his well-being as a member of any group. That I do not subscribe to this view is evident by my claim that the material well-being of individuals is independent of membership in any group. It follows that the description of the overall well-being of an individual is not exhausted by the description of his well-being as a member of a group. This invalidates the subsumption thesis. But I want to make an additional claim—not a philosophical or conceptual claim but a somewhat empirical and transhistorical one—that even the social well-being of any individual is not exhausted by membership in any one group. Individuals interact with different individuals and, at any given point of time, are members of different groups. Therefore, their overall well-being is conditional upon their membership in many groups. The description of the overall social well-being of individuals is exhausted, if at all, by the description of their well-being not in any one group but in many groups. This is not a claim I can substantiate. But it can be elaborated by examining a simple thought. Imagine an individual anywhere, at any time, and it is difficult to visualise his whole life spent exclusively in the membership of one group. If this is true or even plausible, then the subsumption thesis is further invalidated.

I hope to have calmed some of the fears of individualists. But there still exist issues between us that need examining. Simply put, the issue between value-individualists and non-individualists is ancient: the individualist must ask of everything: 'What's in it for me?' And he asks the same of his membership in a group. The non-individualist claims that at least sometimes we must ask: 'What am I required to do for the group, for the sake of collective values?' I wish to offer a tentative defence of this non-individualist morality against its rival.

However, let me first recapitulate my argument so far:

- Social properties are values (goods).
- Social properties belong to individuals in appropriate relations to other individuals.
- Groups are individuals so (appropriately) related.
- Social properties belong to groups.

I assume that groups have an interest in nurturing, sustaining and protecting these social goods. Therefore:

- Such properties ought to be protected.
- The only way in which social properties can be protected is by protecting social relations.
- Protecting such social relations means protecting groups.
- Therefore, groups ought to be protected.

What do groups need protection from? What threatens group values? I believe group values can be threatened in at least three different ways that may lead to demands for their protection:

(a) When values of one group are imposed on another. Here a real, external threat obtains.

(b) When members of the group, out of akrasia, wilful or unwitting neglect (self-interest or laziness), ignorance, confusion or delusion, cease to care for group values. This might be called an internal threat.[4]

(c) When members deliberating over these values realise their inadequacy or limitation and find better formulations thereof or discover still better values.

Notice that (c) threatens the existing formulation of values but rarely the values themselves. Even when values are genuinely threatened, the purported threat comes from new values that sublate (cancel and preserve) older ones. So, (c) never entails insensitive rejection, and need not be counted as a real threat. This is not to say that it is not perceived as one. But perceived threats do not legitimise special protection to values. Some collectivists mistakenly or deliberately subsume (c) under (a) or (b). On the other hand, individualists quite rightly emphasise the importance of (c), but generally tend to think of all changes in value as instantiating (c). And, although the less optimistic among them have begun to see the danger of external threats, they hardly ever recognise internal threats. Anyone pointing these dangers out is instantly seen as harbouring authoritarian intentions, as willing to sacrifice an individual for the sake of the group, as an enemy of (c), in short, as advocating the subsumption thesis.

So, one contentious issue on which individualists and non-individualists stand divided is internal threats to group values. Whereas individualists gloss over these dangers, non-individualists see them as worth combating. However, the problem for the non-individualist is that a fair, non-coercive way of protecting group values has hardly been found or implemented. Generally, four possibilities exist in face of internal threats. The first is to let group values die. Second, to coerce or manipulate some individuals into protecting them. Third, to rely on the heroism of individuals. Finally, to ensure that no one gets a free ride, that each one sacrifices some of his desires and does his fair bit in sustaining group values. Individualists rightly oppose the exercise of the second option. They grudgingly accept the third option but, because they do not see the full force of group values, are unable to grant validity to the fourth option.

I believe societies rarely commit suicide, but they also hardly ever deploy the fourth option. Therefore, grave moral inequalities continue to persist amidst us. Societies perpetually face internal threats and in response they plunge into what can be called an unfair division of moral labour.[5] Group values are preserved by the moral hard work of some (who sacrifice much more of their desires for the sake of groups), while others free-ride. In this context, moral individualism, that denies group value, is the ideology *par excellence* of free-riders.

Thus, groups need protection from internal threats and this sometimes requires that individuals sacrifice their current self-interest. Does this imply a commitment to the subsumption thesis? I do not think so. How and why so? Well, because no group may require that an individual work for it all the time — precisely what the subsumption thesis allows or enjoins. Two reasons suffice to show why not. First, individuals must be exempted from moral work to look after their own material well-being, and to sometimes pursue their desires. Second, they must be permitted to work for other groups. But the difficulty I am pointing to arises because individuals also shirk work when tempted by free rides. In fact, a basic character of groups permits this liberty to individuals on all three counts.

A group survives without all its members working for it all the time. This enables its members, first of all, to lead their material lives (they can sleep, eat etc.). Second, it allows its members to be members of other groups, both over time and at any given point. Third, it allows them to leave one group and join another. Groups can frequently bear the costs of departure of some of its members, a feature that adds to the richness of human existence. But the same attribute of groups that yields positive benefits also secretes a disadvantage. It encourages moral inequalities. Groups generally build into themselves asymmetries such that some persons or types of persons bear unfair costs of nurturing goods that benefit all members. Let me give an obvious example. Most of us value family life for the enduring relations that it makes possible. Both men and women equally share the joys of family, but the burdens generally are unfairly distributed. Women selflessly sacrifice their desires by indirect strategies such as the internalisation of their role as glorified mothers or wives. The fact that such asymmetries exist within the family makes it a repressive group. This is the truth in individualist claims. But it does not follow from this that the institution of family has no independent value, and therefore that the non-individualist claim is false.

What does the presence of internal threats to groups, and of unfair division of moral labour imply? Does it mean that we grant groups a right over their members? After all, rights are accorded in order to secure protection from threats. If internal threats exist, then we might as well immunise groups from those acts of individuals which create these threats. Am I then advocating that groups have rights not only against other groups, but also against their own members? My answer is in the negative. But the reason grounding this answer is different from the one generally offered. I shall be very brief in my response here. In much of the literature on this subject, the very thought of group rights implies the handing over of control to groups over the lives of their members, and this terrible possibility is enough justification against viewing groups and their collective goals as possessing independent value. I think the reason for not granting legally enforceable rights to groups against their own members is the great practical difficulty of (*i*) distinguishing (*b*) from (*c*); and (*ii*) of separating cases of genuine free-riding from those where individuals work to take care of themselves or other groups. Moral complexity makes it prudent that groups at best have moral, not legal, rights over their members.[6]

I end this section with a point that is crucial to my discussion. It is a truism that groups in all societies perpetually face internal threats. It is equally true that enough individuals exist in every society who are engaged in the critical examination and revision of the values of the group to which they belong. It is also a fact that such revision is perceived to be a threat to the very survival of their group by many of its members, particularly by those firmly entrenched within existing power relations, and that a palpable tension exists between free-riders in the group and its committed reformers. In this very complex situation, the birth or consolidation of an external threat has the following negative consequence for the endangered group. The already existing tension between the ultra-individualist tendencies to free-ride and the collectivist tendency to reform one's own group is invariably resolved by loud public proclamations that a challenge to an existing interpretation of values is in fact a real threat to the very survival of the group, by the curtailment of internal debate, and *most of all by the intensification of existing unfairness in the division of moral labour*. Some members of the group are excessively and oppressively burdened with the task of sustaining the group by upholding all its values, including the morally obnoxious ones.

I have argued that groups are more than mere aggregates of individuals, that part of their value is not reducible to their value for individuals understood in abstraction from groups, and that this moral worth of groups needs protection just as the moral worth of individuals does. I admit this creates the potential for conflict between group values and individual rights. I have also argued that some individual rights are more basic than any group rights. It follows that groups which violate these individual rights are in the relevant respect morally guilty. But it is part of my claim that these morally suspect features do not take away from them their entire moral status. It is, of course, true that if the violation of basic individual rights is the sole *raison d'être* of the existence of a group, then this group has no moral value at all. Such groups have no rights against other groups. That such morally depraved groups have existed in the past and have even acquired power is surely the principal reason for the liberal distrust of groups. But liberal individualism wrongly concludes from this that the value of all groups must be their value for individuals.

A final objection is worth responding to. It might be argued that even if groups have collective interests, they cannot really be said to have rights, for rights properly belong only to individuals. Allow me to briefly answer this objection by relying on the very persuasive definition of rights provided by the philosopher, Joseph Raz. According to him, 'X has a right if and only if X can have these rights, and other things being equal, an aspect of X's well being (his or her interest) is a sufficient reason for holding some other person's to be under a duty' (Raz 1986: 166). Such a definition is amenable to both an individualist and a non-individualist construal. For the individualist, X can only be an individual and his interests must also be conceived individualistically. For the non-individualist, however, X can easily be treated as a group that has irreducible collective interests, that is, an interest in irreducibly collective goods. I have argued above that it is legitimate to talk about groups having irreducible properties, some of which at least are its interests. It follows on Raz's definition that groups have rights. Nothing in his definition suggests that the discourse of rights is ineluctably linked to individualism.

Reform of Muslim Personal Law

If what I have said is reasonable, then position A, which denies for one reason or another that groups have value or that they need protection, is indefensible. Ontological and value-individualism are both implausible or false. But B is not justifiable either; it also misunderstands the nature of groups and their relations to individuals. Groups do not hover over and above individuals and, although they have irreducible value, it does not follow that the value of some properties of individuals is any less and can be over-ridden. In short, A does not recognise any group rights, while B recognises them, but in the wrong way, with no place for the value or rights of individuals.

The implication of this abstract philosophical discussion is this. Muslims as a group have rights and, given the importance of law within Islam and the contextual significance in India of the domain of the private, they have a right to their personal laws. It does not follow, however, that Muslims have a right to the protection of existing interpretations of laws grossly unjust to women. For a start, my account rules out, in an unabashedly individualist vein, the violation of basic individual rights in the name of group value. Freedom from domestic violence, a right to share in inheritance, and the right to maintenance for divorced and destitute women (flowing from the agent- and group-neutral reason of fulfilment of basic needs) must be legally enforceable, irrespective of the group to which women belong. The state has simply to enforce the exercise of such rights, no matter how incompatible they are with the personal laws or customary practices of any group. Any custom or law of Muslim orthodoxy that violates these basic rights must be set aside.[7] No Muslim can reasonably argue that the abolition of such laws constitutes an internal threat to his culture. But, and this is the crux of the problem, there also exists a *prima facie* incompatibility of Muslim personal laws with the best available standards of equality and autonomy. Surely, it might be argued, by these standards, polygamy should be abolished, women must have a right to equal share in inheritance, and divorce must be effected by mutual consent rather than by the punitive exercise of an exclusive male prerogative. Should we then proceed with a uniform civil code? Here the need for caution arises. It is not entirely unreasonable to claim that, in the absence of a clear perspective on where Islam stands on the values of gender equality and autonomy, without proper discussion at all levels on these issues, and under conditions where there anyway exists an external threat, any permission to tamper with personal laws is tantamount to an internal threat to the culture of Muslims. I believe there is something to be said in favour of this view, and that we might therefore support a reconciliatory position, C, which is that personal laws need reform, not outright rejection.

However, this position, as it stands, is still morally speaking too simple. To be sensitive to the complex moral dimensions of this issue, we need a better specification of how this reform is to come about. So, C bifurcates further. The position C1 argues that these reforms can be imposed from above, with the initiative of the state, much the same way as reforms were introduced within Hinduism. The other view claims that such reforms must come from within the community. The latter view is subject to further division. The first, C2, argues that reform from within entails that the state adopt a strict policy of non-interference in personal matters of Muslim community. The second, C3, argues for a distinction between paternalistic coercion and parentalistic interference, and further that the rejection of paternalistic coercion is compatible with the obligation of the state to provide conditions which facilitate reform within the community. A combination of C and A, in a contrasting system of priorities, completes the picture. In India, citizens have the option of complying with the uniform civil code rather than with the personal laws of the community into which they are born. Before independence, this option was conditional upon the complete renunciation of one's religion and therefore of one's cultural identity. This precondition virtually blocked the right of individuals to exit from their respective personal laws. Since independence, it has been possible to both keep one's religious identity and opt for the common civil code. This means position D, the policy of an optional civil code, combining B or C with A. Finally, according to position E, there may exist an automatic compliance with a common civil code but citizens can have the option to be governed by personal laws (A is more basic, but an option exists for B or C).[8]

I opt for the solution that advocates D, i.e., a combination of C3 and A. I believe reforms within Muslim personal law must come from within, but that a liberal and democratic state is committed to the provision of conditions that make possible a full and free deliberation over the entire issue, a precondition for any reform. I also believe that Muslim women must be given the right to exit from the system of personal laws. As there are no advocates for the removal of the option to be regulated by a common code (a sign, surely, that the Muslim orthodoxy does not view it as threatening and a sign, too, that Muslim women do not see it as a reasonable option), on the question of the choice between a uniform civil code and separate personal laws, I back separate personal laws, not on the ground that they are sacred, but on the more general ground that Muslims have a right to a separate cultural identity. Since it is this more general reason that grounds the rights of and entails duties for individuals, groups and the state, it would be wholly consistent with my position if, on the more specific grounds of justice, personal laws are eventually overhauled and replaced by something else that better protects their separate identity. My point, however, is that whatever it is that replaces personal law, it is not likely to, and perhaps should not, entail a common civil code. India has and should have a common criminal code. It has a set of fundamental rights which are and should be uniform. Since laws pertaining to contract apply equally to all groups, our civil code is already common enough. Any further uniformity is unnecessary and incompatible with the cultural rights of groups.

What is my defence of this position? I think everything hinges on how Muslim women view their own situation. Do most of them view their situation within the community as similar to being under a bell jar, as must surely be assumed by those who wish a swift imposition of a uniform civil code on liberal-emancipatory grounds? Are Muslim women waiting to break the chains, and only in need of some external aid? Is it purely a gender issue, with men exploiting women? Or is it rather that they have entirely accepted their current role within Muslim culture as dictated by the demands of the *shariat*? Is the division of moral labour seen as legitimate or as unfair by Muslim women? Rather than forcing the situation of women into one or the other pigeonhole, surely it is better — certainly more in keeping with their status as full moral agents—to view it as riven with an internal conflict. Despite all the inequalities of their condition, Muslim women see the importance of their cultural identity just as well as Muslim men do. They realise the value of their group.

Position A denies this and position E does not give it enough importance, at least not in the current context. But Muslim women can also view themselves independently of their current status within the group, as bearers of interests that grant them greater moral worth than they currently enjoy *qua* group members. Such interests are foregrounded when they view themselves either *qua* equal interlocutors deliberating over the values of their group, or as potential members of other groups. It is best to see Muslim women and, to some extent, Muslim men, as playing out this internal struggle. A Muslim cultural identity matters to (the relevant) women. But, despite Muslim orthodoxy that wants it to be so, it is not the *only* thing that matters to them. This clearly is an internal struggle within the Muslim community, between status quoists and pro-change Muslims. The Shah Bano case can surely be read in this manner. The real salience of this point is obscured, however, by the hostility of some Hindus to all Muslims.

This point needs spelling out. It is tempting to see in this situation either a struggle between individual women who happen to be Muslims and an intransigent group led by Muslim men, or to see women as pawns in a fiercely fought game between two rival groups, Hindus and Muslims. I see it somewhat differently. Recall my discussion of the sources of value change. Muslims in India are undergoing all three processes at once (*a, b* and *c*). It is true that Muslims face an external threat (from Hindu militants, surely the reason that grounds their group right). There is also some evidence of an internal threat (the reason why Muslim orthodoxy plays a hegemonic role among Muslims today). But there also exist persistent attempts among Muslims to reinterpret their tradition (see the valiant attempts of both modernist and traditional Muslims, including a large number of liberal men and women and exemplary figures such as Asghar Ali Engineer and Maulana Wahiduddin). It is in the interest of Muslim orthodoxy that the lines between (*a*), (*b*) and (*c*) are blurred. The presence of Hindu militants makes such distinctions even more fuzzy. (Clearly, when the internal struggle within Muslims is warped, both Muslim orthodoxy and Hindu militants benefit.) It is the current difficulty of demarcating (*b*) from (*c*), and the pervasive presence of (*a*), that create the dilemma, above all for Muslim women. Muslims as a group have value. There exist internal and external threats to the group. The line between such threats and (*c*) is blurred. But though the division of moral labour is unjust to women, it helps sustain the group. Muslim women are torn between their group identity and their need for justice. This was strikingly illustrated when Shah Bano withdrew her case following its merciless exploitation by a section of Hindu militants. Now, I believe it is futile to deny that this impasse exists. I see D as a solution precisely because it points to a way out. Positions A, B, C and E do not properly see this impasse: while B and C deny the claims of justice, A and E refuse to give importance to the value of groups.

Notes

1. Under the old criminal procedure code (CPC) of 1898, all neglected wives, including Muslim women, were granted rights of maintenance. Confined to the privacy of her home, with few opportunities for employment, the amount for maintenance was surely a woman's only means of survival. This right, therefore, was grounded in her basic material needs. But frequently, when a Muslim woman sought the help of the court to secure maintenance, the husband divorced her, thus freeing himself from payment of maintenance beyond the required three months. To check this malpractice, the CPC of 1973 amended the relevant act to include divorced women in this category. Muslim orthodoxy mischievously objected to this amendment, complaining that it violated their religious laws. Viewed thus, the conflict between group and individual rights appears irreconcilable, heading for collision between the rival worldviews of modernity and Islam. I deal with this conflict at greater length at a later stage in this chapter.
2. It would be wrong to conclude from the holistic character of groups that they are organisms. In organisms, the link between parts and wholes is much stronger. Each part, more or less, has one fixed place and one distinct role to perform within the whole. There is little possibility of mobility between parts or across different organisms. This is not true of human groups.
3. Nagel here discusses Tim Scanlon's example discussed in his 'Preference and Urgency' (1975).

4. Tocqueville comes immediately to mind as one who warned us of internal threats. A retreat from the public good consequent upon over-privatisation was viewed by him as a serious threat to liberty. See Taylor (1985: 310).
5. The division of moral labour means different things to different people. For example, Nagel uses it to refer to the division within us between the personal and the impersonal standpoints. For others, it is linked to role-morality and to how society divides moral labour into different institutions and roles. I mean something related, but my core idea is dependent upon how the protection of group values requires that its members set aside self-interest or claims of autonomy, and on how the costs of setting these aside are distributed amongst its members.
6. It must be emphasised that this moral right may be exercised in the presence not of (c) but (b), and even here it must be grounded in claims of injustice, in the face of an unfair division of moral labour. A group does not have a moral right to prevent me from working for other groups or for the genuine care of myself.
7. My use of the term 'basic' does not imply that, relative to other rights, they matter more to all individuals. It does mean though that other rights supervene on them.
8. The two policies differ in the relative weight they place on secular-individual and religious-group identity. The one optional in the policy is also given less importance.

References

Bhargava, Rajeev. 1992. *Individualism in Social Science*. Oxford: Clarendon Press.
———. 1999a. 'The Democratic Vision of a New Republic: India, 1950', in Francine Frankel, Zoya Hasan, Rajeev Bhargava and Balveer Arora, eds, *Democracy and Transformation*. New Delhi: Oxford University Press.
———. 1999b. 'Should We Abandon the Majority–Minority Framework?' in D.L. Sheth and Gurpreet Mahajan, eds, *Minority Identities and the Nation State*. New Delhi: Oxford University Press.
Hartney, M. 1991. 'Some Confusion concerning Collective Rights', *Canadian Journal of Law and Jurisprudence*, Vol. 4, No. 2, July 1991.
Nagel, Thomas. 1986. *The View from Nowhere*. Oxford: Oxford University Press.
Raz, Joseph. 1986. *The Morality of Freedom*. Oxford: Clarendon Press.

202   Rajeev Bhargava

Scanlon, Tim. 1975. 'Preference and Urgency', *Journal of Philosophy*, Vol. 72, pp. 655–69.
Taylor, C. 1985. *Philosophical Papers*, Vol. 2. Cambridge: Cambridge University Press.

ten

Elections, Parties and Democracy in India

Peter Ronald deSouza

t he idea of a common political community, as a common set of political institutions and codes, is still in the making in India now fifty years after independence. Not only is the *political community* still in the making, but also the *idea* itself, its shape, contours, founding principles and social relationships. Forging a common political community, through a process of negotiations between social agents, is a multi-level exercise involving, among other things, a politics of compromise. While the experience of being still 'in the making' is not by itself very distinctive, since I suppose it describes the biography of any contemporary democracy, what makes the Indian story worth noting is the complexity of the project.

To 'make' a democracy within fifty years in a social space[1] characterised by a great diversity of language, religion, region, ethnicity and economic interest is an extremely complex task. It is this complexity which renders difficult the exercise of mapping the changes taking place in the different dimensions of this social space. Hence even the more sophisticated readings on democracy in India remain deficient.[2] They are unable to break free of either the ethno-centrism of their approaches, or the hegemony of the dominant discourses on democracy, or the excessive ideological baggage with which they approach the problem for study.[3] Four examples illustrate this point.

The first can be found in the excellent essay by J. Manor on 'Party and Party Systems' who, writing within what can be called the 'decay' model of institutions, raises the question of the very survivability of the 'open political system' in India.[4] The democratic project in India has always had to confront this fear of the 'survivability' of the system in the face of the pulls and pressures that emerge as the polity extends to the social and political periphery. While this model may implicitly concede that democracy is a messy affair, since it involves the participation of large numbers of people, the messiness that India exhibits is often regarded as system-threatening. This characterisation is, I believe, the result of a deeper ethnocentrism within which many such essays are written. Similar challenges to the so-called mature democracies, for example, the declining voter turnout in the US or rising anti-semitism in many countries of Europe, or the dismantling of the welfare state, are not regarded as system-threatening. They are seen as minor challenges to a well-entrenched practice of democracy. India, unfortunately, does not merit such confidence.

The second example belongs to what I call the 'checklist' model of explaining democracy in India. This model merely approaches the Indian project with a checklist and then tries to determine how many items on the checklist are found in the Indian polity. If many are found, then India 'qualifies' as a democracy. If not, then India must wait its historical turn to be admitted to the exclusive club. It must work harder. The best example of this is Lijphart (1996). Writing within a comparative framework, he strives to show that the four features of his consociational model of democracy: (a) grand coalition governments that include representatives of all major linguistic and religious groups; (b) cultural autonomy of these groups; (c) proportionality in political representation and civil service appointments; and (d) a minority veto with regard to vital minority rights, can be found in India, and hence India too is a consociational democracy. This approach, besides being ahistorical, does not sufficiently appreciate the complexity of the transformative process under way. The model has no dynamic to it. It does not strive hard enough to make sense of the plentiful empirical material on Indian politics that contains pointers to the deeper and more enduring processes within the polity. To understand the Indian project of democracy, it is necessary to distinguish the enduring processes from the superficial variations which embroider these processes. Most of the studies within the 'checklist' mode, unfortunately, do not seem to realise the significance of this distinction.

The third example shows how even innovative studies are unable to break free of the hegemony of dominant discourses on democracy. Y. Yadav (1997a), in his rather grand overview of democracy in India, developed with a self-conscious attention to historical process, sees democracy as having been 'creolised or vernacularised' in India. He arrives at this characterisation after a detailed and intricate discussion of stages, perspectives and a shift in the locus of politics from elite-led initiatives to mass-directed determinants. This is very insightful. But to then characterise this as a process of creolisation, I believe, constitutes a major ideological lapse. This language of 'creolisation', in addition to raising the interesting issue of distinguishing between original and settler democratic practices, which in turn raises the question of the distinction between the essentials and derivatives of democracy, also raises the political question of why the Indian experience should be seen as creolisation whereas the European experience should not. While this may appear to be nitpicking, a minor quarrel over words, I have chosen to take note of it to point to the hegemony of dominant discourses which puts studies outside these discourses on the defensive, maintaining thereby the implicit characterisation of democracies in Europe and the US as the original if not authentic ones, whereas all others are merely derivatives, merely creolised.

The fourth case sees the project of democracy in India as an integral part of the larger project of modernising Indian society.[5] One of the most insightful accounts in this mode is that of S. Kaviraj. For him, the critique of the modernity project—its exaggerated faith in the power of enlightenment rationality, its naïve belief that modernity would replace tradition, its unjustified conviction that the scientific temper and the temples of modern India would be the dominant motor of this transformation to modernity, its belied expectation that primordial identities would be replaced by secular identities, and its unfulfilled hope that 'capitalism' would foster 'democracy' — hence becomes also a critique of democracy. The nuanced nature of such analysis, although very seductive, does not treat as qualitatively different the Indian biography from that of any other society. The uniqueness of India's democratic project, if at all referred to in such accounts, lies in its political history and not in terms of the multi-level societal transformation taking place in a short period of time. While this is an extremely rich account of the Indian political landscape, there are two major lacunae in it. The first concerns the link between the project of modernity and that of democracy. While this link provides a grand historical perspective from which to view social change in India, to treat democracy and modernity as 'Siamese twins' — as analytically inseparable — which is how such analyses treat them, is simply impermissible. Democracy in India can be analysed in isolation from an analysis of modernity. This is so because democracy, once introduced into a society, develops a dynamic of its own, producing a series of consequences, some of which may be unintended. To always find deliberateness in the historical process is, hence, not just granting too much to the mind of history but also, I believe, ignoring the significance of the independent, in some senses uncontrollable, momentum that processes develop once they have been initiated. The second lacuna concerns the fact that such analyses have not factored in the aspect of scale, which is central to this transformation.

While all these four cases provide valuable insights into democracy in India, all of them suffer from one major deficiency. They do not appreciate the magnitude of the political and social transformation that is taking place in India. They do not allow for different rates of change in different sectors, or locations. Understanding democracy in India requires one to understand these linkages between rates of change and sectors that are integrated with each other, and to examine the consequences which follow from them for the whole polity. What makes India a unique case is the aspect of scale (Gibson et al. n.d.). It covers not just population and territory but also cultural diversity, since India is not just a 'nation-state' but a 'civilisation state' (Kumar 1990). Scale refers to the number and range of political agents who have been enfranchised by the new constitutional order. They represent each of the dimensions around which individuals and groups are constituted in society, such as language, religion, region, caste, class, interest, ethnicity. Nowhere else has such an ambitious project, of political and social transformation, of converting a hierarchically segmented social space into a common political community based on an overlapping consensus, of building up community relationships between groups that hitherto had only superior–subordinate relationships, been attempted. Creating a strong feeling of 'fraternity' is the challenge of the project of democracy in India.

No study of democracy in India would therefore be adequate if it does not factor in this dimension of scale. Scale underscores the point that one cannot transform a societal space of such proportions without lapses, excesses, inefficiencies, failures, perhaps even disproportionate development. I mention this to highlight the inherent material, cultural, agency and managerial limitations of this transformative process. For example, one may actually have well-designed institutions or even have enlightened policies, but in spite of this one may still be accused of non-delivery because the culture and practice of these institutions become fetters to their capacity to deliver the goods. These practices convert the institution from being a means to an end, in Weberian terms, to becoming an end in itself. Or again, a society may have great historical opportunity to achieve its goals, but the choices made by the political leadership fall short of the optimal choice available, a shortfall which emerges because the proximate and immediate, in the eyes of the agent, trumps the distant and the delayed. It is dilemmas such as these that get captured by any explanation of democracy in India that recognises the dimension of scale. This is not to suggest that there is no place for judgement and criticism or that everything is fine and glorious, and hence that the earlier mentioned judgements were out of place. It is only to provide such criticism with a greater sensitivity to the paradoxes of the transformative process. In fact, the above four narratives would read very differently if they had factored in this aspect of scale.

However, factoring in scale is only part of the challenge of explaining democracy in India. The other part is to address the question: what does it mean to attempt a transformation of a civilisational space of such proportions, a transformation which seeks to invert and replace the earlier principle of societal organisation, that of hierarchical segmentation, by the democratic principle of egalitarian commonality? The revolutionary promise of democracy in India is to create an egalitarian community. The issue therefore is to understand what it takes to establish a society-wide acceptance (this would be a great achievement), or even at the very least some reaction, cultural and political, to the principle of equality.

The choice of a constitutional democracy in 1947, wittingly or unwittingly, set into motion this unstoppable dynamic of political and legal equality. Three aspects of this political equality are noteworthy because the transformative dynamic derives its logic from them. Once introduced, they acquire a momentum. These are: (a) equal *freedom* of participation, seen as freedom of expression, association, movement, etc.; (b) equal *opportunity* of participation, seen as not just the existence of alternatives but also the perception of these alternatives; and (c) equal *participation*, exemplified by the equality of the vote (Oppenheim 1971).

These features of equality, especially equal freedom and equal opportunity, set into motion a struggle of rationalities: between the region and the nation, between the short term and the long term, between the segmental and the universal. This struggle of rationalities has as its objective the evolution of common rules for the political community, the determination of the terms of its interaction. While the roots of this struggle can be traced to the colonial period, in that the contest between the universalising basis of the institutions of colonial rule and the particularistic loyalties of segments of Indian society had already begun, it is mainly after independence, with the adoption of universal franchise, that it has acquired a different tenor and a more ambitious scale. Within this terrain there are very many different groups jostling for a fair share of social resources, competing to make their political agenda the common agenda. This is how the politics of compromise has developed in India. In the following sections of this chapter I shall look at the consequences of this march of equality in the area of elections and political parties.

The significance of elections in India can be appreciated when one examines (a) the nature of the institution entrusted with the job of conducting elections; and (b) the features of the electoral process. The basic principles of the Election Commission (EC) of India which have guided its actions were quite unambiguously set out by the debates in the Constituent Assembly. First of all, the participants were determined to establish the *principle of the equality of voters*. The argument that all citizens are eligible to be on the electoral rolls was made to guarantee inclusiveness of groups, particularly the weaker sections of society, as against the exclusiveness being practised in the regions. Dr B.R. Ambedkar forcefully argued for such inclusiveness based on the principle of equality:

> It has been brought to the notice of the drafting committee as well as Central Government that in these provinces the executive government is instructing or managing things in such a manner that those people who do not belong to them either racially, culturally or linguistically, are being excluded from being brought on the electoral rolls. The house will realise that franchise is a most fundamental thing in a democracy. No person who is entitled to be brought into the electoral rolls on grounds which have already been mentioned in our constitution, namely, an adult of 21 [now 18] years of age should be excluded merely as a result of the prejudice of a local government, or whim of an officer. That would cut at the very root of democratic government (B.R. Ambedkar, quoted in deSouza 1998: 53).

The second important principle was the *independence of the Election Commission* in carrying out its duties. To guarantee this, a separate chapter in the Constitution of India (Part XV, Art. 324–29) dealing with elections was considered necessary. The EC, which derives its authority directly from the constitution and not from some elected government, hence has considerable autonomy of action. The third principle was the *right to representation*. Shrimati Annie Mascarene, attempting to present the discussion on the structure of the electoral system as a conflict between two motivations, that of being expedient and that of being ethical, eloquently reminded the members not to forget the imperatives of the right to representation in their anxiety to design an efficient mechanism (deSouza 1998: 54). The EC has attempted to strengthen this independence through its various instructions and attempts to curb electoral malpractice.

In the thirteen general elections that the EC has conducted so far, it has gained considerable legitimacy among the citizens of India. In a poll conducted in 1996 by the Centre for the Study of Developing Societies, the EC was ranked the highest among political institutions in terms of public support. The lowest-ranked were the police and the bureaucracy.[6] Respondents seemed to be saying that the EC has remained true to its goal of guaranteeing free and fair elections. This task of conducting elections is, at the very minimum, a huge logistical exercise. Some basic statistics of the thirteen general elections will bear this out (see Table 10.1). The cost to the EC of the 11th and 12th General Elections was about US$140 million and US$160 million respectively (1US$ = Rs 42). The number of officials on election duty during the 11th General Election was 3.9 million. And the amount of paper required to print ballot paper was 8,000 and 7,700 metric tonnes respectively. These statistics are provided merely to give a sense of the enormity of the managerial exercise involved in converting votes into seats, an exercise which is completed by the EC in a matter of weeks. In the last fifty years the EC, as an institution, has become a part of the 'overlapping consensus', the common political space of demo-cracy that has emerged in India.

TABLE 10.1
PROFILE OF TWELVE GENERAL ELECTIONS

Year	Seats	Candidates	Electorate	Turnout (%)	Poll Stations
1952	489	1,864	173,213,635	45.70	196,084
1957	494	1,591	193,652,069	47.70	220,478
1962	494	1,985	216,372,215	55.40	238,244
1967	520	2,369	249,003,334	61.30	267,555
1971	518	2,784	274,094,493	55.30	342,944
1977	542	2,439	321,174,327	60.50	358,208
1980	542	4,620	355,590,700	57.00	434,442
1984	542	5,481	399,816,294	64.10	505,751
1989	543	6,160	498,906,429	62.00	579,810
1991	543	8,699	514,126,380	56.70	594,797
1996	543	13,952	592,572,288	57.94	767,462
1998	539	4,708	602,340,382	62.04	765,473

Source: *The Hindu*, 13 February 1998; the Election Commission Statistical
        Report on General Election 1998 to the 12th Lok Sabha, New Delhi.

This profile of elections provides some valuable clues to the political process in India. First, the increasing turnout, from a low of 45 per cent to a turnout ranging from 56.7 per cent to 64.1 per cent in the last five general elections, shows the consolidation of the electoral system. It further shows that, in spite of a big gap between promise and delivery (India still fares poorly on many of the indices of human development [Dréze and Sen 1995]), the electoral system, which is the mechanism through which govern-ments get replaced and punished, still enjoys legitimacy. This is perhaps because it is the only means by which the common voter can register his/her protest. And this they have done with unfailing regularity.

The table also shows the scale of the exercise. The 62.04 per cent turnout of the electorate in 1998 translates into 373 million voters (thirty-seven times the population of Portugal!). When such a large number of people are involved, even in a single act of registering their preference vis-à-vis parties, one is bound to get a plurality. This plurality manifests itself in terms of candidates, parties, perspectives, issues. It results in a broadening and a deepening of the polity as it moves from a restricted centre outwards towards the social and political periphery, thereby involving more and more groups in the political process. Fifty years of this extension has produced a complex polity moving forward at different rates in different domains. This equal opportunity of registering preference initiates a process which has multiple consequences for the polity. Some of these are: the formation of political identities (along old or new lines); the increased political struggle for societal resources resulting in not just competition but also conflict, not just between groups but also between regions; the emergence of a new type of political leadership which has changed the terms of doing politics; and the appearance of new political formations. Table 10.2 shows the number of parties that have secured some representation in the 1996 and 1998 general elections.

TABLE 10.2
PARTIES IN PARLIAMENT

Seats	>120	120–150	49–20	19–10	9–2	1–0	Total
1996	2	0	3	6	9	8+6 (ind.)	28
1998	2	0	2	4	20	12+6	40

From Table 10.2 one can see the increasing number of groups entering the political process. Politics in the 1990s has moved from a time when a single party got over 75 per cent of the seats in parliament to a time when the two dominant parties share between them about 70 per cent of the seats with the balance being shared between a large number of small regional parties. It is significant that most of the parties in these two general elections got less than nine seats. It shows that the bigger parties that aspire to form a government with the help of these smaller parties would have to adopt more centrist policies than they may wish to, because they now have to form both pre- and post-election coalitions to enable them to put together a majority for governance. Devices such as the Common Minimum Programme in 1996 and the National Agenda for Governance in 1998 are used to forge together such a common pragmatic space and form coalition governments. These, however, remain unstable, because smaller parties in such coalitions acquire the veto. The governments of Deve Gowda and I.K. Gujral, in fact, lasted less than a year.

This dual trend of a consolidating and a fractionating polity can be further illustrated by an examination of the results of the 12th General Election. The number of parties which participated is as follows: national parties (7), state parties (30), registered-unrecognised parties (139). In total, 4,708 candidates contested[7] of whom 1,483 were from national parties, 465 from state parties, 860 from unrecognised parties and 1,900 independents. This converts into the picture of constituency-wise contests provided in Table 10.3.

TABLE 10.3
NUMBER OF CANDIDATES PER CONSTITUENCY IN 1998

Candidates	1	2	3	4	5	6–8	9–10	>10
Constituencies	0	4	14	38	73	186	78	176

Source: Election Commission of India, *Statistical Report on General Elections 1998.*

The table shows a picture of intense competition between groups for determining the way in which the state will spend its resources and also for influencing the agenda of politics. From Table 10.3 one can see that most of the constituencies have more than six candidates, with over 176 having more than ten. This is a clear picture of a deepening process, of a political plurality emerging from a latent social one, of a diversity of interests that however accepts (having participated) the unity of elections as a dispute-solving mechanism.

Increasing competition is a measure of the weaker property of the enfranchisement of the citizen, bestowed by the constitution, becoming the stronger property of political empowerment. Mapping this process of empowerment is what makes the transformation so exciting. Here is a societal space, divided on every conceivable fault-line, deprived of surplus by a prolonged period of colonial rule and an unjust international economic order, inching its way towards a common political community. This is not an easy process. The faceless set of statistics given above conceals the pain and turmoil of the transformative process, for there is pain and turmoil in ample measure along with repeated stories of political betrayal by leaders and groups. In spite of their dryness, these statistics yet reveal the historical truth that India is inching towards a democratic polity.

Another feature that emerges from a study of national and state-level elections is the anti-incumbency trend of the vote. Governments get removed peacefully. This happens at every election. Governments that lose an election accept the verdict of the election, thereby recognising and respecting the sovereignty of the citizen. This increasing empowerment of citizens begins to have major impacts on the political system, such as the increasing number of protest movements, the growth of non-governmental organisations (NGOs), the demand for reservations for Other Backward Castes (OBCs), women, Muslims, etc. I shall now examine its impact on the party system. Before I do so, however, I shall attempt a thumb-nail sketch of the evolution of the party system.

The first phase of the party system was characterised as the Congress system (Kothari 1964). This was marked by the dominance of the Congress party, seen as the party of government in contrast to the other parties, which were seen as parties of pressure. This period lasted for the first two decades after independence.

> The second phase, let us call it the 'Congress-Opposition systems' was still characterised by one-party salience though no longer dominance, of the Congress . . . . Despite remaining out of power very often, the Congress retained a salience in the party system not only because it continued to command greater popular support than any opposition party, but also because it was the core around which the party system was structured. This phase saw the emergence of bipolar consolidation in various states without yielding a bi-polarity at the national level (Yadav 1997b: 191).

The third phase, which began with the 1993–95 elections, has re-sulted in a fractionated polity at the national level and an emerging two-party system in most states. The BJP and the Congress have emerged as the two poles around which the other parties have had to regroup. The BJP's emergence is the result of (*a*) the mis-governance and corruption of Congress rule; (*b*) the BJP's success at changing the agenda of political discourse with its appeal to Hindu nationalism, especially after the demolition of the Babri Masjid; and (*c*) the general feeling among the electorate of 'giving them a chance'. The regional parties, too, have consolidated their vote bank. This consolidation of various interests, regional, caste, and community, can be seen in the votes polled by the various parties (Table 10.4).

TABLE 10.4
PERCENTAGE VOTES POLLED BY SOME SIGNIFICANT PARTIES

	BJP	INC	CPM	SAM	BSP	TDP	DMK	SHS	SAD	RJD	SP	ADMK
1996	20.29	28.80	6.12	2.17	3.64	2.97	2.15	1.43	0.76	–	–	0.64
1998	25.47	25.88	5.18	1.77	4.68	2.78	1.45	1.78	0.82	2.71	4.95	1.84

While the national parties, i.e., the BJP, INC and CPM, have polled these votes from the whole country, the regional parties have each polled this percentage of the national vote from mainly one state.

This third phase in the evolution of the party system shows some very interesting trends. The first is that national parties will have to ally with regional parties to form a government at the centre. The growth in the size of the polity because of the extension of democracy has meant that while the national message remains powerful, it has to compete for political attention with regional messages as well. The consolidation of the small, largely homo-geneous constituency has taken place, and constitutes the vote base of the regional parties. The national parties, especially the Con-gress, have lost their vote banks, and will now have to forge new social coalitions to retain their all-India character. While the BJP has grown, its ability to replace the Congress in terms of the old 'one dominant party' system is very limited.

The second trend of interest is that heightened competition, in a polity the size of India, results in the growth of contrasting ideo-logical tendencies. On the one hand there is an increasing pragmat-ism, as shown by the politics of compromise of the major parties, since they have to forge coalitions. On the other hand there is an increasing ideological assertion by the smaller parties as shown by their chauvinism, since they have to consolidate their support base within largely homogeneous communities. Regionalism is hence on the rise, since an appeal to regional sentiment becomes the language of mobilisation of these smaller parties. The party system, that seeks to operate within and also create an overlapping consensus at the national level, hence has to contend with such regionalism.

The third interesting observation that can be made is regarding the role and increasing salience not just of leaders of regional parties but also of a significant number of middle-level leaders in all parties. These middle-level leaders are the main mobilisers in all political parties. The growth in the number of such leaders has meant that the agenda of politics is being rewritten, since these are mainly political entrepreneurs who see politics as the new economic opportunity. They are the fixers of politics. They represent both the petitioners and the policy-makers. They move the files and are responsible for the erosion of institutions. The culture of rule-abidingness, so necessary for the health of institutions and which promotes the 'common good', stands no chance of developing when it has to engage with this kind of political entrepreneurship. These middle-level leaders have brought a new cynicism to politics. This can be illustrated by the defections and splits that have characterised party politics in parliament and in the state assemblies across the country.[8] To accommodate these middle-level leaders, parties have had to offer them plum positions within the state apparatus. Each is given a fiefdom which becomes the basis of his or her patronage network. They have little accountability. Hence, competition generates the democratic paradox, in that it creates on the one hand a new strata of political leaders who emerge because of the extension of the polity, but these produce on the other hand an agenda of politics that is damaging to the culture of impersonality so necessary for democratic institutions. While competition may promote greater accountability of leaders in the long term, in the short term it encourages them to be less accountable.

The fourth trend that is worth noting is the role of the Election Commission vis-à-vis inner-party democracy. In the 1998 election, the EC passed a ruling that only parties that conducted regular elections would be eligible to nominate candidates for elections. This created quite a stir, as it forced many parties that were dominated by coteries to register membership and practice inner-party democracy. This is not to suggest that as a result of the *diktat* of the EC, party politics has suddenly become transparent and democratic, since Michels' Law of Oligarchy also applies to parties in India. It is only to suggest that this limited policing of party organisation by the EC has introduced an element of uncertainty in the control of party affairs, and hence leaders are having to improve their political practices or else lose control of party organisations. This is good for democracy.

The fifth significant trend that I may briefly mention is the changed terms of political discourse in India with the rise of the Hindu nationalist front whose political wing is the BJP. The emergence of the BJP, as the other pole of politics to the Congress, has meant that some of the founding principles of the polity such as secularism and multiculturalism have come to be questioned. This has required all parties to now define themselves vis-à-vis these two principles. Therefore, what at independence was a 'given' of politics has now become a political space that must be negotiated.

The foregoing presents a profile of an intensely competitive polity. The pressures this competition brings to bear on institutions, ideologies and individuals can be mapped, as I have tried to do very briefly, to illustrate the dynamic of democracy. This dynamic, defined earlier as the march of equality, has begun to transform India's societal space in significant ways; a historical process with revolutionary implications for our collective understanding of democracy. While the gains, discussed above, are a cause for celebration, the failures are a cause for worry. The most damning failure is democratic India's inability to eradicate absolute poverty among a large section of its population.[9] No democratic polity should have to carry a sizeable proportion of its population, illiterate and undernourished, insecure about the basics of their material life. No democratic polity should have to record such disproportionately differential rates of accrual of the benefits of democracy, one for the elite and the entrenched who are the main beneficiaries of state developmental schemes, and another for the general mass of citizens, who gain the vote and little else and hence still have to struggle for the basics of life, or wait many lifetimes for these basics. The challenge of democracy in India is the challenge of creating an egalitarian society. To meet this challenge should we have more democracy or less?[10]

Notes

1. The use of concepts such as society, nation, community to describe this social space has been contested. The substance of the contestation is the degree of unity that each words is supposed to imply. It is held that the unity suggested is greater than the social space can support, since India's inherent diversity soon begins to challenge it.
2. The problem extends even to nomenclature. Should one, for example, refer to the project as that of 'Indian democracy' suggesting thereby a greater ontological unity than perhaps there is, which means there is an object called Indian democracy which is to be investigated and explained, or should one refer to the project as 'Democracy in India', a play of words which shifts the emphasis from explaining the features of an object to explaining the features of process. The latter signifies an ongoing historical project in a certain social space called India.
3. Some prominent examples are Brass (1994), Chatterjee (1997), Khanna et al. (1998), Khilnani (1998) and Weiner (1989).
4. 'Political systems in which diverse parties compete freely for mass electoral support are increasingly hard to find in the less developed nations, even in those that experienced British rule — for a long time thought to yield durable systems of liberal, representative government. But India, after nearly four decades of self-government and eight general elections, and despite hair-raising traumas and persisting threats to open, competitive politics, still qualifies. Nevertheless, in recent years, decay within parties and increasingly destructive conflict among parties have so eroded the strength of the open political system that its very survival is in question.' (Manor 1997: 92).
5. 'Universal suffrage was not an isolated innovation. It formed a part of a large, internally consistent plan for the modernisation of India. Representative democracy was only the political aspect of the process of creating modernity, of which development planning, secularisation, elimination of caste practices in favour of a common modern citizenship, were the other, equally necessary elements. An essential part of this theory of historical change was the belief that each of these elements would support and strengthen the others. Capitalist growth would foster democracy. These in turn would reinforce secularisation and the conversion of identities based on the primacy of communities to those based on the primacy of individuals. For the first twenty years after independence, political events seemed to follow obediently the lines laid down by this theory of history. Since the late sixties however some disquieting divergences from this historical script became increasingly evident' (Kaviraj 1997: 14).

6. The scores were as follows: EC 62 per cent, judiciary 59 per cent, state government 59 per cent, local self-government 58 per cent, central government 57 per cent, representatives 40 per cent, political parties 39 per cent, bureaucracy 37 per cent and police 28 per cent. (deSouza 1998: 51).

7. This is a lower number than the 13,952 candidates of the 1996 elections, but this is because the EC's drive to eliminate non-serious candidates from the polls caused it to hike the security deposit, thereby resulting in fewer non-party candidates contesting.

8. The 52nd Amendment to the constitution was enacted to prevent such defections. It has been quite ineffective since; although it has prevented individual defectors it has encouraged mass defections.

9. This damning failure prompted one of India's leading economists Raj Krishna to state, at a meeting to discuss an agenda for India a few weeks after the lifting of the Emergency in 1977, that he would be prepared to forego civil and political liberties if one could guarantee him that by doing so one could eradicate India's debilitating poverty. This debate of whether democracy helps us better address poverty or whether it is a fetter on our ability to tackle poverty, since it constrains the state, is an unresolved debate in India since both positions have evidence in their favour.

10. The 73rd Amendment, giving constitutional status to the Panchayati Raj Institutions, the third tier of government, answers this question in favour of more democracy. By empowering the third tier, much of the unresolved demand on the political system is sought to be addressed.

References

Brass, P. 1994. *The Politics of India since Independence*. New Delhi: Cambridge University Press.

Chatterjee, Partha (ed.). 1997. *State and Politics in India*. New Delhi: Oxford University Press.

deSouza, Peter R. 1998. 'The Election Commission and Electoral Reforms in India', in D.D. Khanna et al., eds, *Democracy, Diversity, Stability*. New Delhi: Macmillan.

Dréze, J., and A. Sen. 1995. *India: Economic Development and Social Opportunity*. New Delhi: Oxford University Press.

Gibson, C., et al. n.d. Scaling Issues in the Social Sciences. IHDP Working Paper No. 1, http://ibm.rhrz.uni-bonn.de/IHDP/WP01.htm

Kaviraj, S. 1997. 'Introduction', in S. Kaviraj, ed., *Politics in India*. New Delhi: Oxford University Press.

Khanna, D.D., et al. (eds). 1998. *Democracy, Diversity, Stability*. New Delhi: Macmillan.

Khilani, S. 1998. *The Idea of India*. New Delhi: Penguin.

Kothari, Rajni. 1964. 'The Congress System in India', *Asian Survey*, Vol. 4, No. 2, December 1964.

Kumar, R. 1990. 'State Formation in India: Restrospect and Prospect'. Paper presented at the IDPAD Seminar on State and Society: Changing Relations between State and Society in India towards an Emerging European State, New Delhi, 5–9 March 1990.

Lijphart, A. 1996. 'The Puzzle of Indian Democracy', *American Political Science Review*, Vol. 90, No. 2, June 1996.

Manor, James. 1997. 'Parties and the Party System', in Partha Chatterjee, ed., *State and Politics in India*. New Delhi: Oxford University Press.

Oppenheim, F. 1971. 'Democracy: Characteristics Included and Excluded'. *The Monist*, Vol. 55, pp. 29–50.

Weiner, Myron. 1989. *The Indian Paradox*. New Delhi: Sage.

Yadav, Y. 1997a. 'Independent India and Half-Century: Democratic Polity and Social Change'. Paper presented at the workshop on Independent India at Half-Century, Institute of Commonwealth Studies, London, 16 May 1997.

———. 1997b. 'Reconfiguration in Indian Politics: State Assembly Elections 1993–1995', in Partha Chatterjee, ed., *State and Politics in India*. New Delhi: Oxford University Press.

eleven

The Human Rights Agenda in India

Nawaz B. Mody

the Preamble to the Charter of the United Nations reaffirms the faith of the peoples of the United Nations in 'fundamental human rights, in the dignity and worth of the human person, in the equal rights of men and women'. One of the purposes of the United Nations is promoting respect for human rights and fundamental freedoms for all without any distinction. The promotion of human rights is seen as an end to be pursued in its own right, and not as incidental to the promotion of any other purpose.

The Charter provisions constituted a radical departure from the traditional view that matters relating to human rights were solely within the jurisdiction of a state and beyond the jurisdiction of international law. The United Nations Charter was followed by the Universal Declaration of Human Rights which was adopted without dissent by the UN General Assembly. This declaration set out, for the first time, the members' common understanding of human rights and basic freedoms and referred to civil, political, economic, social and cultural rights. With the adoption of the Universal Declaration, the ideology of human rights was clearly spelt out. It became the common standard of achievement for all peoples and all nations. More recently, the Vienna Declaration adopted by the World Conference on Human Rights on 25 June 1993 declared that 'Human rights and fundamental freedoms are the birthright of all human beings.'

What then are these human rights? A United Nations publication states: 'Human rights are those which are inherent in our nature and without which we cannot live as human beings.' Essentially, then, there are certain rights of men and women which cannot be violated even by the state. Thus there are limits to the exercise of power by the state over the individual. The individual possesses these rights against the state itself (Rao 1996).

Human rights have been described as those minimal rights that every individual must have by virtue of being a member of the human family, irrespective of any other consideration. They are based on the demand for a life which will protect the inherent dignity of the individual. They are thus the 'inherent and inalienable rights of men', and hence a state which violates them in its laws and its actions breaches one of the basic prerequisites of civil co-existence between states and can legitimately be brought to account.

A number of international instruments have emerged which not only codify human rights but also draw up measures for their enforcement. These include the International Covenant on Economic, Social and Cultural Rights (1966), the International Covenant on Civil and Political Rights (1966) and the Optional Protocol to the Civil Covenant (1976) which provides the rights for individual petitions.

Human rights can be classified into various categories. The traditional distinction has been between civil and political rights on the one hand and economic, social and cultural rights on the other. It was felt that while one set of rights was subject to immediate application, the other set required progressive realisation. However, it is not really possible to make a rigid demarcation between these two sets of rights, as human rights are interdependent and indivisible. Indeed, it is incorrect to think that some of the basic economic rights are mere claims, and are not human rights because they cannot be immediately enforced. This leads to the fallacy that negative rights which gather around our liberties are more important than positive rights that evolve from our needs. It should never be forgotten that poverty is one of the most potent causes of the violation of human rights, particularly in developing countries like India.

Justice P.N. Bhagwati in the Francis Coralic Mullen case expanded the scope of Article 21 of the Indian constitution to incorporate the right to food, clothing and shelter in the term 'life' in the Article: 'The question arises whether the right to life is limited only to protection of limb or faculty or does it go further . . . we think that the right to life includes the right to live with dignity and all that goes along with it; namely, the necessities such as adequate nutrition, clothing and shelter' (Sen 1998a: 28–29).

Of late, third-generation or solidarity rights have become increasingly important. What are solidarity rights? According to Burns H. Weston, these include the right to economic, political, social and cultural self-determination, the right to economic and social development, the right to participate in and benefit from the common heritage of mankind, the right to peace, the right to a healthy and balanced environment and the right to humanitarian disaster relief. Two essential qualities of these rights which emerge are that they are essentially collective in nature and dependent on international co-operation for their realisation (Weston 1997: 7–8). These rights are the consequence of globalisation and increasing realisation of the need for interdependence of peoples all over the world.

India, as a member of the Commission of Human Rights, played a significant role in the drafting of the Universal Declaration of Human Rights. Later, many of the articles of the Declaration were incorporated in the Indian constitution in the form of fundamental rights and directive principles. India has ratified the two international covenants. However, while ratifying the Covenant on Civil and Political Rights, it had certain reservations and did not ratify the Optional Protocol of 1976. In addition, India has also not ratified the Convention on the Rights of Migrant Workers and the Second Optional Protocol which aimed at abolishing the death penalty.

Human rights have the potential to transform the functioning of a democracy and make it more participative in nature. They are a constant challenge to vested interests and authority in societies riven by enormous disparities of wealth and power, by traditions of authoritarianism and the helplessness of disadvantaged communities, and the conjunction of corrupt politicians and pre-datory domestic and international capital (Chopra 1993).

Given India's huge population, large percentage of illiteracy (48 per cent), poverty and backwardness, the problem of enforcing human rights becomes crucial. Adding to this is the plural and feudal nature of Indian society and the large amount of discrimination which still prevails within it. The Government of India, vide its notification dated 23 October 1993 (S.O. No. 816[E]), classified Muslims, Christians, Sikhs, Buddhists and Parsis as minority communities for the purpose of the National Commission for Minorities Act, 1992. However, severe discrimination and exploitation of scheduled castes and backward communities by upper castes still prevail. These problems are of particular relevance to the enforcement of human rights.

Some of the most vulnerable sections of the population are women and children, the protection and enforcement of whose human rights are a dire necessity. Violations of human rights also arise out of political problems and the proactive role that the state in India has chosen to play. This has particularly been the case in Jammu & Kashmir, Punjab and in the states of the north-east. Moreover, the operation of the criminal justice system has resulted in the gross violation of human rights in terms of arbitrary arrest or detention, custodial violence or even death, and the right to a free trial. As will be seen, this is merely an illustrative list, and I will discuss some of these aspects at a later stage in this chapter.

Faced with these problems, the Government of India passed the Protection of Human Rights Act in 1993 which established the National Human Rights Commission (NHRC) on the basis of the Paris Principles adopted by the UN General Assembly in 1993. The Commission is a statutory body with infrastructural support and funding, and bears the responsibility for inquiring into complaints of human rights violations, reporting to the government or other agencies, encouraging the ratification of the international human rights instruments, and assisting in the spread of human rights education and awareness (Pillai n.d.).

According to Section 4 of the Act, the President of India appoints the chairperson and other members of the NHRC based on the recommendations of a committee consisting of the prime minister, the home minister, the speaker of the Lok Sabha, the leaders of the opposition in the Lok Sabha and the Rajya Sabha and the deputy chairman of the Rajya Sabha. It is felt by some that this body is not free from political interference and carries a distinctively pro-government overtone as, of its six members, four belong to the ruling party (SAHRDC 1998: 15–16). There has also been criticism that Section 3 of the Act provides that of the five regular members of the Commission, three will be judges and two will be from among persons having knowledge of human rights. This preponderance of judges in the NHRC is also felt to be undesirable by some groups (Pal 1995: 5–7)

There is also room to provide greater financial autonomy to the NHRC. As the Commission itself stated in its recommendations of 1993–94, it sought to prevent the government from controlling its purse-strings. However, the government did not agree. Moreover, the reports of the Commission are not regularly placed before parliament for consideration. Also, its record of proper and prompt disposal of complaints is poor, since it has only recommendatory powers. At present, a major review of the legislation pertaining to the NHRC is under way.

The Commission has been able to take up a variety of programmes relevant to societal issues. These programmes range from civil rights protection, the police, prisons and a host of statutes impinging on civil rights to the spread of primary education, abolition of child labour, issues of child prostitution, environmental issues such as arsenic contamination of water and nutritional problems of children. Many of these issues have been taken up by non-governmental organisations (NGOs).

The tasks taken up by the Commission reflect the new social equations emerging out of rising expectations and growing awareness among hitherto marginalised communities. For Justice Ranganath Misra, former chairman of the NHRC, the pillars of the Commission's strength on which its performance must rest are its autonomy and transparency (Misra 1995).

One of the issues that the NHRC has taken up very seriously has been the appalling conditions prevailing in Indian jails (NHRC 1993: 23–24). Problems of overcrowding, lack of sanitation, poor medical facilities, inadequate light and diet exist in most jails. Added to this is the unforgivable delay in the disposal of cases, the large numbers of undertrials and the utter mismanagement of jail administration. During 1994–95, the Commission visited various jails and suggested corrective measures. But it is a known fact that conditions in jails continue to be deplorable and that large numbers of undertrials continue to languish in jails. Another major problem is the increasing number of deaths in jail custody. The NHRC has instructed all state governments to report within twenty-four hours all cases of deaths in police and jail custody. Between April 1994 and November 1995, 201 jail deaths were reported to the Commission by different states. Bihar and Delhi, with 40 and 93 cases respectively, figure at the top of the list (Sen 1998a: 200–201).

Of the 922 jails in the country, fourteen are prisons meant exclusively for women. Women prisoners are insufficiently trained and badly treated. This fact has been noted by the NHRC. Women undertrials constitute more than 70 per cent of the female jail population of the country. They languish in jail for five to seven years, and their condition is far worse than that of male undertrials. The NHRC has prepared a Model Prison Bill for replacing the antiquated Prison Act of 1894. However, there is no sign of the legislation seeing the light of day, and inhuman conditions continue to prevail in most jails in the country.

Instances of arbitrary arrest and detention are frequent. Amnesty International, in its submission to the UN Human Rights Committee concerning the implementation of the articles of the International Covenant on Civil and Political Rights, has drawn attention to this and called for further investigations, particularly in the state of Jammu & Kashmir and in areas governed by the Armed Forces (Special Powers) Act. It has specifically sought implementation of Article 9(3) of the Covenant and asked the Committee to enquire into the steps taken by the Government of India to ensure that safeguards to protect detainees during arrest and detention, which exist in law and in directives of the courts and the NHRC, are adhered to in practice (UN Human Rights Committee 1997a: 63–65).

Child-related abuses and violations of human rights are a major blight on the record of human rights in the country. The exploitation of children is intrinsic in Indian society. The state, oddly, legitimates as well as condemns the exploitation of children. The struggle for rights of children necessitates changing the very nature of society itself, rather than merely expecting the state to concede these rights (Roy 1998). Child labour is one of the pressing issues confronting India. It is prevalent in various private enterprises, especially the match industry in Sivakasi, the glass industry in Firozabad, the brassware industry in Moradabad, the carpet industry in Mirzapur and Jammu & Kashmir, lock-making in Aligarh and slate-making in Mandsaur. Despite various legislations and constitutional provisions, child labour persists. In its report of 1995–96, the NHRC opined that the problem of child labour will persist until free and compulsory education is provided for all up to the age of 14. The initiative taken by the NHRC led to the constitutional amendment proposing to make the right to education a fundamental right in the Indian constitution. However, this amendment has lapsed.

The problem of bonded child labour, which refers to the phenomenon of children working in conditions of servitude to pay off debts, also persists in India. Estimates indicate that there are at least fifteen million bonded child labourers who work in appalling conditions to pay off their parents' debts. The government has failed to enforce the Child Labour Act as well as the Bonded Labour Act (Chamaraj 1997; Tucker 1997).

Child prostitution, which is one of the cruellest forms of exploitation, abounds in India. A report prepared by the Ministry of Human Resources Development indicates that about 15 per cent of India's two million sex workers are children. Thirty per cent of the sex workers in six major cities of India — Calcutta, Mumbai, Delhi, Chennai, Bangalore and Hyderabad — are under 20, while about 40 per cent of the women entered the profession before they were 18 years old. Religion and caste in India often seek to sanctify and legitimise prostitution under the *devdasi* system, which still prevails in Andhra Pradesh, Karnataka and Maharashtra. A conservative estimate of prepubescent girls who become *devdasis* annually is 5,000. The growth of tourism in Asia has coincided with the expansion of the child sex industry. Child prostitution has been particularly rampant in Goa and Tamil Nadu. The NHRC even issued notices to the respective states who, oddly enough, replied that 'there were no reported cases of child prostitutes in their areas' (Sen 1998b). This in itself indicates the manner in which the state governments have approached the problem. Female literacy is likely to be the major key to eliminating this type of gender abuse.

Perhaps the most important item on the agenda is the need not only to impart education on human rights but to create a culture of human rights among the people of India. The NHRC has statutorily been given this responsibility and has taken its duties quite seriously in this regard. According to Justice M.N. Venkatachaliah, chairman of the NHRC, education is the solution to many of the problems of human rights (Interview with Justice M.N. Venkatachaliah, *The Hindustan Times*, 15 November 1996).

The UN has assigned a primary role to education on human rights. The International Congress on the Teaching of Human Rights at Vienna in 1978 and the UNESCO International Congress on Human Rights Teaching, Information and Documentation at Malta in 1987 dealt with the formulation of principles to guide human rights education. Such education must aim at fostering an attitude of tolerance, respect and solidarity inherent in human rights, provide knowledge of its national and international dimensions and develop awareness among individuals of the ways of translating them into social and political reality.

Education on human rights is the crying need of the hour. It is only education that can liberate the mind from the thraldom of obscurantism and bigotry, nurture democratic values and promote societal transformation. An on-going debate prevails about the manner in which human rights should be taught in schools, colleges and universities. Some seek to make it optional, while others seek to include it in the curriculum of every subject. The objective, however, has to be to teach the common language of humanity. Human rights should not be merely one subject but should permeate all aspects of education.

In India, where illiteracy abounds, education on human rights is not possible unless literacy levels are raised. The Supreme Court, in a recent judgement, *Unnikrishnan J.P. and Others vs State of Andhra Pradesh* (AIR-1993-SC-2176) held that Article 45 of the constitution confers an enforceable fundamental right to education on all children up to the age of 14 years. The Government of Tamil Nadu passed a law providing for compulsory education for all children below 14 years.

Human rights teaching must be conditioned by the values and ethos of society in order to be effective. In India, the impression that human rights is a western concept imposed by western powers is widespread. This is erroneous. From ancient times, human rights in various forms have been the cultural heritage of mankind. In the final analysis, human rights are about human dignity, a notion familiar in India's civilisation centuries before the west was even born. Way back in 1980 the University Grants Commission (UGC) appointed the Sikri Committee to consider different ways of promoting human rights education in India. The Committee suggested different approaches at different levels. At school, care should be taken to develop positive values and attitudes about human rights. At the secondary school stage, a more systematic approach to the development of curricula, libraries and teachers should be adopted. College students in all faculties should be exposed to human rights. The universities could introduce diploma courses in human rights. Adult education programmes for human rights could also be evolved and become part of the curriculum.

For this mammoth task, the preparation of textbooks and training of teachers is crucial. The National Council for Educational Research and Training (NCERT) has already prepared a manual, *A Source Book on Human Rights*, which has been published by the NHRC (Sen 1997). Teacher training for human rights is a weak area, and needs more attention. Besides, education about human rights cannot remain solely classroom-based. It must perceive the reality of the problems at the grassroots and in the areas where they emerge; field trips, familiarisation visits and interaction with activists are absolutely necessary for any human rights education to be relevant.

A most heartening development was India's decision to sign the UN Convention against Torture, adopted on 10 December 1984. By September 1996, ninety-nine out of 185 member states had ratified it. One of the main reasons why India did not sign earlier was the fear of exposing the country to new and unwarranted forms of external intrusion. Another fear was the provision that compensation would have to be paid for unwarranted acts of physical and mental torture. But though the Gujral government agreed to sign the convention, the required follow-up action has not yet been taken.

Non-governmental organisations (NGOs) play a crucial role in enforcing the practice of human rights and exposing cases of their violation. India too has recognised their effectiveness, since the NHRC has been working regularly with them in its various projects and activities.

It is interesting to go through the contents of the concluding observations of the UN Human Rights Committee (1997b) while considering its third periodic report on India in July 1997. In highlighting the positive aspects, it praised the role of the constitutional framework and the frequent references made to international human rights instruments by the courts. It welcomed the establishment of the NHRC and noted its powers. It also welcomed the setting up of six State Human Rights Commissions. It lauded the lapse of TADA in 1995 and the holding of regular elections in the country. However, it expressed its concern over India's not signing the Optional Protocol by which individuals could approach the Committee, and the continued social discrimination suffered by scheduled castes and tribes. It also deplored the continuing mis-treatment of women and girl children.

The report was particularly harsh about the manner in which the Armed Forces (Special Powers) Act, the Public Safety Act and the National Security Act violated human rights in regions declared as disturbed areas. The Committee expressed its displeasure that civil or criminal proceedings against members of the security or armed forces, acting under special powers, could not be commenced without the sanction of the state government. This deprived people of the remedies to which they were entitled. It was also critical of the widespread use of special powers of detention without complying with the rules of procedure required. The report went on to criticise the conditions in prisons and asked for speedy trial of those charged with offences. It also voiced its concern over the failure to eliminate bonded labour, and over the forcible repatriation of asylum-seekers from Burma and Bangladesh. A number of recommendations were made to alleviate the pitiable conditions of child labourers and child prostitutes.

Significant human rights abuses, despite constitutional and statutory safeguards, continue to take place in Jammu & Kashmir. Many of these abuses are generated by intense social tensions, violent secessionist movements and the authorities' attempts to suppress them. These problems are acute in Kashmir, where the judicial system has been disrupted by terrorist threats, the assassination of judges and witnesses, the judicial tolerance of the government's anti-militant tactics and, often, the refusal of security forces to obey court orders. In fact, of late, a decrease in abuses by security forces in Kashmir has coincided with increased abuses by pro-government counter-militants. Serious human rights abuses include extra-judicial executions and political killings, excessive use of force by security forces including torture and rape and the eventual deaths of suspects in police custody, arbitrary arrests and incommunicado detention (Women's Initiative 1994).

Although an elected government was restored in Jammu & Kashmir in 1996 for the first time in six years, the number of insurgency-related deaths has not declined. International human rights groups have been given permission to visit the state, as has the International Committee of the Red Cross for visits to prisons on a continuing basis. These have demonstrated the government's attempts at transparency on human rights problems.

However, political killings by government forces (including deaths in custody and faked encounter killings), pro-government counter-militants and insurgents have continued to remain at a high level in the state of Jammu & Kashmir. Security forces committed an estimated 100–200 extra-judicial killings of suspected militants. This is believed by observers to be less than in previous years. However, the decline has been partially offset by an increased number of killings by pro-government militants. According to press reports, those killed had typically been detained by security forces, and their bodies, bearing multiple bullet wounds and often marks of torture, were returned to relatives. Security forces claim that these killings, when acknowledged, occurred in armed encounters with militants. Moreover, even the NHRC has no authority to directly investigate abuses by the security forces, and security forces do not report custodial deaths either in Kashmir or the northeast to the NHRC.

Killings and abductions of suspected militants and other persons by pro-government counter-militants have emerged as a significant pattern in Kashmir. Counter-militants are former separatist militants who have surrendered to government forces but have retained their arms and paramilitary organisations. The precise number of counter-militants is not known. The US Department of State Country Report on India, 1997, estimated that 100 to 200 political killings had taken place in Kashmir, including that of the journalist Sheikh Ghulam Rasool who had been publishing news reports criticising the militants. There are also reports that government agencies fund, exchange intelligence with, and even direct, the operations of counter-militants as part of the counter-insurgency effort. By 'sponsoring' or 'condoning' counter-militant activity, which takes place outside the legal system, the government cannot avoid the responsibility for abductions, murders and other abuses by these groups (United States Department of State 1997).

The total number of deaths in Kashmir in 1996 had not changed much in comparison with the total in 1995, although the proportion of civilian deaths had increased. Press reports indicated that 1,214 civilians, 94 security forces personnel and 1,271 militants died in insurgency-related violence in Kashmir in 1996. The corresponding figures for 1995 were 1,050 civilians, 202 security forces personnel and 1,308 militants. The decrease in security forces personnel deaths reflects the increased role of counter-militants. Non-governmental organisations and other agencies agree that civilian deaths attributed to security forces have decreased (ibid.).

The Amnesty International report on disappearances (1999) highlights one of the cruellest aspects of counter-insurgency in Jammu & Kashmir. The report estimates that between 700 and 2,000 persons have 'disappeared' in the state. The 'missing' include children and the elderly, revealing that many persons appear 'to be arbitrarily detained' or 'arrested as the only male member found in their homes during raids', picked up to put pressure on a relative suspected to be a militant 'to surrender', and in some cases for extorting money.

Amnesty International is convinced that the most common motive appears to be to intimidate young people into not joining the militants, or to frighten the general population from joining or supporting armed militancy. As against this, the Government of India keeps claiming that whenever *prima facie* cases of violations are established, exemplary action is taken under the law against the offenders and appropriate relief is provided to the victims. The report provides detailed evidence to the contrary.

The report also surveys the enormous powers given to the security forces under the Jammu and Kashmir Public Safety Act and the Jammu and Kashmir Prevention and Suppression of Sabotage Act, 1965, which was notified in August 1997. But the most severe of the laws operating in the area is the Armed Forces (Special Powers) Act which gives the power of life and death to the forces. Even the recently established State Human Rights Commission of Jammu & Kashmir has endorsed the view that atrocities committed by the forces are endemic (Amnesty International 1999).

In India's north-eastern states civilians continue to be victims of military operations against armed groups seeking autonomy. In September 1998, P.D. Sharma, Additional Secretary, Home Ministry, announced that India planned to recruit former members of the separatist United Liberation Front of Assam (ULFA) into its security forces, including the army, to provide them employment. As in the past, surrendered ULFA members (called SULFA) who aided regular security forces in counter-insurgency operations were implicated in extra-judicial executions and killings (*Human Rights Watch Report*, 1999). The pattern in Kashmir is clearly also operative in the north-eastern states.

These reports are indictments, which the government can choose to ignore at the risk of inviting international opprobrium and dismay. With increasing globalisation affecting the public-image-building exercise of the country internationally, much needs to be done to repair the damage, and to restore the dignity and rights of India's abused citizens. While the NHRC has been able to function, only a few states have set up state commissions. Of these, only the West Bengal Human Rights Commission (1996) and the Jammu & Kashmir Commission have published reports. Moreover, special Human Rights Courts have not yet been established anywhere.

Most crucial here is the need to train and expose members of the armed forces, the paramilitary forces and the police to human rights education. Though human rights programmes form part of the training programmes for the police and paramilitary forces, their content and manner of execution leave much to be desired. The content is routine, and trainers are generally from the forces. These two- to three-day programmes are quite inadequate to create a culture of human rights among the security forces, who, by the time they are exposed to such training have developed their own defence mechanisms to counter human rights education. In fact, human rights education is jocularly held by them as being responsible for an increase in crime. For them encounters are a much more acceptable solution to this problem.

The agenda for human rights in a developing country like India is unlimited, owing to problems arising out of scarcity of resources. The task is of considerable magnitude, and an on-going one which will need strength, resilience and fortitude to succeed. Creating awareness and educating neglected, exploited and marginalised groups will be a great asset in making the process of enforcing human rights meaningful, and enhancing the quality of our democracy.

For political activists, the language of rights is attractive: rights possess both political and moral clout, and rights themselves possess clarity in the sense that they make claims and they compel obedience. Above all, they grant a status to the individual and latterly to the group. To demand a right means that one does not receive anything out of benevolence or charity, but that one is entitled to respect and regard because one possesses properties which are particularly human. Therefore, rights—more so human rights—the world over have become the accepted mode of doing politics. Clearly, as political commitment to human rights has grown, philosophical commitment has waned. Defenders of human rights are somewhat taken aback when they see that political theory and political practice seem to be going their own parallel ways with little prospect of intersection (Chandhoke 1998). These are problems that need to be sorted out.

References

Amnesty International. 1999. *India: If They Are Dead, Tell Us: Disappearances in Jammu and Kashmir*. Amnesty International, London, February 1999.

Chamaraj, Kathyayini. 1997. 'Child Bonded Labour: Shackled Saga', *Humanscape*, January 1997.

Chandhoke, Neera. 1998. 'Thinking Through Rights: Exploring Grey Areas in the Theory', *Economic and Political Weekly*, Vol. 33, No. 5, 31 January 1998.

Chopra, Yash. 1993. 'The Asian Perspective on Human Rights'. Paper presented at the Commonwealth Legal Education Conference on Economic Policies, Human Rights and the Legal Order, Bangalore, 4–6 June 1993.

Misra, Ranganath. 1995. 'Our Aim is to be a Moral Authority', *Business Standard*, 15 December 1995.

National Human Rights Commission (NHRC). 1993. *Annual Report 1993–94*, New Delhi: NHRC.

Pal, R.M. 1995. 'National Human Rights Commission Annual Report: Not a Creative Document', *PUCL Bullettin*, October 1995.

Pillai, R.V. n.d. 'Institutional Framework of the National Human Rights Commission on its Statutory Responsibilities', Unpublished paper.

Rao, P.C. 1996. 'Enthronement of Human Rights', *The Hindustan Times*, New Delhi, 18 March 1996.

Roy, Dunu. 1998. 'Rights of Child Labour—Ethics, Production and National State', *Economic and Political Weekly*, Vol. 33, No. 5, 31 January 1998.

Sen, Shankar. 1997. 'Human Rights' I and II, *The Statesman*, 16 and 17 April 1997.

———. 1998a. *Human Rights in a Developing Society*. New Delhi: APH Publishing Corporation.

———. 1998b. 'Hastening Childhood's End', *The Telegraph*, London, 4 March 1998.

South Asia Human Rights Documentation Centre (SAHRDC). 1998. National Human Rights Institutions in the Asia Pacific, SAHRDC, New Delhi.

Tucker, Lee. 1997. 'Child Slaves in Modern India: The Bonded Labour Problem', *Human Rights Quarterly*, No. 19, pp. 572–629.

UN Human Rights Committee. 1997a. Submission by Amnesty International to the Human Rights Committee concerning Implementation of Articles of the International Convenant on Civil and Political Rights, July 1997.

———. 1997b. Consideration of Reports Submitted by State Parties under Article 40 of the Convenant—India—1997.

United States Department of State. 1997. Country Report on Human Rights Practices for 1996 (India). Bureau of Democracy, Human Rights and Labour, Washington, D.C.

West Bengal Human Rights Commission. 1996. *Annual Report 1995–1996*, Calcutta.

Weston, Burns H. 1997. 'Human Rights', in V. Jocopino, ed., *Rights and Health*, Vol. 1. Berkeley, CA: Odin Readers.

Women's Initiative. 1994. *Women's Testimony from Kashmir: The Green of the Valley is Khaki*. Mumbai: Women's Initiative.

Society
in
Transition

twelve

Caste and the Secularisation Process in India

D.L. Sheth

I ndia has the world's most complex and unique system of social stratification, the 'caste system'. In existence for thousands of years, the caste system got its name about five hundred years ago when the Portuguese landed on the Malabar coast and began to directly experience Indian society. Derived from *casta* in Portuguese, the term caste has since been used generically to describe the whole (*varna-jati*) system, as well as specifically to refer to its various orders and the different units within an order. The Portuguese 'discovery' of caste, however, went much beyond giving a name to India's *varna-jati* system. They were the first Europeans to provide detailed accounts of its functioning. The most perceptive empirical account of caste was given by the 16th-century Portuguese visitor Duarte Barbosa. He identified the main features of the caste system: (*a*) as a hierarchy, with Brahmins at the top and 'untouchables' at the bottom; (*b*) as the practice of untouchability premised on the idea of 'pollution'; (*c*) as the existence of a plurality of 'castes' separated from each other by endogamy, occupation and commensality; (*d*) as a system in which sanctions are applied to maintain customs and rules; and (*e*) as a relationship of caste with political organisation.

Although Barbosa did not provide a 'systematic' account, the elements of caste he identified remain central to any definition even today. Moreover, Barbosa's approach to reporting about caste had some distinctive qualities. First, he described caste as he saw it functioning on the ground. He got his facts by talking not just to the elites, but to common people in their own language. Second, he did not use the religious scriptures as a source of information on caste. There is no reference to the *varna* theory of caste in his narratives. Third, he related the idea of pollution to the practice of untouchability and not to the functioning of the whole system. Fourth, he saw caste not exclusively in ritual-status terms, but also as a plurality of 'self-governing' cultural communities. Fifth, he confined himself to a matter-of-fact account of what he saw and was told about caste, and refrained from moralising and passing value judgements on it (Cohn 1987: 139–40).

The Colonial Discourse

Nothing much of significance was added nor any improvement made to Barbosa's account for the next 250 years by his European successors reporting on caste. It was only after British rule was established in India that a second 'discovery' of caste was made by the Europeans. The western orientalist scholars, the Christian missionaries and the British administrators began, in their different ways, to make sense of this complex phenomenon. A new colonial discourse on caste was born. It marked important departures from pre-colonial accounts of caste.

First of all, the new discourse centred on whether caste was a system beneficial to Indians or whether it worked against them. The orientalist scholars viewed caste as serving some positive functions, whereas the missionaries saw it as an unmitigated evil. Second, both its sympathisers and opponents saw caste in highly schematised and unidimensional terms: as an inflexible hierarchy of vertically ranked ritual statuses. The idea of pollution, which Barbosa saw in the context of untouchability, was now generalised for the whole system, in which the idea of ritual purity and im- purity of statuses was considered the central principle governing the caste system. The reality of caste was reconstructed largely from its depiction in the religious scriptures. In the event, Barbosa's empirical view of caste was now superimposed by the scriptural (ideological) *varna* view of caste. Third, with the 'discovery' of Hindu scriptures by orientalist scholars, caste became a prism through which colonial rulers began to see Indians and the whole of Indian society. Caste was now seen as representing the world-view of Indians and the totality of India's social and cultural life. Certain non-ritual, even non-religious elements, which always existed in the caste system and informed quite a few aspects of inter-caste relations, were theoretically ruled out of the system.

Fourth, in the course of setting up its revenue administration, a number of land and village surveys were launched by the colonial regime in different regions of India. This focused the attention of revenue administrators, many of whom were anthropologically inclined scholars, on the Indian village — which was also a revenue unit. This focus developed into a view of the village as a microcosm of the Indian society, and caste as constituting its social, economic and political organisation, legitimised by its religious ideology. In this village view, caste was seen as an ensemble of local hierarchies, each contained within a village or a group of villages. This view contributed to the image of the village as a stable, unchanging social system. In the later ethnographic studies of caste carried out by Indian sociologists, the *varna* theory was discarded, but caste continued to be seen as a vertical hierarchy of ritual statuses embedded in the religious and cultural context of the village.

Fifth, the administrative and anthropological concerns of the British officers led them to counter both the orientalist and the missionary views of caste. Their concern was utilitarian, about finding administrative and political ways to tame and change this formidable system functioning from ancient times, to suit the needs of the colonial polity and economy. This concern of the colonialists prompted an ideological debate on caste. The debate achieved a degree of political sophistication which was not shown earlier either by the orientalists in their appreciation, or the missionaries in their condemnation, of the caste system. It introduced a new, theoretical-comparative dimension for viewing caste. Caste now began to be seen in comparison with the normative (values of equality, individualism etc.) and social (estate, race, class etc.) categories of western societies. Eventually, with English-educated nationalist Indians joining the debate on the terms set by the colonial regime, caste became a bone of contention between conservatives and progressives, traditionalists and reformers. Valuation became the mode of observation.

Sixth, the method British administrators adopted in reporting about caste, unlike that of the orientalist scholars, was 'empirical'. They saw the caste system not only in terms of the *varna* categories, but also as separate communities often divided by descent, political organisation and custom. Consequently they theorised caste in terms of its racial and tribal origins and character. In fact, multiple and elaborate systems of classification of castes were evolved by them based on a variety of ethnographic materials, officially obtained through various village and caste surveys (Cohn 1987: 141–62).

Seventh, crucial to the colonial discourse was the relationship between caste and the state. From the 1901 Census, the colonial state began caste-wise enumeration of the entire Indian population. The decennial censuses not only updated the population figures for each enumerated caste, but gave it a specific name/label and a rank. In doing so, the census officers tended to rely on their 'reading' of the scriptures as well as on local knowledge and practice. But when a name and/or a rank given to a caste was in dispute — and this happened frequently — the census officer's 'anthropological' judgement, albeit tempered by representations received from leaders of concerned castes, prevailed. Thus, despite the diversity of the debate, at the end of the day the criterion of 'social precedence of one caste over the other', meaning the scriptural principle of ritual-status hierarchy, was explicitly and *officially* recognised.

The colonial state, thus, acquired an agency, even a legitimate authority, to arbitrate and fix the status claims made or contested by various castes about their locations in the ritual hierarchy. At the same time, the enumeration of castes and their ethnographic descriptions compiled by the state highlighted how social and economic advantages accrued to some castes and not to others in the traditional hierarchy. This led to demands from many castes for special 'recognition' by the state for educational and occupational benefits as well as for political representation. The colonial state assumed a dual role: that of a *super-Brahmin* who located and relocated disputed statuses of castes in the traditional hierarchy, and that of a *just and modern ruler* who wished to 'recognise' the rights and aspirations of his weak and poor subjects. This helped the state to protect its colonial political economy from the incursions of the emerging nationalist movement. Among other things, it also induced people to organise and represent their interests in politics in terms of caste identities and participate in the economy on the terms and through mechanisms set by the colonial regime.

On the whole, the colonial regime not only introduced new terms of discourse on caste, but also brought about some changes in the caste system itself. A large part of these changes, however, were the unintended consequences of colonial policies. They were related to the larger historical forces of modernisation, secularisation and urbanisation, which had begun to make some impact on Indian society by the end of the 19th and the beginning of the 20th century. But some specific policies of the colonial regime, aimed at delegitimising the power of the traditional social elites and creating support for its own rule, had direct consequences for the caste system. Towards the end of colonial rule such policies, alongside the larger historical forces, had produced some profound and far-reaching changes in the caste system.[1]

The most important among these changes was the formation of a new, trans-local identity among 'lower castes', collectively, as a *people* with the consciousness of being 'oppressed' by the traditional system of hierarchy. The discourse of rights, until then quite alien to the concepts governing ritual hierarchy, made its first appearance in the context of the caste system. New ideological categories like 'social justice' began to interrogate the idea of ritual purity and impurity, according to which the traditional stratificatory system endowed entitlements and disprivileges to hereditary statuses. The established categories of ritual hierarchy began to be confronted with new categories like 'depressed' and 'oppressed' castes.[2] Second, several castes occupying more or less similar locations in different local hierarchies began to organise themselves horizontally into regional- and national-level associations and federations, as it became increasingly necessary for them to negotiate with the state and in the process project their larger social identity and numerical strength.[3] Third, movements of the lower castes for upward social mobility, which were not new in the history of the caste system, acquired a qualitatively new dimension as they began to attack the very ideological foundations of the ritual hierarchy of castes, not in terms internal to the system (as was the case with the Buddhist and Bhakti movements), but in the modern ideological terms of justice and equality.

Changes that occurred in the caste system during the colonial period have greatly intensified after India's decolonisation. Further, with India establishing a liberal democratic state and with the growth of institutions of competitive, representational democracy, the changes acquired newer dimensions and a greater transformative edge. All this has produced fundamental structural and systemic changes in the traditional stratificatory system.[4]

Despite the fact that such qualitative changes had occurred in the stratificatory system after India's independence, the changes continued to be interpreted in the old colonial ideological-evaluative frame. The terms and categories used for describing these changes — by sociologists studying caste as well as by social reformers and political thinkers wanting India to become a casteless society — were derived from the colonial discourse. This gave rise to two opposite views of change in the caste system, which in fact represented mirror-images of each other. One view, that has long dominated studies of caste in post-independence India, emphasises certain structural and cultural *continuities* that Indian society has manifested in the course of modernisation. In this view, changes in caste are seen in terms of functional adjustments made by the system for its own survival and maintenance. The other view, that dominated the political-ideological discourse on caste until recently, sees modernisation as a linear, universal force of history, transforming the caste system into a polarised structure of economic classes. On the whole, the discourse on caste in post-independence India remained bogged down in the dichotomous debate on 'tradition versus modernity' and 'caste versus class'.

Secularisation of Caste

The dichotomous view of change has prevented scholars, policy-makers and political activists alike from taking a view of the *process* by which caste has changed and by which a new type of stratificatory system has emerged. This process, which can broadly be characterised as secularisation of caste, has detached caste from ritual-status hierarchy on the one hand, and has imparted to it the character of a *power*-group functioning within a competitive democratic politics on the other. Changes in caste thus may be observed along these two dimensions of secularisation: *de-ritualisation* and *politicisation*. These changes have (*a*) pushed caste out of the traditional stratificatory system; (*b*) linked it to the new structure of representational power; and (*c*) made it possible, in their cumulative impact, for individual members of a caste to claim and achieve new economic interest and a class-like identity. Thus, secularisation of caste, brought about through its de-ritualisation and politicisation, has opened up a third course of change. For lack of a more appropriate term I shall call it *classisation*. In the following sections I shall describe these three processes of change in caste and shall examine their implications for the emergence of a new type of stratificatory system in India.

De-ritualisation

Caste has been conventionally conceived of as an insulated *system* of ritual-status hierarchy, embedded in the 'perennial' religious culture of India. Rituality (meaning the rootedness of caste behaviour and organisation in religious ideology and practices) is supposed to constitute the core of the whole system of castes; it has enabled caste to maintain autonomy and stability of status-hierarchy in the face of changes, both economic and political, that occur in the wider society. Caste 'accommodated' these changes only to the extent that the system could absorb them without losing its structural and cultural integrity. In responding to these changes, caste may find 'new fields of activity' or assume new functions, but all this to retain its basic structure and ideological (religious) core. Such insularity of the caste system is guaranteed because it is bounded by certain contexts — ambiences — each articulating a form of rituality. These contexts pertain to: (*a*) the religious ideology of purity and pollution; (*b*) the religiously sanctioned techno-economic and political organisation of the village, especially its food production and distribution system; and (*c*) the customs and traditions of castes evolved over centuries. Caste has not only survived in these contexts, but has grown and acquired its *systemic* character within them. They have provided caste with its 'support system'.

In what follows, I argue that the changes that have occurred in caste, especially after India's decolonisation, amount to de-ritualisation of caste — meaning the delinking of caste from various forms of rituality which bounded it to a fixed status, an occupation, and specific rules of commensality and endogamy. I further argue that, with the loss of rituality, a large part of the 'support system' of caste has collapsed. Uprooted from its ritually determined ideological, economic and political contexts, it has ceased to be a unit of the ritual-status hierarchy. Caste now survives as a kinship-based cultural community, and operates in a different, newly emergent system of social stratification.

First, the modernisation of India's economy and the democratisation of its political institutions have released new economic and political power in the society. The hierarchically ordered strata of castes now function as horizontal groups competing for power and control over resources in society. Alongside this change in organisational structure, meaning horizontalisation, the form that consciousness takes has also changed. The feeling of belonging to a caste is now expressed more in the nature of *community consciousness* rather than in hierarchical terms. Caste consciousness is now articulated as the political consciousness of groups staking claims to power and to new places in the changed opportunity structure. It is a different kind of collective consciousness from that of belonging to a 'high' or a 'low' ritual-status group. The rise of such consciousness of castes has led to a disruption of hierarchical relations and to increase in competition and conflict among them. Far from strengthening the caste *system*, the emergent competitive character of 'caste consciousness' has contributed to its systemic disintegration. The disintegrating system of traditional statuses is now thickly overlaid by the new power system created by elections, political parties and above all by the social policies — such as that of affirmative action — of the state.

Second, fundamental changes have occurred in the occupational structure of the society. A vast number of non-traditional, unbound-to-caste occupations and a new type of social relations among occupational groups have emerged. This has resulted in breaking down the nexus between hereditary ritual status and occupation—one of the caste system's defining features. It is no longer necessary to justify one's occupation in terms of its correlation with the ritual purity or impurity of one's inherited status. The traditional, ritualistic idea of the cleanliness or otherwise of the occupation one follows has become unimportant. The crucial consideration now is activity that brings a good income to the individual. If a Brahmin deals in leather, or an ex-untouchable deals in diamonds, it is no longer looked upon as socially deviant behaviour. That the former is a more frequent occurrence than the latter has only to do with the resources at one's command, and not with observance of ritual prohibitions attached to the statuses involved. More importantly, the cleanliness or otherwise of an occupation is increasingly seen in the physical and biological sense rather than in ritual or moral terms.[5]

Third, significant internal differentiations have taken place within every caste. Traditionally, an individual caste bounded by rituals and customs functioned internally as a truly egalitarian community, both in terms of rights and obligations of members vis-à-vis each other, and in terms of lifestyles, meaning the food they ate, the clothes they wore, the houses they lived in, etc. Differences in wealth and status (of clans) that existed among households within the same caste were expressed on such occasions as weddings and funerals, but rarely in power terms vis-à-vis other members of the caste. Today, households within a single caste have not only been greatly differentiated in terms of their occupations, educational and income levels, and lifestyles, but these differences have led them to align with different socio-economic networks and groupings in the society—categories which cannot be identified in terms of the caste system.

Fourth, the caste rules of commensality (restrictions on accepting cooked food from members of other castes) have become inoperative outside one's household. Even within the household, observance of such rules has become quite relaxed. In 'caste dinners', for example, friends and well-wishers of the host, belonging to both ritually lower as well as higher strata than that of the host, are invited, and are seated, fed and served together with the members of the caste hosting the dinner. Caste panchayats, where they exist, show increasingly less concern about invoking any sanctions in such situations.

Fifth, castes which occupied similar ritual status in the traditional hierarchy, but were divided among themselves into sub-castes and sub-sub-castes by rules of endogamy, are now increasingly reaching out into larger endogamous circles, in some cases their boundaries co-terminating with those of the respective *varna* in the region to which they supposedly belong. More importantly, inter-caste marriages across different ritual strata, often even crossing the self-acknowledged *varna* boundaries, are no longer very uncommon. Such marriage alliances are frequently made by matching education, profession and the wealth of brides and grooms and/or their parents, ignoring traditional differences in ritual status among them. Significantly, such inter-caste marriages are often arranged by the parents or approved by them when arranged by the prospective spouses on their own. The only 'traditional' consideration that enters into such cases is the vegetarian/meat-eating divide, which is also becoming somewhat fuzzy. Although statistically the incidence of such inter-caste marriages is not significant, the trend they represent is. A more important point is that the mechanisms through which castes enforced rules of endogamy have weakened in many castes.

The ideology and organisation of the traditional caste system have thus become vastly eroded. Its description as a *system* of ritual-status hierarchy has lost theoretical meaning.[6] As may be expected, such erosion has taken place to a much greater extent and degree in the urban areas and at the macro-system level of social stratification. But the local hierarchies of castes in rural areas are also being progressively subjected to the same process.[7] In the villages, too, traditional social relationships are being redefined in economic terms. This is largely because in the last three decades, particularly after the Green Revolution and with the increasing role of the state and other outside agencies in the food production and distribution system in rural areas, the social organisation of the village has changed substantively. From the kind of social-religious system the Indian village was, it is increasingly becoming primarily an economic organisation. The priestly, trading and service castes—social groups not *directly* related to agricultural operations—are leaving villages or serving them, if and when such services are still required, from nearby towns. Members of such castes continuing to live in the villages have largely moved out of the 'village system' of economic and social interdependence of castes. They increasingly function in the emergent national-market-related rural economy or the secondary and tertiary sectors of employment.

In this process, many a caste has structurally severed its relationship with the system of ritual obligations and rights which once governed its economic and social existence and gave it an identity in terms of its status in the ritual hierarchy. Inter-caste relations in the village today operate in a more simplified form, as between castes of landholders/operators and those of the landless labour. This relationship is often articulated in terms of the political consciousness of two groups of castes representing different economic interests in the changed political economy of the village.

The socio-religious content of economic relationships in the village has thus largely disappeared; they have become more contractual and almost totally monetised. The traditional *jajmani* relationships, which regulated economic transactions between castes in social-ritual terms, have been replaced by relationships of employer and employee, of capital and wage labour. When the traditional social and religious aspects of economic relationships are insisted upon by any caste, such as traditional obligations of one status group to another, it often leads to inter-caste conflicts and violence in the villages. Briefly, the pattern of social relations sustained by the internal system of food production of a village, and by conformity of status groups to their religiously assigned roles in the system and to norms defining the roles, has virtually disintegrated.

In sum, while castes survive as micro-communities based on kinship sentiments and relationships, they no longer relate to each other as 'units' of a ritual hierarchy. The caste *system*, for long conceived as a ritual-status system, has imploded. Having failed to cope with the changes that have occurred in the larger society, particularly after India's decolonisation, the caste *system* is unable to maintain itself on the basis of its own principle of ritual hierarchy. It cannot sustain vertical linkages of interdependence and co-operation among its constituent units, nor can it enforce its own rules governing obligations and privileges of castes vis-à-vis each other.

In the few specific contexts where ritual relationships between castes still survive, they have acquired contractual, often conflictual forms, negating the system's hierarchical aspect. Ritual roles which members of some castes (like the role of a priest or a barber) still perform have been reduced to those of functionaries called upon to do a job for payment on specific occasions (weddings, deaths etc.). Performance of such roles/functions by a few members of a caste, however, has no relevance for determining its place in the changed stratificatory system. Such roles, it seems, now survive outside the stratificatory system, as a part of Hindu religious practices. But such phenomenal changes have occurred in Hinduism itself in recent years that inter-caste relations can no longer be viewed as constitutive of a ritually determined religious practice. The growth in popularity of new sects, of deities and shrines, the growing importance of gurus and godmen and the new practice of public celebrations of Hindu religious festivals on a much wider social and geographical scale, involving participation of members of a number of castes across ritual hierarchy and regions, have all shored up the popular-cultural and political aspects of Hinduism. These have considerably weakened the traditional ritual and social organisational aspects of Hinduism. In this process, inter-caste relations have not only lost systemic context, but also to a large extent their *religious reference*. Castes now negotiate their status claims in the newly emergent stratificatory system.

The simultaneous processes of detachment of castes from ritual hierarchy and the growth, albeit in varying degrees, of economic, social and cultural differentiations within every caste have resulted in castes entering into various new, larger social-political formations which have emerged in India's changing stratificatory system. As we shall see in the next section, each of these formations grew in the process of politicisation of castes, and has acquired a new form of collective consciousness, a consciousness different from that of a ritual-status group. Yet, the new consciousness is not of a 'class' as in a polarised class structure. This consciousness is based on the perception of common political interest and modern status aspirations on the part of the members of these new formations. In this process, the unitary consciousness of individual castes has diffused into an expanded consciousness of belonging to a larger social-political formation, which cannot be described as a 'caste' or 'class'.

Politicisation of Castes

For about two decades after independence, the political discourse on caste was dominated by left-radical parties and liberal-modernist intellectuals who viewed, rather simplistically, the changes in the caste system in linear terms — as suggestive of its transformation into a system of polarised economic classes. In so believing, they ignored the fact that while caste had lost its significance as a ritual-status group it survived as a 'community', seeking alliances with other similar communities with whom it shared political interest and consciousness. Consequently, political parties of the left, both the communist and the socialist, by and large sought to articulate political issues and devise strategies of mobilising electoral support in terms of economic interests, which in their view divided the social classes in India.[8] In the event, although these parties could credibly claim to represent the poorer strata and even occupied some significant political spaces in opposition to the Congress party at the time of independence, they failed to expand their electoral support in any significant measure for decades after independence.

Put simply, competitive politics required that a political party seeking wider electoral bases must view castes neither as a pure category of 'interest' nor as one of 'identity'. The involvement of castes in politics fused 'interest' and 'identity' in such a manner that a number of castes could share common interests and identity in the form of larger social-political conglomerates. The process was one of *politicisation* of castes which, by incorporating castes in competitive politics, reorganised and recast the elements of both hierarchy and separation among castes in larger social collectivities.[9] These new collectivities did not resemble the *varna* categories or anything like a polarised class structure in politics. The emergence of these socio-political entities in Indian politics defied the conventional categories of political analysis, which is class analysis versus caste analysis. The singular impact of competitive democratic politics on the caste system thus was that it delegitimised the old hierarchical relations among castes, facilitating new horizontal power relations among them.

Congress Dominance: First Phase of Politicisation

The process of politicisation of castes acquired a great deal of so-phistication in the politics of the Congress party, which scru-pulously avoided taking any theoretical-ideological position on the issue of caste versus class. The party, being politically aware of the change in the agrarian context, saw castes as socio-economic entities seeking new identities through politics in place of the old identities derived from their traditional status in the ritual hier-archy. Thus, by relying on the caste calculus for its electoral politics and, at the same time, articulating political issues in terms of eco-nomic development and national integration, the Congress was able to evolve durable electoral bases across castes and to maintain its image as the only and truly national party. This winning com-bination of 'caste politics' and 'nationalist ideology' secured for the Congress a dominant position in Indian politics for nearly three decades after independence.[10] The party rarely used such dichot-omies as upper castes versus lower castes or capitalists versus working class in its political discourse. Its politics was largely ad-dressed to vertically linking the rule of the newly emergent upper-caste and English-speaking 'national elite' to lower-caste support. And the ideology used for legitimation of this vertical social linkage in politics was neither class ideology nor caste ideology; the key concept was 'nation-building'.

The Congress party projected its politics and programmes at the *national* level as representing the 'national aspirations' of the Indian people. At the *regional* level, the party consolidated its social base by endorsing the power of the numerically strong and up-wardly mobile, dominant but traditionally of lower status, castes of land-owing peasants; like the Marathas in Maharashtra, the Reddys in Andhra, the Patidars in Gujarat, the Jats in Uttar Pradesh and so on. In the process, it created patron–client type relationships in electoral politics, relationships of unequal but reliable exchanges between political patrons — the upper and dominant (intermediate) castes — and the numerous 'client' castes at the bottom of the pile, popularly known as the Congress's 'vote-banks'. Thus, in the initial two decades after independence, hierarchical caste relations were processed politically through elections. This ensured for the Congress a political consensus across castes, despite the fact that it was presided over by the hegemony of a small, upper-caste, English-educated elite in collaboration with regional social elites belonging, by and large, to the upwardly mobile castes of landed peasants. The latter, however, were often viewed by the former (the 'national elite', with the self-image of modernisers), as parochial traditionalists. Still, the alliance held.

This collaboration between the two types of elites created a new structure of representational power in society, around which grew a small middle class. This class consisted of the upper-caste national elite living in urban areas *and* the rural social elite belonging to the dominant peasant castes, as well as those upper-caste members living in rural areas. The ruling national elites, although they belonged to upper castes, had become detached from their traditional ritual status and functions. They had acquired new interests in the changed (planned) economy, and lifestyles which came through modern education, non-traditional occupations, and a degree of westernisation which accompanied this process. The dominant castes of the regional elites still depended more on *sanskritisation* than on 'westernisation' in their pursuit of upward social mobility. But they encouraged their younger generations to take to modern, English-medium education and to new professions. In the process, despite their Sudra origins but thanks to their acquisition of new power in the changed rural economy and politics, several peasant communities succeeded in claiming a social status equivalent to that of the *dwija* castes.

Consequently, such communities as Patidars, Marathas, Reddys, Kammas and their analogues in different regions were identified with 'upper castes', and not with 'backward castes'. Acquisition of modern education and interest in the new (planned) economy enabled them, like the *dwija* upper castes, to claim for themselves a new social status and identity — those of the middle class.

At the same time, the caste identities of both these sections of the 'middle class' were far from dissolved. They could comfortably own both upper-caste status and middle-class identity, as both categories had become concomitant with each other. While the alliance between the upper-caste national elite and the dominant-caste regional elites remained tenuous in politics, together they continued to function as a new power group in the larger society. In the formation and functioning of this middle class as a power group of elites, caste had indeed fused with class, and status dimension had acquired a pronounced power dimension. But insofar as this process of converting traditional status into new power was restricted only to the upper rungs in the ritual hierarchy, the latter sought to use that power to establish their own caste-like hegemony over the rest of society. It is this nexus between upper traditional status and new power that inhibited the transformative potentials of both modernisation and democracy in India.

This conflation of the traditional status system with the new power system, however, worked quite differently for the numerous non-*dwija* lower castes. In negotiating their way into the new power system, their traditional low status, contrary to what it did for the upper and the intermediate castes, worked as a liability. The functions attached to their very low traditional statuses had lost relevance or were devalued in the modern occupational system. Moreover, since formal education was not mandated for them in the traditional status system, they were slow to take to modern education compared to the upper castes. Nor did they have the advantage of inherited wealth, as their traditional status had tied them to the subsistence livelihood patterns of the *jajmani* system.

In brief, for the lower castes of peasants and artisans, the ex-untouchables and the numerous tribal communities, their low statuses in the traditional hierarchy worked negatively for their entry in the modern sector. Whatever social capital and economic security they had in the traditional status system was wiped out through the modernisation process; they no longer enjoyed the protection that they had in the traditional status system against the arbitrary use of hierarchical power by the upper castes. On top of that they had no means or resources to enter the modern sector in any significant way, except by becoming its underclass. They remained at the bottom rung of both hierarchies, the sacred and the secular, caste *and* class.

This did objectively create an elite–mass kind of division in politics, but it still did not produce any awareness of the polarisation of socio-economic classes in society. In any event, it did not create any space for class-based politics. In fact, all attempts of the left parties at political mobilisation of the numerous lower castes as a *class* of proletarians did not achieve any significant results either for their electoral or revolutionary politics. Neither did their politics, focused as it was on class ideology, make much of a dent in Congress-dominated politics, for the latter had established the political hegemony of the upper-caste-oriented middle class with the electoral consent of the lower castes! A very peculiar caste–class linkage was forged, in which the upper castes functioned in politics with the self-identity of a *class* (ruling or 'middle'), and the lower castes, despite their class-like political aspirations, with the consciousness of their separate *caste* identities. The latter were linked to the former in a vertical system of political exchange through the Congress party, rather than horizontally with one another.

Politics of Reservations: Second Phase of Politicisation

It took about three decades after independence for the lower castes of peasants, artisans, the ex-untouchables and the tribals, to express their resentment towards the patron–client relationship that had bound them politically to the Congress party. With a growing awareness of their numerical strength and the role it could play in achieving their share in political power, their resentment took the form of political action and movements. Awareness among the lower castes about using political means for upward social mobility, and for staking claims as larger social collectivities for a share in political power, had arisen during the colonial period, but it was subdued after independence for almost three-and-a-half decades of Congress dominance.

It was around the mid-1970s that upper-caste hegemony over national politics began to be seriously challenged. This was largely due to the social policies of the state, particularly that of Reservations (affirmative action). Despite tardy implementation, towards the end of the 1970s the Reservations policy had created a small but significant section in each of the lower-caste groups which had acquired modern education, and which had entered the bureaucracy and other non-traditional occupations. In the process, a small but highly vocal political leadership emerged from among the lower castes.

The process of politicisation of castes, however, came to a head at the beginning of the 1980s. This was when the Second Commission for Backward Classes (the Mandal Commission) proposed to extend reservations in jobs and educational seats to the Other Backward Classes (to castes of lower peasantry and artisans) in *all* states and at the central level. This proposal was, however, stoutly opposed by sections of the upper and intermediate castes. They saw the newly politicised lower castes forcing their way into the middle class (particularly into white-collar jobs), and that too not through open competition but through 'caste-based' reservations. This created a confrontation of interest between the upper and intermediate castes on the one hand and the lower castes on the other. But it led to a resurgence of lower castes in national politics. This resurgent politics, guided by lower-caste aspirations to enter the middle class, was derided as the 'Mandalisation of politics' by the English-educated elite. The so-called Mandalised politics, a euphemism for the politicisation of lower castes, has since resulted in radically altering the social bases of politics in India.

First, the Congress-dominated politics of social consensus, pre-sided over by the hegemony of an upper-caste, English-educated elite, came to an end. The Congress organisation could no longer function as the system of vertical management of region–caste factions. The elite at the top could not accommodate the ever-increasing claims and pressures from below, by different sections of the lower castes, for their share in power. From the mid-1970s through the 1980s, large sections of the lower strata of social groups abandoned the Congress and constituted themselves into shifting alliances of their own separate political parties. The vertical arrangement of the region–caste factions that the Congress had perfected simply collapsed. The national parties — the Congress, the BJP and the Communist parties alike — had to now negotiate for political support directly with the social-political collectivities of the Other Backward Castes (OBCs), the Scheduled Castes (SCs) and Scheduled Tribes (STs), or with the regional–caste parties con-stituted by them.

Second, the categories of OBCs, SCs and STs, expressly devised for the administrative purpose of implementing the Reservations policy, perhaps as an unintended consequence acquired a strong social and political content, and surfaced as new social formations in the macro-stratificatory system. They now operated in politics with the self-consciousness of socio-economic groups. Not content with proxy representations by the upper-caste–middle-class elites, they wanted political power for themselves. Politics now became a contest for representation among horizontal power groups, representing social collectivities as identified by the policy of Reservations. These groups began to bargain with different existing parties or formed their own new parties. Whatever survived of the hierarchical dimension of the traditional stratificatory system in politics was thus effectively horizontalised.

Third, the 'Mandalised politics', by generating aspirations among the lower castes to attain 'middle-class' status and lifestyles, prevented the process of *class* polarisation. This politics created new compulsions in the social arena. The old middle class, dominated by the upper and intermediate castes, was now compelled to admit expansion beyond itself and make space, even if grudgingly, for different sections of the lower castes. At the same time, lower castes, while forming coalitions in politics, began to compete intensely among themselves at the social level for entry into the growing middle class.

In sum, the state policy of affirmative action gave a big impetus to the process of politicisation of castes (as well as to de-ritualisation of inter-caste relations). The policy itself, by providing special educational and occupational opportunities to members of the numerous lower castes, converted their traditional disability of low ritual status into an asset for acquiring new means for upward social mobility. The politicisation of castes, along with the spread of urbanisation and industrialisation, has contributed to the emergence of a new type of stratificatory system in which the old middle class has not only expanded in numbers, but has begun to acquire new social and political characteristics.

Classisation of Caste: Emergence of a 'New Middle Class'

'Classisation' is a problematic, even controversial, concept used for describing a certain type of change in caste. As a category derived from the conventional 'class analysis', it articulates the issue of change in linear and dichotomous terms, asking how caste is (rather, 'why caste is not') transforming itself into a polarised structure of economic classes. Just as the role of *status* and other 'non-class' elements (gender, ethnicity etc.) is routinely ignored in analyses of class in western society, 'class analysis' in India too undermines the role of 'caste' elements in class and vice versa. At the other end of the spectrum are scholars devoted to 'caste analysis', who have little use for a concept like 'classisation'. Accustomed to viewing caste as a local hierarchy and to interpreting changes *in it* in terms of the caste system's own ideology and rules, they view class elements in caste (such as the role of modern education, occupational mobility, and economic and political power) as elements extraneous to the caste system; elements which, of course, it incorporates and recasts into its own image to maintain its *systemic* continuity. Classisation neither follows a linear, teleological course of change, nor does it represent the caste system's own reproductive process. I, therefore, view *classisation* as a twofold process: (*a*) *releasing* of individual members of all castes (albeit the extent of this may vary from one caste to another) from the religiously sanctioned techno-economic and social organisation (the occupational and status hierarchy) of the 'village system'; and (*b*) *linking* of their interests and identities to organisations and categories relevant to the urban-industrial system and modern politics. This process operates not only in urban areas, but also increasingly in rural areas. The two aspects of the process are not temporally sequential, nor spatially separated. They criss-cross, and changes become visible in the form of elements of a newly emergent macro-system of social stratification. Thus viewed, 'classisation' is a process by which castes, but more frequently their individual members, relate to categories of social stratification of a type different from caste.

The emergent stratificatory arrangement, however, is far from having acquired a 'systemic' form. Yet, new and different types of social and economic categories have emerged at all levels of society, by relating to which caste is not only losing its own shape and character, but is acquiring a new form and ideology. Thus, as we saw earlier, caste survives, but as a kinship-based cultural community, not as the status groups of ritual hierarchy. It has acquired new economic interests and a political identity. Its members now negotiate and own larger and multiple social and political identities. In this process, caste identity has lost its old character and centrality. The economic and political activities in which members of a caste are now engaged are of a radically different type from the ones perpetuated by the caste *system*. The ritually determined vertical relationship of *statuses,* which encouraged harmony and co-operation among castes, has been transformed into one of horizontally competing, often conflicting *power* blocs, each constituted of a number of castes occupying different statuses across traditional local hierarchies. In the process, new socio-economic formations, some of 'ethnic type', have emerged at the macro-level of society. They compete for control of economic, political and cultural resources in the society. The idea of upward social mobility today motivates people of all castes (not just of the 'lower' castes) collectively as well as *individually.* For the quest today is not for registering higher *ritual* status; it is universally for wealth, political power and modern (consumerist) lifestyles. In short, caste has ceased to 'reproduce' itself, as it did in the past.

All these changes have imparted a structural substantiality to the macro-stratificatory system of a kind it did not have in the past. In the absence of a centralised polity, the system functioned superstructurally as an ideology of *varna* hierarchy. Lacking structural substance, it served as a 'common social language' and supplied normative categories of legitimation of statuses to various local substantive hierarchies of *jatis* (Béteille 1996; Srinivas 1962: 63–69). But, as we saw earlier, after India became a pan-Indian political entity governed by a liberal democratic state, new social formations, each comprising a number of *jatis* — often across ritual hierarchies and religious communities — emerged at the regional and all-India levels. Deriving its nomenclature from the official classification devised by the state in the course of implementing its policy of affirmative action (Reservations), the new formations began to be identified as: the forward or the 'upper castes', the backward castes (OBCs), the *dalits* or Scheduled Castes (SCs) and the tribals or the Scheduled Tribes (STs).

Unlike status groups of the caste *system,* the new social formations function as relatively loose and open-ended entities, competing with each other for political power. In this competition, members of the upper-caste formation have available to them the resources of their erstwhile traditional higher status, and those of lower-caste formations have the advantages accruing to them from the state's policy of affirmative action. Thus, the emergent stratificatory system represents a kind of fusion between the old status system and the new power system. Put differently, the ritual hierarchy of closed status groups has transformed into a fairly open and fluid system of social stratification.

This system is in the making. It can not be described either in caste terms or in pure class terms. However, the salience of one category in this newly emergent stratificatory system has become visible in recent years. It can be characterised as the 'new middle class'; 'new' because its emergence is directly traceable to the disintegration of the caste *system*. This has made it socially much more diversified compared to the old, upper-caste-oriented middle class that existed at the time of independence. Moreover, high status in the traditional hierarchy worked implicitly as a criterion for entry into the 'old' middle class, and *sanskritised* lifestyles constituted its cultural syndrome. Both rituality and *sanskritisation* have virtually lost their relevance in the formation of the 'new' middle class. Membership of today's middle class is associated with new lifestyles (modern consumption patterns), ownership of certain economic assets and the self-consciousness of belonging to the 'middle class'. As such, it is open to members of different castes — who have acquired modern education, taken to non-traditional occupations and/or command higher incomes and political power — to enter this 'middle class'.

However, the 'new middle class' can not be seen as constituting a pure *class* category — a construct which is in fact a theoretical fiction. It carries some elements of caste within it, insofar as the entry of an individual in the middle class is facilitated by the collective political and economic resources of his/her caste. For example, upper-caste individuals entering the middle class have at their disposal the resources that were attached to the status of their caste in the traditional hierarchy. Similarly, for lower-caste members lacking in traditional status resources, entry into the 'middle class' is facilitated by modern-legal provisions like affirmative action to which they are entitled by virtue of their low traditional status. It seems the Indian 'middle class' will continue to carry caste elements within it, to the extent that modern status aspirations are pursued, and the possibility of their realisation is seen by individuals in terms of the castes to which they belong.

Yet, crucial to the formation of the 'new middle class' is the fact that while using the collective resources of their castes, individuals from all castes entering it undergo the process of *classisation*; this means they (a) become distant from ritual roles and functions attached to their caste; (b) acquire another, but new, identity of belonging to the 'middle class'; and (c) have economic interests and lifestyles which converge more with other members of the 'middle class' than with their own 'non-middle-class' caste compatriots.

The process of middle-class formation in India is empirically illustrated by the findings of an all-India sample survey. The survey, based on a stratified-random sample (probability proportionate to size) of 9,614 Indian citizens (male and female) drawn from all the Indian states, except the state of Jammu and Kashmir, was conducted by the Centre for the Study of Developing Societies, Delhi, in June–July 1996. For lack of space and due to the preliminary nature of the analysis, I provide below a broad profile of the 'new middle class'.

The middle class, which at the time of independence almost exclusively consisted of English-educated members of the upper castes, expanded to include the upwardly mobile dominant castes of rich farmers during the initial three decades after independence. In other words, this period saw the emergence of a small rural-based middle class.

The survey conceived the category middle class in terms of *subjective* and *objective* variables. The subjective variable pertained to the respondent's own identification as 'middle class' and an explicit rejection of a 'working-class' identity for himself/herself. Using self-identity as a precondition, certain objective criteria were applied for inclusion of a respondent in the category 'middle class'. Thus, from among those with middle-class self-identification, respondents possessing two of the following four characteristics were included in the category 'middle class': (a) ten years or more of schooling; (b) ownership of at least three assets out of four— motor vehicle, TV, electric pumpset and non-agricultural land; (c) residence in a *pucca* house—built of brick and cement; and (d) white-collar job. Accordingly, 20 per cent of the sample population was identified as belonging to the middle class.

The survey analysis revealed that even today, the upper and the rich farmer castes together dominate the Indian 'middle class'. While members of the two 'upper' categories, the *dwija* upper castes and the non-*dwija* dominant castes, account for about a quarter of the sample population, they constitute nearly half of the new middle class. But this also means the percentage representation of upper castes has reduced in today's middle class, for the old middle class was almost entirely constituted of them.

About half of the middle-class population came from different lower-caste social formations—the *dalits* (SCs), the tribals (STs), the backward communities of peasants and artisans (OBCs) and the religious minorities. Considering that members of all these social formations constituted 75 per cent of the sample population, their 50 per cent representation in the middle class is much lower than that of the upper and intermediate castes. But seen in the context of their inherited lower ritual status in the traditional hierarchy, this is a significant development. Even more significant is the fact that when members of the lower castes, including those belonging to castes of 'ex-untouchables', acquire modern means of social mobility such as education, wealth and political power, their low ritual status does not come in the way of their entering the 'middle class' and, more importantly, acquiring the *consciousness* of being members of the 'middle class'.

The analysis of the survey data also revealed statistically highly significant differences in political attitudes and preferences between members of the middle class and the rest of the population. More importantly, on certain crucial political variables (like support to a political party) and cultural variables (for example, belief in the *karma* theory), the difference between the lower-caste and upper-caste members of the middle class was found to be much *less* than that between members of the 'middle class' and their caste compatriots not belonging to the 'middle class'.

The Indian middle class today has a fairly large rural component, thanks to the earlier inclusion in it of the rural-based dominant castes, and now of members of the lower castes participating in modern economy and administration. In brief, the 'middle class' in India today is not a simple demographic category comprising certain ritual-status groups. It is a social-cultural formation in which, as individuals from different castes and communities enter, they acquire new economic and political interests and lifestyles in common with other members of that 'class'. Within this 'new' middle class, the caste identities of its members survive; however, operating in conjunction with the new, overarching identity of 'middle class', they acquire a different political and cultural meaning.

To conclude, secularisation of caste, occurring along the dimensions of de-ritualisation, politicisation and classisation, has reduced caste to a kinship-based micro-community, with its members acquiring new structural locations and identities derived from categories of stratification premised on a different set of principles than those of ritual hierarchy. By forming themselves into larger, horizontal, not vertically hierarchical, social groups, members of different castes now increasingly compete for entry to the 'middle class'. The result is that members of the lower castes have entered the middle class in sizeable numbers. This has begun to change the character and composition of the old, pre-independence middle class, which was constituted almost entirely by a small, English-educated, upper-caste elite. The new and vastly enlarged middle class is becoming, even if slowly, politically and culturally more unified and socially diversified.

Notes

1. For a detailed discussion on changes in caste under British rule in India and the impact the colonial policies had on the caste system, see Galanter (1984: 18–40) and Ghurye (1962: 270–305).
2. Collective self-awareness among the lower castes as *a people*, oppressed socially and economically by the ritually high-ranking castes, developed and found organisational articulation through their participation in anti-Brahmin movements which grew in the early decades of the 20th century. See Omvedt (1976); see also Irshick (1969).
3. Galanter sees this development during the colonial rule as having brought about some important changes in the caste system: 'Caste organisation brought with it two important and related changes in the nature of castes. The salient groups grew in size from endogamous *jatis* into region-wise alliances. Concomitantly, the traditional patterns of organisation and leadership in the village setting were displaced by voluntary associations with officials whose delimited authority derived from elections' (Galanter 1984: 23).
4. For a recent argument articulating a contrary position emphasising that the caste system has, even in the face of such changes, maintained systemic continuity, see Shah and Desai (1988: 92–133). Shah sees horizontal divisions as intrinsic to the caste system itself, representing another principle of caste organisation which has always operated in juxtaposition with 'hierarchy'. The horizontal divisions in caste, in his view, are thus produced and reproduced as part of the continuous process *within* the system, a kind of change that a

system undergoes for its own survival and maintenance. Whereas for his interlocutor in the debate I.P. Desai, the horizontal divisions which are prior to caste but were integrated in the *system* of castes by the principle of ritual hierarchy, are now breaking away from that hierarchy and interact in horizontal social and political spaces. In this sense, for Desai, horizontal divisions represent a new principle for the emerging stratificatory system which has undermined the caste principle of ritual hierarchy (see ibid.: 40–49).

5. For an illuminating discussion on the changed relationship between ritual status and occupation and its implications for the emergence of a new type of stratificatory system in India, see Desai (1984).

6. Of late, such recognition of systemic changes in caste has been reflected in the mainstream sociological writings. For example, M.N. Srinivas characterised the changes that have occurred in the caste system as *systemic* in nature: 'As long as the mode of production at the village was caste-based, denunciation of equality from saints and reformers, or from those professing other faiths proved ineffective. It was only when, along with ideological attacks on caste, education and employment were made accessible to all, and urbanisation and industrialisation spread, that *systemic changes* occurred in caste' (italics mine) (Srinivas 1996: xiv).

7. For an overview of comprehensive, systemic changes that have occurred in local hierarchies of castes in rural areas, see Karanth (1996). In his concluding remarks to the essay Karanth observes: 'In the first place, it may not be appropriate any more to refer to caste in rural India as a "system". Castes exist as individual groups, but no longer integrated into a system, with the dovetailing of their interests' (ibid.: 106).

8. The writings and politics of Ram Manohar Lohia, a renowned socialist leader, however constituted an exception to this approach of the left parties to political mobilisation. In his view, horizontal mobilisation of lower castes on issues of social justice had greater political potential for organising the poor and deprived populations of India than the ideology of class polarisation which lacked an empirical, social basis for mobilisational politics. See Lohia (1964). Also see Sheth (1996a, 1996b).

9. The concept 'politicisation of castes' was first used by Rajni Kothari in the early 1970s, to describe changes that had occurred in the caste system with its involvement in democratic politics. See Kothari (1970: 3–25).

10. Rajni Kothari in his pioneering work on the Congress party saw this aspect of Congress politics – the party expanding its social base through management of caste-based political factions regionally and

seeking consensus on issues of development and modernisation
nationally—as crucial to the Congress party's prolonged political
and electoral dominance. See Kothari (1964, 1989: 36–58).

References

Béteille, André. 1996. 'Varna and Jati', *Sociological Bulletin*, Vol. 45, No. 1,
March 1996, pp. 15–27.
Cohn, Bernard S. 1987. *An Anthropologist Among the Historians and Other
Essays*. New Delhi: Oxford University Press.
Desai, I.P. 1984. 'Should "Caste" be the Basis for Recognising Back-
wardness?' *Economic and Political Weekly*, Vol. 19, No. 28, pp. 1106–16,
28 July 1984.
Galanter, Marc. 1984. *Competing Equalities: Law and Backward Classes in
India*. New Delhi: Oxford University Press.
Ghurye, G.S. 1962. *Caste and Race in India*. Mumbai: Popular Prakashan.
Irshick, Eugene F. 1969. *Politics and Social Conflict in South India: The Non-
Brahman Movements and Tamil Separatism 1916–1929*. Berkeley: Uni-
versity of California Press.
Karanth, G.K. 1996. 'Caste in Contemporary Rural India', in M.N. Srinivas,
ed., *Caste: Its Twentieth Century Avatar*, pp. 87–109. New York: Viking.
Kothari, Rajni. 1970. *Caste in Indian Politics*. New Delhi: Orient Longman.
——. 1964. 'The "Congress System" in India', *Asian Survey*, Vol. 4, No. 12,
December 1964, pp. 1161–73.
——. 1989. *Politics and People: In Search of Humane India*, Vol. 1. Delhi:
Ajanta Publishers.
Lohia, Ram Manohar. 1964. *The Caste System*. Hyderabad: Ram Manohar
Lohia Vidyalaya Nyas.
Omvedt, Gail. 1976. *Cultural Revolt in a Colonial Society: The Non-Brahman
Movements in Western India – 1873 to 1930*. Mumbai: Scientific Socialist
Education Trust.
Shah, A.M., and I.P. Desai. 1988. *Division and Hierarchy: An Overview of
Caste in Gujarat*. Delhi: Hindustan Publishing Corporation.
Sheth, D.L. 1996a. 'Ram Manohar Lohia on Caste in Indian Politics',
Lokayan Bulletin, Vol. 12, No. 4, January–February 1996, pp. 31–40.
——. 1996b. 'Ram Manohar Lohia on Caste, Class and Gender in Indian
Politics', *Lokayan Bulletin*, Vol. 13, No. 2, September–October 1996,
pp. 1–15.
Srinivas, M.N. 1962. *Caste in Modern India and Other Essays*. Mumbai:
Asia Publishing House.
—— (ed.). 1996. *Caste: Its Twentienth Centry Avatar*. New Delhi: Viking.

thirteen

Transitions and Reorientations: On the Women's Movement in India

Seemanthini Niranjana

any attempt to map the recent changes in the political and eco-nomic fabric of Indian society, and to examine their imprint on the gender question, will necessarily be an incomplete one. This is because the transitions have not been mere linear move-ments from one point to another, but have involved an interming-ling of several levels — of local issues getting catapulted onto the national scene and international developments coming to affect what have been until recently supremely local matters. The gender question has assumed a rather complex shape within such a context, intersecting with caste, class, regional and religious con-siderations. The proliferation of such differences over the last two decades, as indeed the escalation of tensions between them, has only served to complicate the terms on which women and the conditions of their empowerment can be understood today.

Given the diversity of women's groups in existence and the range of issues they have been taking up, it may be useful and necessary to place the 'gender question' within a larger perspective. Providing a description of the development of the women's movement in India, of the shifts in concerns and strategies that it has undergone, and of the current plurality of perspectives that prevails, would be a part of this exercise. At the same time, it would also be timely to reflect on two issues that tell us something about the political and cultural spaces occupied by the women's movement: one, the relationship between the women's movement and the democratic state, especially how feminism has engaged with the issue of rights through the legal domain (also important here will be the question of women and politics); and two, how the Indian women's movement has engaged with the question of (Indian) culture — how the criticism of the Western origins of feminism has been tackled, whether alternative conceptual strategies have been envisaged, and so on. Tracing some of these contours will familiarise us with the modes in which feminism entangles with citizenship debates and with identity politics of specific kinds, although these are questions I do not directly engage with in this chapter. The attempt here is more to map a trajectory than to elicit an extant formulation.

The Women's Movement in India

No linear narrative of the 'gains' of the women's movement can do justice to the diversity of ideological positions articulated within it. Far from presenting a homogeneous front, the women's movement in India has diversely debated the working and effects of patriarchal oppression, the strategies needed to deal with it and the kind of mobilisation (or mass support base) that it must seek. While the kind of ideology espoused — liberal, socialist, radical, Marxist or Gandhian — would offer a convenient way of distinguishing between different sorts of women's groups, the support base they command has also been a pertinent factor. Even as the issues raised by women's groups have not been any less important, the relatively narrow urban middle-class base of their activism has been questioned. In contrast, the economic hardship of rural women is valorised, as is the latter's attempt to link up with wider ecological, peasant and other social concerns. Though neither of these alignments exhausts the possibilities of women's political activism, they do provide an indication of the heterogeneity it has come to embody.

Assessing the continuities and disjunctures of the gender question in India necessarily involves a reference to its historical and temporal dimensions. The continuous flux characterising the material and socio-cultural patterns of our society has made the context of modernity crucial in any attempt to understand the women's question. A blind adoption of the tradition–modernity framework to explain social change would, however, fail to account for the complexity of the different modes in which women and their lives are defined, affected and refashioned by social change. The process of modernisation has itself been a complex rather than a unidirectional one, often linked to larger social, religious and political movements that seek to effect transformations in material as well as ideological realms. Attempts at framing the women's question cannot be examined, as Sangari and Vaid (1989: 2) recall, independently of 'questions about the politics of social change'; questions which have redefined the relations between patriarchy, cultural practices, social values and political economy. The framing of the question, therefore, has been different at different temporal junctures, reflecting decisive shifts in concerns and contexts. Yet, it also reveals an underlying continuity when viewed in a larger perspective, since these diverse modes of articulating the women's question are all, in a fundamental sense, responding to the manifestations and effects of modernity.

It has been customary to trace the historical growth of the women's question in India to the 19th century (Mazumdar 1985). During this period, both the social reform movement and the nationalist movement were consolidating their bases and attempting to address problems regarding the position of women in 'modern' India. Women's emancipation was central to the social reform initiatives begun largely by upper-caste, western-educated men. The questions they raised — *sati, kulin* polygamy, widow remarriage — have been recognised as specifically upper-caste evils. At times, reform was symbolic rather than real, attempted through appealing to the *shastras* rather than to changing social circumstances. At other times, female education was seen as an important lever with which to effect changes. This 19th-century crusade for *stree-swadhinata*, however, worked within the limits of the reigning patriarchal ideology (Sarkar 1985). The period of the nationalist movement too is significant on several counts. It is often pointed out that in the years of Gandhi's leadership women participated spontaneously in political struggle (for instance, in the civil disobedience movement). Nevertheless, one finds that an ideology of the private as women's space and, indeed, of the sanctity of this sphere, seems to have become entrenched. Although Gandhi himself indicated the radical political stances that women could and needed to take within the familial context, it remains doubtful whether these translated into visible political acts that altered the very structure of these spaces. Chatterjee (1989) has argued that the nationalist movement offers a revealing picture in this regard — on the one hand, it helped chart the social and moral boundaries of/for women by focusing on the 'feminine' as an embodiment of the 'spiritual values' or 'essence' of India; but, on the other hand, by positing that India was materially and not spiritually subjugated by the West, it depoliticised and 'resolved' the women's question. This resolution evokes interest since the women's question, as it surfaced again in the post-independence era, has been marked by a distinct change in its tone and concerns.

In fact, in the period immediately after independence, with the constitutional adoption of the equality principle, the urgency of the women's question seemed to diminish, and as Mazumdar (1985: 4) has remarked, 'for all practical purposes, the women's question disappeared from the public arena for . . . over twenty years.' This was in spite of the fact that the trends of modernisation and social change were generating new questions regarding the role of women in society. Perusing the reasons for such a non-perspective on women, commentators have highlighted '. . . the national consensus to keep the women's question out of the sphere of political controversy, projecting it as a purely social issue of long-term changes in attitudes through education and development' (Mazumdar and Sharma 1979: 115). However, from the mid-1960s onwards, the dormant women's question was resuscitated, and began to configure wider socio-political movements. This was also a time when poverty and unemployment were widespread, especially because planned development (in both the industrial and agricultural sectors) had generated a number of contradictions of its own. Increasingly marginalised and rendered powerless, women registered their protest by figuring prominently in movements like the anti-price-rise agitation in Mumbai/Gujarat (1972–75) and the Bodhgaya peasant struggle for land in the early 1970s. Each of these wider junctures seems to have prompted an analysis of women's oppression, giving rise in turn to more focused demands and agitational strategies; for instance, the demand that women be given land rights in their own names (see Sen 1990).

The ferment on the socio-economic front reached a flashpoint by the 1970s, spurred on by various political crises as well. Several movements emerged — for instance, the Chipko movement — as a challenge to the developmental policies and misplaced priorities of the Indian state. There was also the larger issue of workers' demands within which women's economic rights figured. The emergence of the Self-employed Women's Association (SEWA) in 1972 is often cited as an important development of that decade. While the left and other forces in the country drew attention to the failure of the Indian state in effectively delivering its developmental promises, the realisation also grew that the granting of rights to women in the economic, political and educational fields had hardly any beneficial consequences (Desai and Patel 1985: 992–95). A major landmark was the Committee on the Status of Women in India, which sought to investigate the extent to which constitutional and legal provisions had affected women's status, employment patterns and education over the decades, and to suggest alternative measures wherever required. The mass of data published in the Committee's Report (GoI 1974) revealed a substantial erosion of women's position in India, evidenced by the declining sex ratio, decline in work participation due to labour displacement, as well as an increase in female illiteracy. Against this background, a national debate on the women's question was revived, and an attempt made to scrutinise existing conceptual-methodological frameworks, as part of an effort to generate new data on women which could assist in implementing developmental policies and programmes. An increase in the number of scholarly studies on women — indeed, the very emergence of women's studies as a discipline — must also be viewed against this backdrop.

In addition to all this, the 1970s also saw the emergence of an 'autonomous' or independent women's movement, with an expanding base in urban India. The different levels at which the gender question was being raised yielded a multifaceted analysis of women's oppression, especially of the caste and class basis of oppression. Women's groups across the country began a concerted campaign against a number of important issues, in particular custodial rape and dowry deaths. In many ways, it was these campaigns that provided a new visibility to the autonomous women's movement in the country. Nationwide protests were organised around specific incidents like the Mathura Rape Case (1978) and the Maya Tyagi Case (1980); issue-based groups were formed, like the Forum Against Rape (now called the Forum Against Oppression of Women) in Mumbai in 1981. Besides agitating against the practice of dowry, urban women's groups also began to take up related issues like alcoholism, spouse abuse and sexual harassment. While seeking to create an awareness about these issues, they also sought to develop alternative structures of support for women trapped in abusive circumstances. Legal aid and counselling, consequently, were very much a part of their organisation strategy.

Though the proliferation of women's groups in urban areas was very much a phenomenon of the 1980s, a common charge was that these groups remained cut off from the masses in India. From here, the slippage into arguing that their feminism was Western-inspired has been a routine one, a debate that we will return to in the final section. The entry of non-governmental organisations in a big way and the professionalisation of activism, especially in the late 1980s and early 1990s, added to the emerging scenario. To be sure, wider developments in Indian politics and society (especially the rise of communalism, caste conflicts and religious revivalism of various hues) have imposed a certain disarray upon the women's movement. While feminist responses to the Muslim Women's Bill (1986) and the *sati* incident in Deorala in 1987 brought out the ways in which recent socio-religious developments had foisted a certain inactivity or 'stillness' upon the women's movement (Gandhi and Shah 1992), they also provided a context for invaluable discussion on the prospects of a uniform civil code and the implications of the rise of the Hindu right wing. The appropriation of feminist discourses by mainstream political parties and the media, and the gloss they have spun over images like female power (*stree shakti*) and the new, liberated woman, are matters of concern as well. Similarly, the ways in which emergent identities such as those of caste, region and religion have served to undercut a wider gender identity have had to be engaged with, in both theoretical and practical terms.

In spite of these lines of fragmentation, women's groups have continued to raise a concerted voice against different forms of violence against women; issues like women's health, the negative effects of certain family planning measures targeting women, women's work, wages and employment conditions, and women's legal rights and legal reform have figured prominently. The women's movement in the 1990s has been more or less forced to confront:

> . . . shifts in the locus of control over resources and find new strategic points of intervention implied by the decentralisation process, liberalisation and increasing integration into the global economy, increasing reliance on market mechanism and the growth of non-governmental conflicts between different women will also need to be addressed, in a climate of rising caste and communal tensions and increasing socio-economic inequality (John and Lalitha 1995: 137).

The State and the Women's Movement

The mutual relationships among the various women's groups, and between these and the women's wings of different political parties, are an important dimension of plural feminist politics in India. Equally significant has been the relationship between women's groups (or, more tidily, the women's movement) and the state, which, instead of representing a clear-cut alliance, has been characterised by a shifting ground of strategies. Over the decades, however, what has continued is the ambivalence marking this relation; the women's movement has been both antagonistic towards the state and demanding of it (for instance, through clamour for legal reform) — valences that cannot be captured within a simple 'for' or 'against' rhetoric.

In the initial years, the women's movement directed its actions towards the government, concentrating on transforming state policies, be it in the areas of law, health or employment (to name a few). The mobilisations around issues of rape, dowry and amniocentesis not only compelled the state to take cognisance of women's issues, but also led to the state often consulting women's groups while formulating policies on a range of issues. Yet, rarely did this translate into a gender-sensitive state, for its entire machinery (the bureaucracy included) and state-backed processes (like the developmental and legal processes) continued to be gender-resistant. The scene has changed somewhat with economic liberalisation (structural readjustment and its socio-political consequences) in the 1990s. Not only the role of welfare, but also the expansion of social activism through non-governmental organisations and increased international funding for such activities, has transformed women's groups and rendered them even more diverse. The state itself, to be sure, has not been a mono-lithic structure, but has been a site within which different groups have lobbied for power; how women's groups *strategise* vis-à-vis the state has, consequently, remained a major issue. Apparently in response to the women's movement, the state has enacted pro-women legislation, even attempting female empowerment by providing women spaces within the political arena. The possible repercussions of the recent move towards political decentral-isation, which has opened up a phenomenal space for rural women within the political structures of the state, have yet to be fully understood. None of these recent developments has been easy to conceptualise, given their seemingly contradictory pulls.

For one, though the state and its functioning have been increas-ingly subject to widespread scepticism, it has also managed to extend its reach in new ways; in fact, the involvement of the state in female empowerment—howsoever problematic—is an indi-cation of this. In like fashion, though the women's movement has often manifested a contestatory relationship with the state, women have also sought to redefine their lives using the spaces provided by it. It would be necessary, in this context, to also reflect upon the plural sites of women's mobilisation. At one level would be expressions of women's agency within the space of civil society. At another level are their struggles for equality within the frame-work of the democratic state itself, a struggle alongside other groups for better access to resources. Reflecting on the possible links, or even breaks, between the two spaces would perhaps help us grasp the nuances within women's mobilisation for change. Without aspiring to offer any definitive conceptualisation of these processes, we could briefly refer here to two arenas emblematic of the new interface between the state and women, namely, the

legal domain and the issue of legislative reform, and political reservation for women in local-level institutions.

The Legal Domain and Women

Legal reform has been a major avenue through which feminists in
India have sought to achieve the goal of gender equality. Insofar
as the state is closely tied to the legal domain, feminist demands
for legal reform have been necessarily directed at the state. In the
liberal discourse on equality and rights that has constituted the
basis of the women's movement, the state is at times cast as a protector of women's rights. Indeed, the legal domain is perceived as
the site through which gender inequality in society is challenged
and conventional notions about women and their roles questioned.
Legal reform is aimed at securing (and protecting) the rights of
women (for instance, in property or at the workplace), as well as
clamping down on discriminatory practices and preventing crimes
against women (for example, *sati*, rape and dowry). While all this
is true on a theoretical plane, it is also widely recognised today
that, despite the granting of formal equal rights to women, substantive inequality continues to pervade our daily lives (Kapur
and Cossman 1996). This contradictory scenario has provoked
considerable debate on the role of law in social transformation,
especially with reference to gender issues.

There are some who take a demystificatory view of law, characterising it as a tool of patriarchal oppression. The working of the
legal system, the conduct and practices of the law-enforcers, the
gender biases built into courtroom practices and legal interpretations, all reflect its patriarchal underpinnings. It is implicitly
suggested that an excessive reliance on the law for ushering in
gender equality would be unrealistic and misplaced if wider
exploitative structures are not tackled simultaneously. The more
common view adhered to by a broad spectrum of (liberal) feminists
has been that the law can play a positive and vital role in achieving
a gender-just society. This argument often begins by positing a
genderless citizen bearing equal rights in all fields of life, thereby
suggesting that gender difference should be largely irrelevant to
the law. Yet, there are several steps to be taken before this can be
achieved.

Since women's oppression is understood as being a result of discriminatory treatment, much effort has been directed at the elimination of such discrimination and the provision of equal opportunities for women and men. The bulk of early feminist struggles within the legal domain can be described in these terms. The failure to achieve gender equality was often attributed to disinterest or faulty implementation of existing legal principles or, at times, even to a lack of awareness of legal rights on the part of women themselves. The experiences of women's groups in dealing with the law soon revealed, however, that in spite of being an indispensable strategy, law alone was insufficient to engineer fundamental social transformations, especially in gender-oppressive structures.

Recent feminist scholarship has gone a step further and has begun exploring the links between the law and women's struggles from a variety of perspectives. At one level, this has involved a focus on the multiple, shifting bases of oppression and, concomitantly, of resistance. At another level, feminist legal studies (Agnes 1992; Mukhopadhyaya 1998) have also begun attempting to capture the contradictory nature of the law itself, to show how, while granting formal equality to women, legal discourse has itself been constructing women as gendered subjects (as dependent wives or mothers), reiterating ideas of female duty and sexuality and drawing on an entrenched familial ideology. Such analyses have definitely altered the equation between the women's movement and the state, whereby the latter can no longer remain an unproblematic protector of women's rights.

Women and the Political Arena

The space available to women within the Indian political system has hardly been significant, despite the fact that several political rights for women have been enshrined in the constitution itself. It is in the light of this marginalisation of women in the Indian polity that the reservation of one-third of all seats for women at the various levels of local governance marks a significant turning-point. From being hailed as a 'silent revolution' of the 'emerging millions', to being dubbed as political dummies, women's bid to enter formal political institutions in India has generated much comment, interest and resistance. Most assessments of the political status of women have taken into account obvious indicators like the quality and quantity of women's participation in the political process. External indices, such as women's voting behaviour, and whether they are represented in political parties, are electoral candidates and/or hold public offices, have been often reviewed in discussions of the political empowerment of women. One needs to look beyond numbers, however, to explain possible barriers to women's political participation. Entrenched ideas that politics is the world of men and that women's role is confined to the domestic domain serve to back up myths about women in politics, without addressing or problematising what is at the heart of politics, namely, power. That politics is not simply a struggle for power alone, but about the power to change, is not always recognised, restricting, consequently, the very space of the political to public institutions. In relating women to political processes, then, a widened definition of political spaces would yield a much more fruitful analysis. Such a broad canvas would include observations about women's representation in formal political (governing) bodies, their role in decision-making and the positions they hold, as well as their wider participation in struggles and movements of various kinds outside the formal arena. Our understanding of women's empowerment should be based on the articulation of women's agency at these different levels. Empowerment is not just about individual transformation, but also about changes in unequal institutional arrangements and about changes in access to and control over resources of various kinds.

The terrain of democratic politics offers an important context within which to examine a significant part of this process. While there is a fair amount of consensus on the meaning of democracy itself, *governance* within democracies has been a difficult question to tackle, given the conflicting interests and power lobbies at work. How, and to what extent, the interests of marginalised groups in society come to be voiced has been a constant concern, and has foregrounded representation as a key process in democratic politics. The provision of quota reservations for various disprivileged groups at different levels of governance is meant precisely to achieve a wider representation of the needs and interests of these groups. Yet, most discussions on political processes dwell on the question of reservations per se, rather than examining the axis of representation. It appears that the figure of the political representative and the act of representation need to be understood more deeply than they have been till now, especially when we speak of women's participation in governing bodies.

Though it can be argued that the ideal role of the political representative is to convey without distortion the interests of those represented, the actual process is much more complicated. The political representative has a doubly important role to play in contexts/countries where severe socio-economic deprivation has eroded the social identity of the masses (and consequently their ability to articulate their felt needs in a coherent fashion). S/he may be required to fashion and shape fragmented identities and local interests by couching them in a general (universal) language. To be more explicit, the representative is not just representing a pre-existing collective interest; indeed, there may often be no such well-articulated entity. Rather, the representative inserts an inchoate demand into political discourse such that it gets inscribed as an interest, in the process transforming the represented into identifiable political subjects. As the political theorist Laclau underlines, the task of the representative is a central and constitutive one 'of providing the marginalised masses with a language out of which it becomes possible for them to reconstitute a political identity and a political will'.

Reflecting on the representative–represented relationship becomes all the more relevant given women's marginalisation from politics and the recent endeavour by the state to create political spaces for them. In contrast to peasants, dalits or backward classes, women have rarely been considered a well-formed interest group. Part of the problem is that given the dispersal of identities across caste, religion and other axes, gender alone has rarely been the sole rallying point for women. Whether political reservations alone would be sufficient to transform them into political actors with clear-cut interests remains a doubtful matter. Under such conditions, it is necessary to ask whom the female representative is representing—other women, those of her caste/religion, or the entire community? The woman political representative has a demanding task before her, especially in the first case, that of having to play a major role in the very formation of women as a collective interest group. In the process, she also comes to institute her own political agency and mediate in the agency of those whom she represents. Hitherto unmarked or assumed as unproblematic in political debate, this relation between the representative and the represented could assist in understanding and conceptualising the process of women's politicisation. It also highlights the manner in which the wider concerns of civil society are translated into 'interests' in the political arena, largely through the mediation of the political representative.

The bid to involve women in the governing of local political bodies assumes significance against this background. Part of a wider move towards political decentralisation, the promotion of panchayati raj institutions over the last few years has sought to ensure adequate, active and extensive participation of people in local bodies by providing quota reservations for various disprivileged groups. The use of the system of reservations as a tool of positive discrimination against centuries of neglect, deprivation and particularly caste oppression is not new to India. While the provision has certainly re-scripted the scenarios of caste and identity politics, reservations for women in politics is a comparatively newer issue. The basic argument, however, remains the same; that these measures are 'historical correctives' seeking to undo and alter the older discriminatory structures by ensuring that resources/benefits are distributed equally. One could thus legitimately justify reservation for women on the grounds of their gross under-representation until now in political bodies, which has led to their alienation from the political process itself.

The quota system not only envisages an improvement in the socio-economic and political status of women, but is also an attempt to ensure fair representation to women's viewpoints and concerns in political, developmental and decision-making forums. A number of doubts have been raised, however, about the move towards reservations, ranging from the argument that fixed reservations would ghettoise women in politics, to the fear that women representatives would become mere dummies in the hands of vested interests. Jostling with these doubts is also the expectation that the presence of women will cleanse the political arena of corruption and usher in a different system of governance. The assumption here is that women are intrinsically altruistic, selfless and caring, and that these non-competitive values could help them articulate a new political ethos. This expectation appears to be a trifle misplaced, not only in essentialising certain so-called female qualities, but also in unrealistically placing women outside the prevailing political environment. Rather than proceeding along these lines, moot issues in examining women in politics are whether the priorities being articulated by women are of a different sort, whether resources are being managed more effectively, and how far this could go in improving the quality of life of the communities concerned. A related question that needs to be explored, as highlighted earlier, is the extent to which women have begun to emerge as an interest group with well-articulated political demands.

The point of these two considerations — of women in relation to the legal as well as political domains — has been to demonstrate the tangled links between the state and women. While the legislative domain presents a highly contradictory scenario that has resisted being forced into rigid analytical frameworks, the government's move to bring women into governance threatens to upset conventional understandings of power and its exercise. These are issues very much at the forefront of the women's struggle and reflect their strategic and fluid relation to the state, a relation that can no longer be simplistically described in terms of either co-option or contestation alone. It also serves to foreground vital questions about the empowerment of women within democratic spaces, while drawing attention to numerous other sites of politics that intersect with this process. In other words, the dispersed assertions of women's agency have demanded that we reconsider the divide between state and civil society as markers of the ground of politics. With several struggles for transformation taking place outside or beyond it, the state no longer remains the sole locus of political activity. Civil society often becomes the context in which specific social identities (say, dalit or feminist) are formed and struggles waged. There is, undoubtedly, a clear intermingling of these with the political identity (of citizenship, or political office) conferred by the state. These intricately linked scenarios suggest that women's political agency cannot be confined to a formal political frame, cutting as they do a wide swathe across the state and civil society.

A Question of Culture

Feminism, as a universal movement for women's rights, has been wont to assume a universality of gender oppression and has tended to project a 'universal sisterhood' of women united against exploitation. Yet, as a deeper scrutiny of the international women's movement would reveal, there are several lines of difference that separate women from one another—be it race, nationality, religion, class, caste or ethnic group. It is necessary, therefore, to understand the nature of these differences, to see feminism as a movement rooted in a specific national history. Disentangling the relationships and tensions between the national and the international is no easy task, for it brings us up squarely against the question of culture, or cultural difference.

One of the most frequent questions that feminists in India have been confronted with is about the so-called Western origins of feminism itself. Though the women's movement has had a firm grounding in substantive and empirical realities, it has, from time to time, been castigated for its largely urban, middle-class base and for bringing in 'alien' ideas of women's liberation. While struggling against this characterisation, feminists have also found it necessary to review analytical frameworks, since Western theories have diverged considerably from non-Western contexts. Formulating a theory of gender in the contemporary Indian world has not been an easy task (see Tharu and Niranjana 1994), especially with the new socio-political alignments that feminists have had to contend with. Retrospectively speaking, the Indian feminist movement in the 1970s and 1980s had a clearly marked-out agenda. Attempts were made to highlight asymmetries in gender relations, be it the vulnerability of women workers, sexual harassment or inequities in women's access to health care or development opportunities. Working with the concept of women's rights, demands were made on the legal system to be more sensitive to gender disparities. That clarity of purpose and homogeneous agenda no longer obtains today. The 1990s has been witness to the rise of several new forces such as fundamentalism, economic liberalisation, communalism and casteism. It has become necessary for Indian feminism to define itself anew in the face of these developments, a task rendered all the more difficult due to the different kinds of identity politics in which religious, caste and economic groups have been engaging. Equally problematic has been the manner in which the women's question has acquired visibility (and even acceptability) today. From the media to the political right, we find an appropriation of what was once the critical vocabulary of feminists, forcing the latter to recast their strategies and concepts. The moot question, however, remains: what resources do we draw upon? Though this dilemma is often reduced to one of recognising a mismatch between Western theoretical frameworks and our realities, and doing something about it (such as formulating alternative analyses), the real problem remains one of how to engage with the notion of Indian culture itself. What really do we mean by this catch-all term? Is the idea of an indigenous culture quite as unproblematic as the idea of Western culture is problematic?

These have increasingly become paralysing questions for Indian feminists. Attempts to highlight the uniqueness of the Indian women's movement have involved not just underlining regional or historical specificities, but also focusing on cultural difference, especially on the divergent modes of cultural expression in modern India. This is being done in different ways, ranging from a rejection of everything Western to a more strategic and selective engagement with Indian tradition itself. An extreme position is that of Kishwar (1991), who disavows the label 'feminist' in a bid to detach it from its Western origins and thereby engage with local women's issues on their own terms. While there can be no disputing the need to question the universalism implicit in the term 'feminist', one is left wondering about the curious lack of criticality regarding our own Indianness/tradition. Undoubtedly, to articulate the difference a culture makes is also to entangle with tradition, invented as it may be. It is here that feminists have run up against a conundrum—of how to critique oppressive traditional structures while at the same time drawing out the strengths they may have; and of how to achieve the latter without lapsing into a celebration of the 'power' of Indian women.

The very charge that feminism is a movement inspired by the West seems a misplaced one, rather like suggesting that notions like secularism or even democracy are alien to us. It also fails to take seriously the historicity and richness of the women's movement in India. If feminism is all about women struggling to change oppressive institutional structures, then its form and agenda will clearly be dictated by the unique historical circumstances in which every nation is placed. Feminism in each country will bear the stamp of the cultural, economic and religious forces at work there. Yet, because of the dominant and widespread tendency in India to project women as custodians of cultural values, or to project feminine images as a trope for Indian culture (and even nation), it has become difficult to critique the elements of that very culture that are oppressive towards women. In doing so, one is immediately exposed to the charge of Western influence and of going against 'our' culture. Given the closures this institutes, we could shift the debate a bit and argue for the need to begin conceptualising aspects of Indian culture itself—a task that will enable an understanding of cultural differences as well. It will also help in re-inflecting general concepts like gender inequality, patriarchy or power by grounding them in the actual working of such structures in specific contexts. Political struggle is clearly an inseparable part of this conceptual reworking. A more comprehensive grasp of the transitions undergone by the women's movement in India would become possible when emergent feminist initiatives in reorienting both political strategies and conceptual frameworks are more closely examined.

References

Agnes, F. 1992. *Give Us This Day Our Daily Bread: Procedures and Case Law on Maintenance*. Mumbai: Majlis.

Chatterjee, P. 1989. 'On the Nationalist Resolution of the Women's Question', in Kumkum Sangari and Sudesh Vaid, eds, *Recasting Women*. New Delhi: Kali for Women.

Desai, N., and V. Patel. 1985. *Indian Women*. Mumbai: Popular Prakashan.

Gandhi, N., and N. Shah. 1992. *The Issues at Stake: Theory and Practice in the Contemporary Women's Movement in India*. New Delhi: Kali for Women.

Government of India (GoI). 1974. Towards Equality: Report of the Committee on the Status of Women in India, New Delhi.

John, M.E., and K. Lalitha. 1995. Background Report on Gender Issues in India. Anveshi, Hyderabad, and Overseas Development Administration, UK.

Kapur, R., and B. Cossman. 1996. *Subversive Sites: Feminist Engagements with Law in India*. New Delhi: Sage.

Kishwar, M. 1991. 'Why I Do Not Call Myself a Feminist', *Manushi*, Vol. 61, pp. 2–8.

Mazumdar, V. 1985. 'Emergence of Women's Question in India and the Role of Women's Studies', Occasional Paper 7, Centre for Women's Development Studies, New Delhi.

Mazumdar, V., and K. Sharma. 1979. 'Women's Studies: New Perceptions and Challenges', *Economic and Political Weekly*, Vol. 14, No. 3, 20 January 1979.

Mukhopadhyaya, M. 1998. *Legally Dispossessed – Gender, Identity and the Process of Law*. Calcutta: Stress.

Sangari, K., and S. Vaid (eds). 1989. *Recasting Women*. New Delhi: Kali for Women.

Sarkar, S. 1985. 'The Women's Question in Nineteenth Century Bengal', in K. Sangari and S. Vaid, eds, *Women and Culture*. Mumbai: SNDT.

Sen, I. (ed.). 1990. *A Space Within the Struggle: Women's Participation in People's Movements*. New Delhi: Kali for Women.

Tharu, S., and T. Niranjana. 1994. 'Problems for a Contemporary Theory of Gender', *Social Scientist*, Vol. 22, Nos 3–4, pp. 93–117.

fourteen

Uniform Civil Code and Gender Justice in India

Zoya Hasan

I n the 1990s, religion and gender became intertwined in the political turmoil that currently envelops India. One issue at the centre of this turmoil concerns the question of whether religion-based personal law should be continued or a uniform civil code (UCC) instituted. The UCC, that is, the legal unification of the civil codes of different religious communities, refers to the ideological deployment of uniformity with the double agenda of improving the status of women and of integrating communities through a set of uniform civil laws. At different historical moments, therefore, the UCC has been projected as the most salient emblem of a modern homogeneous nation in contradistinction to that of personal laws which are perceived as a symbol of difference. No other symbol than that of the UCC reconstructs with such force the contention between nation and cultural rights. The state's commitment to a UCC was expressed in the Directive Principles of State Policy in the constitution. But five decades after independence, public opinion still remains sharply divided. Religious personal law in matters of marriage, divorce, maintenance, inheritance and child custody continues to be binding on followers of different communities.

Feminist and other scholars of nationalism in post-colonial societies have drawn attention to the centrality of the 'woman question' in the transition to modernity. In India, the modernising state, in its attempt to undertake a certain form of social transformation that would enable it to weld a nation, formulated laws that would recognise its members as part of the same nation, sharing a common nationality (R. Menon 1998). It would have to grant rights and guarantee equality in an undifferentiated manner to all its citizens. The institution of common laws clearly linked integration to the agenda of modern nationhood. But, as various analyses have shown, the enterprise was confounded from the outset by the dispute over the desirability as well as the feasibility of introducing legal uniformity in a socially stratified and heterogeneous society (see, for example, Parasher 1992; Sangari 1995). In other words, the continuing predicament over the UCC reveals the centrality of the gender question in contemporary critiques of the state. By the same token, increased women's participation and politicisation engendered the formation of a public and collective identity for women which has distanced itself from definitions of separate gender roles within the private and public spheres. Instead, women's groups are focused on gender justice which crosscuts power relations between modernity and tradition, secularism and religion, as well as between men and women and women themselves.

This chapter explores the UCC controversy through an analysis of the changing relationship between state, communities and the women's movement. It is an attempt to unravel some of the strands in the tangled web of interconnection between community identity, nation and gender. Its specific focus is on the role of the state in the promotion of gender-just laws and the various ways in which women's rights have been conceptualised.

State and Community

Until recently, scholarly works have treated gender, religious and community identity as static and unchanging. Those studying identity construction often focus on the social and cultural domain, rather than on the state. Students of the state, on the other hand, are less inclined to examine the processes of identity formation. The debates over the UCC reveal that it is untenable to draw a sharp line of distinction between community and state on the question of religion or gender. This is on account of structural, administrative and ideological linkages between the two (Sangari 1995: 3294–96). Religious communities under discussion have been constituted in relation to the state and, more importantly, by political processes connected to the state. Moreover, successive governments have been involved in the internal affairs of religious communities and in the maintenance of places of worship and other kinds of religious establishments. Thus, the interface between community and the state extends to the sphere of law. This has, consequently, led to a triangular relationship between personal laws, community representatives and the state (Hasan 1994). The state has been asked to protect religious boundaries in two different ways: through the demand for the exemption of minorities from the application of the criminal procedure code made by religious spokesmen, and through the demands for a UCC made by the Hindu communalists.

The demand for a UCC, first aired by the All India Women's Conference in 1937, figured prominently in the nationalist and early feminist agendas in the 1940s and 1950s. Today, however, none of the major women's organisations supports it with the same degree of enthusiasm; in fact, there are serious differences of opinion on the matter. More importantly, the UCC has acquired political salience in part because gender-just laws are conspicuous by their absence, and in part because India's new ruling party, the Bharatiya Janata Party, a right-wing authoritarian formation, has appropriated what was otherwise a feminist demand. The Congress and Left, on the other hand, are opposing the demand for a UCC, though for different reasons.

The contentious issue, one that has engendered controversy, relates to marriage, divorce, maintenance, inheritance and adoption. As is well known, Hindu family laws were changed in 1955–56 through the Hindu Marriage Act, the Hindu Succession Act, the Hindu Minority and Guardianship Act and the Hindu Adoption and Maintenance Act. Yet, there was no attempt to secure a UCC as suggested by the Directive Principles of State

Policy. Still it was argued in different circles that uniformity was essential for national unity. This argument was presented in the Minutes of Dissent submitted by Minoo Masani, Hansa Mehta and Rajkumari Amrit Kaur against the decision to postpone the UCC to the future, through its relegation to the Directive Principles of State Policy. The Minutes of Dissent argued: 'One of the factors that has kept India from advancing to nationhood has been the existence of personal laws based on religion which keeps the nation divided into watertight compartments' (Parasher 1992: 233). Hansa Mehta maintained that a UCC was more important for national unity than a national language. Similarly, the Report of the Committee on the Status of Women in India in 1972 stated that 'the continuance of various personal laws which accepts distinctions between men and women violates fundamental rights, it is also against the spirit of national integration and secularism' (GoI 1972: 142). Likewise, Supreme Court judgements have regularly emphasised the unificatory potential of legal equality. The Supreme Court judgement in the Sarla Mudgal case (1994), for example, said: 'In the Indian Republic, there was to be only one nation—the Indian nation—and no community could claim to remain a separate entity on the basis of religion.'

Though anxious to ensure that religion should not hinder social reform, the advocates of UCC seldom emphasised the reformist potential of the UCC. Set up invariably in terms of secular state versus religious community, the public discourse was largely silent on UCC's significance for women. From the outset the argument was always cast in terms of an opposition between legal integrity and legal pluralism. The case for legal uniformity rests on uniformity as the basis of nationhood, harmony, democracy and individual rights for women,[1] while the case for legal pluralism rests on a presumed antagonism between the religious community and the nation-state, on the right of communities to their own laws and on the presupposition that personal laws are tied up with religious belief.

Underlying the national integrity argument was an assumption that while the secular state has allowed minorities to carry on with their retrogressive personal laws, Hindu laws were changed and the majority community willingly accepted reform. This is a misleading argument for two reasons: Hindu laws were codified and not fully reformed, and this was done in the face of stiff opposition from Congress leaders both inside and outside parliament and from the religious elites. The major groups opposing the legislation were: the conservative hardliners within the Congress party, with leaders like Vallabhbhai Patel, Rajendra Prasad and J.B. Kripalani, who had a completely different worldview from that of Jawaharlal Nehru; Hindu fundamentalists within the Congress, including Deputy Speaker of the Lok Sabha Ananthasayanam Aiyyangar, who opposed attempts by Law Minister B.R. Ambedkar to proceed with the legislation; the Hindu Mahasabha represented by men like Shyama Prasad Mukherjee, N.C. Chatterjee and others who opposed the Bills strongly for threatening the so-called religious foundations of Hindu society and subverting Hindu ideas, culture and religion; the Sikh groups represented by men like Sardar Hukam Singh who resented being clubbed with Hindus in the broad framework of reform; and the Muslim groups led by Naziruddin Ahmed who were clearly encouraged by the conservatives in the Congress to tilt the balance in their favour. Every single clause of the Bill was opposed and the cry of 'religion in danger' was repeatedly raised. The property clauses giving property to daughters were most vehemently opposed, as was the abolition of polygamy. Pandit Thakur Das Bhargava, a strong opponent of the Bill, summed up the opposition when he condemned the Bill as 'equality run mad' (cited in Som 1994).

The storm raised by the Bill took Nehru by surprise. The principle of equal rights between men and women was accepted at the Karachi Congress in 1931 and enshrined in the constitution. The easy acceptance at Karachi of the Fundamental Rights resolution ensuring sex equality, and its subsequent incorporation in the constitution, led Nehru to believe that the Hindu Code Bill could be easily passed. But he realised that while accepting equality on paper, there had been no serious contemplation by his colleagues of what it implied. For Nehru, however, the Hindu Code Bill was a necessary measure which fitted into his overall perspective of national development, for which the uniformity of legal practices was a vital element.

The Hindu Code Bill was considerably watered down as Nehru came to accept that the opposition to the Bill could not be wished away and in its existing form it could never get parliamentary approval. As he explained to B.R. Ambedkar, who resigned as Law Minister because he thought Nehru tended to compromise: 'With the best will in the world we cannot brush aside this opposition and get things done quickly. They have in their power to delay a great deal. We must, therefore, proceed with some tact' (cited in Som 1994). His strategy was to bide time. After the Congress victory in the 1951 elections, Nehru went ahead with the Bill, but the Bill was separated and the Bills were themselves made more acceptable by whittling down the controversial points.

The Hindu Code Bill was by no means an unqualified advance for women's rights. Some provisions clearly discriminated against women (see Kishwar 1994). Women parliamentarians criticised the Bill for not going far enough. Hansa Mehta said that the Succession Bill did not go far enough, as sons were regarded as being more equal than daughters. For instance, in the case of the Hindu Succession Act, there were several compromises: the joint family system was retained; retention of coparcenary, whose membership was restricted to males, meant that sons would not only get a share of their father's property but also their own interest as coparceners in the joint family property; by excluding agricultural land from legislation relating to succession, its benefits were restricted; the unrestricted right of testation—right to make a will—often led daughters to be dependent upon their fathers' goodwill for being provided for life. In view of these limitations, not surprisingly, the Bills were ultimately passed with the total approval of parliament.

Hence 'Nehru's victory was largely symbolic' (Som 1994: 172–73). Nehru himself regarded the Hindu Code Bill as 'a very moderate measure of social reform ... indeed very largely a codification of the existing law'. But he considered the symbolism important since it would be the first major shake-up of the system of Hindu personal law. In the event, he remarked that the passage of the Bill 'constituted the greatest advance of his career' and an 'outstanding achievement of his time'. As he explained later to the chief ministers: 'They are not in any way revolutionary in the changes they bring about and yet there is something revolutionary about them. They have broken the barrier of the ages and cleared the way somewhat for our womenfolk to progress' (ibid.: 178).

Minority Rights and the Constitution

The Congress government was unwilling to press for similar changes in the laws of the minority communities or to legislate a UCC. The question of personal law had come up for debate on several occasions in the Constituent Assembly. Muslim members emphasised the unchanging nature of Muslim personal law and also that it could not be changed by the state. Any changes, they argued, should be initiated by the Islamic community. As this line of reasoning confirmed government suppositions, it was effective. In the process of these negotiations Muslim political leaders represented both Islamic law and their own community as more unified than they actually were or had been. They succeeded in establishing that legal codes and religion were interlinked, and that personal laws formed an integral part of the socio-religious identity of Muslims.

In such a situation, the government refrained from interfering in the regime of personal laws. Jawaharlal Nehru was reluctant because he felt that in the aftermath of partition his government should avoid any step that would offend the religious sensibilities of minorities, especially the Muslims. Instead, he wanted to assuage Muslim anxieties regarding their status in independent India. Nehru said: 'If anybody brings forward a civil code bill, it will have my extreme sympathy. But I confess I do not think the time is ripe in India for me to push through it.' Although he considered a UCC for the whole country essential, Nehru was apprehensive that any imposition on minorities, without their consent, would be imprudent. Hence, the policy of merging religious communities in a single citizenship remained a pious hope enshrined in the Directive Principles of State Policy. But given the changeable nature of cultures, Nehru, the architect of this policy, expected that these provisions and concessions to minorities would themselves be subject to change. He hoped that Muslim communities would, in the fullness of time, respond to the winds of change. Meanwhile he insisted they should have the right to decide the timing of their response.

Nehru's expectations have not been fulfilled. The last fifty years have witnessed little effort towards reform. By contrast, the two decades preceding independence saw considerable reformist activity, albeit of a type which stressed a return to pristine Islam and the need to observe the *Shariat* in everyday life. Nevertheless, there was agreement among reformers, who included a coalition of the ulema, middle-class reformers and westernised politicians, that the status of Muslim women required amelioration (Minault 1998: 139). Often reformers recommended eliminating custom. In some cases they advocated legislative enactments in order to bring personal law closer to the scriptures. But a series of legal changes, which included the Muslim Dissolution of Marriage Act of 1939, led to some improvements in women's rights in the context of family relations (ibid.: 140–42).

After independence, Muslim political leaders were able to hold off the legal advance of women's rights by taking shelter under the special provision for minorities and its overall significance in a multicultural, heterogeneous society. The constitution provides for the religious liberty of both the individual and associations of individuals united by common beliefs, practices and discipline. This has given rise to tensions between two different conceptions of rights, the rights of individuals and the claims of communities. Through special provisions for scheduled castes, scheduled tribes and other backward classes, the constitution introduced the principle of positive discrimination in favour of the poorest and lowest in the social order, especially those excluded from the caste system. The grant of universal equal rights to all was offset by the recognition of injustice suffered by particular groups, especially the scheduled castes, and thereby the recognition that preferential treatment be given in the form of reservations in government jobs and educational institutions for members of these groups (Austin 1966: 50–74).

The implicit recognition in the constitution that religions have both sustained and legitimised caste and gender discrimination led the state to being at once a reformer of injustices based on religion as well as a protector of religious freedom. Hence, the minorities were granted some degree of control over their own affairs, including the right to express their cultural particularity. This took two forms: the inclusion of the freedom of religion in the fundamental rights, and safeguards for minority rights, includ-ing the right to maintain their own educational institutions (Smith 1963: 100–134).

The incorporation of these rights was undoubtedly influenced by the context of partition, when the state endeavoured to gain the trust of Muslim communities that opted to stay in their country of birth. The spectre of Hindu–Muslim communalism hung over the subcontinent when India became independent. The partition meant that Pakistan might become a homeland for Muslims, but India would remain a home for Hindus, Muslims, Christians and others, and though Pakistan was a Muslim state, there were more Muslims in India than in Pakistan. One way of facilitating the integration of minorities was to recognise them as members of religious communities. From the standpoint of universalism and egalitarianism, such group-specific rights were a violation of liberal principles, but in India they were seen not as privileges, but primarily as safeguards against larger majority groupings.

This, however, did lead to a recognition of minority identity in the legal structure of the state. Hence, personal laws, which were often disadvantageous to women, were allowed to function without any reform. While these safeguards are important, no effort has been made to ensure that they are not monopolised by the most conservative elements within the minority. The controversy over the Shah Bano judgement is a case in point.

Community Identity and Women

The turning point in the debate on gender justice was the famous Shah Bano case. The Supreme Court, in a landmark judgement delivered in April 1985, granted a small maintenance allowance to Shah Bano, a 73-year-old divorcee, to be paid by her husband Mohammed Ahmed Khan, under the provisions of the Criminal Procedure Code. Ahmed Khan had argued in an appeal to the Supreme Court that since he had fulfilled his obligations under Muslim personal law by paying her an allowance for three months of the *iddat* period and *meher* as well, he was not bound to maintain her any further. The Supreme Court, however, ruled that criminal laws override personal laws and are applicable to all, including Muslim women. This judgement sparked off a political furore. To soothe ruffled feelings, the Rajiv Gandhi government enacted a legislation, the Muslim Women (Protection of Rights on Divorce) Bill, 1986, to explicitly exclude Muslim women from the purview of the Criminal Procedure Code, to which all citizens otherwise have recourse.

The controversy around the judgement and the public as well as the parliamentary debate tended to focus on the conflict between the right of the religious minority to cultural autonomy and to a separate civil code as an important guarantee of its identity on the one hand, and the claims of the state legitimised through representative institutions to articulate and realise the common good on the other (Jayal 1998: 161). The critics ignored the important question of women's rights, which remained confined to feminists and the Left parties. The Muslim leadership focused on legal issues that linked women and family life to Islamic legal identity and defended the definition of the Muslim community as a legal entity. The government defended the legislation on the ground that it conformed to the wishes of the Muslim community and should be conceded irrespective of the opinion of other communities or society at large. The law minister stated that:

> We have to tread very carefully for the Muslim personal law is linked to the Muslim religion in the mind of Muslim . . . . . We must look at it from the point of view of Muslims and then try to find out what is the law which governs the Muslims and which according to them is not merely a law of man's making as a law ordained by God. This is the belief of Muslims (GoI 1986).

The primacy of community rights over citizenship was once again endorsed by the state which willingly limited the application of its own laws to exclude citizens from the rights available to others. The controversy signifies the important role played by official state discourse in safeguarding community identity. The Congress party legitimised it, in terms of both state policies and strategies of mobilisation. In the absence of a reformed divorce law, Muslim women were unequal vis-à-vis men, and were now rendered unequal vis-à-vis women from other communities who have access to the law in respect of maintenance. To be sure, these issues raise questions that are not easily reconciled: the claims of rights of women and of individuals as against those of cultures and groups. The problem is undoubtedly compounded by the substantial purchase that community identity has on the polity.

However, the recent debate among social scientists on notions of community makes it clear that community identity is not natural or primordial. Communities are constituted in distinct ways at different historical junctures. Thus, it is well known that personal laws are constructions of the 20th century. As with the Hindu Code Bill, the Shariat Act of 1937 and the Dissolution of Muslim Marriages Act, 1939, demarcated the boundaries of the Muslim community. Nonetheless, the historicity of community construction does not deny the reality that these identities exist and that they matter to large numbers of people. Yet, it is a fact that community identity can be punitive, and there is little evidence to show that communities are committed to internal democratisation of gender differences. Personal laws deny women the rights that communities claim for themselves vis-à-vis the state: autonomy, selfhood and access to resources.

From the women's standpoint, the difficulty lies in marking the identity of the community exclusively by defining its women. Failing to define the community in broad terms, the Muslim leadership conflates religion and culture, identifying only one area as the essence of cultural identity, which boils down to personal laws. By defining community identity entirely with reference to a strict code of laws, legal change is ruled out because the survival of cultural identity depends on a codified identity. But the reform of personal laws does not mean the end of community or community identity, because there is a vast array of things which constitute the identity of the community, including language, religious rituals, pilgrimage to Mecca, fasting and prayers.

Hindu Communalism, Minorities and Women's Rights

During the last decade, many in India have asked why action has not been taken to bring about the fulfilment of the constitutional ideal. It has become a source of political conflict and polarisation between secularists and communalists, that has engaged political parties and mass media in a fierce polemic. But foremost, it has revealed deep social and political cleavages between the secular state and the Hindu organisations, and between them and women in particular.

The state has had to steer a precarious course between the norm of secularism and the norm of religious pluralism. The conflicts between the two positions coexisted for four decades after independence. There were moments when the contradictions came to the fore, but not many appear to have been troubled by their disagreement. At any rate, these points of discordance were not widely contested and they did not appear to be seriously divisive (Béteille 1998). But the relative accommodation was upset in the late 1980s, which has much to do with changes in India's politics: the growth of communal politics and the controversies surrounding it.

The decision to put off consideration of legal equality created a major area of tension between the Hindu nationalists and the minority communities. Until it came to power in March 1998, the BJP had raised the issue mainly to draw a parallel between the Congress party's capitulation to Muslim conservatives in the 1950s and then again in the 1980s, in the Shah Bano case. The lack of reform in Muslim personal law and its stout defence by the Congress party was exploited by the BJP to build a critique of secularism and of the Muslim community. It became a rallying point for communal groups campaigning against secularism and the secular practices of the state run by the Congress party.

Epitomising a long-term tendency in politics and society, the design of the Hindu nation, in contrast to pluralistic nationalism, stands for emphasising the distinctness of Hindu civilisation, and, playing down horizontal divisions among Hindus, the integration of all castes, communities and sects into a homogeneous whole. In some respects Hindu nationalism is, however, different from fundamentalism. Whereas fundamentalism rejects the separation of religion and state, Hindu communalism accepts this separation in principle. Partha Chatterjee argues that:

> The persuasive power, and even the emotional charge the Hindutva campaign appears to have gained in recent years do not depend upon its demanding legislative enforcement of ritual or scriptural injunctions, a role for religious institutions in legislative or judicial processes, compulsory religious instruction or state support for religious bodies, censorship of science, literature and art in order to safeguard religious dogma or any other similar demand undermining the secular character of the existing Indian state (1994: 1768).

This has crucial implications for women because the major alternative to secular law is community-based religious law (Basu

1998: 170–72). By virtue of its supposed commitment to secular principles, the BJP can uphold constitutional protection of sexual equality, and in fact adopt a high moral posture to castigate secular governments for being pseudo-secular owing to their indulgence of minorities. 'Personal law', Uma Bharati argues, 'defies the spirit of the constitution' (ibid.: 172).

By decrying the actions of successive Congress regimes on the issue of family law, the BJP seeks to demonstrate its own commitment to constitutional principles. The BJP uses the language of legal and constitutional rights to pit women's rights against minority rights. As some feminist legal scholars point out, it interprets secularism to mean that Muslims and Hindus should be treated alike, thereby disregarding the vulnerabilities to which Muslims as a minority are subject (Kapur and Cossman 1995). This is because Hindu nationalists, unlike their counterparts in many Muslim countries, identify their principal enemies as internal rather than external (ibid.: 171). By comparison, Islamic fundamentalism in West Asia, for example, is inseparable from the nationalist opposition to westernisation and modernity in its various guises. Nilofer Gole (1996: 5) notes that veiling in Turkey embodies the battleground for two competing conceptions of self and society, Western and Islamist. Similarly, Valentine Moghadam (1994: 13) observes that fundamentalists in Iran consider the veil as an antidote to the virus of 'Westoxication' and 'Euromania'.

Until the BJP-led government decided to conduct a series of underground nuclear tests, Hindu nationalists had not expressed any open anti-western sentiment. Rather, their targets were the 'outsiders' located within the nation, that is, Muslims, whom they regard as foreign even though Indian Islam is no more derivative than Chinese, Tibetan, Thai or Japanese Buddhism. Yet the idea that Islam is foreign is axiomatic for Hindu nationalists and for their agenda of removing the protective safeguards for communities and regions in order to produce a uniform, homogeneous code.

It is clear that the ideological consensus formulated by the state on issues of secularism and minority rights during Nehru's regime has given way to a politics of intolerance that now pervades the culture. The controversy over the UCC provides the BJP with a crucial means of challenging the ideological legitimacy of the secular state. The compulsions of coalition politics have forced the BJP government to shelve the immediate introduction of a UCC. It has to wait until the party gains a majority in parliament to unfold its *Hindutva* agenda of cultural homogenisation. Meanwhile, in the Hindu nationalist discourse, the UCC continues to be a touchstone of what it means to be an Indian, and a struggle over what the conditions of belonging are.

Women's Groups and Gender Justice

In the larger body politic, gender construction, identity formation and citizenship continue to be formulated within the rhetoric of binary opposition. Salient among these are: universalism/difference; uniformity/plurality; state/community. Rather than accepted as logical and necessary oppositions, these categories need to be historicised and subjected to closer scrutiny. Women's groups have attempted this by taking a fresh look at the process and mechanics of gender construction, especially the role of the state in this process.

From the 1940s, there was a general consensus that the state should legislate gender-just laws for all communities. This was part of the larger understanding that the state ought to play an important role in progressive social and political transformation. However, by the mid-1970s this consensus had broken down with the economic and political crisis of the state, engendered by the failures of development planning and socialism. This period saw a significant growth in women's participation in mass struggles on every front. The mass discontent brought about a radical rethinking in the women's movement on the role of the nation-state. The reluctance to universalise women's rights was illustrated by the pragmatic compromises of the state and its complicity in encashing on religious difference, for instance through the Muslim Women's Bill. Not surprisingly, there was growing disquiet over state-initiated legislation in areas of marriage, divorce, maintenance and inheritance, including the Hindu Code Bill (see, for example, Anveshi Law Committee 1997). The reform of Hindu laws did challenge the religious elites, but it culminated in the promulgation of laws that are not entirely just to women.

The makers of the constitution believed that the constitutional right to equality would be reinforced by the social policy of equality. This belief informed the policy of affirmative action for the scheduled castes which sought to reinforce equality as a right with public support for equality as a policy. When it comes to rights of women, equality as a right is enshrined in the constitution, but with no support for gender equality as a policy. Though the state is theoretically committed to ensuring the rights of its citizenry, it has been constrained by the dilemma of whether to support reforms from above or to support reforms from within. Significant initiatives to reform personal laws have been thwarted as often by the state as by pundits, mullahs and priests. Even the strategy of reform from within in the case of the Christian community has met with prevarication from the state.[3] The legal reform of personal law becomes a bargaining counter for the state which retains the power to decide whether or not to reform the personal law of any community.

The decisive shift came in the wake of the Ayodhya movement and the dramatic growth of the BJP. The BJP's ambition is to establish a singular citizenship by obliterating the legal recognition of religious and cultural differences. Hence the focus on Muslim personal law. The feminist groups are clearly uncomfortable with its appropriation of the UCC, particularly because in the hands of the BJP it becomes a rhetorical device to attack minorities. This created a dilemma for feminist politics, and more generally for secular democratic politics, between two conflicting norms: the norm of religious tolerance and the norm of equality between men and women. The women's movement remained committed to equality, but it did not want changes forced upon personal laws by the militant Hindu communal forces who saw the Muslim resistance to the UCC as a sign of their inability to integrate into the nation. Aware that legal change cannot be isolated from the wider political contradictions in the context of communal politics, women's groups began to seriously rethink the demand for a UCC (Agnes 1994). This gave rise to two kinds of approaches: one proposed that the present historical moment of heightened religious identities requires working within them, while the other foregrounded gender justice by delinking it from national integrity.[4]

From the early 1990s, the opposition to uniform laws was marked by a simultaneous critique of the UCC and personal laws. It signalled an acknowledgement that gender justice needs to be delinked from uniform laws. Groups which earlier supported uniform legislation jettisoned it in favour of common, gender-just or egalitarian laws, as against uniform laws. It is worth noting that the term uniform was practically dropped within the women's movement, even by those groups who endorsed state legislation (N. Menon 1997: 253–63). The change is visible in the repudiation of the UCC by all political parties, the BJP excepted. The change is most explicit in the case of the All India Democratic Women's Association (AIDWA), the largest women's organisation in the country. Like other feminist groups, AIDWA has had to reckon with a political climate vitiated by communal politics and religious identities. Not too long ago, the AIDWA promoted common laws, but at this juncture it champions a gradual approach to legal reforms in recognition of the difficulty of pushing change in the present communal climate, encouraging community initiative and demanding fresh legislation with regard to matrimonial property and the custody of children.

A number of proposals have been mooted by women's groups to enlarge the scope for gender justice. While distancing themselves from a state-imposed UCC, feminist positions differ both from the national integrity argument and from an unqualified defence of community rights. The national integrity argument is problematic owing to its implicit and sometimes explicit rebuke of minorities as 'anti-national'. The communitarian argument is equally problematic because it endangers women's rights. Moving away from both, women's groups have given priority to the notion of women as individual citizens with inalienable rights.[5] Some groups, such as the Mumbai-based Majlis, prefer to maximise the space for women within communities, which means reform within personal laws rather than legislation by the state. Then there are others who want to devise genuinely egalitarian or secular laws and allow people to opt for these.[6] The Forum Against Oppression of Women, Mumbai, has evolved such a code.[7] The Working Group on Women's Rights, Delhi, put forward a proposal that blends state legislation in both private and public domains and also provides the option of a return to personal laws.[8] This option would turn the regime of personal laws into something voluntary and yet leave open the possibility of transformation of a community through its own initiatives, rather than by the state.

The key to understanding these shifts lies in the specificity of the Indian discourse on secularism. Secularism in India simultaneously posits the disengagement of religion from the public arena and the need for the state to regulate religious practices, either by non-intervention, for example, declaring certain areas of jurisprudence to be the prerogative of religious leaders, or by intervention, for example, ensuring financial accountability of religious trusts (N. Menon 1997: 264–65). The critique of the state in this context is either that it intervenes too much, as when the government passed the Muslim Women's Bill, or too little, as in its reluctance to enact a UCC. This is the peculiar predicament of the state, to understand which we have to keep in mind not only India's composite cultural tradition but also its present demography and heterogeneity. The presence of social pluralities makes it difficult to conceive of a stable political arrangement without religious tolerance and secularism. However, the definitions of 'secular' and 'nation' take place in a political field where certain identities are privileged—even while equality is emphasised— and others subordinated. As Deniz Kandiyoti argues, whenever women serve as markers between different ethnic and religious collectivities, 'their emergence as full-fledged citizens' with concomitant rights 'will be jeopardised'.

The goal of gender equality cannot be indefinitely postponed. It is by seeking rights as citizens that women aspire to actively redefine the contours of the debate and shape new laws. 'The legitimacy of new common laws', as Kumkum Sangari argues, 'should be based on a secular and democratic horizon that seeks justice for women within a wider egalitarian project. As such it cannot be formulated by the state or the BJP, or through a consensus of religious communities' (Sangari 1995: 3386). Such laws can only be made from a non-religious location, and they would have to take into account both similarities and differences, and allow the individual's right to choose where to belong. In sum, common laws have to be based on a principle of access to inalienable rights that are the same for all.

Notes

1. For details on this debate see Parashar (1992).
2. Despite centuries of Muslim rule, the community did not adopt the *Shariah* as the basis of law; consequently, women's rights in the *Shariah*

were seldom complied with or enforced. As a result, the opportunities of exercising their Quranic prerogatives, especially in claiming ownership of landed estates and property, were denied to women. Until the introduction of the Shariat Act in 1937, legal and social codes observed by Muslim communities in different parts of the country were varied and diffused. Thus began an effort by the ulema to work for a complete supersession of non-Islamic customary practice and compulsory enactment of an Islamic legal system. The enactment of the Muslim Personal Law Shariat Application Act, 1937, signalled the acceptance by the state legal system of the principle that in all personal matters such as marriage, divorce, maintenance, inheritance and custody, Muslims would be governed by the Muslim personal law. Similarly, the Dissolution of the Muslim Marriages Act, 1939, represented yet another attempt by the ulema to rectify what they perceived as a lacuna in the existing laws which had left Muslim women without the option of divorce, except through apostasy from Islam. For the first time, this Act gave Muslim women the right to seek judicial dissolution of marriage (Fyzee 1974).

3. In 1993, a Christian Marriage Act was proposed by the government with the approval of all Christian churches and Christian women's organisations. Despite the Christian community's support for changes in divorce laws, the Bill has not yet been debated in parliament.

4. Three kinds of interventions were made with regard to legal reforms. First, there were attempts by women's groups all over the country to evolve a common package of laws that are free of gender bias. Second, there was the effort to reform from within communities. Third, a number of judicial interventions addressed themselves to discrepancies in law to reduce inequalities between men and women. For example, a recent Supreme Court judgement gave the widow and daughter of a deceased coparcener equal rights to property left by him. Another judgement granted a divorced Hindu woman the right to sell, use for income or dispose in any way she likes the land given to her in lieu of maintenance. In another case, the widow was granted full ownership rights of the premises given to her as part of her maintenance. Such verdicts have greatly helped to reduce the existing inequities between men and women in matters of inherited property.

5. For an explication of this argument, see Sangari (1995).

6. This idea was put forward as early as 1945, when it was suggested that the UCC be made optional. After independence, the Special Marriages Act or the Indian Succession Act offered a number of options. Yet the government did not endeavour to create a machinery for implementing an optional code. Had it done so, it may well have expanded the ground of secular laws, besides building up pressure for reforms within community laws.

7. The proposal includes the following: (a) the need for changes and modifications in the procedures of law to ensure effective implementation; (b) the demand for a system of social security benefits for women; and (c) the demand that the state take on the responsibility for imparting legal education to women at all levels.

8. The proposal has three features: (a) comprehensive package of legislation providing equal rights for women in terms of access to property, guardianship, right to matrimonial home, and equal rights in the workplace, anti-discriminatory provisions in recruitment and promotions; (b) all Indian citizens would come under the purview of common laws at birth; and (c) all citizens would have the right to choose at any point to be governed by personal laws, if they so desire, while retaining the option to revoke this choice. See Working Group on Women's Rights (1996).

References

Agnes, Flavia. 1994. 'Women's Movements within a Secular Framework: Redefining the Agenda', *Economic and Political Weekly*, Vol. 29, No. 19, 7 May 1994.

Anveshi Law Committee, Hyderabad. 1997. 'Is Gender Justice Only a Legal Issue? Political Stakes in UCC Debate', *Economic and Political Weekly*, Vol. 32, Nos 9–10, 1 March 1997.

Austin, Granville. 1966. *The Indian Constitution: Cornerstone of a Nation*. Oxford: Clarendon Press.

Basu, Amrita. 1998. 'Hindu Activism in India and the Questions It Raises', in Patricia Jeffrey and Amrita Basu, eds, *Appropriating Gender: Women's Activism and Political Religion in South Asia*. New York: Routledge.

Béteille, André. 1998. 'Conflict of Norms and Values in Contemporary Indian Society', in Peter Berger, ed., *Limits of Social Cohesion: Conflict and Mediation in Pluralist Societies*. Boulder, CO: Westview Press.

Chatterjee, Partha. 1994. 'Secularism and Toleration', *Economic and Political Weekly*, Vol. 20, No. 28, 9 July 1994.

Fyzee, A.A.A. 1974. *Outlines of Muhammedan Law*. Delhi: Oxford University Press.

Gole, Nilofer. 1996. *Forbidden Modern: Civilisation and Veiling*. Michigan: Michigan University Press.

Government of India (GoI). 1972. Towards Equality: Report of the Committee on the Status of Women in India, Ministry of Education and Social Welfare, Government of India, New Delhi.

———. 1986. Lok Sabha Debates, Fifth Session, Eighth Lok Sabha, Vol. I, XVII, Government of India, New Delhi.

Hasan, Zoya (ed.). 1994. *Forging Identities: Gender, Communities and the State*. New Delhi: Kali for Women, and Boulder, CO: Westview Press.

Jayal, Niraja Gopal. 1998. 'Secularism, Identities and Representative Democracy', in Mushirul Hasan, ed., *Islam, Communities and the Nation: Muslim Identities in South Asia and Beyond*. New Delhi: Manohar.

Kandiyoti, Deniz. 'Identity and Its Discontents: Women and Nation', *Millennium Journal of International Studies*, Vol. 20, No. 3, pp. 429–43.

Kapur, Ratna, and Brenda Cossman. 1995. 'Communalising Gender/ Engendering Community: Women, Legal Discourse and the Saffron Agenda', in Tanika Sarkar and Urvashi Butalia, eds, *Women and the Hindu Right: A Collection of Essays*. New Delhi: Kali for Women.

Kishwar, Madhu. 1994. 'Codified Hindu Laws: Myth and Reality', *Economic and Political Weekly*, Vol. 29, No. 33, 13 August 1994.

Menon, Nivedita. 1997. 'Women and Citizenship', in Partha Chatterjee, ed., *The State and Politics in India*. Delhi: Oxford University Press.

Menon, Ritu. 1998. 'Reproducing the Legitimate Community: Secularity, Sexuality and the State in Postpartition India', in Patricia Jeffrey and Amrita Basu, eds, *Appropriating Gender: Women's Activism and Politicised Religion in South Asia*. New York: Routledge.

Minault, Gail. 1998. 'Women, Legal Reform and Muslim Identity', in Mushirul Hasan, ed., *Islam, Communities and the Nation: Muslim Identities in South Asia and Beyond*. New Delhi: Manohar.

Mogadham, Valentine. 1994. 'Introduction: Women and Identity Politics in Theoretical and Comparative Perspective', in Valentine Mogadham, ed., *Identity Politics and Women: Cultural Assertions and Feminisms in International Perspectives*. Boulder, CO: Westview Press.

Parasher, Archana. 1992. *Women and Family Law Reform in India*. New Delhi: Sage.

Sangari, Kumkum. 1995. 'Politics of Diversity: Religious Communities and Multiple Patriarchies', *Economic and Political Weekly*, Vol. 30, No. 51, 23 December 1995.

Som, Reba. 1994. 'Jawaharlal Nehru and the Hindu Code: A Victory of Symbol over Substance', *Modern Asian Studies*, Vol. 28, No. 1.

Smith, Donald Eugene. 1963. *India as a Secular State*. Princeton: Princeton University Press.

Working Group on Women's Rights. 1996. 'Reversing the Option: Civil Codes and Personal Laws', *Economic and Political Weekly*, Vol. 31, No. 20, 18 May 1996.

fifteen

The Media in Contemporary India

B.G. Verghese

may 1998 saw the fifth centenary of Vasco da Gama's landing in Calicut marking the commencement of what was to be a lasting encounter between Asia and the West. Columbus had, a few years earlier, 'discovered' America while searching the seas for India. At the dawn of the new millennium, contemporary India is emerging to take its place in what increasingly appears likely to be an Asian century.

Vasco da Gama's charter was to navigate the oceans, explore new lands and learn more about their people, paving the way for conquest and the spread of the Christian faith and commerce. A printing press intended for Abyssinia accidentally found its way to India in 1556. The vessel halted in Goa en route and there the press remained. It was used to print a Catechism, believed to have been authored by St Francis Xavier. One of the technicians accompanying the press prepared the first set of Indian language types, the *Lingua Malabar*, a combination of Malayalam and Tamil characters, in which was printed in Quilon in 1577 the first Indian language text, Xavier's *Doutrina Christa* (*Priting Times*, 1993, New Delhi).

Spanish, Portuguese, Danish and English missionaries further developed printing and typography in Bombay, Madras and Bengal. The printing press followed the Bible and other religious texts, and 1805 saw the publication of the *Bhagwad Gita* through block printing under the patronage of the Raja of Miraj. A decree in 1684 barred Goans from printing in the local language. This crippled the printing industry in Goa as Portuguese texts were presumably sent out from Lisbon. It was not until 1821 that a press was imported from Bombay to print a weekly, *Gazeta de Goa*.

However, by 1780, the first modern Indian newspaper had been born with the publication of James Augustus Hickey's *Bengal Gazette*. It was lively, irreverent, probing, scandalous and irrepressible, telling all that the honourable East India Company and the genteel society of Calcutta wished to hide. Things changed over the years. Independence in 1947 marked another watershed. The Indian press never looked back.

Information is power, and transparency imposes accountability. The colonial period, therefore, saw a divide between establishment journals and the nationalist press. Media laws and regulations were enacted to curb seditious writing. The press became an important instrument of India's largely non-violent freedom struggle under Gandhi, himself a remarkable communicator. The motto the country adopted after independence was, not surprisingly, 'Let Truth Prevail': easy to proclaim, not so easy to follow, as idealism everywhere slowly yields to *realpolitik* and, at another level, to the market.

India stands apart from nearly all other newly independent nations spawned by decolonisation after the Second World War. It deliberately chose full-blown liberal democracy as the instrument of effecting an economic and social revolution, rather than having it as a possible end-product of such a process. This was a total inversion of the Western model which was regarded as the natural and proper sequence. It inevitably meant giving pride of place to freedom of speech and expression, not as some kind of theoretical constitutional doctrine to which occasional lip-service might be paid, but as a fundamental, living, societal value.

In a democratic society, it is the free flow of information through independent media and a plurality of sources that empowers the people and renders accountable the rulers and all others in authority. Else, the citizen would remain ignorant and easily misled and manipulated. This is well documented by reference to so many countries where authoritarian or military rule has inevitably been accompanied by curbs on the media. In contrast, a free press has been integral to India's democratic ethos and has played a critical role in the governance of the country.

The experience of the constitutional Emergency imposed by Indira Gandhi on India for twenty months between 1975 and 1977 is instructive. Of all the instruments used to subvert democracy, the most effective and pervasive was censorship. No one knew what was happening. Each person or community was divided from the other and intellectually and emotionally boxed into little compartments. Isolation bred insecurity and fear and impeded concerted action.

During the grim days of Emergency, it came home even to the most unlettered that of all fundamental rights, that of freedom of speech and expression, from which media freedom derives, is indeed and must always remain paramount. With parliamentary and judicial proceedings subject to censorship, the legislative and judicial branches of government were rendered impotent, leaving the executive with unbridled power. The Gujarat High Court's ruling striking down the government's censorship order as *ultra vires* was itself censored, thus perpetuating a gross illegality.

Communication is the basis of community. In its absence, even the freedom of association or trade union rights were affected and protest was weakened if not nullified. It took time for citizens to develop alternative means and codes of communication. Once that happened, elements of solidarity returned and in due course the Emergency was overturned. It can truly be said that though India won independence in 1947, it won freedom in 1977. That was the substance and meaning of the electoral verdict. The poorest and most underprivileged discovered that denial of the right to free speech and expression had deprived them of a crucial instrument in the struggle for dignity and betterment. Lawyers, academics, parliamentarians, workers and peasants, civil servants, writers and artists, indeed, just about everybody other than courtiers and sycophants, felt helpless and suffocated.

Parenthetically, a growing, insistent demand for legislating the right to information in place of the prevalent official secrecy regime, a legacy of colonial rule, is noteworthy. Transparency enhances participation and accountability, and is undoubtedly a powerful instrument in fighting corruption and malfeasance. This is of particular relevance to the poor for whose upliftment vast sums are annually allocated and special programmes devised. Where does all this money go? Who are the beneficiaries? There is ample evidence to show that large sums are siphoned away by corrupt contractors, bureaucrats and politicians working in collusion. A movement to secure public access to public records— from village to district level—of development and poverty alleviation programmes in Rajasthan in 1997 revealed massive fraud. Information can truly empower people. A draft Freedom of Information Bill, 2000, is under consideration by the central government (see *Lokayan Bulletin* 1999).

Subsequent to the Emergency, whenever federal or state governments attempted to impose curbs on freedom of expression in the name of dealing with scurrility, defamation, the right of reply or whatever—all pertinent in some degree but miscast in their sweep and, perhaps, hidden intent—every section of society rose in protest and marched to block any illiberal legislation. They had come to recognise freedom of speech and expression, and especially media freedom, as their sword and shield and not something removed from their day-to-day lives and well-being.

This revelation is in sharp contrast to the attitude of influential sections of society and the media to press freedom in the 1950s and 1960s. At that time, it was common enough to hear of the dangers and misdeeds of the so-called monopoly or 'jute' press owned by large business houses with a range of manufacturing or trading interests. There was a tirade against the alleged sins of omission and commission of these large newspaper groups on the ground of furthering vested interests at the cost of the national interest. This was an ideological rather than an objective judgement, as there was never a newspaper monopoly in India and the plurality of media voices precluded any semblance of narrow control over the flow of information.

There followed a clamour to 'delink' newspaper ownership from large industrial houses and to 'diffuse' ownership among newspaper employees and others. Even successful family-owned newspapers came under fire merely because of their growing circulation. Newspapers may and do support vested interests of various kinds from time to time in India, as anywhere else in the world. But this has little to do with their size or ownership. A Bill to effect 'delinking' and 'diffusion' was indeed drafted but met with such fierce opposition that it was dropped.

These misconceived theories were themselves a product of a mistaken view of the nature of press freedom, which is but the collective manifestation of the citizen's right to freedom of speech and expression. Although India was an early signatory to the United Nations Human Rights Charter and the International Covenant on Civil and Political Rights, the extended definition of freedom of speech and expression as the right to receive and impart information without restriction, irrespective of national boundaries, was neither widely known nor understood, and was certainly not incorporated in Indian law until somewhat later. Rather, press freedom was regarded as a proprietorial or, at best, a newspaper freedom and not as the citizen's right to know.

The courts recognised this much earlier, and from the start consistently ruled to enlarge press freedom against attack or encroachment by the state. Article 19 of the Indian constitution sets out a Bill of Rights. First in this listing is freedom of speech and expression. This is constrained by a proviso that enables the government to impose 'reasonable' restrictions in the interests of the sovereignty and integrity of India, security of the state, public order, incitement to offence, friendly relations with foreign states, morality and decency, contempt and defamation. This has compelled the media to act with sobriety and a sense of responsibility and is intended to ensure that freedom does not degenerate into licence. Were that to happen, credibility would be lost and public sympathy forfeited.

The safeguard, however, lies in restraints being reasonable, which renders them justiciable. The courts have not merely struck down arbitrary executive action but, through creative jurisprudence, have steadily widened the ambit of freedom of expression. In so doing, they have relied on other rights such as equality before law and the right to life and liberty. The Supreme Court quite early on warned the state against using newsprint control (at a time of foreign exchange shortage and import regulation) as a means of newspaper control. Other judgements have upheld the freedom of the editor against day-to-day proprietorial interference in the discharge of his professional duties; barred prior restraint on the media even with regard to publication of material defamatory to the state or public officials; and held that defamation of public officials in the discharge of their official duties cannot rest merely on the fact of publication or inaccuracies but must prove personal malice or animosity, so as not to impart a chilling effect on investigative reporting.

In an important judgement in 1995, the Supreme Court declared the airwaves or electromagnetic spectrum to be public property and not a government monopoly as theretofore. It reiterated that the citizen's right to freedom of speech and expression guarantees the citizen's right to inform and be informed across national frontiers. The Court accordingly directed the government to set up an independent broadcasting authority to license the airwaves. At the same time, it warned against 'private oligarchies' gaining control over the airwaves, as that could equally defeat the purpose of plurality in expression and the kind of free debate that is the hallmark of a truly democratic society. This landmark judgement spurred long pending legislation to de-governmentalise the state-controlled radio and television channels and transfer these to an autonomous public service broadcasting corporation, Prasar Bharati, managed by an independent board funded by and accountable to Parliament. This has been done and, teething troubles notwithstanding, a new chapter has opened in Indian broadcasting.

The conversion of the two previously state-owned radio and television organisations into public broadcasting services (PBS) constitutes a landmark, a transfer of power, a shift from government to governance, from state to civil society. Many countries have found it necessary to encourage and even protect PBS systems to ensure quality, balance and cultural enrichment and to reach out to niche audiences with low market ratings or audience size. In a developing and extraordinarily diverse society like India, a modern nation still in the making, this must be a paramount consideration.

Huge cohorts are in transition from mere vote-banks to socially and politically conscious citizens in steady succession. They seek information, access and participation to become full and equal partners in governance and civil society. Broadcasting, and the media generally, must change from being 'for' to 'of' and 'by' the people. Millions live at, or just above, the level of subsistence. Their educational, informational and cultural needs cannot merely be left to the dictates of the market which, for them, lies on the

other side of the rainbow. This is not to oppose commercial broadcasting by any means, but only to emphasise that it simply does
not cover a large part of the social spectrum. Democracy and
plurality call for inclusion and not exclusion, whether by policy
or the purse. Interactive local and community broadcasting or
'narrow-casting' will, above all, reach the many, many 'publics'
that an Indian public broadcasting system must serve.

It is interesting to recall that direct-to-home broadcasting, that
is being bruited as the next wonder, was first tried out in India in
1976–77. An American Advanced Technology Satellite was leased
for a Satellite Instructional Television Experiment (SITE) for direct
community broadcasting to six clusters of 400 villages and some
cities scattered hundreds of kilometres apart all over India. The
programmes were beamed in six languages on a time-sharing
basis. The experiment was a huge success and demonstrated the
educational, awareness-building and integrative role of broadcasting in a large developing society.

A separate, independent regulatory authority is currently in the
process of being legislated to license private commercial radio and
television broadcasters in the terrestrial, satellite, cable or direct-
to-home mode. However, even pending such legislation, a number
of private commercial satellite television channels, Indian and
foreign, have been permitted to operate in India which offers a
huge broadcast and advertising market. India also has the largest
film industry in the world in eight or more major languages, with
a hardware and software capability that makes for great multi-
media possibilities, internal and international. Controversy sur-
rounds three issues: the move to mandate that satellite broadcast
providers shall up-link from India; limitation of satellite broadcast
service equity holdings to 24 per cent rather than 49 per cent as
originally proposed; and a limitation on cross-media holdings to
no more than 20 per cent of the market. Terrestrial broadcast services will have to be wholly owned by nationals, as in most countries in the West.

There has been similar controversy over permitting foreign
newspapers and journals to publish from India. Other than the
Reader's Digest, for some reason no other commercial venture has
been allowed, though there is absolutely no bar on the free circulation of foreign journals. This policy was designed in 1955 as a
measure of infant-industry and cultural and political protection

in the early years of independence. The Indian print media has grown and matured greatly since then and the social and political environment has also changed. Nevertheless, the prevalent weight of opinion appears to favour continuation of the prohibition despite the arrival of satellite broadcasting, fax, international dialling and Internet.

More urgent issues clamour for attention. While India's print media continues to grow in strength, technological capability and circulation, there are certain disconcerting trends. With economic liberalisation and globalisation, some newspapers are more marketed than edited. There has been a tendency to trivialise the news. Cynicism prevails and, with it, a certain arrogance of power exemplified by trial by the press. A 'north–south' divide exists, as in many societies. Sensation, colour and body-counts are part of a process where events take precedence over processes. Yet, in an immensely variegated, large, developing society in the throes of several levels of transition, the processes of development and social change are vital indicators of 'growth' that cannot be ignored. The concept of news calls for redefinition, and not only in India.

Armed militancy, terrorism and fundamentalism pose new challenges. Media freedom has at various times been gravely imperilled by the gun in Punjab, Jammu and Kashmir and India's North-East. How should the media and society contend with such extra-legal situations? There have been instances of both courage and compromise. And in situations of war or internal conflict, official news management and jingoism have not always been kept at bay successfully. The record, though mixed, is improving.

The information revolution has created an instant, universal world with the news available on the hour, every hour. Information flows have multiplied manifold; with it disinformation of every kind. This has come to acquire menacing proportions everywhere. So too in India. Television has emerged as a most powerful and seductive medium. Yet the 'news' television captures is often limited to the pictures that the camera can or does record, depending on what it focuses on, and when and where. What it does not or cannot record is not 'news'. So there can be a large gap between image and reality, between disinformation and information, with truth very often chasing illusion and maybe only catching up with it when new images have supplanted old realities. The show goes on. The media is the message, and the vertical integration or convergence of medium and message, hardware and software, could pose new dilemmas.

The Press Council of India and professional associations have intervened to admonish and correct. A code of journalistic ethics has emerged through such 'case law'; but this is only a moral and not a legal corrective. The latter only exists for statutory violations, defamation and contempt. Efforts to impose a code of conduct on the media have been rightly resisted as this could be misused as a means of licensing or policing journalists. A broadcast complaints mechanism is also in the process of being set up to adjudicate on issues of fairness and standards. These are useful and necessary, but are they sufficient? The debate rages.

Freedom and responsibility go hand in hand. Gandhi's aphorisms survive. One, inscribed on the portals of All-India Radio, proclaims: 'I do not want my house to be walled on all sides and my windows to be stuffed. I want the cultures of all lands to be blown about my house as freely as possible. But I refuse to be blown off my feet by any.' Another is that 'rights come from duties well performed.' These are apt maxims for the media in the new millennium.

References

Lokayan Bulletin. 1999. 'The Right of Information', Vol. 16, Nos 1–3, July–August 1999.

Goa
in
Transition

sixteen

Economic Policy and Development in Goa

Errol D'Souza

Contemporary Goa, the tiny region of approximately 3,700 square kilometres situated on the west coast of India, draws a lot of attention from 'scribblers' such as scholars and journalists in the fields of politics, language, religion, culture, tourism and the environment. Writing on the recent and present economy of Goa is correspondingly meagre and deals mainly with sectoral issues such as the impact of mining, the employment potential of tourism, the demographic profile of the population, the fragmentation of landholding in agriculture, and the like. There is accordingly no eagle-eye view or perspective readily available that provides a framework which may be deployed to make sense of the broad economic development in Goa. In this chapter, I shall hazard the proposal of such a perspective where the focus will be mainly on contemporary Goa, that is, from the time the region achieved statehood in 1987.

Before getting down to that task, however, I cannot resist briefly sketching out some facets of history. Goa was the administrative, trading and ecclesiastical capital of *Estado da India* (Boxer 1969). As the military and political centre of *Estado da India*, a state based on a network of trade routes rather than on territorial integrity (Pearson 1989), Goa gained its economic hegemony from the control of maritime connections rather than from rule over the land. Portuguese mercantile activities were essentially devoted to the extraction of commodities and control of the movement of goods from Asia to Europe rather than outright control of production. Accordingly, even in 1630, after the decline of the Portuguese seaborne empire had set in, 47 per cent of the revenue in Portuguese India came from seaborne commerce, while 31 per cent came from agriculture and other land-based taxes (Pearson 1990). The Portuguese had preserved the pre-colonial village structures and had not introduced much change in the tax structures and village productive systems. So they did not in any way contribute to the transformation in the mode of production (De Souza 1990), unlike in other parts of colonial India and Asia. Most of the revenue was used to finance military expeditions and missionary activities outside Goa (Rodrigues 1977). Also, a large amount of state revenue throughout the colonial period was spent on salaries and benefits for the bureaucracy (De Souza 1979; Fernandes 1923–24). This, according to some writers, led to the adoption of a bourgeois lifestyle by a minority in the population who held positions in government (Cunha 1939; Fernandes 1940).

This extremely short account of Goa's past has been given here because of some of the parallels it presents with Goa after gaining statehood in 1987. Goa has joined the process of planned development only since 1962–63, when the rest of India was halfway through the Third Plan. However, due to the crisis of the Indian economy in the mid-1960s which resulted in three Annual Plans, planning for long-term economic development commenced in the state only with the Fourth Plan. The post-liberation economy of Goa is marked by a rapid growth of population. While the population rose from 596,000 in 1950 to 627,000 in 1960, registering a decennial growth rate of only 5.14 per cent, during 1960–71 and 1971–81 it registered an increase of 36.88 and 26.15 per cent respectively. This spurt in population is attributed to net in-migration after liberation. During 1981–91, however, the population increased by 15.96 per cent only, bringing the total population in 1991 to 1.17 million. The sex ratio, which was favourable to women prior to liberation, turned adverse to women during the post-liberation period with 969 females for every 1,000 males, as compared to

929 females in the rest of India (1991 Census). The literacy rate in Goa steadily increased from 35 per cent in 1960 to 75.5 per cent in 1991. The male literacy rate of 83.6 per cent in 1991 was much higher than the female literacy rate of 67.1 per cent. Net state domestic product (NSDP) at current prices increased from Rs 270 million in 1960 to Rs 3.15 billion in 1980–81, and further to Rs 10.24 billion in 1990–91 and Rs 18.49 billion in 1994–95. The primary sector (agriculture, animal husbandry, fisheries and mining) contributes around 22.6 per cent of NSDP, the secondary sector (manufacturing, industry, construction, electricity, gas and water supply) around 30.9 per cent, and the tertiary sector (trade, transport, banking, insurance, real estate, public administration and other services) 46.5 per cent. The sectorwise shares in real terms are similar.

The economic growth rate in Goa was higher than the all-India growth rate for the 1970s and 1980s. The growth rate of 8.2 per cent for the period from 1986–87 to 1994–95 was much higher than the growth rate of national net domestic product, which was 5.3 per cent during the same period. Goa has the highest per capita income among all the states. Maharashtra holds second rank, followed by Punjab, Haryana, Sikkim, Arunachal Pradesh and Gujarat. In 1988–89, Goa's per capita income was higher than Maharashtra's by 39.8 per cent, and higher by 26.4 per cent in 1994–95. One simple way of understanding what contributes to regional disparities in income generation is to decompose per capita income into its components in the following way:

$$\frac{\text{NSDP}}{\text{Population}} = \left(\frac{\text{NSDP}}{\text{No. Employed}}\right)\left(\frac{\text{No. Employed}}{\text{Labour Force}}\right)\left(\frac{\text{Labour Force}}{\text{Population}}\right)$$

$$= \left(\frac{\text{NSDP}}{\text{No. Employed}}\right)(1 - \text{Unemployment Rate})\left(\frac{\text{Labour Force}}{\text{Population}}\right)$$

Thus, one of the factors responsible for inter-state disparities is purely demographic — the population of working age, or the total labour force. Other factors include economic conditions, namely, earnings per worker (NSDP/No. Employed), and the unemployment rate. This sort of decomposition indicates that a region may be poorer because wages per employee are lower, or because there are fewer people working, and so on. The income per employee in Punjab for instance is 16.5 per cent less than that in Goa. The high income per employee in Goa is a result of the highly endowed workforce, labour quality being high. Goa has the third highest percentage of literates to population aged 7 and above among all states in India (Kerala and Mizoram being the first two in this regard). In terms of this decomposition, it turns out that the unemployment rate of 9.37 per cent in the state is significantly higher (143.38 per cent higher) than the all-India unemployment rate of 3.85 per cent. Also, in Goa, the demographic composition is not favourable to the process of income generation as the labour force participation rate, at 37.57 per cent, is lower (10.68 per cent lower) than the all-India labour force participation rate of 42.06 per cent. Obviously, accounting for the high level of unemployment in Goa is very much an agenda item for anyone attempting to trace the broad contours of the development of the region. I shall have something to say about this a little later.

The Nature of State Intervention

The high unemployment rate is surprising given that state intervention dominates the economy. A summary measure of state intervention is the proportion of total income earned in the state as a result of expenditure decisions by the government through the budget. This measure shows that state government expenditure as a percentage of state domestic product has been fairly constant over the years, as Table 16.1 demonstrates.

TABLE 6.1
GOVERNMENT EXPENDITURE AS A PERCENTAGE OF NSDP

1988–89	1989–90	1990–91	1991–92	1992–93	1993–94	1994–95
37.96	40.82	41.69	43.72	34.93	39.53	39.87

Source: Basic Statistics, Department of Planning and Statistics, Government of Goa.

The government has thus been intervening in a steady way in the economy and this prompts the question: how has the steady rate of government intervention been maintained, and is it sustainable? As will soon be obvious, the nature of government intervention is constraining the economy, and such intervention is not sustainable. First, developmental expenditures have been falling quite significantly over the years since Goa has become a state. Developmental expenditures, which were 79.5 per cent of total government expenditures in 1988–89, fell to a budgeted 58.1 per cent in 1997–98. Two years – 1994–95 and 1995–96 – show a rise in the share of developmental expenditures, but this is an aberration due to the fall in repayment of loans and internal debt in those years. The reduction in the repayment of loans, for instance, was from Rs 1.9 billion in 1993–94 to Rs 1.2 billion in 1994–95, and internal debt decreased from Rs 1.74 billion in 1993–94 to Rs 1.2 billion in 1994–95. This occurred due to the reduction in a major item of non-plan expenditure, ways and means advances from the central government, from Rs 130 million to nil in subsequent years. Also, repayments on account of ways and means advances from the Reserve Bank of India (RBI) fell from Rs 1.59 billion in 1993–94 to Rs 1 billion in subsequent years. The fall in repayment of loans was the result of the external imposition of the writ of the RBI and the central government as regards ways and means advances, and had nothing to do with internal financial planning by the state. Without this imposition of limits to non-plan financing by the central government and the RBI, the state would have continued the policy of increased borrowings to splurge, as is evidenced by the quick return to reduced developmental expenditures in 1996–97, financed through the route of raising the internal debt component of market loans bearing interest. The fall in developmental expenditure is significant, because it is precisely these expenditures which stimulate growth in an economy and any deceleration in them implies that budgets have not been growth-oriented. It is developmental expenditure that results in a growth of incomes and employment, and if this is not forthcoming, then the lack of a commitment to development and growth is the responsible factor. Developmental expenditure can be disaggregated into two types – current and capital. Of the two, capital developmental expenditures are more significant, as they increase the capacity to produce of the economy and so ensure that bottlenecks do not occur. Such expenditures stood at Rs 1.08 billion in 1991–92, Rs 995 million in 1992–93, Rs 896.2 million in 1993–94, Rs 1.04 billion in 1994–95, Rs 1.15 billion in 1995–96, Rs 1.22 billion in 1996–97 and about Rs 1.44 billion in 1997–98. Thus, only recently has there been a pick-up in expenditures on this front, and in real terms capital expenditures have been falling through the decade.

The fall in developmental expenditures and, significantly, in those of the capital type, has been one of the ways in which the government has been constraining the growth rate of the economy.

Second, from the financing point of view there has been a rise in the state's own revenue, whereas grants-in-aid and contributions to the state government have fallen. In fact, the rise in the state's own revenue from 41.04 per cent of total expenditure in 1988–89 to 55.23 per cent in 1997–98 (budgeted) was matched by a fall in grants-in-aid and contributions from 33.69 per cent in 1988–89 to 14.48 per cent in 1997–98. To make up for the declining share of grants-in-aid, the state government has been resorting to boosting sales tax rates and receipts from departmental commercial undertakings. Sales taxes rose from 14.82 per cent of government revenue in 1988–89 to 22.44 per cent in 1997–98, a rise of about 8 percentage points. Receipts from departmental commercial undertakings were up by 6 percentage points; from 13.34 per cent in 1988–89 to 19.43 per cent in 1997–98. This mode of government intervention is also a constraint on the growth of incomes and employment, because jacking up the rates of sales taxes and the like pushes up the prices of commodities, which has a differential impact on the community. Those who have bargaining power are able to maintain their real incomes despite the inflationary impetus generated, while those whose incomes do not increase in tandem with increases in the cost of living find themselves relatively worse off in real terms. Also, those who face declining real incomes demand fewer commodities, as a result of which the receipts from sales begin to decline. Businesses begin to cut back production plans as revenues decline, and there is a move to cut variable costs by pruning the labour force employed. There are thus two effects: the distributional situation worsens, and there results a decline in demand and deceleration in the growth of incomes. Besides, as a result of the rise in prices of commodities, the government finds it must increase its expenditures in nominal terms in order to be able to control the same amount of real resources—to keep its command over goods unchanged. This accounts for a part of government intervention in the economy. On the one hand the government raises extra revenues from sales taxes, but as this generates a rise in prices, government expenditures—which are a major component of the total expenditure in the economy—are increased in order to keep expenditure in real terms from being eroded. Thus, in real terms there is no release of resources for development.

The principal objective of grants-in-aid and devolutions is to secure equity between populations living in different fiscal jurisdictions. Ideally, the principles of federal finance suggest the sharing of revenues between the central government and lower levels of government such as the states, because of differential access to buoyant sources of revenue. This helps to neutralise differences in the level of services provided by governments in different areas—these services depend on the needs of a population, the costs of providing for those needs, and the resources available in a fiscal jurisdiction. In 1990–91, central grants-in-aid and contributions paid for 32.2 per cent of total expenditures, while in 1997–98, this was budgeted to be less than half that figure at 14.48 per cent. Grants-in-aid and contributions are devolved to states in accordance with criteria which give weightage to population, backwardness, tax effort, state domestic product, etc. Goa merits little attention for transfers from the central government in this regard as its record in these areas is good. Planning Commission transfers to the state fell after 1990–91 with the acceptance of the Mukherjee formula of devolution.[1] From 1992–93, Finance Commission grants have also been declining—the state's share of income and excise taxes declined from 13.97 per cent in 1992–93 to 10.15 per cent in 1997–98. Other Finance Commission transfers such as grants under Article 275 of the Constitution[2] also fell from 6.39 per cent in 1992–93 to 1.08 per cent in 1997–98.

If a major source of revenues such as grants-in-aid and contributions is declining, then the only way that the pace of government expenditure can be maintained is by increasing fiscal deficit. This was 25.27 per cent of government expenditures in 1988–89, and was budgeted to be 30.29 per cent in 1997–98. The ratio of fiscal deficit to state domestic product was 9.2 per cent in 1988–89, 11.89 per cent in 1990–91 and 10.9 per cent in 1994–95. These figures are much higher than the fiscal deficit/gross domestic product ratio of 5 per cent that is taken to be an upper limit indicator of fiscal discipline in India. The high fiscal deficit also means that debt servicing, measured as interest payments and repayment of loans, eats up a high proportion of total expenditures (23.5 per cent in 1997–98), reducing the resources available for developmental purposes. Debt servicing was 94.8 per cent of borrowings in

1997–98 and 108 per cent of borrowings in 1996–97, indicating that all the borrowings do not make resources available for effective state intervention. It is often pointed out that the high proportion of debt servicing to borrowing need not be a faithful indicator of the lack of resource mobilisation when revenue surpluses are high, because revenue surpluses do make funds available for expenditure on capital account items. The revenue surplus and the recovery of loans given by the state government comprise the own resources of the government that are available for spending on the capital account. However, an important item of capital expenditure is the repayment of the principal sum on loans taken earlier. Accordingly, if the own resources of the government available for spending on the capital account are less than the repayment of loans expenditure item on the capital account, the state is not in a position to discharge its debt obligations from its own resources. It must borrow to repay old loans and that is the essence of a *debt trap*. Table 16.2 shows that this is true of Goa. As the last row of the table reveals, 69.21 per cent of the borrowings in 1993–94 and 62.51 per cent in 1997–98 were just intended to repay old loans.

Also, the financial situation has deteriorated sharply in the last few years with the revenue account going into a deficit.

Coalitions and Deficits

What this amounts to is that in the Goan economic scenario, citizens prefer low taxes but politically support governments that undertake increased expenditures (on health, roads etc.) which benefit them. Borrowing allows governments to increase expenditures and garner political support by not imposing higher taxes. As a consequence, due to the high debt servicing, developmental expenditures fall, the state government perpetually nurses a large fiscal deficit, and there is a reduction in the growth of incomes and employment. The asymmetrical behavioural response which demands low taxes but high expenditures results in shifting the burden to future budgets and future taxpayers. This is a major challenge for any democratic society, as a governing principle of citizenship is that citizens may be taxed if they express their preferences through voting for representatives who further their interests. Currently, due to high borrowings, future taxpayers are

TABLE 16.2
GOA'S FINANCIAL HEALTH IN RECENT YEARS

	1993–94	1994–95	1995–96	1996–97 (RE)	1997–98 (BE)
1. Revenue A/c surplus	3,322.64	2,755.53	3,228.41	581.75	–3,684.40
2. Recovery of loans	312.78	312.09	374.60	426.91	438.97
3. Resources available (for capital expenditure)	3,635.42	3,067.62	3,663.01	1,008.66	–3,245.43
4. Repayment of loans	19,056.86	12,065.48	2,381.20	12,781.09	13,109.40
5. Repayment of loans (less Row 3)	15,421.44	8,997.86	–1,281.81	11,772.43	16,354.83
6. Row 5 as percentage of borrowings	69.21	49.16	–	54.77	62.51

Source: Basic Statistics, Department of Planning and Statistics, Government of Goa.

being taxed by a government which they have not voted in, and thus does not represent them. The principle that motivates economic policy then is the 'taxation without representation' of future generations.

This situation occurs because the government budget implies expenditures which have distributional effects in the sense that some individuals gain at the expense of others — there is considerable rivalry to appropriate the gains from government regulations, tax-subsidy policies and contracting. Given that the share of government expenditure in the state domestic product is 40 per cent, meaning that of every rupee spent in Goa, 40 paise is spent through the government budget, the government holds considerable sway in the economic life of the state. As a result, interests in preserving existing policy or supporting the creation of new policy are also significant. Various interest groups accordingly struggle for the policy-induced benefits which are at the discretion of politicians. This struggle can be considered to have four characteristics. First, a number of groups compete to appropriate the benefits of government policy outcomes. Second, these benefits of policy are individually allocated in the sense that a single group benefits at the expense of other groups. Third, the benefits of government policy decisions are divided among the members of the winning or favoured group. Fourth, group members voluntarily decide the extent and nature of participation in efforts to influence the policy decisions of government.

Identifying interest groups and the co-operation and conflict between them is one way of coming to grips with the economic ferment in the state. However, I would argue that the implications of the distributional effects of government policies and expenditures that various interest groups seek to appropriate are much wider, and are more informative about the prospects of development in the state. One implication is that governments do not come into existence to satisfy the collective needs of all members of the community but rather to gratify the wants of only a part of the community. The aim of politics accordingly is redistribution towards favoured interest groups. Second, for any policy proposal with its associated re-distributive implications to be passed in the legislature, a government must obtain a controlling number of seats in the legislature. Accordingly, it is sensible for a party, not to maximise votes, but rather to seek a win in the simple majority of the number of constituencies represented in the legislature. Third, as politics is the business of redistribution, we must specify the vehicles of this redistribution. The vehicles are the various ministries through which government policies are implemented, and thus the cabinet is a part of the essential definition of a government. In terms of the division of labour within a cabinet, ministers are assigned particular policy jurisdictions or portfolios. These give a minister the job of initiating and implementing policy within a particular ministry. The resources (financial, human etc.) commanded by a minister to facilitate this task give him/her considerable de facto power over policy outputs in his/her jurisdiction. Given that the charge of formulating and implementing policy within a ministry has its own work pressures, and that a minister cannot easily call for the advice and expertise of the manpower of another ministry, it is extremely difficult for a cabinet minister to poke his nose deeply into the goings-on of other ministries headed by his cabinet colleagues. This gives each minister the ability to act in his ministry independently of other members of the cabinet. A cabinet portfolio is accordingly associated with jurisdiction over salient policy dimensions, and it is difficult to implement a policy which is actively opposed by the relevant minister. Since individual ministers will then have the incentive to act autonomously, there exists a potential tension between the collective decisions of the cabinet and the individual decisions of its members.

We can then think of a government as a set of individuals that has a controlling number of seats in the legislature, as well as a certain distribution of cabinet portfolios among the members of the set, with its associated policy position. The set of individuals can be a single party or a coalition of parties, as has been the case in Goa. As there is only a finite number of possible cabinet portfolios, which is smaller than the set of individuals forming the government, and as a portfolio signifies de facto power over salient outputs as well as the transferable benefits that go along with a cabinet rank, the essence of any proposal by a set of individuals to form a government is the portfolio allocation that it involves. Any proposal to form a government is also vulnerable to losing its majority in the legislature if individuals withdraw their assent to being members of the government. Those who have not been allocated portfolios or have not been given preferred portfolios are likely to do this, as a cabinet rank carries substantial transferable benefits as well as the ability to dictate policy. In this sense, the distribution of portfolios is a determinant of the durability of a government within the normal gap between electoral periods. A ministerial berth can therefore be viewed as a pre-specified reward which elected individuals contest for. Within a set of individuals who form a majority in the legislature, though all may contend for this reward, only some can become ministers. As a government functions mainly through institutional bodies such as cabinets and committees, it is important to be in such bodies in order to be able to decide policy that caters to the interest groups which support a politician. Anyone who cannot be accommodated with a ministerial berth would thus have some motivation to join another set of individuals who can form a majority in the legislative assembly as well as offer him a ministerial berth.

It is because politics has re-distributive goals that this tendency arises. In fact, the tendency can get aggravated and degenerate into what may be called 'contender cycles' as has been the case in Goa. To consider the essence of how this may arise, assume for the moment that the transferable benefits associated with two ministerial berths have a monetary equivalent of Rs 100. Also assume that of the three persons in an assembly, only two can become ministers. The three must decide by majority rule whom to elect as ministers. Suppose now that individuals A and B team up to form a majority and decide to divide the Rs 100 between themselves, 60/40. C has much to gain in trying to break this agreement, and he may propose to B that they split the amount in the proportion 50/50. This implies a gain to B, who we can expect will accept the offer, and a new coalition government forms. A now has much to gain from breaking this and trying to form a new coalition government and so might offer C a 55/45 split. When issues of redistribution are involved, those who lose out always have an incentive to attempt to become members of a winning coalition, and this has the potential of generating contender cycles.

A blown-up version of this phenomenon has been occurring in Goa. The Pratapsingh Rane government in late 1989, for example, had 21 members of whom 10 were ministers. All the remaining 11 members of the legislative assembly (MLAs) were contenders for the post. As they did not constitute a majority, they could only become ministers through the formation of a coalition and so some of them joined hands with the Maharashtrawadi Gomantak Party

(MGP). Also, the constitutional constraint of a minimum of one-third defecting in order not to be disqualified from being MLAs implied that the MGP would bargain to join hands with exactly 7 (one-third of the 21 Congressmen in the Rane government) of the 11 MLAs, so that the remaining ministerial berths could be given to the MGP. The ensuing Barbosa government, thus, had 12 ministers of whom 7 were from the Goan People's Party (the name the faction which broke from the Congress gave itself).

However, the Barbosa government had 15 ordinary MLAs who were all from the MGP. Being contenders, 7 of them (over one-third of the MGP strength) had an incentive to defect and join hands with the 14 MLAs of the Congress. This was the situation which led to the formation of the Ravi Naik government in 1991. However, in a significant move the number of ministerial posts was increased to 14. This one move resulted in the durability of the Ravi Naik government. This is because the contenders at the time could only form a coalition if the 7 Congress MLAs (one-third of 21) who were not ministers defected and joined hands with the 6 GPP and 12 MGP MLAs in the assembly. As the 7 Congress and 6 GPP MLAs were contenders, the assumption was that they would demand ministerial status and only one MGP MLA could then become a minister out of 14 ministerial posts. Having only one out of its 12 members as a minister in a coalition government was too high an opportunity cost for the MGP to even consider the proposed coalition seriously. The politics of government formation in Goa as a result of the logic of coalitions as outlined here implies that whoever forms a government will carry on the policy of jumbo cabinets in order to forestall the possibility of being dislodged from power, and subsequent governments in Goa have borne this out.

Large cabinets and the interest groups they represent result in large fiscal deficits and an overextended pattern of government expenditure. With each minister seeking to expand the budgetary allocation under his command, this results in inflated demands on the budgetary resources shared by the government. Each minister is aware that whatever government resources he does not exploit may or may not be available for his use, depending on the spending decisions of the other ministers. Hence, each minister exerts a negative externality on the other, and that is what generates an expansionary government expenditure programme. With such expenditures outstripping current revenues, the only way to finance them is through the creation of debt obligations which have grown over time and pre-empted large chunks of the resources of government, thereby leaving little for developmental expenditures. This has resulted in a decline in the capacity of the government to intervene effectively in the economy and to help in the generation of employment. However, apart from this macro-economic, direct impact, where government intervention has become unsustainable, I submit that the significantly high unemployment rate in Goa is not the involuntary unemployment that is the focus of discussion among development policy makers, but is rather a form of luxury unemployment. We turn to this now.

The Nature of Unemployment and Tourism

From the late 1970s the outflow of workers to the Middle East has been a major factor affecting regional employment. The migration of such workers—and an estimated 35,000 have so migrated—is normally temporary and distinguishable from permanent migration for resettlement. The domestic–foreign wage differential has had consequences for labour supply in the region of Goa. The high wage abroad provides an incentive for the migrant to work harder and for much longer hours abroad, and on his return home to compensate for this by choosing to enjoy more leisure. Besides, the increased financial wealth accumulated from working abroad is likely to have a negative effect on his offer to work on returning to his home town. Given the cushion provided by the migrant's earnings, his spouse and family members find that their reservation wage has increased and would offer to work less for the same wage. Moreover, the cushion of remittances relaxes the constraint of the need for an immediate source of income, and encourages pursuing the search for a job overseas or a government sector job, as the reward for searching for such employment is increased. The preference of the migrant for leisure on his return home, the increased reservation wage of the migrant's family, as well as the higher reward in searching for a job overseas or in the formal sector at home, gets reflected in a higher rate of unemployment in Goa, which is three times the national average. Moreover, the high outmigration has contributed in large measure to making the status associated with a job an important decision variable when considering an employment offer. Given the high regard and admiration that workers who migrate derive from society, the remainder of the workforce looks upon occupations as rewarding individuals not just by wage payments but also the social status they confer. In a labour market transaction, accordingly, it is not just the amount an employer pays for the services of workers that is significant but also how much he offers in terms of job attributes such as social status. If certain jobs do not have the right attributes deemed to be socially necessary, then individuals would prefer to remain unemployed in the hope of finding appropriate employment later, and this worsens the unemployment rate. However, unemployment due to high reservation wages is a form of luxury unemployment.

Macro-development is mainly about the effectiveness of state intervention and outcomes such as unemployment and inflation, and we have dealt with these issues at some length. Now we move on to some sectoral issues such as tourism and the power sector. As is well known, Goa is on the international tourist circuit, the number of tourists arriving here having gone up to about 1.18 million in December 1997, of which 262,000 were foreign tourists. There are 18,000 beds in 1,286 hotels and lodging places of different categories. Foreign tourists stay on an average for fifteen days, and domestic tourists for about four-and-a-half days. Also, a large proportion of domestic tourists (64.2 per cent, according to a survey done by Tata Economic Consultancy Services in 1976) stay with friends and relatives instead of at hotels. Tourism planners and policy makers are fond of reeling off statistics regarding the direct and indirect income and employment multipliers generated due to the economic activity of tourism. What is not discussed is the fact that tourism is subject to seasonal variation, with a busy season and a slack season. And as tourism is a service industry where the moment of production and that of consumption are contemporaneous, inventory accumulation or decumulation is not possible. Thus, the industry reacts to fluctuations in demand by varying output itself. Firms in the tourism sector cannot adjust output to demand variations by immediately hiring or firing the necessary or surplus labour, as customer satisfaction is sensitive to the speed of delivery. Quality variations and a customer badly served can damage reputation and reduce the flow of future customers to the firm. Employers thus react to the early stages of tapering off of demand from a peak season by reducing the hours of work. Skilled workers (receptionists, telephone operators, cooks etc.) have high fixed recruitment and screening costs. So the longer such a worker remains with an employer, the longer is the time span over which the cost can be spread, and hence such workers are generally kept underemployed during the slack season. On the other hand, unskilled workers (waiters, roomboys, sweepers, kitchen-helpers etc.) have low turnover costs for an employer as the search and training costs for such individuals are low. Such workers are therefore easily laid off during the off-season. The seasonality of incomes and employment is thus a major social cost of tourism that is ignored in the debates on tourism in the state (D'Souza 1993). The state is currently attempting to shift towards the high-paying tourist through plans to privatise historical forts and monuments, introducing adventure tourism such as bungee jumping and watersports, encouraging private parties to build golf courses, and recently clearing a plan to encourage gambling through allowing the installation of slot machines on offshore vessels.

Manufacturing, Tax Holidays and the Power Sector

In 1990–91, there were forty-two large and medium industries in the state with a total investment of about Rs 2.21 billion and providing employment to 9,120 persons. Likewise, there were 4,763 small-scale industrial units with an investment of Rs 903.4 million and providing employment to 30,073 persons. These units produced a range of products like TV sets, watches, auto components, ceiling fans, nylon fishing nets, processed food, cotton yarn, IMF liquor, fertilisers, pesticides, tyres, drugs and sugar. By 1996, there were eighty large and medium industries with a total investment of Rs 8.21 billion and employing 13,717 persons. The number of small-scale industrial units had increased to 5,118 with an investment of Rs 1.34 billion and employing 33,136 persons. The share of the manufacturing sector in state domestic product was 17.6 in

1990–91 and 23.6 in 1994–95. A tax holiday scheme that was introduced in 1993 and ended in March 1998 had mixed results. The five-year tax holiday was availed of by 962 industries, roping in an investment of Rs 9.3 billion. These industries included 904 small-scale units which invested Rs 817 million and fifty-eight large and medium-scale units with an investment of Rs 8.48 billion. When the scheme began in April 1993, seven or eight big industries set up projects in Goa in the first two years, while over 400 local entrepreneurs set up small units. This increased to forty-five big projects in 1995–96, roping in an investment of around Rs 4 billion. Due to the worsening power situation since then, the response dropped to only five more units in 1996–97 with a meagre investment of around Rs 350 million. Over twenty-five multinationals, mainly in the fields of pharmaceuticals, electronics and industrial accessories, have availed of the tax holiday. Seven projects were set up by non-resident Indians, and German units set up by Hoechst, Benchemie, the Bosf group and Siemens accounted for 39 per cent of foreign investment. About 8 per cent of foreign investment was accounted for by US MNCs such as Kodak, Richardson Vicks and Essef Corp. Firms from the UK, Portugal, Australia, Luxembourg, Korea, Switzerland, Canada, the Netherlands, Hong Kong and Taiwan have also come into Goa mainly to set up industrial accessories in steel, aluminium and plastics. Due to the lack of power, some twenty-three big companies have 'officially' begun production as a symbolic gesture to avail of the tax holiday facility, and are waiting for an improvement in the power situation before going in for full-fledged production.

Goa has come a long way from the situation prior to liberation when electricity was generated from diesel engines, which supplied a total of 2.2 MW catering to 6,000 consumers. Currently, the requirement of power is met by supplies from the Korba and Vindhyachal NTPC stations (135 MW) in the western grid. Besides, there is an additional 150 MW allotted from the national grid. However, Goa is able to draw only 220 MW availability from the grid and the total requirement is estimated to have reached 445 MW. The transmission and distribution losses of power at 26 per cent are much higher than the national average, and attributed to overloading of old, poor-quality and badly maintained distribution lines and transformers. Power shortage is today the biggest infrastructural bottleneck that Goa faces, with industries suffering a 30 per cent loss in production in 1998 due to power cuts. The state-run Goa Medical College was receiving only 22 KVA against its 33 KVA requirement, and had postponed all routine operations due to non-functioning of equipment, including the X-ray and the CT scan apparatus, at the time of writing. There is no dedicated power line connecting Goa to the national power grid in Maharashtra, and upgrading the distribution system to minimise losses, it is estimated, would cost more than Goa's annual budget. Given the seriousness of the problem, the state has recently opened up its power sector to private investment in both generation and transmission and distribution. The policy allows for the setting up of power generation plants, including captive power plants, without restrictions on capacity, and for the transmission and distribution of power by raising one's own infrastructure. State control would only be on tariffs through a State Power Regulatory Authority. There are over 4,500 employees in the state electricity department and the government has engaged the International Finance Corporation as consultants on how to corporatise the departmental structure of power supply in the state. The first private sector project is a Rs 1.62 billion, 50 MW naphtha-based plant in Sancoale being set up by Reliance-Salgaocar Power Private Limited, with an estimated per unit cost of Rs 2.02. The government has guaranteed purchase of 80 per cent of the plant load factor, and has agreed to pay deemed generation charges in case of strikes, lockouts and natural calamities, and also to supply water to the plant at January 1996 frozen rates. Without additional power capacity being set up, however, it is not going to be possible to attract new industrial units into the state — tax holiday or not. This will affect employment generation. Besides, as hotels and restaurants are forced to shut down their central air-conditioning units, the effects on tourism will be adverse and, of course, the direct impact on the comfort of the local population is an omnipresent concern.

Miscellaneous Issues and Conclusion

There are numerous other issues that would properly find a place in any discussion of development in Goa. Agriculture, for instance, is still an occupation pursued by 24 per cent of the working population (1991 Census). Approximately 39 per cent of the state's geographical area constitutes net sown area, and some 7.6 per cent of this is cultivated twice annually. Nearly 46 per cent of the gross cropped area is under cashew and coconut, 35 per cent is under rice, and the remaining under miscellaneous crops like vegetables, pulses, groundnut and sugarcane. A large proportion of operational holdings are below 2 hectares in size and so not economically viable. The problem of agriculture is a large number of tiny farms, which often makes the produce on the farm insufficient for home consumption. Issues such as uneconomic holdings, intensity of cultivation, lack of motive power and irrigation (15 per cent of net sown area is irrigated), are high on the development agenda.

Mining is estimated to employ some 8,500 persons directly, while an equal number of persons are employed in transport and other allied activities relating to this industry. The mining of iron ore has been on the increase whereas that of bauxite and ferromanganese on the decline. The export of iron ore was of the order of 13.36 million tonnes in 1990–91 and 14.51 million tonnes in 1995–96, and is estimated to earn foreign exchange of over Rs 2 billion. The rising costs of excavation and environmental issues have dogged this sector's development.

The fisheries potential in Goa is assessed at around 70,000 tonnes per annum with an average of 2,500 tonnes of prawn exported every year. Overfishing by trawlers using purse nets, the development of prawn farming in brackish water, and the concentration on sales for exports and to tourists to the exclusion of the local population are issues in this sector. Goa's social sector indicators are good with above-average literacy rates and low birth and death rates, and an excellent doctor–population ratio (1:869 as against 1:2,100 for India). With declining birth rates, there has been a fall in enrolment at the primary school stage. However, retention in the school system is low, with 70 per cent of those enrolling in the first standard dropping out before they can attain secondary education. Also, the vocationalisation of education has not been successful in providing employment-oriented training, and a large number of those with higher education are unemployed or unable to find jobs in the area of their expertise, thus spawning outmigration.

Goa enjoys pride of place in the economy of India with a high per capita income and social indicators that are indicative of high levels of human development. However, the state has been able to get to this position more due to its strategic location and natural resources, rather than from a thriving economy. It has not been able to sustain government intervention, with the chunk of government resources being pre-empted by wages and salaries to an enlarged bureaucracy (there are about 42,195 employees in government and aided schools and colleges, making Goa the state with the largest ratio of government employees to population in the country), and interest payments on debt. Unemployment is high. The internal demand generation process is weak and the income generation process has been kept up by exports of mining ore and fish, by the non-tradable tourism sector, and by migration of the population which has been remitting incomes in a major way. Goa is a young state—just thirteen years old—in the Indian Union. It is a state in transition that has yet to find a balanced and sustainable growth path.

Notes

1. The formula gives a large weightage to population (55 per cent) and per capita income (25 per cent), a weightage of 15 per cent to special problems and 5 per cent to fiscal management in the devolution of resources to the states. The lower weightage given to per capita income has not been in Goa's favour.
2. These are essentially gap grants given to cover revenue deficits to states deemed to be 'in need of assistance'.

References

Boxer, C.R. 1969. *The Portuguese Seaborne Empire, 1415–1825*. London: Hutchinson.

Cunha, T.B. 1939. 'Portuguese India: A Survey of Conditions after 400 Years of Foreign Colonial Rule', in T.B. Cunha Memorial Committee, *Goa's Freedom Struggle*, Mumbai.

De Souza, T.R. 1979. *Medieval Goa: A Socio-economic History*. New Delhi: Concept Publishers.

———. 1990. *Goa through the Ages: An Economic History*, Vol. II. New Delhi: Concept Publishers.

D'Souza, E. 1993. 'Fluctuations and Employment Institutions in the Tourism Sector', *Indian Journal of Labour Economics*, Vol. 36, No. 4.

Fernandes, A.C. 1923-24. 'The Population Problem in Goa', *Indo-Portuguese Review*, Vol. 6, pp. 22–26.

——. 1940. 'A Renovacao Economica da India Portuguesa', *Boletim do Instituto Vasco da Gama*, Goa.

Pearson, M.N. 1989. *The New Cambridge History of India: The Portuguese in India*. New Delhi: Cambridge University Press.

——. 1990. 'Goa's Overseas Trade', in Teotonio R. De Souza, ed., *Goa through the Ages: An Economic History*, Vol. 2. New Delhi: Concept Publishers.

Rodrigues, L.A. 1977. *The Portuguese Army of Goa*, Goa.

Appendix

TABLE 16.A.1
HOW A RUPEE OF GOVERNMENT EXPENDITURE IS SPENT

	1988–89	1989–90	1990–91	1991–92	1992–93	1993–94	1994–95	1995–96	1996–97 (RE)	1997–98 (BE)
Index of government expenditure (Rs 24,472.94 lakh = 100)	116.50	133.80	162.62	190.53	220.43	293.04	301.20	296.46	377.16	431.36
Developmental expenditure (of which)	79.50	76.18	76.78	73.34	68.23	55.75	62.12	71.57	63.40	58.10
Medical, family welfare & public health	7.64	8.28	8.19	7.95	7.02	5.86	5.98	6.83	5.95	5.26
Water supply & sanitation	7.16	7.30	6.59	6.82	6.11	6.11	5.61	6.90	5.84	7.91
Education, sports, art & culture	21.29	20.30	18.86	17.45	16.57	13.49	14.93	17.21	16.05	12.99
Water and power development	21.50	19.80	20.47	18.38	19.94	15.58	20.62	23.84	20.08	20.01
Non-developmental expenditures	20.50	23.82	23.22	26.66	31.77	44.25	37.88	28.43	36.60	41.90
Interest payments	5.50	7.82	7.53	12.29	10.85	9.51	10.47	12.40	11.30	11.08
Repayment of loans	2.75	3.40	3.68	3.50	10.72	26.57	16.37	3.28	13.85	12.42
Debt burden	25.97	36.46	38.06	124.19	99.59	116.12	108.10	129.37	108.03	94.80

Source: Government of Goa, Budget Documents, various issues.

TABLE 16.A.2
HOW A RUPEE OF GOVERNMENT EXPENDITURE IS FINANCED

	1988–89	1989–90	1990–91	1991–92	1992–93	1993–94	1994–95	1995–96	1996–97 (RE)	1997–98 (BE)
State's own revenue	41.04	40.56	39.28	43.32	46.60	45.59	52.20	63.42	55.74	55.23
State excise duties	2.59	2.83	3.17	3.21	3.54	2.94	3.60	3.71	3.15	2.99
Sales tax	14.82	14.93	14.75	17.42	19.30	18.90	21.32	26.67	23.39	22.44
Receipts from departmental commercial undertakings	13.34	12.76	12.12	12.85	13.90	14.18	15.86	18.48	17.48	19.43
Grants-in-aid and contribution	33.69	26.49	32.20	26.31	25.95	19.51	20.54	19.89	16.98	14.48
State's share of income and excise taxes	12.85	7.97	13.39	13.50	13.97	10.93	11.79	9.79	9.81	10.15
Other finance commission transfers	8.37	5.65	8.83	7.51	6.39	4.72	4.70	5.60	3.16	1.08
Planning commission grants	9.36	9.46	7.45	2.87	3.08	1.72	2.49	2.55	2.49	2.19
Discretionary grants	3.11	3.41	2.53	2.43	2.52	2.14	1.56	1.95	1.52	1.06
Fiscal deficit	25.27	32.95	28.52	30.37	27.45	34.90	27.26	16.70	27.29	30.29
Internal debt	3.19	3.03	2.66	2.10	12.10	24.23	16.23	3.71	14.68	17.75
Planning commission loans	20.96	21.27	16.64	6.01	6.58	3.83	5.41	5.36	5.54	4.89
Discretionary loans	7.63	6.46	10.16	4.60	2.97	3.02	3.18	3.05	3.06	2.15
Public account net (small savings, provident fund etc.)	-6.32	2.55	-1.65	17.16	8.52	2.62	2.68	2.94	4.88	4.81
Overall deficit (+) or surplus (–)	-0.19	-0.36	0.71	0.50	-2.72	1.20	-0.24	1.64	-0.87	0.69

Source: Government of Goa, Budget Documents, various issues.

seventeen

The Development–Environment Interface in Goa

Maria Ligia Noronha

In advanced capitalist economies, the growth versus environment debate in policy has moved decisively from a discussion of the nature and extent of trade-offs between the two to one of how material and environmental objectives can be made more complementary. While economic interest may still predominate, goals are rarely pursued to the exclusion of environmental objectives (Rees 1985). In less developed countries such as India this is often not the case, and the trade-off is almost always in favour of economic goals. The fact that such growth has implications for the environment is almost a secondary consideration that needs to be brought to the attention of decision-makers but is not central to their worldview. One of the reasons for this lopsided approach is the dominant perception of the differential temporal scale of impacts of environment and of development activity. A decision relating to development, such as the setting up of an industry, will involve employment of people, provision of jobs and generation of income. The impacts are immediate. The environmental impacts of such decisions, however, are observable only after a period of time, and hence are given less importance in decision-making and policy formulation. Even in the enforcement of existing environmental policy, one tends to observe an almost in-built bias in favour of lax enforcement when these policies conflict with economic goals.

This chapter discusses this bias in the context of Goa, a small state of the Indian Union, where the environmental impacts of development are easily observable because of the fragile nature of the ecosystem as well as the existence of active and articulate environmental groups and citizens. It does this through a focus on two main ongoing activities — mining and coastal tourism — as these have been around for many decades and contribute significantly to income and jobs in Goa.

The Goan Economy

Goa is one of the most developed states in India, with a per capita income which is considerably higher than the all-India figure. In terms of other human development indicators too, such as infant mortality, birth, death and literacy rates, availability of drinking water and the status of women, Goa is better off than the country as a whole (see Errol D'Souza, this volume).

Some of the main features of Goa's development over the last thirty years can be summarised as follows:

1. Agriculture progressed well during the period immediately after liberation, but has been stagnant since the 1970s. The reason for this slowdown varies among regions; in some, the alternative land-use opportunities are more lucrative causing agriculturists to find reasons to move away from agriculture; in others, the tenurial laws have made agriculture a non-remunerative proposition as holdings have become small and fragmented; in yet others, agriculture has been steadily expropriated by the externalities caused by mining activity.
2. The fishing industry has grown in terms of capital employed. There has been a shift towards offshore and deep sea fishing, and small boats have been replaced by trawlers. The markets targeted by the industry too have moved away from the local

population of fish-eaters to serving the tourist industry and the export market. Thus, while the industry has grown, fish has increasingly become a luxury item for the local population.

3. Mining continues to be an important activity for both income generation and foreign exchange earnings, with a contribution of 7.7 per cent to net state domestic product (NSDP). The activity has over the years resulted in a number of environmental externalities that the producers and consumers of iron ore have not taken into account in their costing and development decisions.

4. The manufacturing industry contributes about 20 per cent of NSDP. Some of the large industrial units have caused certain pollution problems, documented in Alvares (1993). A number of small units in the industrial estates are also polluting the local environment.

5. Tourism is an important industry, contributing around 13 per cent to NSDP, and attracting both Indian and foreign tourists. According to the Department of Tourism, Goa, the number of domestic and foreign tourists who visited Goa in 1997 were 928,925 and 261,673 respectively. Tourism is estimated to contribute 7 per cent to employment and 7 per cent to state tax revenues, according to the Department of Planning, Statistics & Evaluation.

6. In terms of infrastructure, Goa has an extensive transport network with 196 km of road per 100 sq km as against the national average of 66 km per 100 sq km; an all-weather port, and air, rail and sea links with the rest of the country. Goa depends for power on its neighbouring states. It has just commissioned a private power plant of 50 MW. It is currently in the grip of a severe power crisis, not having had a proper power policy since liberation in 1961. A tax holiday and a 25 per cent subsidy on power, given in 1991 to attract investment to Goa, has resulted in a number of industrial units, both large and small, being allowed to be established. This was done without a proper assessment of the availability of power. A growing gap between demand and supply, and high transmission and distribution losses, have ensured that power is emerging as a major bottleneck for the growth of the economy and the well-being of the local residents.

Goa is gearing up for further growth, as is evident in the efforts of the state government to lobby for regional co-operation with the other states of the western region, the building and the commissioning of the Konkan Railway, the announcement of a new private airport and the discussion relating to the potential of Goa to be a Free Port. This article, while being optimistic about Goa's development potential, attempts to raise a cautionary note by drawing attention to the environmental feedbacks that some development activities are generating, which, if unattended, can reduce 'well-being' in Goa over time.

Tourism

Tourism as an economic activity can be traced back to the 1960s. Goa had the right blend of history, culture and sun to attract the tourist of the west, which effectively put it on the tourist map. More recently, there have been two types of tourists coming to Goa — the international in search of the sea, sun and sand, and the domestic who comes in search of a culture that is 'different' in the sense of dress-style, a sense of freedom and a western flavour. The industry has been exploiting this, and particularly the Portuguese connection, as is evident in the mushrooming of resorts and restaurants carrying names such as Dona Sylvia, Cidade de Goa, O. Pescador and Aldeia Santa Rita.

The local government embraced this activity but without a clear focus on how it should develop. The result of this lack of focus meant that tourism developed in an ad hoc manner (Wilson 1997a). In subsequent decades, and especially since the late 1970s, the growth of tourism has been rapid. According to official tourist statistics, while the period 1981–86 saw an increase in the number of domestic and international tourists, the period 1986–91 saw a slowdown in growth rates for domestic tourists and a fall in growth rates for international tourists (Table 17.1).

Tourist arrivals in Goa increased over 1991–92 to 1995–96 with the rate of growth of international tourists being higher than that of domestic tourists. This is largely due to the fall in the value of the rupee in the 1990s, which has made holidaying in Goa that much more attractive. While in the early 1980s, the share of international tourists who came to Goa was less than 3 per cent, it

TABLE 17.1
GROWTH OF TOURISM IN GOA

	Average Annual Growth Rates (per cent per annum)	
	Domestic	International
1981–82 to 1986–87	7.98	27.20
1986–87 to 1991–92	2.75	–1.34
1991–92 to 1995–96	3.90	31.00

Source: Directorate of Tourism, Goa.

increased steadily to over 10 per cent by the mid-1990s. During the period 1995–97, the average earnings in foreign exchange were US$43–57 million.[1] This has increased the importance of Goa as a tourist centre in the perception of the central government. A consequence of this is the increased clout that those who wish to promote tourism-related infrastructure in the state enjoy with the central government. A number of hotels and resorts built over the last fifteen or so years, have been set up in violation of existing rules and regulations (see Alvares 1993).

It cannot be denied that tourism has had a number of positive benefits for Goa, in terms of increased incomes, employment, foreign exchange and state revenues, and the provision of avenues for upward mobility for locals (Sawkar et al. 1997). However, there is increasing concern that tourism also has some negative social impacts and is stressing the Goan coastal ecosystem. In the long run, this will have an adverse impact on the industry itself. Figure 17.1 illustrates these various impacts by way of a Venn diagram, underscoring the point that some of the consequences of tourism may have impacts along multiple domains.

For example, the construction boom that has tracked the growth of tourism since the 1990s has had a positive economic benefit, but it is also responsible for negative environmental impacts due to congestion and sprawl in certain coastal areas.[2] Shifts in occupation, say from agriculture or fishing to tourism, may have resulted in increased incomes and allowed upward social mobility. But they have also had negative impacts as, for example, where agricultural wetlands have been converted into built-up areas, or sections of fishing villages which earlier protected the beaches from concretisation have been given up to the tourist industry.

FIGURE 17.1
IMPACTS OF TOURISM IN GOA

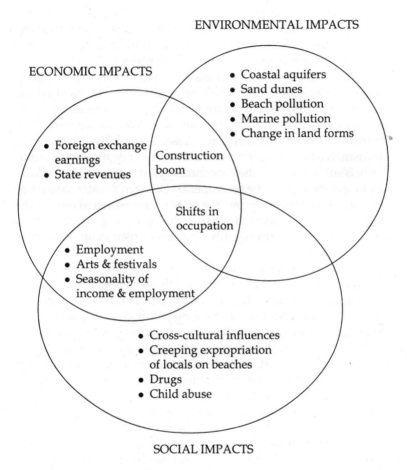

ENVIRONMENTAL IMPACTS

ECONOMIC IMPACTS

- Coastal aquifers
- Sand dunes
- Beach pollution
- Marine pollution
- Change in land forms

- Foreign exchange
  earnings
- State revenues

Construction
boom

Shifts in
occupation

- Employment
- Arts & festivals
- Seasonality of
  income & employment

- Cross-cultural influences
- Creeping expropriation
  of locals on beaches
- Drugs
- Child abuse

SOCIAL IMPACTS

Beach-based tourism has over the years resulted in a spatial concentration of buildings in some coastal areas, leading to a heavy demand for resources in these places.[3] A visit to any of the four main coastal areas of Goa — Bardez, Salcete, Tiswadi and Mormugao — immediately reveals the concentration and congestion of constructions and related infrastructure and facilities catering to the tourist industry, resulting in major changes in land use, serious shortages of resources such as land and water, and potential damage to coastal aquifers, the sand dune system, and coastal and riverine vegetation.[4] While Goa is not yet a Benidorm, some villages are moving that way. One journalist, for example, has described the village of Calangute, as the 'largest land grabbing centre in the state' due to the pace at which land is being converted and construction activity is taking place there.[5]

Land transactions have, in many cases, involved a change in land use from agriculture or fishing, settlement or orchard to land put under tourist infrastructure such as hotels, shops and bedsits. A major concern with changes in land uses to accommodate tourism is the recognition that tourism, especially international tourism, is a fickle industry, and that a tourist destination's popularity is subject to the fads of the industry. An approach that allows the face of the coast to be permanently changed to cater to tourism without simultaneously putting in place measures to ensure the longevity of the industry is a narrow approach to its sustainability. There is in Goa a concern with whether tourism as an industry is sustainable at all.

This concern with sustainability arises not only because of the whimsical nature of the industry and the permanent changes that construction and concretisation create, but also because of the rate at which the beaches in Goa are being polluted and are allowed to be polluted. Any casual visitor to the local beaches will be struck by the garbage — bottles, plastic bags, empty packets of crisps and cans of beer and soft drinks — littering most of Goa's popular beaches.[6] The same visitor will also be struck by the absence of any rubbish bins around to enable the beach user to get rid of the litter that s/he creates. Some local resorts offer water sports as an attraction to their hotels, but do little to make sure that the water around is not polluted by the diesel discharges or leaks from these boats. The waste produced by a number of resorts is also often piled up on the side of the resort; the wind picks these up and strews the countryside with the products of this callous environmental behaviour. A myopia is evident here. In the haste to increase incomes and profits, the hoteliers/resort-owners and the various service providers do little to ensure that the best practices are followed. In the long run, this will affect the hotel itself, as the beach and the water around it become unattractive for swimming and other uses. Quite apart from the long-term impacts that the polluter himself/herself and the industry as a whole face, this cavalier attitude on the part of hoteliers (and this is also true of restaurant and shack owners along the beach), coupled with a singular inaction on the part of government, has resulted in a significant reduction in the quality of the environment for the local population.

Tourist villages in Goa are now increasingly marked by an over-investment in buildings and an under-investment in conditions that can ensure that their attractiveness is maintained and sustained. If this orientation continues, the very resource upon which this industry is based will cease to be a resource. This will not only slowly kill the industry, but the processes and impacts that it has already set in motion will have long-term implications for Goa's overall development, unless government policy puts in place remedial measures and adopts a more environmentally friendly tourism.

Mining Activity

Another important economic sector in Goa is mining, popularly known as the backbone of Goa's economy. It has indeed been a very important element of the economic history of modern Goa since the mid-1940s. This importance has, however, been falling off over the last twenty-five years. In 1970–71, the share of income from the mining sector was 11.7 per cent; by 1980–81 it had fallen to 5.5 per cent, and further to 4.7 per cent in 1990–91. This trend has changed since 1990–91, with the sectoral contribution rising to 7.7 per cent in 1994–95. At present there is no local market for its low-grade ore, and all of it is exported. In terms of exports, Goan ore represents over 60 per cent of India's exports of ore. The value of iron ore exported from Goa is roughly equal to the tax and non-tax revenues of the Goa government, which for 1996–97 was estimated at Rs 7,000 million, pointing to the importance of the industry to the economy of Goa.[7] In order to comply with export specification, the ore from Goa is beneficiated, and is used for blending by foreign steel mills with higher-grade ore imported from other countries. The destinationwise share of exports is as follows: Japan, 56 per cent; Europe, 21 per cent; South Korea, 10 per cent; China, 9 per cent; and others, 4 per cent. The high dependence of exports on the Japanese market is evident.

A recent socio-economic survey conducted by the Tata Energy Research Institute (TERI) revealed that about 37 per cent of the total households in the mining belt are economically dependent on the mining sector. Of this, economic dependence through direct employment is above 60 per cent (TERI 1997). Economic activities related indirectly to mining are also important sources of employment for the households forming about 30 per cent of the total employment in the mining sector. From an economic point of view, therefore, the mining sector is of importance to Goa.

Mining operations are carried out in small leases of about 100 hectares or less, which is atypical of the industry. This is due to historical reasons. In the 1940s, there was a rush for mining rights in Goa, and the entire mining belt, which extends over an area equal to 18 per cent of Goa's land area, was given out as mining concessions by the erstwhile Portuguese colonial government. The concessions were given to private owners and were for ninety-nine years. Because the demand for mining rights was high, the Portuguese government had to parcel out small areas of land. Hence the large number of lease-holders and the small size of holdings (Noronha 1996).

Fifty years of mining have provided Goa with income and employment, created a class of industrialists who have been able to invest the surpluses from mining in a number of other activities such as tourism, power or the marketing of consumer products, and generated foreign exchange for the country. On the flip side, however, mining has left huge mountains of dumped mud in the countryside and large waterlogged holes in the ground, reduced air and water quality in the region, changed land use and land cover in the region, and is slowly but surely expropriating the farmers around the mine areas (Alvares 1993; CRE 1992; Modassir 1994; Nayak 1994; TERI 1997). It is evident that there is a mismatch between the boundaries of mine management and the ecosystems in which the mines are nested. The small size of holdings has been one reason for the lack of proper planning of mine operations. This, coupled with the large number of lease owners seeking to make profits out of their share of the resource in the ground, has resulted in a despoliation of the surrounding area in terms of air, water and land quality. No one is attentive to the region, as each minds his own interest.

As a result of this, over the period 1988–97, area under mining activity in the mining region of Goa increased by 46 per cent, while wetland agriculture declined by 14 per cent; area under forest cover declined by 14 per cent and water bodies shrank due to silting by 2 per cent (TERI 1997). Agricultural land has been affected by mining in three ways: (*a*) land has been diverted from cropping to dumping of waste material; (*b*) runoff from dumps has silted croplands and either reduced their productivity or made them unsuitable for agriculture; and (*c*) runoff has silted streams used for irrigation.

Air quality in the region is affected due to the fugitive dust from mining operations and truck movements, exhaust from the many transportation trucks, dumpers, dozers and shovels, and the dust blown off from waste dumps and ore stacks along water bodies. It is estimated that 20 per cent of the villages in the mining belt have poor to bad air quality and, in many locations, concentrations of suspended particulate matter exceed standards (TERI 1997).

Major water quality problems occur in important river stretches and streams upon which local communities depend for their water consumption, due to dewatering of mine pits, the discharge of partially treated or untreated waste water from beneficiation plants, the surface runoff from dumps, and the movement of barges. In many villages, the need to pump out water in mine operations that occur below the water table to allow ore to be recovered has caused a lowering of surface wells, and thereby reduced water availability to villagers.

It is evident that mining has created, and is creating, a number of environmental impacts in the region. This has occurred despite a plethora of rules and regulations that govern mining and the environment in Goa and India. A strong mining lobby, the foreign exchange argument, and a perennial cry that mining operations are occurring in a buyer's market with a low profit margin, have enabled the mining companies to get away with very little by way of rehabilitation and remediation of the surrounding region.

The Regulatory System

An assessment of both the mining and the tourism sectors in Goa reveals that their income and revenue generation functions have overshadowed their environmental impacts on the Goan eco-system. Despite elaborate rules and regulations that exist both at national and at state levels to monitor and manage environmental impacts and land uses, it is evident that such monitoring by state authorities has been absent. Apart from the absence of monitoring, it is evident that a number of rules have not been implemented.

Environmental policy in India, as in many other countries both developed and developing, has concentrated on regulatory rather than economic instruments. The approach has been one of regulating behaviour directly through applying water and air quality standards, bans, permits, land zoning and various other restrictions.[8] The policy regime has thus laid a strong emphasis on approaches of the 'command and control' variety rather than those of the economic or persuasive variety.

Under the Environmental Protection Act of 1986, a coastal zone notification was issued in 1991 setting out various rules and requirements and prohibitions for the coastal regions. It required all coastal states to prepare a coastal zone management plan that would classify the beach areas in terms of the three coastal regulation zones. Restrictions were imposed on the setting up and expansion of industries, operations and processes in the zones. The coastal zone notification and the subsequent amendment to it in 1994 are of particular importance to tourism and the development of tourism-related infrastructure in Goa, as most resorts are in, or being planned for, beach areas. The violations of this notification have resulted in a number of writ petitions being filed by the prominent environmental group in Goa, the Goa Foundation.[9] Many state-level Acts are also powerful instruments for environment management. Town and Country Planning Acts are effective tools for regulating land use and urban and regional development. Municipal and Panchayat Acts also have numerous clauses relevant to environmental concerns.[10]

It is evident from this brief description that India is well armed with a defined set of environmental regulations. The truth, however, is that these laws and rules are not well implemented at the state level, if at all. Even the central government's policies on pollution control tend to be unclear and ambivalent. Decisions taken by the Ministry of Environment are often side-stepped, and rules violated by other departments.[11] Stringent action is taken only in the wake of protest by environmental groups, especially if the latter take the case to court. But the effects of such actions are often shortlived and transient, and industry reverts to its earlier behaviour when the dust of protest dies down and after a show of environmentally friendly symbols.

A careful study of the failure of implementation of rules and regulations in Goa points to a weak institutional capacity; weak in terms of both ability and willingness to implement these regulations. Poor ability can be attributed to a number of factors:

1. The unclear linkages between concerned agencies and a poorly defined allocation of responsibilities. This is so both when there are a number of institutions regulating the same resource/ activity, and when there are a number of agencies dealing with different consequences of the same activity. For example, in the case of tourism, land use in villages is regulated by traditional ward committees, village-level panchayats, district-level planning and development authorities and the national coastal zone regulation rules. This results in a number of agencies having poor linkages among themselves and being unclear about how to deal with the complexities of issues that arise at each level of authority. In the case of mining, there are a large number of government agencies responsible for monitoring mining operations and for protecting different ecosystems. The end result is a tendency always to pass on the responsibility to another department/agency.

2. A lack of knowledge and information about what constitutes good and bad practices in tourism and mining. In the absence of a benchmark against which to compare local practices, well-advertised but cosmetic environmental improvements by the industry become the evidence of good behaviour, and hence an excuse for public officials to 'leave them alone to create jobs and income'.

3. Lack of resources, financial and human, to pursue enforcement. This is the excuse most often put forward by government departments to explain their inaction.

Coupled with a low capacity is the lack of political will. In part, this is because the environment often has a low priority for public officials when it conflicts with economic goals. But it is also because these activities are controlled by groups in society that have close links with the political leadership and the middle- and low-level bureaucrats, who have the actual responsibility of monitoring environmental behaviour. For some of them, regulations have become a means of dispensing patronage and, in many cases, of self-enrichment.[12] These bureaucrats are too embedded in the system to be able to push for environmental change, or even to want to push for change. It is the senior bureaucracy, the non-governmental organisations (NGOs) and the courts, which are not part of the local dominance, which need to push for the required changes.

It would be incorrect to explain away policy failures entirely by pointing to weak ability or unwillingness to act. There is also an institutional dilemma at work here. Regulating authorities find themselves caught between conflicting needs: the need to implement rules on the one hand, and the need to respond to the demands of local residents and groups which they represent on the other. Take the case of tourism. In many tourist villages, locals have been at the forefront of demands for land conversions, and have been instrumental in selling land to the tourism industry in order to appropriate some of the benefits of tourism. Land-holding patterns have helped this process. The villagers are often owners of shops, restaurants and small resorts, and have contributed to the growth of congestion in the region by providing land and/or capital. Those charged with implementing rules relating to land and to the environment (for example, members of the ward committees and of panchayats), are often drawn from the villages. They find it difficult to resolve the trade-off between local need fulfilment and rule implementation. There is a need for environmental education, both of the regulated and the regulator, to enhance the understanding of what is in the real short- and long-term interests of the community.

Conclusion

This chapter has discussed some of the environmental consequences of two major ongoing activities in Goa. Some of the main observations that arise from this discussion are as follows.

First, because of its small size, Goa is unable to influence national policy where activities involving foreign exchange are concerned.

There is also a tendency for national policy to disregard local concerns of a social and environmental kind. A more local orientation to policy does raise, however, the political question of competitive politics within a democratic society. This competition is intense not only between interests in the locality, but also between regions, and between the federating states and the centre. Small states do not have adequate representation at the centre, and what representation there is often speaks on behalf of the dominant interests. In an era of globalisation, one aspect of which is the opening up of the country for the development of its natural resources, it is important that the regional dimension, seen in terms of the environmental impacts of the development of resources and its local linkages, be integrated in a policy aimed at the sustainable development of the region.

Second, laws and regulations by themselves have not worked. They do not work unless there is a capacity to implement them. The institutional capacity has been weak in terms of both ability and willingness to implement these regulations. Industry, especially mining and tourism, operates very much in an 'implementation' vacuum, since most of the bodies charged with implementation of environmental rules have not taken their roles seriously. Some of the reasons for this are to be found in the political economy of the state, and others in the informational, technical and financial constraints faced by these bodies. Unless there is an attempt to strengthen these agencies and 'free' them from the political constraints they face, offences will continue to occur with impunity.

Third, despite several studies and protests about the environmental impacts of mining, not enough has been done by way of remediation.[13] It is evident that the greater the time lapse between the occurrence of environmental damage and its remediation, the greater (in most cases) will be the resources (both human and financial) necessary for addressing the problem. Hence the need for action where damage has already occurred, for monitoring and management of ongoing activities, and for the study of the environmental impact of future development choices.

Fourth, notwithstanding the relatively higher environmental awareness of the Goan polity, not enough is done by way of careful study when new development activities are on the drawing-board. One such major change that is being planned for Goa is according it Free Port status, to give the country a major point of entry for activities that can earn foreign exchange due to free trading and an unfettered policy environment.[14] Such a status can change the environmental face of Goa, not only because of the economic activities that may be set up here and the possibility of large influxes of population attracted by the pull of prosperity, but also because of an inability to monitor and manage environmental impacts (Noronha 1998). If the state is not able to monitor the mining and tourism industries, how can it control the many more economic activities that will come in the wake of a free policy regime? If the state is constrained by local vested interests, how will it be able to withstand the pulls and pressures created by the multinationals and transnationals that may be attracted to a Free Port? Unless an attempt is made to develop a policy framework that works, to nurture a bureaucracy that makes it work, and to foster a political culture that allows it to work, it would be environmentally foolhardy to give Goa Free Port status.

Fifth, in contemporary, globalised India, states are vying with each other to attract new, especially foreign, investments. Lax environmental policies and enforcement practices may increasingly be used by states as a means of differentiation to attract new industry. An analysis done by Mani et al. (1998) on the impact of environmental regulations on locational choice for greenfield investment in India in 1994, however, leaves us with some hope. The study found that stringency of enforcement of environmental regulations does not have an adverse impact on the relative attractiveness of sites for location of new industry, and that, in fact, there is a positive correlation with environmental spending by the state. This finding lends support to the argument that states do not have to be soft on the environmental front to attract industry. On the contrary, concern with environment is an indicator of other variables in a state, such as good governance.

A choice of development options based on careful advance planning and subsequent monitoring is so much more valuable than the fire-fighting evident today. The closing down of an industry is a difficult option once the industry has been set up; hence the need to examine in careful detail the type of technology that is being imported, the methods of waste disposal and waste discharge, and the possible environmental impacts of any industries and development activities planned by the state.

Goa could be a model of sustainable development for the rest of India. It is small and, therefore, manageable. It has a high level of literacy, skilled labour, an articulate and concerned polity, and is already well placed relative to other states in terms of human and economic development indicators. However, development in Goa is not being monitored for its environmental implications. Development in Goa occurs sometimes at the *expense* of the environment. These negative feedbacks will, over time, reduce the well-being of people in the state, unless they are recognised and an explicit effort is mounted to make development and environmental management objectives more complementary in the design of policies and strategies to tap the potential of this well-endowed state.

Notes

1. This is probably an underestimate as it is a record of foreign currency converted in Goa. However, a considerable amount of foreign currency that is meant to be spent in Goa is converted at the first port of entry which is normally Mumbai or Delhi. If the all-India foreign exchange earnings from tourism are considered and Goa is apportioned a share based on the share of tourists who come to Goa, then the amount rises to around US$115 million.
2. For a discussion on the impact of the ad hoc growth of tourism on the northern beaches and villages of Goa, see Wilson (1997a, 1997b).
3. See 'Industry and Tourism Take Toll of Goa's Coastline', *The Navhind Times*, 4 June 1998.
4. The Tata Energy Research Institute (TERI) has recently concluded a research project that has studied the impact of these transient population movements and other tourist-related migrations on coastal environments in Goa, focusing on the driving forces and mechanisms by which these result in changes in coastal land use.
5. 'Blind Tourism Policy Encourages Illegal Constructions', *O Heraldo*, 5 March 1998.
6. A. Wilson, 1997, 'Garbage, Vendors Turn Idyll into Nightmare', *O Heraldo*, 3 March 1998, p. 1.
7. Almeida, 1997, *The Economic Times*.
8. There are four main statutory Acts that seek to preserve the environment: The Water Pollution Act, 1974; The Air Pollution Act, 1981;

The Forest Act, 1980, and The Environment Protection Act, 1986. For details, see Rosencranz et al. (1991).

9. For details of these violations and the legal battles being fought by the Goa Foundation, see Alvares (1993).
10. See, for example, the Goa Panchayat Act, 1993, Section 66.
11. For some examples, see Vyas and Reddy (1998).
12. 'Blind Tourism Policy Encourages Illegal Constructions', *O Heraldo*, 5 March 1998.
13. This is however beginning to change as the government has begun to adopt a more proactive role in improving environmental behaviour through consultation with industry, environmental NGOs and research institutes.
14. *The Times of India*, 2 March 1998.

References

Alvares, C. 1993. *Fish, Curry and Rice: A Citizen's Report on the Goan Environment*. Goa: EcoForum.

Centre for Resources Engineering. 1992. Environmental Impact of Iron-Ore Mining in Goa. Project submitted to the Ministry of Environment, Mumbai, April 1992.

Mani et al. 1998. World Bank Policy Research Working Paper 1718, Washington, D.C.

Modassir, M. 1994. Impact of Current Iron Ore Mining Activities on the Environment of Goa and Proposed Measures to Minimise Long Term Environmental and Economic Damage. MBA Thesis, University of Hull, UK.

Nayak, G.N. 1994. Impact of Mining on Environment in Goa — Present Status. Report to the Ministry of Environment and Forests, Government of India, Goa University, Taleigao.

Noronha, L. 1996. 'Mining in Goa: The Need to Integrate Local, Regional and National Interests'. Paper presented at the UNCTAD Expert Group Meeting on Development Policies in Resource-Based Economies, Geneva, 21–22 November 1996.

———. 1998. 'Understanding the Environmental Implications of a Free Port for Goa'. Paper presented at the Free Port for Goa seminar at the Indian International Centre, Goa, 10 January 1998.

Rees, J. 1985. *Natural Resources: Allocation, Economics and Policy*. London: Methuen.

Rosencranz, A., S. Divan and M.L. Noble. 1991. *Environmental Law and Policy in India: Case Materials and Statutes*. Mumbai: Tripathi.

Sawkar, K., L. Noronha, A. Mascarenhas and O.S. Chauhan. 1997. 'Tourism and Environment: Issues of Concern in Goa'. Symposium on Economic Globalisation and Environmental Sustainability in SAARC Countries, 2–6 June 1997.

Tata Energy Research Institute (TERI). 1997. *Areawide Environmental Quality Management Plan for the Mining Belt of Goa State*. Project Report for the Government of Goa, New Delhi.

Vyas, V.S., and V.R. Reddy. 1998. 'Assessment of Environmental Polices and Policy Implementation in India', *Economic and Political Weekly*, 10 January, pp. 48–54.

Wilson, D. 1997a. 'Paradoxes of Tourism in Goa', *Annals of Tourism Research*, Vol. 21, No. 1.

———. 1997b. 'Strategies for Sustainability: Lessons from Goa and Seychelles', in Stabler, ed., *Sustainable Tourism? From Policies to Practice*. Wallingford: CAB International.

eighteen

Pragmatic Politics in Goa: 1987–99

Peter Ronald deSouza

a review of the past twelve years of politics will allow us to move beyond the tumult of the movement to a study of the patterns which emerge, to a deeper evaluation of political events, issues, trends and personalities. When these twelve years are read not as a series of weeks but as the *longue duree* of a society, some interesting insights concerning the politics of democracies emerge. In this chapter I shall stand back from the tumult of these twelve years and try and find, amidst the din and dust, something of 'significance'.

Changing Profile of the State

The story begins with Goa's attainment of statehood on 30 May 1987. From a union territory with an assembly comprising thirty members, the new state now has an enlarged assembly of forty members, a change in numbers symptomatic of the increasing power of the state. This shift has consequences for the different

I should like to thank Adi H. Doctor for comments and Alito Siquiera, Aureliano Fernandes, Venecia Cardoso, Santosh Vernekar and Mohan Mangueshkar for assistance with data. An earlier version of this paper was published in the *Economic and Political Weekly*, Vol. 34, Nos 34–35, 21–28 August 1999, pp. 2434–39.

domains of social life. In the economic domain, for example, the state has now to be fiscally more independent since it is less eligible for grants from the centre. This has resulted in a decline in state development expenditure (D'Souza 1997: 17). The shift has also had symbolic consequences, in that now the citizens of Goa are on par with the citizens of other states in their ability to select the president and to decide their own futures. It has also had political consequences, in that statehood has given greater autonomy to the political leaders, thereby reducing the *de jure* power of the central bureaucracy and of the lieutenant governor (now a governor). Decisions concerning items on the state list can now be taken in Goa and do not need the approval of the bureaucracy in Delhi, as had been the case earlier under union territory status (Rubinoff 1998: Ch. 5). These consequences, economic, symbolic, political, have taken place during a period of dramatic change in national politics; changes which, when read together with changes at the state level, present a picture of politics in Goa that is fairly complex. Let me elaborate.

In addition to the usual issues of agriculture, mining, transport, industry, unemployment etc., that impact upon politics, the issues that need to be noted, if not analysed, with respect to their significance for state politics in the years 1987–99 are the following: (*a*) the transformation of land from a tool in the production process into an alienable commodity in an emerging market in/for land; (*b*) the growing role of tourism in expanding the contribution of the services sector in the economy (Sawkar et al. 1998), and in its effects on identity politics; (*c*) the demographic changes brought about by in- and out-migration and the consequences of this migration for political and social life; (*d*) the controversies centring around large development projects such as the Konkan Railway and the proposal for a Free Port, with respect to their irreversible impacts on Goa; and (*e*) the expansion in the size of the state bureaucracy as a result of which there is one government employee for approximately every twenty-six citizens, making the state a rent-seeking rather than just an enabling state. I have thought it fit to foreground these five issues here because the dynamics of party and electoral politics in Goa have in considerable measure been influenced by them.

However, before I get into an analysis of the politics of the period, let me say something especially about the market in land because of the enormous impact it has had on the politics of this period. My comments will be in the nature of a series of propositions, a potential research agenda perhaps, since unfortunately there is little systematic study on this issue on which I can draw. I should like to begin by stating that the most significant factor in this decade of politics is the dramatic change in the status of land. Whereas earlier the value of land was assessed in terms of its contribution to agriculture, now it is assessed in terms of its worth as a tradeable commodity. A new group of players has emerged in this market in/for land, the most significant of which is the political class of bureaucrats and elected representatives. The growth in this market has been because of the role of many actors, like builders, landlords, tenants and politicians, each of whom has a stake in the network of transactions. The dynamics of this market has as yet not been mapped in terms of (*a*) the interests and strategies of each actor; (*b*) the monetary volume of the transactions in the sector; and (*c*) its contribution to the economy; but suffice it to say that it is very large, as can be gauged from the changing physical landscape of the towns and beaches of Goa.

These transactions are further strengthened by the expansion of the tourism industry. Some of the instruments that the industry has developed for raising capital, such as the 'rent-back facility', where builder, hotelier, house-owner and regulatory agency collude to create large properties in tourist sites, strengthen this market in land. Since all these activities involve getting many government permissions, covering the whole range from planning permissions to occupancy certificates, to loans from the Goa Economic Development Corporation (EDC), a state-owned entity, the politician and bureaucrat become key figures in the various transactions involved. Further, since these transactions involve large sums of money, and since they constitute one of the major economic activities in the state, the political economy of government in Goa has begun to be constituted around this market in land. Goa has also emerged as a society with a significant middle class which brings new meanings to politics — it likes to see politics as spectacle. I have made mention of this class here because its internal dynamics has significance for politics, particularly democratic politics.[1]

The foregoing is a profile of a society undergoing change at many levels, and as a result of many forces, some of which are government-induced, some because of other agencies. The parameters of this change are vigorously contested on every plane, cultural (Angley 1999), environmental,[2] economic,[3] social and, of course, political. This last is the theme of this chapter, which I shall examine a little later. Before I do so, however, I need to locate this reading of politics in Goa within the larger frame of Indian politics. This is necessary because the process of linking up with the larger Indian polity shows impacts of the larger on the smaller which are both direct and delayed, superficial and more enduring.

Three aspects of these linkages could perhaps be mentioned here to illustrate the point. The first is the culture of party politics in Goa. Party politics has acquired the same internal logic, perhaps through imitation, as party politics at the central level in terms of palace intrigue, factions, the authority status of the high command, the etiquette of subservience and sycophancy, and most significantly the blurring of the distinction between the personal and the public. The second is the centrality of politics to daily life, not just in a removed sense of 'everything is affected by politics,' but in a more immediate sense of politics as spectacle, of a curiosity to know about the latest episodes in the long-running and popular political drama. A measure of this centrality is the fact that Goa supports eight daily newspapers in three languages. The third aspect is the political-cultural impact of the mobilisation around the demolition of the Babri Masjid. This mobilisation has affected the way the communities have constituted themselves, an observation that will become more apparent when we look at the election results of the last decade, particularly the rise of the Bharatiya Janata Party (BJP) and the decline of the Maharashtrawadi Gomantak Party (MGP).

The preceding elaborate prefatory note is intended to provide the perspective within which the high stakes that parties and politicians play for can be understood. The market in land is the text within which the actions and choices of political agents can be understood. This must be borne in mind when I discuss the politics of the period. My reading of the changes at the surface level of politics must be seen in terms of its base in the political economy of land. I will discuss the politics of the state in three sections: (*a*) the changes in the institutions of the polity; (*b*) the trends within party organisations and the party system; and (*c*) the emerging electoral landscape. Since elections are a sort of diagnostic tool for examining the state of the polity, this last section will help us understand better the consequences of the interaction between the domain of society and that of politics.

Changes in Political Institutions

An analysis of the experiences of political institutions in these twelve years establishes one clear fact: that an aggressive and aspiring political class, made up of different segments, has emerged, which has taken possession of political institutions and begun to fashion them after its own interests. The extent of this fashioning will depend upon the tension between the flexibility and resilience of the institution, flexibility to accommodate interests/directives, and resilience deriving from the logic of its rules and beyond which it cannot go. The agency of this political class, brought in through individuals, such as faction or party leaders like Churchill Alemao, Ravi Naik, Ramakant Khalap, Manohar Parrikar, Wilfred de Souza and Luizinho Faleiro, or through groups, such as Bahujan Samaj, Kshatriya Bhandari Samaj, the Mool Goenkarancho Ekvott and the Catholic Church, and through the cultural perspectives within which they are located, begins to cause a strain on institutions which now have to negotiate a balance between the 'public interest', ostensibly expressed through their impersonality, and the 'particular interests' represented by the interventions of the political class. The outcomes of this struggle between the two interests can be seen as the episodes and events that make up the history of our institutions, in this case those of Goa during the years 1987–99. Let me illustrate with a few cases.

I shall begin with the institution of the legislature. Let me draw attention to some of the significant events that occurred during the period under review when the assembly completed two terms (1989–94 and 1994–99), the third just begun in June 1999. The most repetitive aspect of this period was the act of defections when members of the legislative assembly (MLAs) left one party and joined another without resigning and facing the electorate. Regardless of the constraints of the 52nd Amendment, members, after elections, saw politics only in terms of their personal, short-term interests and, unconstrained by party ideology, changed sides quite often, establishing firmly the politics of pragmatism (deSouza 1998a). Such pragmatism appears to have a considerable elasticity.

The data in Table 18.1 gives us a synoptic account of the movement of defectors between parties, the role of the speaker, and the time taken to pronounce judgement during which the defector

TABLE 18.1: DEFECTIONS AND THE OFFICE OF THE SPEAKER

Speaker	Period	Political Party	Date of Defection	Petitioner	Against Defection	Petition Filed	Order Given	No. of Months	Verdict
Luis P. Barbosa	22-1-90 to 14-4-90	Congress	–	–	–	–	–	–	–
Kashinath Jalmi (Member u/10th Schedule)	29-3-90 to 14-12-90	MGP	24-3-90	Luizinho Faleiro (Congress)	L.P. Barbosa	17-3-90	14-12-90	9½	Disqualified
Surendra Sirsat (Speaker)	26-4-90 to 4-4-91	MGP	1) 24-3-90 2) – 3) 24-3-90 4) 3-1-91	1) D. Fernandes (Congress) 2) V. Naik (MGP) 3) Amshekar (MGP) 4) K. Jalmi (MGP)	1) 6 Members (GPP) 2) C. Pegado (Individual) 3) 7 members (GPP) 4) Ravi Naik (Congress)	1) 28-3-90 2) 30-11-90 3) 22-11-90 4) 25-1-91	1) 13-12-90 2) 7-2-91 3) 6-2-91 4) 15-2-91	1) 9½ 2) 2½ 3) 2½ 4) 22 days	1) Petition dismissed 2) Petition dismissed 3) Petition dismissed 4) Naik disqualified
Simon D'Souza (Acting Speaker)	5-4-91 to 25-7-91	Congress	Review Petition	1) Ravi Naik (Congress) 2) Bandekar/Chopdekar (Congress)	1) Speaker Surendra Sirsat's decision 2)	1) 4-3-91 2) 4-3-91	1) 8-3-91 2) 8-3-91	1) 4 days 2) 4 days	(1) & (2): Speaker's decision reversed
Shaikh Hassan Haroon (Speaker)	26-7-91 till 1994	Congress	24-3-91	1) Victor Gonsalves (Congress) 2) P. Raut (Congress)	1) 6 members (GPP) 2) Chodankar (MGP)	1) 4-1-92 2) –	1) 15-9-94 2) –	1) 2½ years 2) –	1) Petition dismissed 2) –
Tomazinho Cardozo (Speaker)	16-1-95 to 10-2-99	Congress	27-7-98	Pratapsingh Rane	Willy de Souza and four others	27-7-98	1) Interim: 28-7-98 2) Final: 29-7-98	1) 24 hours 2) 48 hours	Interim disqualified (ex parte); final confirmed

continued to enjoy parliamentary privileges and, in some cases, even the exercise of power. It is a picture of the new culture of pragmatic politics that is emerging.

The next interesting aspect of the period is the ten changes in government that took place in these two terms, indicating that the assembly developed an autonomy of its own, with its forty members willing and able to work out short-term coalition combinations arrived at through constructed legislative majorities. Election opponents became allies and allies traitors (see Fernandes 1997). The frequent changing of coalition partners, and the language acrobatics that were employed to provide justifications for it, resulted in the moral cement of society suffering a severe erosion. The domain of public morality lost its ability to deter public men and women from transgressing the limits that underlay the ethics of representation, that constituted the evolved codes of political behaviour in a representative democracy. Not one MLA, during these twelve years, thought it fit to get an endorsement from voters for these shifts in association. Nobody resigned and sought re-election. While the initial defections caused some outrage, resulting in voters punishing the defectors in the 1994 elections, their continued occurrence dulled public morality, with most of the habitual defectors returning in the 1999 elections. The only democratic code that seems to have retained some force is majority rule within the assembly. All else was negotiable. During this period, seven governments lasted for less than one year, one for less than two years, just two for more than two years; and one for only two days (see Table 18.2).

TABLE 18.2
DURATION OF CABINET GOVERNMENTS SINCE 1990

Churchill Alemao	March 1990–April 1990	17 days
Luis Proto Barbosa	April 1990–December 1990	9 months
Ravi Naik	January 1991–May 1993	28 months
Dr Wilfred (Willy) de Souza	May 1993–April 1994	16 months
Ravi Naik	April 1994–April 1994	2 days
Dr Willy de Souza	April 1994–December 1994	8 months
Pratapsingh Rane	December 1994–July 1998	48 months
Dr Willy de Souza	July 1998–November 1998	4 months
Luizinho Faleiro	November 1998–February 1999	3 months
Luizinho Faleiro	9 June 1999–	in power

These changes in government in some cases also involved changes of assembly speakers who, empowered by the 52nd Amendment to the constitution, the Anti-Defection Act, acted in a blatantly partisan manner in deciding on the legality or illegality of defections on the basis of whether the defectors were changing over to the speaker's party or not. In some cases these decisions were taken in a matter of days, in some cases months, making a mockery of the spirit of the Act (deSouza 1998a; see Table 18.1, column headed 'No. of Months'). In one case, a member (Kashinath Jalmi) appointed under the 52nd Amendment to decide on the legality of a speaker who defected to become chief minister served, during the period of the decision, as the law minister of the very same chief minister. The office of the speaker lost its high status as an office impartially regulating the discursive dynamics of the polity. It came to be seen as an office that is purchasable, not earned. These defections resulted in jumbo cabinets with the number of ministers growing to fourteen in a house of forty members.[4] Since members from the opposition, in alliance with factions from the ruling group, formed new governments, one could reasonably argue that during the assembly term, particularly 1989–94, many members in the legislature, because of jumbo cabinets and repeated defections, became members of the executive thereby undermining the doctrine of separation of powers between the executive and the legislature, an important principle in a democracy (deSouza 1998b). The principle of collective responsibility also faced erosion since members from an earlier cabinet joined the following cabinet, which was formed through defections, and in their justifications challenged the integrity of the cabinets they had just left. These happenings in the assembly have shown (and no political party is exempt from this charge) that the moral force of the concept of the *Laxman Rekha*, the limiting codes constraining behaviour in a democracy, is very weak in Goa.

During this period, the institution of the governor also came under a cloud. Governor Bhanu Pratap Singh had to resign because of his dismissal of the Dr Wilfred de Souza government without consulting either the president or the majority group in the legislative assembly, thereby violating the letter and spirit of Article 164 of the Constitution of India. Further, this political competitiveness between groups brought the courts into the picture, requiring them to now resolve issues of defection within the legislature. This is an undesirable development, since it weakens the doctrine of separation of powers and sovereignty of jurisdiction. Now matters of defection and the decisions of the speaker, because of the slovenly way in which they have been handled, have been linked to issues of 'due process' and 'natural justice' thereby making them eligible for judicial review (D'Mello 1994).

In contrast to these negative trends, however, the institutional topography of Goa also witnessed some positive developments. Since the 73rd Amendment gave the third tier of government constitutional status, the Conformity Act in Goa also incorporated some of its provisions. As a result, one-third of the seats in the 182 panchayats were reserved for women. Many new faces entered the political system, generating a new dynamism and extending the range of representation. Since panchayati raj institutions (PRIs) are still in their early stages, they are still going through their learning curve, exhibiting characteristics of collusion and competition with vested interests and dominant groups.

Trends within Party Organisations

There are five major players in the party system. The first is the Congress, which I will call the 'dominant party' in a sense akin to Rajni Kothari's classification, since it sets the terms of party competition and since all the other parties develop their strategies, or owe their existence to it. The second, in terms of its salience (although declining) during this period, is the MGP which has developed a peculiar master–slave relationship with the Congress. The third is the BJP which has grown by cannibalising the MGP with which it once had a relationship, converting a vote bank that was rooted in a strong Bahujan ideology into one that can perhaps best be described as soft *Hindutva*. The fourth and not insignificant group is the small, local, personality-based parties such as the UGDP and the GRCP, who have the ability to win a few seats in the assembly and who, again to borrow Rajni Kothari's terms, can be described as parties of pressure with respect to the Congress.[5] The fifth significant group is the independents who have, as in the

1989–94 assembly, sometimes held the balance of power. It is the dynamics between these five players which sets the character of the party system.

Of all the above it is the Congress that best exemplifies the politics of pragmatism. This is evident in its success in accommodating opposed factions; in its converting into a fine art the practice of expelling and re-admitting politicians who had left the party bringing down its government on several occasions;[6] in its stressing 'winnability' rather than venality; in its manipulation of the election of the speaker;[7] in its splitting of opposition parties, especially the MGP and the UGDP;[8] in its expansion of the cabinet and appointment of MLAs to 'lucrative' posts such as the chairmanships of the two planning authorities and of the Economic Development Corporation etc. These are just some of the practices of the Congress which have ensured its dominance during the decade, except for brief periods when large sections left to form the GPP (Alemao and others, in 1990) or the Goa Rajiv Congress Party (GRCP) (Dr Willy and others, in 1998) (see Table 18.1). More than any other party, the Congress has demonstrated an ability to manage dissidence in that it has even got implacable enemies to work together. In the 1999 cabinet, for example, Faleiro has managed to have both Ravi Naik and Churchill Alemao in the cabinet, even though it was Naik who had imprisoned Alemao and proceeded against him when he (Naik) was chief minister. This success is because of a dual strategy of invoking the 'mind' of the high command, which few ambitious Congressmen would like to go against, and of tactically being one step ahead of the dissidents. Faleiro in 1999 has succeeded so far in curbing open revolt by having Rane as speaker, thereby holding the threat of disqualification over any dissidents, by accommodating major faction leaders within the cabinet, and by making regular trips to meet Sonia Gandhi.

The MGP is a party with its eyes on the past. Unlike the Congress it had a mass base across most of Goa, based on its Bahujan ideology (I will discuss this later when I discuss the vote), and a fairly strong network of local leaders and followers which it has succeeded in frittering away. Unlike the Congress, the MGP has not had the capacity to manage factions and hence has bled regularly. Factions have left and joined the Congress. Dayanand Narvekar,

Ravi Naik, Wilfred Misquita, all felt at various times that it would be better for their interest, and that of their constituency, if they bargained their way into (or back into) the Congress. The time horizon of most of these politicians is just one assembly, and hence, when they saw themselves in the opposition, they strove to become members of the ruling party by defecting from the MGP to the Congress. As a result the politics of the palace replaced the politics of social classes, within which the MGP was earlier rooted because of its Bahujan ideology. The MGP has also suffered because of poor organisation skills, and because of a paucity of funds (unlike the Congress), since it has been in opposition for too long and dominant interests which depend on the goodwill of the state such as the mining lobby, or the industrialists and builders, do not contribute in large numbers to its coffers. Another factor that has probably led to an erosion of the MGP social base is the in-migration from other parts of India, a demographic change that favours national parties especially since this migrant population is concentrated in certain constituencies. It is estimated to be over 20 per cent of the total population. The final factor that has compounded the MGP's woes is the cannibalising of its mass base by the BJP with whom it aligned in the 1994 assembly elections when it tried to consolidate what it perceived to be a cohesive Hindu vote. The strategy did not succeed (see Table 18.4).

The BJP is a new party in Goa and has grown significantly from 0.47 per cent of the assembly vote in 1989 to 26.19 per cent in 1999. The BJP has succeeded by presenting itself in multiple ways: (a) as an alternative to the Congress, a picture which has found some appeal, especially amongst a middle class disgusted by the politics of defection and pragmatism represented by the Congress — even Catholics in some constituencies voted for the BJP; (b) as a soft *Hindutva* party, which has enabled it to poach on the MGP vote bank and to attract those who have a communal ideology; and (c) as state representative of the government at the centre. It has benefited by the Vajpayee and the Kargil factor, where the BJP has got considerable media mileage. Its organisational strength comes from its close links with the Sangh combine, particularly the secretive RSS. These have so far been inadequately probed and so the extent of control by this extra-constitutional authority — the remote-control syndrome — is not properly understood. Its leader, Manohar Parrikar, has been able to portray himself as an alert and aggressive 'Leader of the Opposition', a title which the party has now wrested from the MGP. When I disaggregate the votes of the last three assembly elections, I shall comment on the character of its social base and on its potential to challenge the Congress as the party of governance.

The smaller parties, such as the UGDP, GPP and GRCP, came into existence because of the political manoeuvrings of their leaders, like Churchill Alemao, Luis Proto Barbosa and Dr Willy de Souza. They have no ideology, and no potential to dethrone the Congress. They apply pressure on the Congress since they draw their support from the Congress vote base. Most of them are located in areas where the Congress is strong, and have no potential to threaten the BJP or MGP. In fact, they have formed governments by forging alliances with the MGP and BJP (March 1990–December 1990 and July 1998–November 1998) (see Table 18.2). They achieve as groups what independents achieve as individuals, which is to apply pressure on the Congress and to create the conditions for their merger or admittance into the Congress. The vote base of this group is sizeable, since it contains the protest vote against the politics of the Congress, which through the period has been in excess of 19 per cent of the vote (see Table 18.3). These broad trends that I have identified have not dealt with:

1. the importance of power brokers;
2. the intensity of constituency-level competition;
3. the role of personal charisma; and
4. the differences in voter preferences between new and old voters, men and women, urban and rural, educated and illiterate etc. It does not illustrate the social profile of the vote.

These aspects also need to be mapped for any comprehensive picture of politics in Goa.

I present in Table 18.3 a summary of aggregate votes polled and seats won by each party to give a sense of the strengths of each group. The small parties and independents have been clubbed together.

TABLE 18.3
PARTY SEATS AND VOTING PERCENTAGE, 1989–99

Year	Congress %	Congress Seats	MGP %	MGP Seats	BJP %	BJP Seats	Individuals & others %	Individuals & others Seats
1989–A	40.52	18	39.52	18	0.47	0	19.50	4
1989–P	46.18	1	27.13	1	0.68	0	23.34	0
1991–P	57.65	2	20.57	0	15.61	0	6.15	0
1994–A	36.90	18	20.74	12	8.89	4	33.46	6
1996–P	34.36	0	26.77	1	13.75	0	25.10	1
1998–P	31.59	2	13.17	0	30.04	0	29.19	0
1999–A	38.55	21	14.03	4	26.19	10	21.21	5

Note: P=Parliament; A=Assembly.

The Electoral Landscape

During this decade the most significant aspect of the electoral land-scape has been the rise of the BJP, the decline of the MGP, and the spirited continuance of the Congress. In this section I shall not undertake the dissection of each assembly and each parliamentary election, since there are too many particularities to each and these do not lead up to or contribute towards a trend (for details see Fernandes 1997). For example, the 1994 assembly election was a protest vote against the politics of defection when nineteen new members, many independents, and some small parties, were elec-ted in the place of many stalwarts such as Ravi Naik, Francisco Sardinha, Shaikh Hassan Haroon and Ramakant Khalap (deSouza 1996); or the 1996 parliamentary elections when the Congress lost both seats, one to the MGP and one to the UGDP; or the 1998 par-liamentary elections where they won both back. There were too many contingent factors unique to each election for us to be able to derive a trend by focusing on them. The significant feature of the 1989 election was the tie of eighteen seats for both the Congress and the MGP; that of 1994, the alliance of BJP–MGP to consolidate the Hindu vote[9] which instead was further fragmented since the MGP got less than it got in 1989; and that of 1999, the return of many of the party stalwarts who had been punished in the 1994 elections. Instead of looking at episodes or contingencies, I shall look at aggregate voting figures to see if there are any significant trends emerging that have implications for the polity.

To assist me in this I shall divide Goa into four regions: NN (North New Conquests), NO (North Old Conquests), SO (South Old Conquests), and SN (South New Conquests), which were impacted differently by Portuguese rule. In the old conquests, Portuguese rule extended for over four centuries whereas in the new conquests it was for less than two centuries. This resulted in a demographic concentration of the Catholics in the old conquests. These are also the more developed regions, where the population is more mixed and in which most of the big towns are located. This means that singular appeals are unlikely to produce results since the interests of one group are unlikely to harmonise with the interests of another group. The ideological politics of the BJP hence is likely to exclude groups which the pragmatic politics of the Congress is likely to accommodate. Hence the Congress, seen as a party of factions, always under internal stress in contrast to the BJP whose internal politics remains largely unreported and hence unknown, has a greater chance of forging an electoral majority. In these regions the division of assembly seats is as follows: NN–12, NO–11, SO–11, and SN–6 . Table 18.4 gives the regional profile over the three assembly elections.

TABLE 18.4
ASSEMBLY PARTIES, BY REGION AND PER CENT VOTE POLLED

Year	Region	Congress	BJP	MGP	IND
1989	NN	34.43	0.81	53.72	11.04
	NO	40.59	0.49	40.30	18.63
	SN	38.17	0.00	54.54	7.29
	SO	49.04	0.30	13.00	37.66
1989 Total		40.52	0.47	39.52	19.50
1994	NN	31.64	11.95	34.11	22.30
	NO	44.02	10.91	20.05	25.02
	SN	36.75	0.00	24.56	38.69
	SO	35.28	8.15	4.99	51.57
1994 Total		36.90	8.89	20.74	33.46
1999	NN	36.97	31.09	23.3	8.64
	NO	34.31	25.09	10.22	30.38
	SN	31.80	29.33	19.39	19.47
	SO	49.43	19.75	4.25	26.58
1999 Total		38.55	26.19	14.03	21.21

A study of the table reveals three interesting trends. The first is the obvious one of the BJP's growth at the expense of the MGP, a shift in the ideology of the social base from strong Bahujan to soft *Hindutva*. The BJP has gained because of the vote against Congress misrule, because the MGP has been unable to present itself as an alternative to Congress; the MGP's important leaders have, time and again, post-election gone and joined the Congress because of the absence of any alternative to the Congress, and because of the Vajpayee factor. This growth has been remarkable in all regions, even SO, and strongest in NN, which had been the bastion of the MGP in 1989. The MGP has declined in all regions, dropping from an aggregate of 39.52 per cent in 1989 to 14.03 per cent in 1999. It remains to be seen whether this is a terminal trend, and whether soft *Hindutva* can replace strong Bahujan, the former being only a community-based ideology whereas the latter ideology has characteristics of both class and caste. It also shows that the *Hindutva* line has made inroads into the strong Bahujan social base, even if only in a soft form, because its more strident version, espoused by members of the RSS combine such as the Bajrang Dal and VHP after the demolition of the Babri Masjid, have few takers in Goa.

Alternatively, one could ask whether the failure of the MGP lies more at the level of logistics, such as party organisation, poor campaign and inadequate resources, a failure which can be remedied through new leadership restating the Bahujan ideology which has an independent existence and which is experiencing a resurgence in other parts of India. The future of the MGP will be decided by the vision of its leaders.

The second important trend is the bargaining position of the independents and the other smaller parties. The vote of 19.5 per cent in 1989 going up to a high of 33.46 per cent in 1994 and steadying at 21.21 per cent in 1999, shows that there are some leaders who have localised support, and who can and have used it to gain positional advantage for themselves either as ministers or as chairpersons of corporations. This is where the GRCP and UGDP, and some independents, have the power to be spoilers. They are largely located in the old conquests, especially SO. They have little influence in NN. This sizeable vote shows that there is a large floating voter group which is searching for a new practice of politics. It gets focused either through a charismatic leader like Churchill Alemao in 1996, or a localised party like the UGDP in 1994, to register disaffection with the Congress. This floating voter represents the search for 'good governance' which the Congress is not seen as providing, and which the electoral system does not seem to offer either. The consequence hence is to apply pressure on the Congress by voting for what I referred to earlier as the 'parties of pressure'. This is not a vote that will go to the MGP or the BJP, since it is essentially a secular vote.

The third important factor, paradoxically, is the continuing consolidation equally in all the regions of the Congress. While the defection factor may have benefited the BJP, in that a population that believes that the voting calculus should be driven by principles voted for it in disgust against the Congress, it also helped the Congress in that it gained new supporters brought in by those who had defected to it. The Congress seems to have maintained a steady support base across all three assembly elections and in all the four regions. This is significant because if it can retain its hold over SO and NO, as it appears to have done, because of the anti-communal and thereby anti-BJP vote, and because of the more mixed populations of these areas, then it can continue to be the party of governance; because these regions may have been willing to vote for the MGP because of its Bahujan ideology, but not for the BJP because of its *Hindutva* ideology. The BJP therefore faces a glass ceiling beyond which it cannot rise. Defection thus has a double impact on the Congress, depleting and replenishing its support base. It helps the Congress to retain its mixed, secular character. So even though the Congress rule has meant instability because of defections, during election time the Congress benefits because the alternatives appear less desirable, especially to populations in SO and NO. In addition to this the Congress benefits from political leaders who have considerable skill in managing elections and who have large war chests. Politics is good business for the Congress, in some cases a family one. The Congress dominance shows that pragmatic politics gives better dividends than ideological politics.

The foregoing has shown that politics in Goa seems to have developed a considerable autonomy in that the actions and decisions of groups and leaders are hardly constrained by either the rules that govern institutions or the moral codes that underlie democratic politics. The mechanisms of accountability, which is democracy's USP, also do not seem to deter this class of political leaders since, in the decade under review, they seem to have worked out strategies to overcome them. The examples of defections, of the role of the speaker, of winnability in elections, are cases in point. The managing of elections and of defections has become the key to ensuring a continued capacity to govern. The Congress leads in this capacity. This is still a long way off from democratic governance. The Congress, and the others, lag in this capacity.

Notes

1. Some valuable data on Goa: (*a*) per capita net state domestic product at current prices in 1998: Rs 19,719; (*b*) per capita bank deposits in 1998: Rs 41,380; (*c*) birth rate per thousand of population in 1998: 17.97; (*d*) death rate per thousand of population in 1998: 7.54; (*e*) literacy in per cent, males in 1998: 83.64, females in 1998: 67.09; (*f*) roads per 1,000 sq km of area in 1998: 2,038; (*g*) urban population to total population growth: 1987=32.03 per cent up to 1998=41.01 per cent; (*h*) agricultural workers to total workers in 1998: 23.94 per cent; (*i*) per capita domestic consumption of electricity: 1987=77.39 up to 1998=208; (*j*) motor vehicles per 100,000 of population: 1987=7,876 up to 1998=22,483; (*k*) population served per hospital in 1998: 10,662.
2. The discussion on the Konkan Railway is a case in point. See the note prepared by the Citizen's Committee (1993), where the pros and cons of the three routes are presented in terms of (*a*) costs, (*b*) environmental impacts, (*c*) safety, and (*d*) development consequences.
3. The proposal to convert Goa into a Free Port raised a host of issues. Noronha (1998) sets the agenda clearly for such a debate.
4. Jumbo cabinets became an election issue in 1999, resulting in the Congress giving an assurance that the cabinet size would not exceed '15 per cent of the size of the assembly' as the first point on its manifesto. However, this was later 'creatively' reinterpreted to indicate that the cabinet size would not exceed eight.
5. The parties' names are: MGP—Maharashtrawadi Gomantak Party; GPP now defunct)—Goan People's Party; UGDP—United Goan's Democratic Party; GRCP—Goa Rajiv Congress Party, GLP—Gomant Lok Pokx.
6. Narveker, Alemao, Shirodkar, Willy, Mauvin, etc., are just some of the regulars.
7. In 1994 the Congress had the speaker *pro tem* manipulate the secret ballot to declare a tie, then cancel it and use the method of a voice vote to elect Tomazinho Cardozo as speaker of the legislative assembly.

8. There are many instances of this in the last decade, like in 1994 when Wilfred Misquita and some others left the MGP and joined the Congress, or in 1999 when Parulekar and Jose Philip left the UGDP to align with the Congress.
9. Since the MGP has its base in the Bahujan Hindu vote and the BJP in the Saraswat Hindu vote, it was felt that an alliance would consolidate the Hindu vote; an argument that overlooks the internal contradictions of caste and class within the Hindu community.

References

Angley, P. 1999. 'A Culture Conceived and Misconceived', in N. Dantas, ed., *The Transforming of Goa*. Goa: Other Indian Press.

Citizen's Committee. 1993. 'Summary of Main Issues/Arguments related to the Konkan Railway Route Alternatives', 19 May 1993, Panaji.

D'Mello, Pamela. 1994. 'The Role of Courts in the Goa Case'. Paper presented at the seminar on Anti-Defection Law and the Goa Case, Goa University, 24 September 1994.

D'Souza, Errol. 1997. *Economy and Institutions*. Mumbai: Himalaya Publishing House.

deSouza, Peter R. 1996. 'Goa: A Democratic Verdict?' *Economic and Political Weekly*, Vol. 31, Nos 2–3, 13 January 1996.

———. 1998a. 'Speaker on the Wrong Side of Right', *The Navhind Times*, 30 July 1998.

———. 1998b. 'A Problem with Governance', *Goa Messenger*, November 1998, p. 8.

Fernandes, A. 1997. *Cabinet Government in Goa*, Panaji: Maureen and Camvet Publications.

Noronha, Ligia. 1998. 'Understanding the Environmental Implications of a Free Port for Goa'. Paper presented at the Free Port for Goa seminar at the Indian International Centre, Goa, 10 January 1998.

Rubinoff, A. 1998. *The Construction of a Political Community: Integration and Identity in Goa*. New Delhi: Sage.

Sawkar, K., et al. 1998. 'Tourism and the Environment: Case Studies of Goa, India, and the Maldives', EDI Case Studies Series, Economic Development Institute of the World Bank, Washington, D.C.

About the Editor and Contributors

The Editor

Peter Ronald deSouza is Professor at and currently Head of the Department of Political Science, Goa University. A member of the International Political Science Association's Research Committees on Political Philosophy and Political Sociology, he has also worked as Consultant to the World Bank on rural decentralisation, and to the International Institute of Democracy and Electoral Assistance (IDEA) on the 'State of Democracy' Project. Professor deSouza is State Coordinator of *Lokniti*, and a member of the UGC expert panel in political science (1997–2000). He has contributed several articles in the area of democratic politics in India to journals and edited volumes.

The Contributors

U.R. Ananthamurthy has been Chairman of the Sahitya Akademi, New Delhi, and has also been Vice-Chancellor of the Gandhi University, Kottayam, Kerala. Author of several books including the award-winning masterpiece *Samskara*, he was conferred the Jnanpeeth Award in 1996.

S.S. Bhandare is Economic Advisor, Tata Services Limited, and Trustee, IMC Economic Research Foundation. He is also Co-Chairman of the Economic Affairs of Assocham, and Member of the Economic and Business Reform Committee of the IMC.

Rajeev Bhargava is a political philosopher at the Jawaharlal Nehru University, New Delhi. His previous publications include *Individualism in Social Science; Secularism and Its Critics* (edited); and *Multiculturalism, Liberalism and Democracy* (co-edited).

Rustom Bharucha is an independent writer, director and dramaturge based in Calcutta. He is the author of several books including *Theatre and the World; The Question of Faith*; and *In the Name of the Secular*.

Errol D'Souza is IFCI Professor of Economics, University of Mumbai. He has been a Consultant to the Finance Department, Government of Goa, and a Member of the Economic Committee of the Goa Chamber of Commerce and Industry. He is the author of *Economy and Institutions: Essays on Goa*.

Bhupat M. Desai is at the Centre for Management in Agriculture, Indian Institute of Management, Ahmedabad. A Visiting Fellow at the International Food Policy Research Institute, Washington, D.C., he specialises in agriculture and rural development, agricultural finance, and agricultural economics. He is also a consultant to several international organisations including NABARD, FAO, the World Bank and ADB.

Gopal Guru is Mahatma Gandhi Professor at the University of Pune, and is a scholar and activist in the area of dalit affairs. He has worked extensively on the political thought of B.R. Ambedkar, and is the author of several works on dalit culture. He is the Convenor of the Dalit Intellectuals Collective, and a frequent contributor to *The Hindu*.

Zoya Hasan is at the Centre for Political Studies, Jawaharlal Nehru University, New Delhi. She is the author of several books including *Quest for Power* and *Forging Identities: Gender, Communities and the State*.

Nawaz B. Mody is Sir Pherozeshah Mehta Professor of Civics and Politics, University of Mumbai. She has authored several books including *India's Role in the United Nations*, and *Pherozeshah Mehta: Maker of Modern India*.

Seemanthini Niranjana is an independent researcher based in Hyderabad. Previously a Lecturer in Sociology at Goa University, she specialises in the area of gender and civil law. She is the author of *Gender and Space: Femininity, Sexualization and the Female Body* (forthcoming).

Maria Ligia Noronha is a Fellow of the Tata Energy Research Institute (TERI), and Convenor, Western Regional Centre, TERI. She is also Member, Mining and Environmental Research Network, UK; Member, Global Assurance Group of Mining and Mineral Sustainable Project of IIED, UK; and a member of several expert committees of the Government of Goa. She has edited (jointly with Alyson Warhurst) *Environmental Policy in Mining: Corporate Strategy and Planning for Closure.*

Ghanshyam Shah is at the Centre for Social Medicine and Community Health, Jawaharlal Nehru University, New Delhi. He has previously been Director of the Centre for Social Studies, Surat, and Ambedkar Professor at Lal Bahadur Shastri National Academy of Administration, Mussoorie. The recipient of various prestigious awards, he has also published several works including *Public Health and Urban Growth: The Study of the Surat Plague*; and *Social Movements in India.*

D.L. Sheth is a Fellow of the Centre for the Study of Developing Societies, Delhi, and has also been a Member of the Backward Classes Commission of India. His previous publications include *The Multiverse of Democracy* (co-edited with Ashis Nandy); *Alternatives* (edited); and *Minority Identities and the Nation State* (co-edited).

Soli J. Sorabjee is Senior Advocate, Supreme Court of India, and the Attorney General of India. An eminent jurist and constitutional expert, he is President of the United Lawyers' Association; Chairman of the Advisory Board of Transparency International (India); President of Capital Jazz; Convenor of the Minority Rights Group (India); and Personal Envoy of the UN High Commissioner for Human Rights for East Timor. His several publications include *The Law of the Press Censorship in India.*

Romila Thapar is an Honorary Fellow of Lady Margaret Hall, Oxford, and of the School of Oriental and African Studies, London.

She is also Corresponding Fellow, The British Academy, and Emeritus Professor, Jawaharlal Nehru University, New Delhi. Her previous publications include *Asoka and the Decline of the Mauryas*; *Ancient Indian Social History: Some Interpretations*; *History and Beyond*; *Sakuntala: Texts, Readings, Histories*; and a children's book entitled *Indian Tales*.

B.G. Verghese is at the Centre for Policy Research, New Delhi. Winner of the Magsaysay Award in 1975, he is a Member of Prasar Bharati, Government of India, and a Member of UNESCO's Macbride Commission on International Communication Policies (1977–99). He is also a board member of the Centre for Science and Environment, India, and of the Population Foundation of India. Author of several works including *Waters of Hope* and *Winning the Future*, he has also been Editor of two leading national dailies, *The Indian Express* and *The Hindustan Times*.

Index